The Presidency of
THEODORE
ROOSEVELT

AMERICAN PRESIDENCY SERIES

Donald R. McCoy, Clifford S. Griffin, Homer E. Socolofsky
General Editors

George Washington, Forrest McDonald
John Adams, Ralph Adams Brown
Thomas Jefferson, Forrest McDonald
James Madison, Robert Allen Rutland
John Quincy Adams, Mary W. M. Hargreaves
Martin Van Buren, Major L. Wilson
William Henry Harrison & John Tyler, Norma Lois Peterson
James K. Polk, Paul H. Bergeron
Zachary Taylor & Millard Fillmore, Elbert B. Smith
Franklin Pierce, Larry Gara
James Buchanan, Elbert B. Smith
Andrew Johnson, Albert Castel
Rutherford B. Hayes, Ari Hoogenboom
James A. Garfield & Chester A. Arthur, Justus D. Doenecke
Grover Cleveland, Richard E. Welch, Jr.
Benjamin Harrison, Homer E. Socolofsky & Allan B. Spetter
William McKinley, Lewis L. Gould
Theodore Roosevelt, Lewis L. Gould
William Howard Taft, Paolo E. Coletta
Woodrow Wilson, Kendrick A. Clements
Warren G. Harding, Eugene P. Trani & David L. Wilson
Herbert C. Hoover, Martin L. Fausold
Harry S. Truman, Donald R. McCoy
Dwight D. Eisenhower, Chester J. Pach, Jr., & Elmo Richardson
John F. Kennedy, James N. Giglio
Lyndon B. Johnson, Vaughn Davis Bornet

The Presidency of
THEODORE
ROOSEVELT

Lewis L. Gould

UNIVERSITY PRESS OF KANSAS

© 1991 by the University Press of Kansas
All rights reserved

Published by the University Press of Kansas (Lawrence, Kansas 66049),
which was organized by the Kansas Board of Regents
and is operated and funded by Emporia State University, Fort Hays State
University, Kansas State University, Pittsburg State
University, the University of Kansas, and Wichita State University

Library of Congress Cataloging-in-Publication Data

Gould, Lewis L.
The presidency of Theodore Roosevelt / Lewis L. Gould.
p.   cm. — (American presidency series)
Includes bibliographical references (p.   ) and index.
ISBN 0–7006–0435–9 (alk. paper)
ISBN 0–7006–0565–7 (pbk.)
1. United States—Politics and government—1901–1909.
2. Roosevelt, Theodore, 1858–1919. 3. Presidents—United States—
Biography. I. Title. II. Series.
E756.G62   1991
973.91'1—dc20   90–11184

British Library Cataloguing in Publication Data is available.

Printed in the United States of America

10 9 8 7 6 5 4 3 2

The paper used in this publication meets the minimum requirements
of the American National Standard for Permanence of Paper
for Printed Library Materials Z39.48—1984.

CONTENTS

FOREWORD

The aim of the American Presidency Series is to present historians and the general reading public with interesting, scholarly assessments of the various presidential administrations. These interpretive surveys are intended to cover the broad ground between biographies, specialized monographs, and journalistic accounts. As such, each will be a comprehensive, synthetic work which will draw upon the best in pertinent secondary literature, yet leave room for the author's own analysis and interpretation.

Volumes in the series will present the data essential to understanding the administration under consideration. Particularly, each book will treat the then current problems facing the United States and its people and how the president and his associates felt about, thought about, and worked to cope with these problems. Attention will be given to how the office developed and operated during the president's tenure. Equally important will be consideration of the vital relationships between the president, his staff, the executive officers, Congress, foreign representatives, the judiciary, state officials, the public, political parties, the press, and influential private citizens. The series will also be concerned with how this unique American institution—the presidency—was viewed by the presidents, and with what results.

All this will be set, insofar as possible, in the context not only of contemporary politics but also of economics, international relations, law, morals, public administration, religion, and thought. Such a broad approach is necessary to understanding, for a presidential administration is more than the elected and appointed officers composing it, since its work so often reflects the major problems, anxieties, and glories of the nation. In short, the authors in this series will strive to recount and evaluate the record of each administration and to identify its distinctiveness and relationships to the past, its own time, and the future.

The General Editors

PREFACE

Eight decades after he left the White House, Theodore Roosevelt remains the most exciting of the twentieth-century presidents. Candidates evoke the name of "Teddy" Roosevelt to show that they are strong in foreign policy and devoted to the environment.* His phrases— the "bully pulpit," the "big stick," and the "strenuous life"—are part of the language. Roosevelt was more than an important contributor to the evolution of the modern institution of the presidency. He personalized the office in a way that had not occurred since Andrew Jackson. In many respects, none of Roosevelt's successors since 1909 has equaled his impact on the popular mind.

Despite Roosevelt's importance to the presidency and despite the force of his personality, no book-length analysis devoted to the presidential experience has been written. His formative years have received rich attention. There are also good studies of the period after he retired to private life on 4 March 1909. Although Roosevelt's two terms were not a time of intense foreign-policy crisis or social upheaval, the problems that the twenty-sixth president faced were formidable and complex. The documentary record of the administration is large. There is also the assumption that the main facts of what Roosevelt accomplished are known. These considerations have helped to push historical inquiry away from Roosevelt in office.

Yet the presidency was the centerpiece of Theodore Roosevelt's life.

*In fact, no one who knew Roosevelt well ever called him Teddy.

ix

Without it, he would be a fascinating minor figure in American history. In office, he addressed the issues that dominated the national agenda in this century—the government's power to regulate an industrial society, the conservation of natural and human resources, and the role of the United States in an interdependent and dangerous world. The answers he developed have been superseded, but he deserves credit for having articulated many of the right questions. This book sets out how Roosevelt shaped his presidential policies and the fate they encountered in the political life of his day.

Theodore Roosevelt was a strong president. For many years, strength alone was enough to establish claims to presidential greatness for those who exercised it. During the 1960s and 1970s the nation perceived that presidential strength is a morally neutral attribute. Not all who wielded executive power had benevolent motives or achieved praiseworthy results. While much of what Theodore Roosevelt did was admirable and while his goals were necessary, the methods he employed sometimes raised legitimate questions regarding the consequences of unchecked presidential discretion. This analytic narrative of his two administrations tries to place into their historical context both his constructive and his troubling contributions to the emergence of the modern presidency.

Accounts of Roosevelt's life usually emphasize the departures that he made in how the presidency was conducted. While he brought freshness, youth, and energy to his duties, he did not work in a historical vacuum. William McKinley had revitalized the office between 1897 and 1901, and Roosevelt built on those accomplishments. In time his flair and charisma eclipsed the work of his predecessor. Nonetheless, Roosevelt was a key player in a general strengthening of the presidency that took place during the quarter century after the election of 1896. It does not diminish his record to recognize that he was never the sole architect of the modern presidency in its formative stage.

Four years after Roosevelt left office, the Republican party had split into two warring factions. Much of the blame for that unhappy result rests with William Howard Taft. Yet the tensions and strains that the Grand Old Party experienced after 1909 had their origins in the policies and political style of Roosevelt's two terms. The growth of presidential power and the rise of governmental regulation under Roosevelt tested the durability of the Republican coalition that had taken national power during the 1890s. The record of Theodore Roosevelt's presidency must address the background of the process that led the Republicans to the disastrous schism in 1912.

Scholarship on specific aspects of Roosevelt's presidency, especially in foreign affairs, is rich and varied. The work of such historians as John M. Blum, George E. Mowry, William H. Harbaugh, and Howard K. Beale laid a foundation of basic information and interpretation on which all who follow them have depended. The excellent edition of *The Letters of Theodore Roosevelt* that Elting E. Morison and his colleagues produced during the 1950s made modern writing about Roosevelt a much easier task. While this study of Roosevelt's presidency draws on research in primary sources, it could not have been completed without the contributions of all the historians who have made the Roosevelt literature as exciting and vibrant as its subject.

The limits of space and the format of this series make discursive footnotes impractical. In many instances, I have chosen to cite secondary sources to give readers a better indication of the depth of writings on Theodore Roosevelt.

A number of friends, colleagues, and students have aided in the research and writing of this book. Members of my undergraduate and graduate seminars over the years have conducted research on Roosevelt that helped me to understand the president more fully. I am indebted to Thomas M. Anderson, Bill Childs, David Crosson, Aaron Forsberg, Walter Gaffield, Sally Hunter Graham, John Leffler, Brenda Loudermilk, James B. Martin, Lois Martin, Craig H. Roell, Stacy Rozek, and Steve Stagner.

Charles W. Calhoun, Paul E. Isaac, Peter Larsen, Michael McGerr, Kristie Miller, Nan Netherton, Bradley R. Rice, Stefan Rinke, and Fred Shoemaker kindly either sent me materials on Roosevelt that they had located in their own work or shared with me their books and articles in unpublished form.

The librarians who helped me are too numerous to thank individually, but the superb staff of the Manuscript Division, Library of Congress, have been of great assistance for almost three decades and deserve a word of recognition. Richard Holland, a bibliographer at the Perry-Castaneda Library, University of Texas at Austin, was a valuable ally for many years in acquiring Roosevelt-era manuscripts on microfilm.

Quotations of Crown-copyright records in the Public Record Office, London, appear by permission of the Controller of H.M. Stationery Office. Quotations from *The Letters of Theodore Roosevelt*, selected and edited by Elting E. Morison et al., 8 volumes (Cambridge, Mass.: Harvard University Press, 1951–54), are used by permission of Harvard University Press.

Friends and colleagues read portions of the book in draft form. I am grateful to Kathleen Dalton, John A. Gable, Paul S. Holbo, and Kate

Torrey for their timely criticisms and suggestions. John Gable has been a source of encouragement and help, as he is for all who work on Theodore Roosevelt. Herbert F. Margulies read the text in its entirety and made many perceptive and incisive comments based on his wide knowledge and thoughtful insights into Roosevelt and his time. None of these individuals is responsible for the use I have made of their help, but I do appreciate their kindness.

I also owe thanks to Donald R. McCoy and Clifford S. Griffin of the University of Kansas and Homer E. Socolofsky of Kansas State University—the general editors of the American Presidency Series—for their constructive criticisms and thorough review of the manuscript.

Helen Keel once again gave generously of her time and energy as a proofreader. Karen Gould was patient and understanding about the hours that I spent with Theodore Roosevelt; her good humor and insight helped me to keep the book in perspective.

Lewis L. Gould

Austin, Texas
March 1990

1

★ ★ ★ ★ ★

"HERE IS THE TASK"

Theodore Roosevelt became the president of the United States on 14 September 1901. After taking the presidential oath at the home of a friend in Buffalo, New York, the city in which William McKinley had been shot a week earlier, Roosevelt addressed public concern about continuity in the presidency. He pledged to "continue absolutely unbroken the policy of President McKinley for the peace, the prosperity, and the honor of our beloved country." A conservative Republican senator observed: "That simple declaration immediately restored confidence in the business world."[1]

There was only time for a brief meeting of the cabinet on 17 September before the new president went to Canton, Ohio, for McKinley's funeral. By 20 September, Roosevelt was at the White House for his first day of official business. The energy and determination that marked the day's work set the tone for the presidency of Theodore Roosevelt.

He drove to the Executive Mansion from the train station in an open carriage despite the fears of other assassination attempts. He began reading the mass of papers that had accumulated since the attack on McKinley. A meeting with the members of the cabinet followed at 11:00 A.M. He asked them to stay on, and he received reports on the varied business of their departments. After the meeting, Roosevelt talked with his comrade from Cuba, Gen. Leonard Wood, and then lunched with Secretary of State John Milton Hay at his home nearby. Roosevelt strode out of the White House by himself, "brushing hurriedly past the uniformed guards and ushers in the hallways and doors." His disregard for

1

security caused some comment in a city still apprehensive about presidential safety. The new president would do as he pleased about his personal style.[2]

Roosevelt's first night at the White House came on 22 September. He recalled to the family that it was his late father's birthday. "I feel," he said, "as if my father's hand were on my shoulder, and as if there were a special blessing over the life I am to lead here." The new president was also a talented politician who understood at once the implications of his situation. A friend said to him that Roosevelt might easily expect to have seven years in the presidency because "no man had ever entered upon the office more absolutely free than he was of all obligation to anybody." Measuring his words carefully when he knew that they might be remembered and recorded, Roosevelt responded that he was "going to be President for three years, and I am going to do my utmost to give the country a good President during that period." He intended to be "full President, and I [would] rather be full President for three and a half years than half a President for seven and a half years." His remarks gave early evidence of the sure political touch that marked his presidency in its relations with the American people.[3] The assertion of presidential vigor was characteristically Rooseveltian. The incoming president did not, however, dwell on the sad circumstances that had brought him to power. "It is a dreadful thing to come into the Presidency this way; but it would be a far worse thing to be morbid about it," he said to his best friend, Henry Cabot Lodge, on 23 September 1901. "Here is the task, and I have got to do it to the best of my ability; and that is all there is about it."[4]

Theodore Roosevelt had been a public figure for almost two decades. He was born on 27 October 1858 in New York City. His father, Theodore Roosevelt, Sr., first a glass importer and later a renowned Manhattan philanthropist, was "the most wise and loving father that ever lived." The elder Theodore encouraged his second child's physical development, helped him overcome childhood asthma, and offered in his own political failures a stimulus for the son's political career. The father, married to a southern wife who had relatives in the Confederate service, hired a substitute in the Civil War. The younger Theodore felt impelled in later military crises to seek active duty. "I did not intend to have to hire somebody else to do my shooting for me," he said in 1907.[5]

Several important influences shaped Roosevelt's boyhood. His illness aroused his determination to carry out his father's command to "make" his body. Although full vigor did not come until early manhood, Roosevelt acquired the taste for sports and robust activities that made him the exemplar of what he called "the strenuous life." As an

2

indoor alternative to full participation in nature study that asthma sometimes prevented, he became a trained and expert amateur naturalist. He
collected diverse and often smelly stuffed birds, and he embalmed small
animals. At thirteen he was fitted with glasses that corrected his defec-
tive eyesight. Despite his poor vision, he had long been a voracious
consumer of books. Eventually he would be among the best read of all
American presidents.[6]

Roosevelt grew up in a loving and comfortable family environment.
"Old money" in New York City gave his father the chance to do good
works. It also ensured that Roosevelt, his younger brother Elliott, and
his two sisters, Anna ("Bamie") and Corinne, would have the core of a
secure income when they became adults. Martha Bulloch Roosevelt,
their mother, grew increasingly detached from the world in later life.
Still she imparted to her son some of the elan of the Old South and the
politically useful gift of roots in Dixie. The Roosevelts traveled extensively in Europe, and the young Roosevelt acquired a sense of European
culture that was richer than most of his political contemporaries. When
Theodore left for Harvard in September 1876, his father called him "a
boy in whom I could place perfect trust and confidence."[7]

In Cambridge, Roosevelt had a "royally good time" as an undergraduate. He studied hard, boxed and rowed, and edited a student
newspaper. His personal income exceeded that of Harvard's president,
and he belonged to the prestigious Porcellian Club. His father's death
from cancer in early 1878 was a severe personal blow, but the resilient
youth recovered to enjoy a golden experience during his last college
years. As a senior he wrote to his sister: "I stand 19th in the class, which
began with 230 fellows. Only one gentleman stands ahead of me."[8]

In October of his junior year, he met his first wife. Alice Hathaway
Lee was seventeen and came from a well-to-do Boston family. She was
"my first love, too," although there had been earlier an infatuation with
a childhood friend, Edith Kermit Carow. Theodore pursued Alice ar-
dently throughout the winter and spring of 1879. The first time he proposed, in June 1879, she rebuffed him, and he spent nights thinking
about her. Then in January 1880 she accepted, and they were married on
27 October 1880, his twenty-second birthday.[9]

After graduation in 1880, Roosevelt began the varied life that he
would follow until his presidency and beyond. He studied the law,
invested in western cattle ranching, and wrote the thorough and dry *The
Naval History of the War of 1812*, the first of numerous books on history,
nature, politics, and other subjects. Election to the New York Assembly
in 1881 marked his entry into politics. Despite later legend, his family
generally approved of his candidacy. Roosevelt took readily to the new

3

and colorful world of Republican municipal and state politics. He won over his fellow lawmakers with his sincerity and energy. Reelected in 1882 and 1883, he sponsored legislation to regulate the conditions of cigar workers in New York, opposed the railroad magnate Jay Gould, and even jousted with Governor Grover Cleveland. Roosevelt reveled in the spotlight, but did so at some cost to his relations with the Republican leadership.

Tragedy came early in 1884. Alice Roosevelt contracted Bright's disease during pregnancy. After her daughter was born, Alice slipped into unconsciousness. Roosevelt's own mother fell ill of typhoid fever at the same time. The two women died within hours of each other on 14 February 1884. The baby, named Alice after her mother, survived. A stricken Roosevelt prepared a memorial to his wife later that year; then he never mentioned or spoke Alice Lee Roosevelt's name again.

The presidential election of 1884 compelled Roosevelt to define his attitude toward the Republican party. He opposed the candidacy of James G. Blaine for the presidential nomination. The most popular Republican of his time, Blaine easily defeated Roosevelt's choice, George F. Edmunds, and became the party's standard-bearer. Eastern Republicans, who disliked Blaine's financial dealings and his standing with the rank and file, urged Roosevelt to join those party dissidents who were bolting to the Democratic nominee, Grover Cleveland. Roosevelt wavered, but in the end he decided, along with a new friend, Henry Cabot Lodge of Massachusetts, that support of Blaine was a necessity for a rising professional politician.[10]

During the mid 1880s it seemed that Roosevelt's destiny lay in the American West. After making initial investments in western ranching during 1882, a year later he put his money, ultimately almost 20 percent of his estate, into two cattle ventures in the Badlands of Dakota. Roosevelt's years in the West infused his life with drama. Cowboys remembered his orders to them: "Hasten forward quickly there." Men spoke of the way he knocked down an armed, drunken tormentor in a Montana saloon. He killed grizzlies, battled storms, and was always reading. By the autumn of 1886, the cattle boom was ending, and the hard winter of 1886/87 completed the loss of most of Roosevelt's investment. The monetary setback was large. The gains in his physical well-being, emotional release, and political appeal lasted throughout his life.[11]

Roosevelt also returned from the frontier because of marriage and politics. On a visit to New York in September 1885 he met Edith Carow again. By November they were engaged secretly and agreed to marry later the following year. New York City Republicans asked him to run for mayor in 1886 against the land reformer Henry George and the Democratic candidate Abram S. Hewitt. The "Cowboy Candidate" made a vigorous campaign but ran a poor third as a sacrificial choice. Edith and Theodore were married on 2 December 1886 in London. The best man was a young British diplomat, Cecil Spring Rice, whom the Roosevelts met on the boat.

The newlyweds brought little Alice to live with them at Sagamore Hill, the hilltop house Roosevelt built at Oyster Bay, Long Island. Soon the Roosevelts started their own family. Theodore, Jr., came in September 1887, followed by Kermit (1889), Ethel (1891), Archibald (1894), and Quentin (1897). Edith brought calm and balance to her husband's life; she treated him as the oldest of her brood of children. To his own offspring, Theodore was playmate, leader, and often a daunting example. "I love all these children and have great fun with them," he wrote, "and am touched by the way in which they feel that I am their special friend, champion, and companion." When he became president, Roosevelt's family was one of his most striking political assets.[12]

The election of Benjamin Harrison in 1888 brought a Republican administration back to Washington. Having campaigned for the ticket, Roosevelt now wanted a federal job. After Secretary of State Blaine ruled out a position as an assistant secretary, the president picked Roosevelt for the Civil Service Commission. For six years under Harrison and Grover Cleveland, Roosevelt learned national politics from the inside as he supervised the patronage practices of both parties. His performance was so good that Cleveland did not remove Roosevelt when the Democrats took power in 1893.

Roosevelt was ready for a change by 1895. There were limits on how much more he could accomplish for honest politics as the Cleveland presidency faltered. He turned aside Republican overtures to run for mayor of New York in 1894, largely because of Edith's opposition. When the GOP elected Mayor William L. Strong in November, Roosevelt told friends that he would like to be one of the city's four police commissioners. In April 1895 his appointment came, and he was chosen president of the commission. Over the next two years, Roosevelt stamped his personality on the city. As "Haroun-el-Roosevelt," he went with his face covered through Manhattan's streets at night to find policemen sleeping on their beats or passing time in saloons. His teeth and pince-nez eyeglasses became public trademarks.

Vigorous enforcement of the state's liquor laws during the summer of 1895 brought closed saloons on Sunday and political resistance to the commissioner. Faced with the opposition of the Democratic machine, Tammany Hall, infighting among his fellow commissioners, and Republican qualms about the effect of his policies on voters, Roosevelt still had a positive impact on the operations of "New York's Finest." He loosened its ties to the criminal element and improved the professional techniques and overall quality of the force.

By 1896, as a Republican victory in the presidential election loomed, his interest in a federal post reappeared. By campaigning for William McKinley, he built up political credits. The sponsorship of now Senator Henry Cabot Lodge of Massachusetts and the eagerness of New York's Republican leaders to have him out of the state were elements in McKinley's decision to name Roosevelt as assistant secretary of the navy in April 1897.

During his service in the McKinley administration, Roosevelt believed in overseas expansion, and he favored a war with Spain over Cuba. He told a friend: "I wish to heaven we were more jingo about Cuba and Hawaii!" He did not, despite what his biographers have repeated, create the tensions between Spain and the United States in 1897. Nor was he a large element in the conduct of William McKinley's diplomacy. Roosevelt helped to prepare the United States Navy to fight the Spanish; he did not bring on the war.[13]

Nor did Roosevelt's celebrated telegram of 25 February 1898 to Commodore George Dewey cause American intervention in the Philippines. With Secretary of the Navy John D. Long away that day, Roosevelt wired Dewey: "In the event of declaration of war on Spain, your duty will be to see that the Spanish squadron does not leave the Asiatic coast, and then offensive operations in the Philippine Islands." But this was not the act of an impetuous, imperialistic subordinate pursuing a "Large Policy" of American expansionism. It reflected naval planning that dated back to 1895; it was also part of an ongoing preparation for hostilities. Long did not rescind the order when he came back to the office the next day, and the actual attack directive came from McKinley himself on 24 April 1898, as the war began.[14]

Nothing could keep Theodore Roosevelt out of the conflict. He volunteered, even though Edith was convalescing from surgery. He brushed aside arguments that he could contribute more to the war effort as an assistant secretary of the navy than as another volunteer officer in his late thirties. Roosevelt believed that he had to seek combat to be true to his own principles. There was always the memory of his father's course during the Civil War. Roosevelt entered the army as a lieutenant colonel in a volunteer regiment whose commander was Col. Leonard Wood. Twenty-three thousand men volunteered for service in what the newspapers decided to call "Roosevelt's Rough Riders." By mid May

1898, the regiment, its leader, and its new second in command were in San Antonio, Texas, to begin training.[15]

Journalists loved the combination of eastern aristocrats, western cowboys, and Indians that composed the Rough Riders. When the group had finished its preparations, Roosevelt boasted that his men could "whip Caesar's Tenth Legion." Their actual task became to defeat Spanish troops in Cuba that were defending the city of Santiago de Cuba. After a stay in Tampa, Florida, the regiment sailed to Cuba in the middle of June, disembarked a week later, and encountered the enemy first in a skirmish at Las Guásimas on 24 June. By the morning of 1 July 1898 the Rough Riders were ready to join an American assault on the San Juan Heights surrounding the city. Roosevelt was now a colonel and the commander of the regiment after Wood's promotion to brigadier general.[16]

After a morning of intense fighting, Roosevelt received orders in the early afternoon to attack the hills in front of his lines. Kettle Hill lay ahead, and on horseback, he took his men through the lines of regulars and up the slope. Jumping off his horse halfway up, he ran forward, killing at least one Spaniard. From the top of Kettle Hill, he joined the charge on the San Juan Heights. For Roosevelt the experience became "the great day of my life," and he long believed that he deserved the Medal of Honor.[17]

A siege of Santiago followed until the Spanish capitulated. Roosevelt worked with other officers to warn Washington and the nation of the dangers of disease if the army stayed in Cuba. By August 1898 he was home to find popular acclaim and political opportunity waiting for him. The Republicans of New York, beset with scandal and an unpopular incumbent, saw a winning strategy in a campaign for governor that a war hero and champion of imperialism could lead. Roosevelt— assuring the party boss, Senator Thomas C. Platt, that as governor he would consult the GOP organization on policy and patronage, holding independents at arm's length, and fending off challenges about his legal residence—got the party's nomination and hit the campaign trail with the Rough Riders beside him. His personal magnetism brought him a narrow 17,000-vote margin over his Democratic opponent.

Roosevelt's two years as governor anticipated many of the themes of his presidency. Daily press conferences kept the public informed about the affairs of the state and about its dynamic young chief executive. He worked closely with Senator Platt and the party regulars as much as possible, but he went his own way in some appointments, on conservation policy, and increasingly about the control of corporate power. His advocacy of enhanced publicity as a means of regulating big business carried over into his early years in the White House. It also worried Senator Platt's campaign contributors. By 1900 Roosevelt felt pressure to move on to the vice-presidency.[18]

After William McKinley's vice-president died in November 1899, a strong effort commenced to put Roosevelt on the Republican ticket in 1900. Roosevelt would have preferred to keep his options open for 1904 by becoming secretary of war or governor general of the Philippines or by staying as governor. He also knew that the vice-presidency was the most available national post the Republicans had in that year. He made all the right moves to take himself out of the race without going the extra step that would have placed him beyond the reach of a draft. Despite these public disclaimers and disavowals, Senator Platt's desire to see Roosevelt out of New York and the absence of a credible alternative made him the logical choice for vice-president. Had he stayed away from the Republican National Convention in Philadelphia, he might have avoided being chosen. When he appeared "wearing an army hat and awakening enthusiasm wherever he went," his selection became inescapable. The ticket of McKinley and Roosevelt swept over William Jennings Bryan and Adlai E. Stevenson—the Democratic candidates—in the election of 1900.[19]

As Roosevelt was being nominated, the angry Senator Mark Hanna, McKinley's close ally, said: "Don't any of you realize that there's only one life between that madman and the Presidency?" Now that Roosevelt had become president, the nation waited to learn how the youngest chief executive would carry out his duties. "In the East, at any rate," a long-time financial columnist recalled in his memoirs, Roosevelt "was regarded with more or less amusement, as a creature of eccentricity and impulse." The theme of impetuosity marked the early appraisals of the new man in the White House. A staff member of the British Embassy told his superiors that Roosevelt had "more than an ordinary share of impulsiveness" and possessed "a firm determination to impose his will upon others." A friend described him as "the meteor of the age."[20]

The man who evoked these comments was seven weeks short of his forty-third birthday on 14 September 1901. The president stood five feet, eight inches in height and was marked by his abundant mustache and familiar pince-nez eyeglasses. He weighed two hundred pounds. To the young friends of his children who composed "the White House Gang," his most noteworthy feature was "the amazing thickness of his girth, and the two buttons on his frock coat set directly in the middle of his back. He was thick *right through*, and we knew it to be muscle." Other visitors remarked on the famous Roosevelt teeth. "He knew that his display of teeth was as effective as a gesture of humor or of rage," recalled William Allen White.[21]

Those who saw Roosevelt in his presidential office expected a more active and frenetic figure than they in fact encountered. "His nerves are so steady that he doesn't even twirl his fingers," said a 1904 commentator, "and if you will note closely you will see that not a muscle of his features twitches." If Roosevelt remained physically quiet when receiving visitors, he did not listen silently. His mind was so quick that he often told people who were speaking to him what they were going to say before they finished. Often he was right; sometimes he was not. The effect was to leave those who spoke to him unsatisfied that they had gotten their message across in the way they wished to state it. "Now talking with Roosevelt often does no good, because he does all the talking," William Allen White told a friend in December 1901. "But when you write to him and he can't talk back, you get a chance to put in more."[22]

As a political leader, Theodore Roosevelt combined innovative and traditional characteristics that he fused into a singularly attractive public personality during his presidency. Although he did not like the motion-picture camera and was uncomfortable with the telephone, Roosevelt was very modern in his recognition that the embryonic instruments of mass communication gave politicians a powerful means of putting across ideas, issues, and their individual messages. He devoted close attention to the ways that the newspapers covered him, and he often acted as his own press secretary. Leaks, background interviews, exclusive stories—all these techniques Roosevelt used adeptly with an often adoring press corps.

Beyond these matters of journalistic adroitness lay Roosevelt's hold on the American people while he was in the White House. The president knew that his fellow citizens found him fascinating, and he gave them a portion of himself in a way that fostered an impression of intimacy between leaders and people. Comparative youth was part of the Roosevelt mystique, as was his energetic and lively family. He knew how to play the chords of shared experience with Americans. His ethnic heritage was elastic enough to embrace all the major nationalities of white, Protestant America. His ancestry and life history took in all the geographic sections of the nation.

For a man in his forties, Roosevelt's life was rich in experience of animals hunted, storms endured, and combat survived. Although he was aristocratic and well-off financially, he lacked affectation and haughtiness. He seemed a president whom one could get to know and who would understand the situation of any reputable citizen who was

9

trying to do the right thing. And the American people responded. In 1906 the novelist William Dean Howells heard "an average American who had been all our average variety of citizens" talking politics on "a westward Pullman." After a time, Howells said: "What about Roosevelt. He turned on me vividly: 'Just love him, just *love* him.' "[23]

On those occasions when Roosevelt spoke to the nation, using the presidency as "the bully pulpit," he was careful to make his ideas clear, his language direct, and his message striking. It was still a time when the president wrote his own speeches, and his words reflected his personality. The phrases—such as the big stick, the Square Deal, malefactors of great wealth, and muckrakers—captured national attention and represented Roosevelt's deft use of language. He did not exploit all his opportunities to communicate with the people. It still seems odd that he did not think of addressing Congress in person, as Woodrow Wilson would do in 1913.[24]

Matchless in his day as a campaigner and popular politician, Roosevelt did not display comparable excellence in his relations with Congress and his party. When it came to dealing with individuals, the president lacked a shrewd sense of why men behaved the way that they did. Flattery could sway him, and he preferred those who told him to follow a course he had already decided to pursue. He boasted about his capacity to listen to those who disagreed with him and to accept their dissenting advice. When critics charged that he was impetuous and too quick to act, he responded that he only moved after consultation with his advisors. Persistent discord, however, usually brought an end to a working relationship with Roosevelt.

The president gave careful attention to the patronage aspects of the Republicans, as they related to his own nomination in 1904 and to the ambitions of Taft in 1908. He was also attuned to the impact of intraparty disputes on his own political standing. Roosevelt did not share the instinctive devotion to the GOP among the Republican professionals, and he was not a committed partisan in the vein of a Nelson W. Aldrich or a Joseph G. Cannon. The politicians respected Roosevelt's power and ability, but they knew that he was not truly one of them.

Roosevelt and Congress were destined for divisiveness. He came to office at a time when the decades of legislative ascendancy in Washington were ending. There had been a gradual rise in presidential power after 1877, culminating in the emergence of the modern office under McKinley. The decline of congressional supremacy did not please the elders on Capitol Hill, and they would likely have resisted the extension of presidential power during McKinley's second term in any case. Despite the secure Republican majorities over the Democrats of twenty-four seats in the Senate and forty-six in the House, there was still the potential for tension between president and lawmakers.

Roosevelt regarded Congress as indecisive and irresolute as an institution, and he distrusted the motives of his opponents in both houses. He made no secret of his open disdain for congressional sensibilities. His cutting remarks about the "scoundrels and crooks" or the "fools" on Capitol Hill rapidly circulated throughout Washington, where political gossip was the primary recreation. When legislators came to see him as president and wished to speak to him quietly about delicate matters, he talked in a loud voice about their business, to the embarrassment of the politicians.[25]

Although he never addressed the lawmakers in person as a body, Roosevelt sent Congress more than four hundred presidential messages. The technique worked during the initial stages of Roosevelt's tenure, but it became an irritant on the Hill during his second term. Lawmakers resented the president's telling them what they must do as well as the public criticism they encountered if they failed to act. Criminal prosecutions of senators and representatives who had engaged in possibly illegal activities seemed to Roosevelt to be his official duty. To those congressmen who were affected, persecution was the more appropriate label, especially when it involved agencies of the executive branch, such as the Secret Service, in gathering evidence. Roosevelt usually won the battle for public opinion when he quarreled with Congress, but these successes were achieved at some cost to the president's legislative record as time went on.

When he assumed the presidency, Roosevelt had a strong will, but did not bring with him an explicit program that he wished to implement. "In internal affairs," he wrote in 1913, "I cannot say that I entered the presidency with any deliberately planned and far-reaching scheme of social betterment." Instead he had "certain strong convictions" about how to conduct himself with a view to "making the government the most efficient possible instrument in helping the people of the United States to better themselves in every way, politically, socially, and industrially." These general principles grew out of Roosevelt's political apprenticeship within the Republican party and out of the ideological commitments he had made to the GOP during the Gilded Age. For all his martial flair and public bravado, Roosevelt would not have been nominated for vice-president in 1900 had he not stood close to the center of the nation's dominant political party.[26]

The new president shared the prevalent conviction among Republicans in 1901 that they represented the constructive nationalism that had preserved the Union during the 1860s and had promoted industrialization across the postwar decades. "It remained the Nationalist as against the particularist or States'-rights party," Roosevelt wrote in his autobiography. Republicans believed that the power of the government should be employed with vigor and purpose in order to spread the benefits of an expanding economy to all classes of society. Republicans thought that their Democratic opponents, on the other hand, stood for negation and governmental weakness, as their ineptitude during the administration of Grover Cleveland had demonstrated, and that William Jennings Bryan and his followers, who had captured the Democracy from the Cleveland men in 1896, constituted "a foolish and ill-judged mock-radicalism." Whether it was in acquiring overseas possessions or achieving recovery from the hard times of the 1890s, the Republicans, Roosevelt believed, could point to a legacy of positive action that made them the natural governing party of the country.[27]

Roosevelt's political career had occurred during the Republican emergence from a position of virtual deadlock with the Democrats during the 1870s and 1880s to a clear electoral supremacy by the presidential race of 1900. After long years of stalemate and frustration between 1872 and 1892, the congressional elections of 1894 and William McKinley's defeat of Bryan in 1896 had established a Republican majority that would be a fact of life throughout Roosevelt's two terms. The central element in Republican success had been the inability of Grover Cleveland and the Democrats to alleviate the distress that accompanied the Panic of 1893 and the ensuing four years of economic depression. Republican arguments that theirs was the party of prosperity convinced voters to end Democratic power and install the GOP in the White House and both branches of Congress. All these developments received Roosevelt's enthusiastic public approval.

What then made Republican politicians uneasy about the new president in September 1901? Throughout his rise in the party, Roosevelt had shown a streak of independence and a skepticism about party dogma. There was also the question of where he stood on the protective tariff, the central economic policy of the Republicans during these years. At Harvard and during the early years of his political life, he had flirted with the doctrine of free trade. Once in office, Roosevelt would follow protectionist policies, but the conservatives would also be suspicious of his commitment to party orthodoxy. The new president found the tariff boring; he never really understood it as a policy. He preferred not to deal with it, if possible, and to leave the political hazards of tariff revision to his successor.

On the issue of business consolidation, however, Republican regulars had reason to be concerned about Roosevelt's fidelity to the GOP precepts that encouraged large enterprises and limited the government's interference with them. Roosevelt was no enemy of private property or the rights of entrepreneurs and corporations. He believed that big business was the natural outgrowth of the nation's industrial expansion since the Civil War. Coming from the aristocratic world of old money in New York City, he did not have a great deal of empathy or respect for the actual process of business. Nor had Roosevelt even been closely involved with the spread of industrialization itself. From this position of distance and detachment, he saw his role as president to represent the balanced judgment of the American people and not to become the advocate of large-scale capitalism. For Roosevelt the problem of industrial size was the kind of large social issue that in the abstract engaged his abundant energies. Fear of an adverse reaction from his party or the business community would not constrain him.

If his domestic goals for the United States were somewhat vague in the autumn of 1901, Theodore Roosevelt had more precise ideas about what he wished to achieve in foreign policy. "Whether we desire it or not," he told Congress in December 1901, "we must henceforth recognize that we have international duties no less than international rights."[28] The emergence of the nation as a world power after the Spanish-American War confirmed in the new president's mind that the United States must have both the will and the power to carry out its world responsibilities. Among the most significant obligations that the nation had was to promote order in a world of empires and nationalistic rivalries. To that end, Roosevelt believed that the president must carry forward a consistent foreign policy that would live up to the commitments the United States had assumed in 1898 and afterward.

The correct approach for the nation was to enhance its prestige and influence in world affairs. This would often involve the exercise of power, but it should be done carefully and with restraint. The United States, said Roosevelt, should act "with scrupulous regard in word and deed, not only for the rights, but for the feelings, of other nations." Moreover, the country should not assume commitments or make pledges that it did not intend to honor. When he was president, Roosevelt wrote proudly in his autobiography: "We made no promises which we could not and did not keep. We made no threat which we did not carry out." It troubled him when public opinion pushed the nation to begin a duty from which the American people were likely to retreat as problems arose.[29]

Roosevelt knew, however, that the citizens of his country were not disposed to support the larger international role that he envisioned. By 1901 it was apparent that Americans did not wish to relinquish the gains

13

of imperialism, but neither did they want to see the United States take on an expanded agenda in the world. With peace abroad, geographic isolation from Asian and European problems, and the absence of any immediate foreign threat, the citizens of the United States could feel reasonably secure. They did not want to embark on additional foreign adventures or see their president engaged in international diplomacy.

So Roosevelt had to move cautiously in his campaign to have the United States play what he considered to be its appropriate role as a world power. Much of the secrecy with which he surrounded his diplomatic initiatives reflected his worry about the potential absence of domestic political support for what he sought to do. Within these limits, however, he wanted his country to be a force for stability in the world. The nation needed to have the means to exercise its influence, and this required that it maintain an adequate navy and a modern, efficient army. Roosevelt pursued the doctrine of military readiness throughout his presidency to an often unreceptive Congress and to a less than enthusiastic public.

Despite the domestic obstacles that limited his power overseas, Roosevelt saw no escape from the exercise of American influence in the world. The Spanish-American War had made the country a Pacific power. Protecting the Philippines and maintaining the Open Door in China necessarily entailed a concern for the power relationships in Asia "and by that route to the general European balance upon which that was contingent." As he confronted the shifting alignments of international rivalries, Roosevelt sought to maintain balance. While his natural sympathies lay with Great Britain and France, he also cultivated the Germany of William II. He pursued a similar middle course between Russia and Japan in Asia. Everywhere he wished to shape United States commitments to fit the nation's capacity to keep its word.[30]

Roosevelt divided the world into those people whose heritage and experience equipped them for self-government and other nationalities who lacked these important traits. While he was careful not to use offensive language in public statements, his contempt for countries that lacked the civilizing virtues often broke through in his private correspondence. Despite these personal feelings, Roosevelt was neither a mindless jingo nor an apostle of American military intervention in underdeveloped areas of the world. Apart from the Philippines, where the native insurgency against the United States continued during the early years of his presidency, Roosevelt sent no troops into action, and no Americans died in armed combat while he was in office.

There was a functioning White House and a presidential administration at Roosevelt's disposal in September 1901. While the new presi-

dent soon put his own stamp on the office, he also left in place many of
the procedures and key officials of McKinley's term. There were important continuities at first between the two Republican presidents. In
many senses, Roosevelt's first term also remained McKinley's second
term.

It aided Roosevelt that McKinley had been his predecessor. The
murdered president had strengthened the power of the office during the
war with Spain. He had adopted techniques of press relations and presidential travel that Roosevelt extended. While McKinley was popular, he
was never exciting or fascinating to the public at large. After McKinley's
grey respectability, Roosevelt seemed a roman candle of exuberance and
fun. Becoming the president in the first year of a new century also
helped Roosevelt convey a symbolic sense of change and vitality.

A significant holdover in the White House was the president's secretary, George B. Cortelyou. Forty-one when Roosevelt took office, Cortelyou had come to the presidency during the Cleveland years as a
stenographer. He became indispensable to McKinley in the crisis that
preceded the war with Spain. The prototype of the modern White
House staff member, Cortelyou managed the dissemination of press
releases from the president, organized the frequent trips that McKinley
made, and provided daily briefings for the journalists who gathered on
the second floor, where tables had been provided for them.

Most of the bureaucratic innovations that McKinley and Cortelyou
had developed carried over into the Roosevelt years. However, the new
chief executive adapted the emerging techniques of the modern presidency to his own personal style. He did not like the telephone, and that
instrument received less use than it had with McKinley. Roosevelt also
took a greater part in press relations and news management, but he did
so in an informal and somewhat sporadic way. To some degree the
impulses that Cortelyou had displayed during the McKinley years toward bureaucracy, rationalization, and order in handling White House
press coverage actually slowed under Roosevelt. The president wanted
to be able to play favorites among the press corps, to issue leaks when he
chose, and to escape the restrictions of an office routine.

By 1901 the work of the presidency was already unrelenting, and it
was conducted in "space not much larger than the vestibule in many a
New York office building." By modern standards, where hundreds of
people serve the president, Theodore Roosevelt had a tiny staff. In addition to Cortelyou, there were two assistant secretaries during the first
year, B. F. Barnes and William Loeb, Jr. Barnes was there when
Roosevelt arrived in September 1901. The thirty-three-year-old Loeb
had begun working with Roosevelt in Albany as a stenographer and had

continued as private secretary for the governor and vice-president. He became a fixture in the administration as the president's secretary after Cortelyou moved on to the cabinet in 1903. Loeb did not mind Roosevelt's hours. "He is always on the spot," Roosevelt said in 1908, "and that means everything to me." The rest of the regular staff consisted of two executive clerks, eleven clerks, and seven messengers. Three other clerks and two messengers were detailed to the White House according to records compiled in July 1902.[31]

The White House never closed, and the staff processed the average daily flow of one thousand letters, hundreds of telegrams, and numerous official documents that reached the president's office. Dozens of newspapers also arrived, and extensive clipping files and scrapbooks were maintained of these items. An elaborate system of cross-filing and indexing kept track of all the paper as it moved past Cortelyou and his associates. The most significant documents went to Roosevelt for a reply. Others were routed to the appropriate department or agency.

Within the Executive Mansion, the business of government went forward with quiet efficiency during the autumn of 1901. Informed observers in Washington knew, however, that the old building did not "adequately meet the requirements either of public service or private use and is not in any respect creditable to a wealthy and powerful nation like the United States."[32] There was not enough room for the clerks, filing space was running out, and library facilities were sparse and overcrowded. The press corps required formal working space rather than tables in corridors, the reception areas needed to be enlarged, and the private and public sections of the Mansion had to be set off from each other. Most important, the White House was not structurally sound, and President Roosevelt would make major renovations to the building.

When he took office, the president deliberately said that he would not be reshaping the cabinet that had served under McKinley. That announcement was part of the process of reassurance that marked the opening days of his presidency. Crucial positions in the cabinet did not change until the election of 1904 neared. As time passed, however, much reshuffling of individual posts occurred, as Roosevelt made frequent shifts in cabinet personnel.

The two leading members of the administration at the outset were the secretary of state, John Hay, and Elihu Root, the secretary of war. Hay was nearing his sixty-third birthday after a distinguished career as Abraham Lincoln's secretary and biographer, a diplomat, a noted author, and ambassador in Great Britain. With his hair parted in the middle and his neat whiskers, Hay was "a nervous, civilized, sensitive man, spruced to the tips of his mustache and beard, with eyeglasses pinching his fastidious little nose."[33] McKinley brought Hay into the cabinet in September 1898 as secretary of state. Hay became famous for the Open Door notes of 1899 and 1900, which asserted the United States' interest in the trade of China and in the territorial integrity of that nation.

Hay took McKinley's death very hard. He had been close to Lincoln and to James A. Garfield; a third presidential assassination was a heavy blow. The death of his son earlier in the summer added to Hay's melancholy. He submitted a letter of resignation to Roosevelt but was gratified when the president asked him to stay at his post. A friend of Roosevelt's father, Hay lost few chances to flatter Roosevelt. A working relationship endured until the secretary's health failed in 1904. Although they agreed on the fundamentals of foreign policy, Hay and Roosevelt experienced more tension in their collaboration than either admitted during the secretary's lifetime. Where McKinley regularly consulted Hay about diplomatic issues, Roosevelt operated more freely in the areas that interested him.

The other imposing figure in the cabinet was Elihu Root. The secretary of war, who was nearing his fifty-seventh birthday, had just completed two full years in governmental service. President McKinley had asked Root to leave his corporate law practice in New York during the summer of 1899. Root proved to be an excellent appointment. He brought a superb administrative capacity to his job, and he was adept at handling the complex issues that the nation faced in Cuba and the Philippines. Root also launched reforms in the army to address the deficiencies that the war with Spain had disclosed in the organization and operation of the service.

Roosevelt had known Root for many years in the Republican politics of New York, and their personalities meshed effectively from 1901 to 1904 and again when Root succeeded John Hay as secretary of state in mid 1905. The secretary of war regarded Roosevelt with a detached amusement that enabled him to joke with the president at moments of crisis. Roosevelt used Root in settling the anthracite-coal strike in 1902 and as part of the negotiations over the Alaska boundary a year later.

The remaining members of the cabinet reflected McKinley's governing style, and changes came early in the new administration. There were some fixtures. The secretary of agriculture, James ("Tama Jim") Wilson of Iowa, had ties to the Republican farm vote that enabled him to serve through both of Roosevelt's terms and on through the Taft administration. Wilson was a valuable source of political intelligence. The secretary of the interior, Ethan Allen Hitchcock, lasted until 1907, when his order to enforce the land laws and his conflicts with influential senators made him a political liability. The attorney general, Philander C. Knox, had joined the cabinet earlier in 1901, and he proved to be an important participant in the implementation of antitrust policy.

The three other cabinet members had less chance of working successfully with Roosevelt. John D. Long was still secretary of the navy. Roosevelt had disliked Long's management practices as a subordinate; he deemed them even less palatable as Long's superior. Charles Emory Smith, the postmaster general, who had been a close friend of McKinley's, was likely to move on at an early date. Finally, the secretary of the treasury, Lyman J. Gage, was a Chicago banker who held the position because of McKinley's confidence in him. All three were soon to be replaced.

Edith Roosevelt arrived in Washington to join her husband on 25 September 1901 and quickly found the living quarters in the White House too small for their active family. "Edie says it's like living over the store," Roosevelt observed. The new president was beginning to settle into his job and the routine that shaped it. "He says to his friends quietly but firmly: 'I will be President,' " and Washington and the nation were realizing that he meant what he said. A newspaperman predicted that "Roosevelt will be the most interesting president we have had in many years and the easy-goers will find that the Rough Rider is a stayer and that he is a horseman."[34]

The first occasion that Theodore Roosevelt had to speak to the nation directly came in his annual message to Congress, delivered when the lawmakers reassembled in December 1901. In that written communication, the president revealed the extent to which he would continue McKinley's policies and the extent to which he would embark on his own initiatives. With his family now beside him in the White House and with his colorful apprenticeship for the presidency behind him, Roosevelt used his ample energies to cast up his own evaluation of the state of the union in the first year of the twentieth century. The resulting document underscored how much the personal character of the new president would shape the course of his administration in the years ahead.

2

★ ★ ★ ★ ★

THE PERSONALIZED
PRESIDENT

On 3 December 1901 clerks read the first annual message of President Theodore Roosevelt to the two houses of Congress assembled for the first session of the Fifty-seventh Congress. The message was sent from the White House in print for the first time, and commentators remarked about its length. In the Senate, the reading "was listened to with marked respect by the Senators" as the more than twenty thousand words took two and one-half hours to read. Secretary of the Navy John D. Long wrote: "It might have been shorter, and I have heard one or two people speak of its having a sort of academic flavor. But it certainly is so hearty and frank and aboveboard that everybody seems to like it, although there are points to which it is not expected that everybody will agree."[1]

By the time he made his report to Congress, Theodore Roosevelt had already shown that he would be a more visible and controversial president in a personalized way than his late-nineteenth-century predecessors had been. He displayed early the capacity to fascinate and captivate the American people that characterized his leadership style. The annual message was the culmination of this early phase when the nation got to know Theodore Roosevelt as a presidential leader.

After the month of mourning for McKinley had ended, the new president became a fixture in the news columns. The announcement was made that the official name of the president's residence would be changed from the Executive Mansion to the White House. Roosevelt took his cabinet members to the Army-Navy football game in Philadelphia. At half time the president led his entourage from the Navy's to the Army's side of the field.[2] During his afternoons in Washington, Roosevelt went horseback riding. Sometimes he took his family on a day trip on the presidential yacht. Of an evening the family attended plays at local theaters. Energy and youth became the hallmark of his administration at the outset, in contrast to the more sedate pace of the Cleveland and McKinley administrations.

Theodore Roosevelt knew that most Americans learned about presidential actions and policies from the press. At the start he endeavored to shape how reporters treated him. On the day he returned from McKinley's funeral, he said to the men from the Associated Press, the United Press Association, and the *New York Sun* Press Association that "if any of the reporters should at any time violate a confidence or publish news that the President thought ought not to be published, he should be punished by having legitimate news withheld from him." The newsmen told Roosevelt that he could not make such an edict effective, but his response was: "All right, gentlemen, now we understand each other."[3]

The reporters who covered the president respected his mastery of their craft. They appreciated his accessibility, the leaks he made to them, and the confidential background information that he shared with them. Most of all, they valued the good copy that he provided. The president knew how to time his statements and press releases for maximum exposure. His announcements often came on Sundays so as to dominate the headlines on Monday, a traditionally slow news day. Roosevelt also played favorites among the press, and eventually a "newspaper cabinet" of friendly reporters evolved. As long as he could dominate the front page, the president was willing to abide the criticism of the editorial section.

To be in Roosevelt's good graces, reporters had to be favorable observers of his record. Newsmen who betrayed his confidence, displeased him, contradicted him, or disclosed what he wished kept private, were enrolled in the Ananias Club, Roosevelt's label for those who had lied to him or about him. If the transgression had been particularly severe, the president wrote to the publisher of the paper involved or tried to cut the reporter off from official White House sources. "The President is a great 'news man,' but he wants to give out the news himself—to control the source of information," a disillusioned reporter concluded in 1906.[4] From the outset there was a strong element of personal news management in Roosevelt's press relations, an arena in which he tried out techniques that succeeding presidents would use.

During the autumn of 1901 most of the news coverage from the

White House was all that Theodore Roosevelt could have wished. The press applauded the president's decision not to appoint officeholders on the basis of regional, sectional, or partisan considerations. His assurance that civil-service principles would govern appointments overseas also received praise. "This office will be administered with an eye single to the interests of efficiency and integrity" was how the president phrased it.[5]

Roosevelt had the advantage of a relatively tranquil honeymoon period. John Hay was handling the negotiation of the second Hay-Pauncefote Treaty with Great Britain to make possible an isthmian canal under United States control across Central America. The two nations signed the treaty, which had been cleared in advance with key senators, on 18 November 1901. Presidential instructions also went out to the United States delegation to an international conference of the American states.

Patronage decisions and other appointments took up most of Roosevelt's available time. The selection of William Dudley Foulke of Indiana for the Civil Service Commission in mid October, and the naming of James R. Garfield, son of the president, to the same panel in early 1902 bore out Roosevelt's commitment to meritorious candidates for these important posts. In the case of individual states, Roosevelt made appointments that bolstered his own political fortunes against potential rivals such as Mark Hanna. The president devoted attention to Colorado, where his men, led by Philip B. Stewart, supplanted the followers of former senator Edward O. Wolcott. In Kansas, Roosevelt favored those who opposed the leadership of the dominant Republican, Cyrus Leland. He also undercut the power of Richard Kerens in Missouri, began a protracted involvement in GOP politics in Illinois, and endeavored to deal with the power of the faction that J. Edward Addicks led in Delaware.[6]

Such work allowed Roosevelt to show his sensitivity to the ethnic and religious elements in the electorate. He wrote to a Roman Catholic clergyman about potential chaplains for the navy and asked for the nomination of "a first-class man, who will be a credit to the navy, a credit to America, and a credit to his church." Similar letters went out to other denominations and to other branches of the government. "The President is of the opinion that there should be a Catholic on the Board of Indian Commissioners," the White House informed the secretary of the interior.[7] These decisions rewarded Roosevelt handsomely among Catholic voters in the 1904 election. For the powerful lobby of Civil War veterans, he eased out McKinley's controversial commissioner of pensions, Henry Clay Evans, who was replaced with a more pliant man from Kansas, the sometime poet Eugene F. Ware.

21

The most delicate patronage choices for any Republican president in these years lay in the South. Roosevelt's initial moves in the region led to the first public commotion of his presidency during October 1901. By the early years of the twentieth century, the Republican party did not exist in the South as a genuine electoral force. The rise of segregation during the 1890s, Democratic election laws that excluded blacks from the polls, and the racism that pervaded the South and the nation—all had led the GOP to become a paper organization that persisted for only two reasons, patronage and convention votes. Those southerners, both black and white, who claimed Republican allegiance looked to their presidents for patronage posts when the party held power. Every four years, delegations from these states made up a significant bloc of votes at the Republican National Convention. With his own nomination in 1904 far from a certainty in the autumn of 1901, Roosevelt had good reason to be attentive to the delegate potential of the South.

The key to controlling Republican politics in the South was influence with the black party members who made up the rank and file of the Dixie GOP. Their leader was the educator Booker T. Washington, of the Tuskegee Institute in Alabama, who by 1901 was the dominant national political figure among blacks. Access to northern philanthropists gave Washington the money that fueled the "Tuskegee Machine," a network of black newspapers, spies, and loyal officeholders dedicated to advancing the cause of "The Wizard of Tuskegee." His conservative social philosophy about black/white relations, expressed in his 1895 speech to the Cotton States Exposition, made him an acceptable spokesman for blacks to white America.

Roosevelt had known Washington since 1898 when they first talked about "what ought to be done by a President to the South."[8] Believing that Reconstruction had actually hurt the interests of blacks, they proposed in the South to appoint some former Confederates and Democrats who had stood for the gold standard in 1896 and 1900. These responsible white conservatives would join with enlightened blacks to safeguard the political position of other southern blacks. During the summer before he became president, as part of his potential presidential campaign in 1904, Roosevelt was planning a visit to Tuskegee in November 1901.

After McKinley's death, on the day Roosevelt took office, he asked Booker T. Washington to see him "as soon as possible," to discuss "the question of possible future appointments in the south exactly on the lines of our last conversation together." The two men met on 4 October 1901 and explored the candidacy of Thomas Goode Jones, a Gold Democrat, for a federal judgeship in Alabama. The selection of Jones was formally announced a few days later. During the next two weeks, agents of Washington saw Roosevelt while information flowed between the White House and the black leader about southern patronage.[9]

When Washington came back to the District of Columbia in mid October, he received an invitation to dine with President Roosevelt on the sixteenth at 7:30 P.M. The other guest was Philip B. Stewart of Colorado. Edith Roosevelt and some of the Roosevelt children were also at the dining table. News of Booker T. Washington's visit appeared as a routine item in New York and Washington, D.C., newspapers after a reporter saw the name in a White House guest register.[10]

The southern press, ever apprehensive about the prospect of social equality between whites and blacks, reacted angrily to the disclosure. A Memphis newspaper termed the occasion "the most damnable outrage that has ever been perpetrated by any citizen of the United States," and the *Richmond* (Virginia) *Times* believed the invitation showed Roosevelt's willingness "that negroes shall mingle freely with whites in the social circle—that white women may receive attentions from negro men."[11]

The furor over the Roosevelt-Washington dinner illustrated the extent of racism in the nation that Theodore Roosevelt governed. The ten million African-Americans, most of whom lived in the South, confronted a rigid system of racial segregation. Poverty, illiteracy, and powerlessness were the lot of the majority of blacks. Life expectancy in 1901 among white men and women in the United States was almost 49.5 years. For nonwhites, life expectancy stood at 33.7 years. The gap persisted during the first decade of the century, part of a general trend that saw life-expectancy rates for black women worsen between 1865 and 1915. Lynchings, which averaged about one hundred a year, were a constant warning of the danger to those who crossed caste lines in the South. Few of Roosevelt's predecessors had mentioned the race issue as president, and substantive actions to help African-Americans had been virtually nonexistent during the 1890s.

Theodore Roosevelt had told Booker T. Washington that he would "help not only the Negro, but the whole South, should he ever become president." His sense of what blacks should receive grew out of his conviction that "as a race and in the mass" they were "altogether inferior to the whites" and were not intellectual and social equals. The impact of their divergent cultural heritages, he believed, kept blacks and whites apart. The president did not intend to use his office to attack racial barriers. The invitation to Washington was a personal gesture done for electoral reasons. Roosevelt told a correspondent, "The very fact that I felt a moment's qualm on inviting him because of his color made me ashamed of myself and made me hasten to send the invitation."[12]

23

Roosevelt and Washington made no public statements about their meeting during his presidency, and their political collaboration continued. The president did not apologize to his critics for his courtesy to Washington, but he did not repeat the action or invite other blacks to the White House for dinner. In time he said to friends that it had been a mistake to entertain Washington. By the time Roosevelt had submitted his annual message, the nation, outside the South, had forgotten about the episode.

The president's main policy task during these autumn months was the preparation of the annual message itself. Two issues posed crucial choices. What policy was he going to adopt on the tariff, the basis of Republican economic policy? Should he extend the program of tariff reciprocity that McKinley had advocated in his last public address? Second, there was the issue of corporate regulation and the trusts. Would the message address the public's concern about monopolies and bigness, or would it be silent?

William McKinley had been vague about where his tariff policy might have gone during a second term. As president he had supported the high rates in the Dingley Tariff (1897), which imposed protective customs duties on wool and woolens, cattle hides, silk, and countless industrial products. To dedicated Republicans the Dingley law was the key to the prosperity that returned during the late 1890s. McKinley's commitment to protectionism, so strong when he came to the White House, shifted as his presidency progressed. He gave signs that he saw reciprocal trade agreements as a way to maintain the essentials of the existing tariff system while at the same time lowering rates on foreign goods and deflecting consumer animosity against high prices. McKinley also regarded reciprocity treaties as an effective way to open up foreign markets for American products. In his last speech, he predicted: "By sensible trade arrangements which will not interrupt our home production, we shall extend the outlets for our increasing surplus."[13]

To achieve this goal his administration had negotiated treaties with France, Argentina, and several other countries. Framed by the State Department's reciprocity commissioner, John A. Kasson, these pacts had run into Senate opposition during 1900/1901 and had not even come to the floor before McKinley died. The policy divided Republicans. Party members in the Middle West found that some of their constituents who sold heavy machinery and farm equipment liked reciprocity as a means of entering markets in Latin America and Europe. The prospect of lower duties on raw materials was also pleasing. There was sentiment in Iowa and elsewhere in the Middle West that products of trusts which were sold more cheaply abroad than in the United States no longer needed protection. This "Iowa Idea" appeared in the state's Republican plat-form in early August 1901. It advocated "any modification of the tariff schedules that may be required to prevent their affording a shelter to monopoly."[14] Reciprocity had behind it as well the momentum that McKinley's assassination gave to his political legacy.

The opposition to reciprocity within the GOP also ran deep and probably represented the attitude of a majority of the Republican leaders in and out of Congress. Any effort to lower the tariff, even on a gradual and controlled basis, would encounter the opposition of "strong man-ufacturing influences" in New England and Pennsylvania who were "fearful of any attempt to reduce duties." In the Senate there was little support among the conservative Republicans "to disembowel the pre-sent tariff act which has given us, in our added power to compete, about all the trade of the world that is worth having." The most important opponent of the reciprocity treaties was Nelson W. Aldrich of Rhode Island, the party chief in the Senate.[15]

During his first weeks in office, Theodore Roosevelt assumed that McKinley's reciprocity policy would go forward easily. A draft of Roose-velt's annual message contained approving references to what McKinley had proposed. On 16 October, Joseph Wharton, a Pennsylvania steel maker and a dedicated protectionist, came to the White House to talk about reciprocity. After reading the message, Wharton expressed his disapproval of the tariff language. Faced with this negative reaction, Roosevelt decided to arrange a meeting with Aldrich that took place on 28 October 1901.

The president and the senator talked during lunch and then spent two more hours in conference. Aldrich indicated that there should be "no tinkering with the tariff" either by reciprocity treaties or laws to lower duties on the products of the trusts. After this conference, the White House cooled toward reciprocity. Senators and representatives who saw Roosevelt in early November concluded "that his first message to Congress will be less radical than has generally been supposed." Senator Hanna, noting that the Republican victory in the recent Ohio elections argued for letting "well enough alone," told the press after seeing Roosevelt: "It is difficult to predict what will be done on the subject of reciprocity." When Henry Cabot Lodge addressed the Mid-dlesex Club in Boston, his carefully hedged remarks on reciprocity were taken as a sign of the president's attitude. Roosevelt and Congress would give the subject "most anxious consideration," but it was "as yet too early to say" whether there should be a general reciprocity law enacted or Senate action on the individual treaties.[16]

Senator William Boyd Allison of Iowa was pushing for consideration of the treaties, if only to quiet the sentiment in his state against high protection and the presumed linkage of the tariff with the trusts. He wrote to Roosevelt on 2 November that "it is the duty of the Senate" to act on the reciprocity pacts. He sent along a copy of an Iowa speech that made this case. "It seems to me that good faith to other nations requires this," Allison wrote, and he noted "a strong feeling in Iowa" that something should be done about reciprocity.[17]

Roosevelt sent Allison's letter and his speech to Aldrich. The Rhode Island senator responded that the president should have "no special anxiety" about whether the Senate would consider the treaties. He interpreted Allison's letter as saying that the president need only indicate a general approval of reciprocity and did not have "to make any specific recommendations either as to the old treaties or as to new ones hereafter to be negotiated." That was not quite what Allison had meant, but it suited Roosevelt's mood about reciprocity after the protectionists had worked on him. The president told Aldrich that he would keep the wording of the section with the changes that the senator had suggested. "All I shall do about the treaties will be to say I call the attention of the Senate to them. I think that if I did not make any allusion to them, some unfavorable comment would be excited."[18]

The decision to drop the McKinley campaign for reciprocity made good political sense to Theodore Roosevelt during the early days of his presidency. A direct confrontation with the Senate over the treaties would likely have brought a presidential defeat. The fifty-five Republicans there, most of them staunch protectionists, would not have given a majority of their votes to the treaty with France. Working with a coalition of Democrats and sympathetic Republicans was not something a partisan Roosevelt envisioned in 1901. Even had the Senate acted favorably, the nature of the Dingley Tariff of 1897, which had authorized the reciprocity negotiations, might have made the concurrence of the House of Representatives necessary. Since the treaties involved revenue, the House asserted a constitutional right to participate through enabling legislation. It was equally unlikely that the 197 House Republicans would endorse tariff revision.

Nonetheless, Roosevelt's decision had lasting consequences for his party and his presidency. The general issue of tariff revision did not come up again during his first term, largely for institutional reasons. There were four annual sessions of Congress during a presidency, two of which had statutory limits on their length. These sessions began in December of even-numbered years and had to adjourn on 4 March of the following year. Three months was not enough time to address the tariff problem when a few determined lawmakers could filibuster to delay meaningful action. The other two sessions started in odd-numbered years. Their length was not fixed. The session that met in a presidential election year was usually empty of significant legislation. Special sessions were theoretically possible but were not often used. A decision not to take up the tariff or reciprocity in 1901/2 meant that Congress would not address them again before 1905/6 at the earliest.

Roosevelt's decision about reciprocity also reflected his own uncertainty and lack of confidence about the tariff, as well as his unwillingness to risk his political future as president. The consequences for the Republican party were significant. The internal division over the tariff festered between 1901 and 1909 and led to animosities that finally erupted when William Howard Taft called for tariff revision in 1909. The party also had to deal with the negative effects of Democratic arguments that the tariff raised consumer prices and helped only big business. As inflation rose after 1900, the opposition case made sense to the American public. Reciprocity might have offset some of these political losses.

For the new president a more significant part of his first message had to do with the national government's power to regulate large corporations. "The absolutely vital question was whether the government had power to control them at all," Roosevelt recalled in 1913. "This question had not yet been decided in favor of the United States Government."[19] Theodore Roosevelt made the issue of regulating the trusts the most distinctive policy of his first term, and he sought to establish the supremacy of the federal government in this area.

The trust issue arose because of the substantial expansion of the nation's manufacturing sector that had occurred by 1900. In 1889 the amount of capital in manufacturing was almost $5.7 billion. Despite the depression of the 1890s, the figure increased to $8.2 billion in 1899. It soared to $20.8 billion by 1914. There were 5.9 million people employed in manufacturing in 1900. The number increased to 8.3 million by 1910. The output of the manufacturing sector was impressive. American mills produced 108.4 million bushel barrels of wheat flour in 1901, and the steel mills turned out almost 13.5 million long tons of ingots and casings.

As part of this industrializing process, large integrated manufacturing companies emerged. In their number of employees and in the size of their capitalization, these firms were unprecedented in the nation's experience. Several of the biggest railroads had more than 100,000 employees by the 1890s. Decisions in corporate board rooms could affect the lives of tens of thousands of people at a time. Standard Oil had almost $125 million of capitalization by 1900, while the American Tobacco Company increased its capitalization to $500 million four years later. The most notable example came in 1901, when United States Steel was organized with a capital of $1.4 billion.

The growth of these large companies during the 1890s renewed fears that the growth of trusts and holding companies might stifle economic opportunity for the middle class. Similar apprehensions during the 1870s and 1880s had led to the enactment of the Interstate Commerce Act in 1887 and the Sherman Antitrust Act in 1890. Now the process of consolidation had resumed despite these legislative barriers. Recovery from the depression of 1893–97, a growing market for industrial securities, and the economic advantages that consolidation presented in the industries that stressed large capitalization and continuous production—all these causes fueled the merger process. Between 1898 and 1902, more than twenty-six hundred firms were absorbed into other companies as a result of mergers. The one hundred largest corporations in the United States grew "by a factor of four" and exercised control of "40 per cent of the national industrial capital." Newspapers, popular periodicals, and a government commission tracked the emergence of these giant companies, including United States Steel. Plans for organizing that company appeared in the press the day before McKinley's second inauguration. Newspapers warned of "the growing antagonism to the concentration of capital" and feared that it might "lead to one of the greatest social and political upheavals that has been witnessed in modern history."[20]

The prospect of social unrest was one of the elements that went into Theodore Roosevelt's thinking about the trusts, first as governor of New York and then as he prepared his opening presidential message. In August 1899 he wrote a friend that he was "exceedingly alarmed at the growth of popular unrest and popular distrust" about corporate size. He also worried that "the multitudes will follow the crank who advocates an absurd policy, but who does advocate something."[21]

The prospect that Roosevelt found most appealing in 1901 was to publicize corporate affairs. Like many in his party, Roosevelt distinguished between good trusts, which were socially useful, and bad trusts, which injured the public welfare. Since big business was an accomplished fact growing out of powerful social and economic forces, it was pointless to try to break up large corporations. The government should inform citizens about trust activities so that the public could make appropriate decisions about investment and policy. In the last speech he made before becoming president, he said: "It is evident that the state, and if necessary the nation, has got to possess the right of supervision and control as regards the great corporations that are its

28

creatures." This control was particularly necessary for "the great business combinations which derive a portion of their importance from the existence of some monopolistic tendency."[22]

This position did not differ dramatically from what other Republicans believed. The GOP platform in 1900 had called for a department of commerce, in part to promote publicity about corporate behavior. President McKinley also saw trusts as either good or bad businesses, and he was contemplating some antitrust actions before he was killed. Roosevelt, with his characteristic flair for public attention, asserted his position more forcefully than had his predecessor, and he showed a theoretical grasp of why the federal government had the right to regulate business.

As he did with the tariff, Roosevelt circulated relevant portions of his message to friends in the financial and business world. Newspapers reported that the president was being urged to "content himself with the merest and most glittering generalities." Senator Hanna gave such advice, as did George W. Perkins, a partner in J. P. Morgan's firm. Roosevelt told his brother-in-law Douglas Robinson, another advocate of caution, that he intended "to be most conservative, but in the interests of the big corporations themselves and above all in the interests of the country I intend to pursue, cautiously but steadily, the course to which I have been publicly committed again and again, and which I am certain is the right course." When Paul Dana, owner of the *New York Sun*, advised more temperate language about business, Roosevelt replied: "You have no conception of the revolt that would be caused if I did nothing in the matter."[23]

Roosevelt's trust proposal was far from radical. What disturbed businessmen in 1901 was the president's assertion that the national interest transcended any individual private economic interest. Roosevelt understood that a do-nothing policy toward corporations would leave the political initiative to the Democrats. More important, the president also knew that it was no longer enough for a modern nation to promote economic growth alone and not to regulate the excesses and the socially harmful actions of corporations.

The annual message largely consisted of reports and comments that the departments and agencies had sent to the White House. Roosevelt also consulted a broad range of Republican opinion inside and outside of Congress. With so much of the message in circulation, leaks about the substance of the tariff and trust sections occurred. None of this bothered Roosevelt much in 1901 when he wanted no public surprises. "President Roosevelt is taking up his work with great vigor," a friend wrote on the eve of the message, "and he holds the confidence of the country to a marvelous extent, and even the politicians, who do not really like him, do not dare to say a word publicly to his disparagement."[24]

In its material resources and the growth of its population, the United States was ready to play a larger part in the coming century than it had in the one just concluded. "At the opening of the twentieth century," Roosevelt remarked in September 1902, "we face conditions vastly changed from what they were in this country and throughout the world a century ago."[25] Two immediate and striking differences lay in the land area of the nation and in the size of its population. In 1790 the United States of America covered 888,811 square miles. By 1900 its mainland area stood at 3,026,789 square miles, not counting its new Caribbean and Asian possessions. A population of 5,297,000 in 1800 had grown to an estimated 77,585,000 persons by 1901.[26]

The pace of change during the preceding ten years for the population had also been impressive. In 1890 there had been more than 63,000,000 Americans. The 1900 census put the official total at 75,994,575. By the time Theodore Roosevelt was succeeded by William Howard Taft in March 1909, estimates had more than 90,000,000 people in the United States. At the turn of the century the balance of men and women was very nearly equal—38,869,000 males to 37,226,000 females. Within the general populace, there were 68,270,000 whites, 9,315,000 blacks, 237,916 Native Americans, 24,226 Japanese-Americans, and 89,863 Chinese-Americans.

The census figures also reveal that Americans were living longer and experiencing a lower death rate during the first decade of the century. Life expectancy rose almost three years for the whole population—from 49.1 in 1901 to 52.1 in 1909. Deaths per thousand in the country decreased from 16.4 in 1901 to 14.2 in 1909. In the population as a whole, infant mortality rates for males under one year of age fell from 179.1 per thousand in 1901 to 139.9 per thousand in 1909. For female infants the figures were 126.1 per thousand in 1901 as compared with 113.2 per thousand in 1909. The available information on infant mortality rates among African-American children is fragmentary for this period, but it suggests that the situation was dramatically worse for them than it was for white infants.

Most of the population lived in what the census defined as the northeastern and north-central areas. In 1900, 47,379,699 Americans resided in these developed, urbanized, and industrialized sections; 55,715,115 did so a decade later. The South had 24,523,527 residents in 1900, 7,922,969 of whom were black; in 1910 there were 29,389,330 southerners, with blacks numbering 8,749,427. The great migration of African-Americans to northern cities was still a decade and a half in the future when Roosevelt entered the White House. The West, which consisted of the Rocky Mountain and Pacific Coast states, had just over 4,000,000 inhabitants as the century began; that number had risen to 6,825,821 by 1910. New York, Pennsylvania, Illinois, and Ohio headed the list of most populous states. California had the most residents among the western states. Texas, Georgia, Kentucky, and Tennessee were the southern leaders in population.

Urbanization was becoming an increasingly common experience for Americans by 1900, and the trend continued while Theodore Roosevelt was president. The urban population in 1900 stood at 30,160,000 with rural citizens totaling 45,834,654. By 1910 the difference had narrowed; 41,998,932 Americans lived in urban territory, and 49,973,334 were classified as rural residents. Those who lived in cities larger than one million increased from 6,429,474 in 1900 to 8,501,174 in 1910. The most populous city in the nation was New York, whose five boroughs had been consolidated during the 1890s. In 1900, 3,400,000 people lived in New York, compared with 1,699,000 in Chicago, and 1,294,000 in Philadelphia. Theodore Roosevelt's childhood and early career in New York City made him a novelty among recent presidents because of his background and upbringing in a large city.

The president began his message with a tribute to William McKinley. "The Congress assembles this year under the shadow of a great calamity." McKinley, who was "the most widely loved man in all the United States," had been struck down by "an utterly depraved criminal" who disliked "all governments, good and bad alike." After his remarks about the fallen president, Roosevelt proposed that Congress consider barring anarchists from entry into the United States and deporting those found in the country. He also advocated that the murder or attempted murder of the president, or of any person in the line of succession to the presidency be made a federal crime. All civilized powers should declare that anarchy was against the law of nations through treaties that would make the doctrine and its adherents subject to the jurisdiction of the federal courts.[27]

Even though the shooting of President McKinley had aroused animosities against anarchists, these proposals came to very little in Congress. The lawmakers proved unwilling to make the killing of a president a federal crime or to authorize enhanced protective measures for the safety of the chief executive. Congress did decide to pass restrictive measures regarding the exclusion, deportation, and naturalization of anarchists, but a law to impose penalties on native-born or naturalized anarchists failed in the Senate during 1903.

In the main body of the message, Roosevelt asserted that during the preceding five years, "confidence has been restored, and the Nation is to be congratulated because of its present abounding prosperity."[28] The depression of the 1890s had been severe, but the McKinley administration had enjoyed a resurgence of business activity that had contributed to Republican success in the election of 1900. In constant 1929 prices, the gross national product had averaged $29.6 billion annually between 1892 and 1896, surged to $37.1 billion between 1897 and 1901, and would rise to $46.8 billion between 1902 and 1906. Per capita income went up from an average of $434 in the 1892 to 1896 period to $569 in the years 1902 to 1906. Farm products had risen in annual value from $6.8 billion during the Cleveland years to $8.4 billion under McKinley. They went up again, to $8.9 billion, during Roosevelt's first term. Nonfarm products shot up from the depression level of $21.7 billion to an annual figure of $27.4 billion between 1897 and 1901; and they continued upward, to $36.3 billion between 1902 and 1906.

The source of the prosperity, Roosevelt believed, rested "upon individual thrift and energy, resolution and intelligence."[29] For the American workers, these qualities were displayed in a labor force that mirrored the continuing importance of farming as well as the emerging industrial energies of the nation. More than 29,070,000 citizens were employed in 1900. Of them, 10,710,000 worked in agriculture; this figure had climbed to 11,340,000 by 1910. The number of individuals who worked in manufacturing and hand-trade enterprises rose from 6,340,000 to 8,230,000. Among the other occupations in 1900, 1,660,000 people were in construction; 2,100,000 in transportation; 2,760,000 in what were described as trade, finance, and real estate; 3,860,000 in service occupations; and 300,000 in government service.

Early in his message, Roosevelt addressed the issue of corporate regulation, the subject of so much concern during the preparation of the document. He dismissed the idea that the protective tariff had promoted the growth of trusts. Combination occurred because of "natural causes in the business world, operating in other countries as they operate in our own." It was wrong to say that "as the rich have grown richer the poor have grown poorer. On the contrary, never before has the average man, the wage worker, the farmer, the small trader, been so well off as in this country and at the present time." Businessmen, especially those who had established great enterprises, had "on the whole done great good to our people." With American firms involved in international commerce, it was equally important not to jeopardize the nation's competitive position. "The fundamental rule in our national life—the rule which underlies all others—," Roosevelt maintained then and later, "is that, on the whole, and in the long run, we shall go up or down together."[30]

After emphasizing the need for caution, Roosevelt argued that there were "real and grave evils" connected with the trusts, "one of the chief being over-capitalization because of its many baleful consequences." Equally important, "a widespread conviction" existed "in the minds of the American people that the great corporations known as trusts are in certain of their features and tendencies hurtful to the general welfare." It followed, then, that "corporations engaged in interstate commerce should be regulated if they are found to exercise a license working to the public injury." Roosevelt was explicit about the form of that regulation: "Publicity is the only sure remedy which we can now invoke." Other answers would emerge after the facts of business practices became public.[31]

In fact, the president suggested where some additional regulatory measures might go. State laws had not worked to halt the trusts, and it had "proved impossible to get adequate regulation through State action." As a result, "the Nation should, without interfering with the power of the States in the matter itself, also assume power of supervision and regulation over all corporations doing an interstate business." Banks were already subject to such regulation, and it would be no more restrictive than the corporation laws of Massachusetts.[32]

One objection to national supervision was the Supreme Court decision in *U.S. v. E. C. Knight* (1895), which ruled that the Sherman Antitrust Act did not outlaw monopolies of manufacturing. Roosevelt contended that notwithstanding the *Knight* decision, a federal law similar to the Interstate Commerce Law could be enacted. If Congress disagreed about its power to pass such a law, then "a constitutional amendment should be submitted to confer the power." Lastly, a cabinet department and a secretary for commerce and industries should be created, with jurisdiction over industrial, labor, and merchant-marine questions. His corporate program would be one phase of "a comprehensive and far-reaching scheme of constructive statesmanship" to broaden markets, safeguard business interest, and solidify the nation's international economic position. In language that foreshadowed the Square Deal, Roosevelt wrote that his proposals would accomplish these ends "while scrupulously safeguarding the rights of wage worker and capitalist, of investor and private citizen, so as to secure equity as between man and man in this Republic."[33]

Having dealt with corporations, the president turned to the nation's working population. "With the sole exception of the farming interest, no one matter is of such vital moment to our whole people as the welfare of the wage workers." Roosevelt was gratified to proclaim that "on the whole wages are higher to-day in the United States than ever before in our history, and far higher than in any other country."[34] In 1901, wages in the United States were higher than they had been for the past ten years and had surpassed the levels that had existed before the 1893 depression. For all industries, including farm labor, the average annual wage stood at $454. With farm workers excluded, the figure rose to $508 per year. Workers in manufacturing enterprises received $456 a year. Those who were employed by steam railroads earned $549 per year; employees of street railroads made $601 each year. Some clerical workers exceeded $1,000 in yearly earnings. Farm laborers made $255 a year on average, while public-school teachers were paid $337 yearly. The mythical average worker labored almost fifty-nine hours each week, and 1,750,000 children between the ages of ten and fifteen were counted as gainful workers in the labor force.

Did these aggregate figures bear out Roosevelt's claims for the favored position of American workers? Estimates of what constituted a living wage varied. One student of the problem argued in 1906 that $600 per year was a minimum needed for subsistence. Another survey contended that two-thirds of the nation's adult male workers did not make as much as $600 annually. In a substantial percentage of all American families, only the father brought home any income. Only 17.3 percent of white women were in the labor force in 1900; the figure for black women stood at 41.2 percent. In his pioneering study *Poverty*, published in 1904, Robert Hunter maintained that as many as ten million people in the United States lived below the poverty line. A critical Canadian author concluded in 1902 that half the population of the United States was "ill-housed, ill-fed, and ill-clothed."[35]

Throughout the opening years of the twentieth century, the economic situation became more difficult for Americans who depended on a salary. After a period of deflation and falling prices between 1873 and 1897, the price level began to rise as the economy came out of the depression of the 1890s and as gold discoveries in Canada and South Africa increased the world's supply of money. Employed Americans had experienced some rise in real wages during the 1890s. For the ensuing decade and a half, the higher cost of living played a larger part as an economic and political issue. Using a cost-of-living index that stood at 100 in 1897, the price level had gone up to 108 by 1901, 119 by 1906, and 128 by 1910. Newspapers and popular journals discussed in detail the mounting consumer prices, and Democratic orators associated the tariff with the higher cost of the necessities of life, such as food and fuel.

Labor unions had not yet become a significant economic or political force by 1901. The number of workers in unions had risen from 447,000 when McKinley took office to 1,125,000 by the year Roosevelt came to the White House. Labor organizations were most prominent in railroading, mining, and the building trades and in the metals, machinery, and shipbuilding industries. The most important union was the American Federation of Labor (AFL), headed by Samuel Gompers. Composed of unions that enrolled skilled workers, the AFL reached a membership of 1,676,000 by 1905 and was debating whether to become more involved in electoral politics as an organization. Other significant unions were the Railroad Brotherhoods and the United Mine Workers. Most unskilled workers had no union protection of any kind, and organized labor did not endeavor to enlist the mass of laborers into their ranks.

The lot of most American laborers was harsh and exacting. Relatively precise figures for industrial accidents did not appear until the end of Roosevelt's presidency, but estimates put work-related deaths at twenty thousand per year, and at least five hundred thousand other workers were injured or maimed. Little insurance or medical assistance existed for these victims. The first several years of the Roosevelt administration were a time of comparative calm in labor relations before employers began the open-shop and union-busting tactics that came after 1904. Still, in 1901 there were more than three thousand work stoppages and strikes. The potential for discontent fueled the membership drives of the Industrial Workers of the World (IWW) and its philosophy of one big union. Its organizing militance would bring the IWW into direct confrontation with Theodore Roosevelt by 1906.

In his annual message, however, Roosevelt's comments about labor reflected his own recognition, gained in part from his experience in the New York legislature during the early 1880s, of genuine inequities in the treatment that working people received. He asked Congress to help individual states address the problem of convict labor that competed with ordinary workers, and he called for enforcement of the eight-hour day in all governmental work. Women and children who were directly or indirectly employed by the government should not have to work long hours in unsafe conditions. He also advocated a factory law for the District of Columbia and measures to improve that city's inhabited alleys. "The most vital problem" that the nation confronted was to improve urban life and to deal with labor issues. "Very great good" could be done by well-managed unions, he wrote, "when they combine insistence upon their own rights with law-abiding respect for the rights of others." In the end, although there were steps the states and the national government could take, "the rule of brotherhood remains as the indispensable prerequisite to success in the kind of national life for

35

which we strive."[36] The tone of moral exhortation, which accorded well with the outlook of most Americans, became a characteristic of Roosevelt's presidency.

The president stated flatly that "our present immigration laws are unsatisfactory."[37] The murder of McKinley had directed public attention toward immigration because of the widespread belief that anarchism was a foreign doctrine. Although Leon F. Czolgosz, McKinley's assassin, was the child of immigrant parents, he had been born in the United States, and that aspect of the issue received less emphasis. The larger conclusion that immigration into the United States represented a growing social problem made the issue of restricting foreign entry into the country a continuing question for Roosevelt's presidency.

Between 1880 and 1930, about 22,000,000 people entered the United States. Almost 8,000,000 did so during the Roosevelt administration. Of the 488,000 immigrants in 1901, 135,996 came from Italy, 133,390 from what the government called Central Europe, and 85,257 from the Russian Empire. These totals far outweighed the 15,000 from Great Britain, the 39,000 from Ireland, and the more than 39,000 from Scandinavia.

These numbers represented a trend that continued for the next eight years. By 1902, 648,743 immigrants were recorded at ports of entry. A year later the number had swelled to more than 800,000, and by 1907 the totals reached a record high of 1,285,349. There were 1,830,000 immigrants from Italy during these years, another 1,886,000 from central Europe; and Russia contributed 1,410,000 from its territories, including Poland. By 1910 the twelve largest cities of the United States had a population that was one-third foreign born. Children of immigrants contributed another third to the population of these cities. "New York had more Italians than Naples, more Germans than Hamburg, twice as many Irish as Dublin, and more Jews than the whole of western Europe. Chicago was more cosmopolitan still."[38]

The "new immigration" from southern and eastern Europe aroused xenophobic and ethnocentric passions in the United States during the Roosevelt years. "If we ever had a chance to avoid the evils of the slum," said World's Work in 1903, "the coming of great numbers of southern European folk brings this Old World curse in spite of all that we can do." On the West Coast, racial fears about Chinese and Japanese newcomers made Asian exclusion a popular answer among the native-born majority. These sentiments would cause diplomatic problems for Roosevelt throughout his presidency. The Immigration Restriction League, to which Roosevelt's friend Henry Cabot Lodge belonged, pushed for laws to impose stricter tests on entrants into the country or for measures to limit immigrants altogether. On the other side of the issue were business interests who found the ready supply of cheap labor an attractive alternative to the power of organized labor.[39]

Theodore Roosevelt took a more tolerant view of immigrants and the ethnic diversity of the United States than did the proponents of restriction. During the 1890s, for example, he had opposed the American Protective Association, an anti-Catholic organization, and he did not display the intense prejudices that marked the anti-immigrant cause. Some of the exclusionary concepts did appeal to him, however, as the message showed. He said that efforts should be made "to exclude absolutely" not only anarchists and their followers "but also all persons who are of a low moral tendency or of unsavory reputation." Tests should be given to determine whether immigrants had "some intelligent capacity to appreciate American institutions and act sanely as American citizens." Immigrants should also demonstrate the ability "to earn an American living" so that "the influx of cheap labor" would be stopped. The president believed that such a measure "would dry up the springs of the pestilential social conditions in our great cities," where anarchism might occur.[40]

The president next turned his attention to tariff policy, in which he found "general acquiescence." He came out against any revision of protection itself. "Nothing could be more unwise than to disturb the business interest of the country by any general tariff change at this time."[41] The tariff system was still a major source of revenues for the federal government. In 1901 the Treasury had revenues of $587,685,000 and expenditures of $524,617,000, for a surplus of $63,069,000. The total national debt was $1,221,472,000. There was no federal budget to measure the cost of government; that reform would come in 1921. Of the government's revenues, customs duties supplied $238,585,000; and internal revenue, in the form of alcohol, tobacco, and stamp taxes, brought in another $307,000,000. During the 1890s, the Supreme Court had declared an income tax unconstitutional; the Sixteenth Amendment was still a dozen years in the future.

The message called reciprocity "the handmaiden of protection." Reciprocity could only be achieved safely if it occurred "without injury to our home industries." Duties must remain high enough to protect the American worker. Reciprocity under Roosevelt was so hedged with safeguards against reducing protective duties that it was little more than a rhetorical gesture toward McKinley's policy. In the last sentence of the formal tariff section, Roosevelt deferred to Aldrich, the other protectionists in the Senate, and the high-tariff attitudes of the GOP. "I ask the attention of the Senate to the reciprocity treaties laid before it by my predecessor."[42]

Separate and distinct from his tariff remarks, in his review of the condition of the territories that the nation had acquired or controlled from the war with Spain, Roosevelt alluded to another aspect of reciprocity. The Congress should consider "the vital need, of providing for a substantial reduction in the tariff duties on Cuban imports into the United States." Since the Cubans had accepted the political dominance of the United States that was expressed in the Platt Amendment of 1901, "we are bound by every consideration of honor and expediency to pass commercial measures in the interest of her [Cuba's] material well-being."[43] Neither the domestic sugar producers nor the powerful beet-sugar lobby in the Republican party agreed with Roosevelt on this point.

After the tariff came the merchant marine, the financial system, and the need for government economy. The nation's merchant fleet in 1901 was "utterly insignificant" when compared with the countries that competed with the United States. In 1901, American vessels brought in $93 million worth of imported goods; foreign ships accounted for $683 million. For exports, American ships carried $84 million; foreign ships hauled products worth $1,292 million. "It should be made advantageous," Roosevelt argued, "to carry American goods in American-built ships." Higher construction and labor costs in the United States made that goal difficult to achieve. The proposal to subsidize American shipping, pushed by Mark Hanna and others, divided the Republicans in Congress along sectional lines: those from the East Coast and the West Coast were in favor of government aid, whereas the Middle West was strongly opposed to it.[44]

Roosevelt praised the Gold Standard Act of 1900 as "timely and judicious." Although William Jennings Bryan had sought to revive the free-silver crusade in the presidential election of 1900, the monetary passions of the 1890s had cooled by 1901. The nation's currency in that year was made up of gold coin ($621,791,000), gold certificates ($247,036,000), silver dollars ($66,921,000), silver certificates ($429,644,000), treasury notes of 1890 ($47,525,000), subsidiary silver ($79,235,000), minor coins ($27,890,000), U.S. notes ($330,045,000), and national bank notes ($345,111,000).[45]

The categories of bank notes represented the subject that animated politics and finance in banking until the passage of the Federal Reserve Act in 1913. Roosevelt thought the National Banking Act, under which the banking system functioned, was adequate for normal circumstances, "but there seems to be need of better safeguards against the deranging influence of commercial crises and financial panics." The currency "should be made responsive to the demands of our domestic trade and commerce." The Treasury and the banking community were even more critical of the financial structure. The retiring secretary of the treasury, Lyman J. Gage, said that the nation's banks stood "isolated and apart, separated units with no tie of mutuality between them." Unless a central bank was created, Gage feared "a repetition of the disastrous phenomena of 1893," which led to a prolonged depression.[46]

The finances of the government, however, were in good condition with the surplus of revenue. Roosevelt emphasized that "strict economy" in spending was needed. Although the cost of government rose during his presidency, Roosevelt was able to reduce the overall size of the national debt. Governmental spending rose to nearly $659,000,000, with a deficit of $57,334,000 by the last year of Roosevelt's second term. Previous years of governmental surpluses, keyed to the economic prosperity of 1902/3 and 1906/7, produced a reduction in the federal debt from $1,221,572,000 in 1901 to $1,148,315,000 in 1909.[47]

Roosevelt's discussion of the Interstate Commerce Act of 1887, a measure that he called "largely an experiment," introduced his thinking about a problem that would lead to one of the significant battles of his campaign for governmental regulation. There were 1,213 railroad companies of all sizes in 1901, with 265,352 miles of track. The lines moved 607,278,000 passengers over 17,534,000 passenger miles and earned revenues of $351,356,000 from that activity. Freight revenues came to $1,118,534,000 in that year. Railroad lines and equipment totaled more than $10,405,095,000 of investment book value. The American railroad system functioned with a high degree of efficiency and a generally decreasing cost at the beginning of the century.[48]

What made the railroads a controversial political issue in 1901 was the consolidation that the industry had experienced at the end of the 1890s. By 1910, there were 1,316 companies, but the thirty-two railroads that were each capitalized at over $100 million controlled nearly 80 percent of the railroad mileage in the United States. Shippers claimed that these large railroad lines gave unfair advantages in the form of rebates to large corporate customers of the railroad service. This had the effect, as Roosevelt summarized it, of driving "out of business the smaller competitor." Some railroad rates were regarded as excessive. There were allegations that the lines favored one locality or another over rival cities or regions. In response, the industry contended that the Interstate Commerce Act, by outlawing pooling and other practices, deprived rail companies "of that right of concerted action which they claim is necessary to establish and maintain non-discriminating rates."[49]

Roosevelt asserted that "the act should be amended" so that railroad rates would be "just to and open to all shippers alike." The federal government should promote this condition and "provide a speedy, inexpensive, and effective remedy to that end." The president opposed "legislation which would unnecessarily interfere" with the railroads and said that Congress should give the problem its "earnest attention." A month before Roosevelt's message, the Northern Securities Company had been incorporated on 12 November 1901 to bring together the Great Northern, the Northern Pacific, and the Chicago, Burlington and Quincy railroads in a giant consolidated northwestern company. The appearance of the Northern Securities Company, as well as the immediate public reaction to it, shaped both Roosevelt's antitrust and railroad-regulation policies as president.[50]

The conservation of natural resources, a subject that Roosevelt's presidency would be identified with, received extended attention in his first annual message. He considered the issue of national forests at the outset. He did not envision "the withdrawal of forest resources" from what he described as the contribution of "their full share to the welfare of the people." A key to his conservation philosophy lay in his next sentence: "The fundamental idea of forestry is the perpetuation of forests by use." Preserving the forests, he argued, "is an imperative business necessity."[51]

Theodore Roosevelt became, with Franklin D. Roosevelt and Lyndon B. Johnson, one of the great conservationist presidents in the nation's history. He was the first national leader to espouse this important and lasting principle. He recognized the need to preserve some wilderness areas untouched, and he was sensitive to the place of animals and plants in the natural order. "When I hear of the destruction of a species, I feel just as if all the works of some great writer had perished," he wrote before he became president. In 1901 he urged that some of the forest reserves should "afford perpetual protection to the native fauna and flora, safe havens of refuge to our rapidly diminishing wild animals of the larger kinds." These lands could also provide "free camping grounds for the ever-increasing numbers of men and women who have learned to find rest, health, and recreation in the splendid forests and flower-clad meadows of our mountains." He believed that the "forest reserves should be set apart forever for the use and benefit of our people as a whole and not sacrificed to the short-sighted greed of a few." The government's forest reserves were portions of the public domain that had been withdrawn from settlement and development.[52] In early November, because of his own concern for the forest system, Roosevelt had asked the secretary of the interior why permits to graze sheep had been issued for a forest reserve in Arizona.

The most powerful intellectual influence on Roosevelt in conservation matters was Gifford Pinchot, chief of the Bureau of Forestry in the

Department of Agriculture. The president invited Pinchot and an aide, Frederick H. Newell, to submit drafts of the sections on forests and irrigation for his message. The resulting language embodied Pinchot's conviction that orderly, planned, and managed economic development of the nation's natural resources was the approach for the Roosevelt administration to follow. The object with the national forests, Pinchot contended, was not to preserve them "because they are beautiful . . . or because they are refuges for the wild creatures of the wilderness." The important goal was for lumber companies to harvest timber and for settlers to use the resulting products to build "prosperous homes." In comparison with this aim of development and economic growth, Pinchot said, "every other consideration comes as secondary." Like Roosevelt, Pinchot was convinced that overall guidance on resource policy was a national function that should not be left to wasteful and probably corrupt states and localities. In time the two men became convinced, as Roosevelt put it in 1913, that "the Executive is the steward of the public welfare," especially on conservation issues.[53]

Roosevelt argued that all aspects of forest management should be unified in Pinchot's bureau. He asked Congress to give the Agriculture Department the statutory power to transfer government land to use as forest reserves. "The present diffusion of responsibility is bad from every standpoint," Roosevelt wrote, because it prevented "that effective co-operation between the Government and the men who utilize the resources of the reserves, without which the interests of both must suffer." In the West, "wise administration of the forest reserves" would also address the region's problems of water supply and aridity. "The forest and water problems," he concluded, "are perhaps the most vital internal questions of the United States."[54]

The second phase of Roosevelt's early conservation program lay in irrigation projects for the western states. A properly watered West could support a much larger population and relieve some of the nation's social problems. Creating the "great storage works" needed was beyond the capacity of business or individual states. The federal government "should construct and maintain" the storage reservoirs, and it should earmark the irrigated land for agricultural settlement. From this policy, Roosevelt argued, would come an increased demand for factory products and an expanded agricultural capacity to serve both the home market and the potential trade of Asia. At the beginning, the irrigation program should move cautiously without extravagance. He also directed attention to those who were already farming on irrigated land, some 7,543,000 acres in seventeen western states in 1899; and he underscored the need for clear legal title to water rights and for wise irrigation laws in the region. Finally, he called for a study of irrigation conditions in the West and abroad. By these remarks, Roosevelt laid the basis for what was to become the Newlands Reclamation Act of 1902.[55]

The president's concern for irrigation was part of his larger interest in the well-being and future of the nation's agricultural sector. In many respects, his administration was an era of unmatched prosperity on the American farm. The value of farm property doubled between 1900 and 1910; the number of farms rose from 5,737,000 to more than 6,361,000 during the decade; and farm income also increased by more than 100 percent. The prices for major farm products reflected the good times. Wheat brought more than sixty-three cents a bushel in 1901. By 1909, wheat farmers were receiving almost one dollar per bushel. In the South the cotton crop rose from ten million bales in 1900 to sixteen million by 1914. The price for the South's staple crop rose from seven cents a pound in 1901 to more than ten cents a pound for three of the eight years that Roosevelt was in office. As the president observed in 1907, "agriculture in the United States has reached a very high level of prosperity."[56]

Roosevelt knew, however, that serious problems existed on the farm. One worrisome trend was a relative decline in farm ownership in the South and the Middle West. The number of tenant farmers, both white and black, was increasing in the South, and a similar trend could be detected among white farmers in the Middle West. In the South, moreover, many African-American farmers were caught in a state of peonage that approached a return to slavery. What also bothered Theodore Roosevelt was the "growth of the city at the expense of the country." In his judgment the movement away from rural life to an urban setting was potentially dangerous because "the permanent greatness of any State must ultimately depend more upon the character of its country population than upon anything else." These considerations supported the president's conservation campaign and found tangible expression in the Country Life Commission at the end of his administration.[57]

After agriculture, the 1901 annual message turned to the nation's new overseas possessions. Roosevelt found conditions in Hawaii and Puerto Rico satisfactory, argued for tariff reciprocity with Cuba, and then took up the American role in the Philippines. During 1901 the United States had apparently made progress in its drive to establish its rule in the Philippines, create a civil government, and quell the indigenous resistance that had begun in 1899. The capture of the Filipino leader, Emilio Aguinaldo, in March 1901, the action of Congress in creating a civil government for the islands, and the actual transfer of control from military to civilian rule on 4 July 1901—all indicated that the United States had overcome the obstacles to colonial dominance.

Roosevelt had long defended the policies of the McKinley administration in the Philippines. He promised that William Howard Taft, the colonial governor, would carry out the national commitment "to give the islanders a constantly increasing measure of self-government, exactly as fast as they show themselves fit to exercise it." The president recognized that "there are still troubles ahead in the islands." Despite the capture of Aguinaldo, the insurrection continued. Finally, Congress needed to pass laws to regulate the business affairs of the Philippines, including franchise laws and other economic incentives.[58]

The signing of the second Hay-Pauncefote Treaty enabled Roosevelt to deal positively with the issue of a canal to connect the Atlantic and Pacific oceans. Creating such a canal in Central America was "one of those great works which only a great nation can undertake with prospects of success." He promised that the treaty would soon be sent to the Senate, after which Congress could commence work on laws to facilitate the construction of the canal.[59]

"Over the entire world, of recent years," Roosevelt continued, "wars between the great civilized powers have become less and less frequent." Wars that European nations waged with "barbarous or semi-barbarous peoples" were a different matter, more in the nature of "necessary international police duty" for the benefit of humanity. The nations of the Americas should emulate the United States and take the Monroe Doctrine as a central principle of their own foreign policies. That declaration of 1823, the president said, "is a declaration that there must be no territorial aggrandizement by any non-American power at the expense of any American power on American soil." Anticipating his posture toward Venezuela in 1902 when that country could not meet its foreign debts, Roosevelt wrote: "We do not guarantee any state against punishment if it misconducts itself, providing that punishment does not take the form of the acquisition of territory." Meanwhile, the United States had no aims to secure additional territory in the Western Hemisphere.[60]

Roosevelt wanted greater attention paid to and more support for the armed forces. The navy must be strengthened because "an adequate and highly trained Navy is the best guaranty against war, the cheapest and most effective peace insurance." The United States Navy ranked fifth in the world in 1900 in overall strength. However, with seventeen battleships either built or being built, it stood second to Great Britain in that important category. Roosevelt wanted to close the gap with the British, and he recommended an increase in the number of battleships and cruisers, as well as additional supporting vessels. In the ensuing four years the president secured congressional funding for another ten battleships, in addition to four armed cruisers and seventeen other ships. The navy had almost twenty-one thousand officers and men when Roosevelt took office. He now sought five thousand more enlisted men and an increase in the size of classes entering the Naval Academy.[61]

Roosevelt's experience persuaded him that "the officers and men alike should be kept as much as possible on blue water, for it is there only they can learn their duties as they should be learned." He stressed that "above all, gunnery practice should be unceasing." Roosevelt wanted additional crews to man the new battleships, praised the navy's General Board as a coordinating force, and advocated the creation of a national naval reserve. "The American people must either build and maintain an adequate Navy," he said, "or else make up their minds definitely to accept a secondary position in international affairs, not merely in political, but in commercial, matters." Roosevelt's use of the presidency as a pulpit to communicate with the American people was evident in this first encounter.[62]

For the army, which numbered 85,557 officers and men in 1901, Roosevelt did not believe that an increase in size was needed. The army must be kept, however, "at the highest point of efficiency." He wanted riflemen who could ride effectively, the creation of a general staff, and less reliance on seniority in promotions. He favored merit promotions, reduced paperwork, and annual field maneuvers. West Point should relax its requirements about mathematics and should endeavor to produce officers "who are good in actual field service." Meanwhile, the nation's militia law, which relied on the National Guard and the states, was "obsolete and worthless" and should be reformed to promote better integration with the regular army.[63]

Roosevelt praised the Union veterans for what they had done for the country, spoke out for the merit system in government appointments, and recommended other changes in the consular service. Every Native American should be treated as "an individual and not as a member of a tribe." The 238,000 people whom Roosevelt called Indians should be made to function "like the white man," and the number of governmental agencies that supervised their conduct should be reduced. He also denounced the liquor traffic among "the aboriginal races" at home and abroad.[64]

As he neared the end of his long message, Roosevelt spent his last sustained discussion on Chinese-American relations. The final act of the antiforeign Boxer Uprising of 1900 had occurred on 7 September 1901, when the Chinese and Western governments had signed a protocol indicating compliance with the demands of the European nations whose armies had suppressed the Boxers. Roosevelt also reaffirmed American belief in the Open Door policy of John Hay and William McKinley to preserve American trade opportunities in China. With a comment about the Pan-American Congress in Mexico and a statement about some Mexican claims, Roosevelt closed the substantive part of the message. In his last paragraph, he thanked other nations for their sympathy on President McKinley's passing, and he promised a foreign policy of "mutual respect and good will."[65]

Press reaction to Roosevelt's message was one of surprise and some sense of anticlimax that the qualities for which he was famous before the presidency were absent. "The 'Rough Rider' and 'the Jingo,'" the impetuous youth of a year ago, has disappeared," concluded the *New York Evening Post*. If the annual message was any indication, its editors added, Roosevelt "might be a man of sixty, trained in conservative habits." Most attention centered on the discussion of the trust issue. The *Chicago Tribune* called Roosevelt's ideas "moderate and safe" and his program one in which "Republicans and Democrats should be able to join hands with ease regarding it." The Irish dialect humorist Finley Peter Dunne caught the ambivalence of Roosevelt's attitude toward big business when he had his character Mr. Dooley say of the president: " 'Th' trusts,' says he, 'are heejoous monsthers built up be th' inlightened intherprise iv th' men that have done so much to advance progress in our beloved counthry,' he says. 'On wan hand I wud stamp thim undher fut; on th' other hand not so fast.' "[66]

Private responses to Roosevelt's statements echoed what the newspapers reported. A Connecticut congressman wrote that the document "seems to be giving general satisfaction throughout the country from its novel character and for the frank and straightforward way in which he presents the several propositions contained in it." In his first several months as president, Roosevelt had moved cautiously within the limits of the policies of the McKinley years. His annual message in 1901 gave few indications that he would soon depart from that approach. Such incidents as the Booker T. Washington episode revealed that Roosevelt had the capacity to engage the public's attention as few recent presidents had done. When Roosevelt attacked the trusts and intervened in a labor dispute during 1902, his personalized presidency took on the controversial character that established his historical reputation in the White House.[67]

3

★ ★ ★ ★ ★

"IMMEDIATE AND VIGOROUS EXECUTIVE ACTION"

On 19 February 1902 the Department of Justice announced its intention to file an antitrust suit against the Northern Securities Company, the railroad holding company formed late in 1901 in the Northwest. The action stunned Wall Street and signaled that Theodore Roosevelt would act quickly and decisively as president when it suited him. The assertion of his independence in economic policy opened a year during which Roosevelt showed how purposeful a president he intended to be.

The attack on Northern Securities was all the more unexpected because the three months after the annual message had been relatively calm. Even cabinet changes had not aroused much public notice. Although Roosevelt had asked all the members of the McKinley cabinet to stay on, rumors of imminent changes soon floated in Washington. Postmaster Charles Emory Smith, a close friend of McKinley's, left in November, and the president replaced him with Henry Clay Payne, a conservative Republican from Wisconsin. Payne was loyal to Roosevelt, had no affection for Senator Marcus A. Hanna, and knew the Grand Old Party from the inside. Payne's selection evoked some protests because of his business connections, but Roosevelt maintained that there was "not one shadow of truth in the accusations" that Payne had been a corporate lobbyist.[1]

Secretary of the Treasury Lyman J. Gage had planned to retire for some time. Roosevelt's willingness to go outside normal channels for information about the Treasury Department led Gage to move up his date of departure. Roosevelt tried to persuade Governor Winthrop Murray Crane of Massachusetts to succeed Gage, but Crane decided not to leave his state office. Roosevelt then turned to Leslie M. Shaw, the retiring governor of Iowa. Shaw had impressed the president when he defended the gold standard during the 1900 campaign. Shaw's selection also removed a possible rival in 1904.

Roosevelt and the secretary of the navy, John D. Long, were awkward collaborators. Long told his son that he had not "had five minutes conversation with the President alone, or fifteen minutes, even in the presence of others, with regard to the business of the Department." Long soon knew that Roosevelt intended to be his own secretary of the navy, and it was decided that Long would announce his retirement. When the news was released in March 1902, Roosevelt named another Massachusetts politician, Congressman William H. Moody, to succeed Long. Roosevelt had known Moody for several years and respected his ability. Senator Henry Cabot Lodge also pushed Moody for the post, in part to open up a seat in Congress for Lodge's son-in-law.[2]

A public squabble with the commanding general of the army, Nelson A. Miles, was the other newsworthy event of this period before the Northern Securities announcement. Roosevelt was irritated when Miles commented in public about a dispute that was raging within the navy over the performance of the admirals who had defeated the Spanish at the battle of Santiago in 1898. In an interview that received extensive attention, Miles contradicted the position of the White House. The president did not believe that a military officer should differ with administration policy. Roosevelt was also aware that Miles had long-standing presidential ambitions. At the instructions of the president, the secretary of war, Elihu Root, reprimanded Miles for his conduct.[3]

Roosevelt had a strong case. Miles had acted with his characteristic indiscretion, so he deserved the censure. The general had once again demonstrated that he was politically inept. But the president was not content to let Root's statement stand by itself. During the last weeks of 1901 and on into 1902, Roosevelt wrote to editors and journalists to shape public opinion toward the general. "Any man who fails to back me up," the president said, "is either a fellow incapable of reasoning or else a man who has never taken the trouble to reason, or, a wrongheaded person who deliberately desires the growth of a spirit which would render the army and the navy not merely useless but a menace to the country."[4]

The Roosevelt/Miles feud raged as the general came up with a proposal to end the insurgency in the Philippines through personal negotiations with the enemy. He also alleged that American troops had inflicted "cruelties and barbarities" on the Filipinos, which he would stop once he had reached the islands with authority to act. Roosevelt and Root rejected the scheme in March 1902 and were irritated when Miles then leaked it to the press. The administration had enough problems with anti-imperialist criticism of its actions in the islands without having Miles himself corroborate the charges. The White House launched a trial balloon by sending out word that Miles's retirement was under active consideration. But with Congress debating Elihu Root's bill to reform the army and with Miles still popular among the Civil War veterans, Roosevelt backed off from ousting the general in April 1902.[5]

The disclosure of the Northern Securities suit in mid February 1902 quickly relegated the Miles case to the background and added a new dimension to Roosevelt's presidency. He demonstrated that as president he intended to diverge from the course of his predecessors about the problem of corporate regulation. Roosevelt believed that this decision represented a key event of his administration. In his autobiography, written more than ten years later when he was a private citizen again, he said that the issue in 1902 was not about how large corporations should be controlled. "The absolutely vital question was whether the government had power to control them at all." The E. C. Knight decision of 1895 had limited the government's authority to regulate interstate corporations. After the fact, Roosevelt wrote proudly: "This decision I caused to be annulled by the court that had rendered it."[6]

The Northern Securities company was the result of a struggle for control of railroads in the Northwest among James J. Hill, E. H. Harriman, and J. P. Morgan during the spring of 1901. The company held the stock of both the Great Northern and the Northern Pacific railroads and of their subsidiary line, the Chicago, Burlington and Quincy Railroad. Hill, of the Great Northern, said that the aim of the combination was to secure "permanent protection for their interests, and a continuation of the policy and management which had done so much for the development of the Northwest and the enhancement of their own property in the Northwest and elsewhere."[7]

The political leadership in Hill's home state of Minnesota responded with less sympathy. The Republican governor, Samuel R. Van Sant, wrote to the chief executives of neighboring states asking them to join him in exploring ways "to fight the great railway trust." Opposition to the Northern Securities Company was expected to help Van Sant's chances for relection. A conference was called for Helena, Montana, on 31 December 1901. The governors of Washington, Oregon, and the Dakotas agreed to support a court test, filed by Minnesota, of the merger.[8]

Van Sant was determined to make "every possible effort to prevent the thwarting of the will of the people." He asked W. B. Douglas, the state's attorney general, to begin legal action against Northern Securities. That was done on 7 January 1902, when Douglas applied to the United States Supreme Court for permission to "file a bill of complaint in equity against the Northern Securities Company." There was, however, a problem of jurisdiction with a state suit against a Minnesota corporation such as the Great Northern Railroad; so it was not at all clear that the Supreme Court would agree to hear the case. During their visit to Washington to file the papers with the Supreme Court, the lawyers for Minnesota met with Attorney General Philander C. Knox on 6 January. As Douglas recalled the conversation, Knox said: "Should you fail in bringing your proceeding under the Minnesota laws, and you bring reasonable proof to me to show that any act of Congress is being violated by the Northern Securities Company, I will bring an action myself."[9]

There is other evidence, too, to indicate an interest within the federal government during this period about the Northern Securities merger. The Justice Department opened a file on the matter early in December, and the Interstate Commerce Commission (ICC) adopted a resolution on 20 December to conduct an inquiry into "the method of association known as the 'community of interest' plan" that mergers such as Northern Securities represented. The ICC held a hearing in Chicago and offered to supply Knox with whatever it found. One business journal reported on 11 January 1902 that Roosevelt had directed Knox to look into the merger case.[10]

In fact, the president and the attorney general informally concluded that the Northern Securities Company was probably in violation of the Sherman Act, and they explored legal action. The two men did not tell anyone else of their intention. Elihu Root, with his corporate background, long resented being shut out of the process, after the announcement was made. In Roosevelt's mind, there was good reason for silence. Root might have mentioned something to his friends in New York. Roosevelt could easily recall the private and public pressure of the previous autumn when he had discussed with members of the New York business elite the sections of his annual message that dealt with reciprocity and corporate regulation. Any leak about what he and Knox intended to do against Northern Securities would have allowed Wall Street to mount a public campaign against the antitrust suit.

Knox pulled his information together in mid February. He wired Douglas for data about litigation in Minnesota, where other private suits had been filed. The state's attorney general replied that he was "glad indeed that you purpose making a personal investigation of the matter."

He sent Knox a rationale for launching a case against the railroad combination. At some point during the next several days, Knox officially informed Roosevelt of his conclusion that the merger was illegal under the Sherman Act. The president then directed that a lawsuit be filed to stop it. They also decided, Roosevelt said later, to issue a public statement that the suit would occur "in order to prevent violent fluctuations and disaster in the market."[11]

The announcement came on 19 February 1902, late in the afternoon, after the end of trading on the stock market. "Some time ago," said the attorney general's release, "the President requested an opinion as to the legality of this merger, and I have recently given him one, to the effect that in my judgment it violates the provisions of the Sherman Act of 1890; whereupon he directed that suitable action should be taken to have the question judicially determined." The effect of this action was felt strongly on the market the next morning. The shares of Northern Securities went down several points, and the rest of the market experienced what a reporter termed "a sudden and severe shock," similar to what had occurred when McKinley had been shot. Critics noted that the Supreme Court had not yet ruled on Minnesota's petition about the merger. The point, so far as Roosevelt and Knox were concerned, was to have the national government act independently.[12]

Toward the end of his life, Roosevelt told his authorized biographer about J. P. Morgan's response to the announcement of the suit. The two men met on 22 February 1902, and Morgan reportedly said: "If we have done anything wrong, send your man to my man and they can fix it up." Roosevelt's man was Knox, and he was already present at the meeting. "That can't be done," Roosevelt responded, and the attorney general added: "We don't want to fix it up, we want to stop it." Morgan inquired about the president's plans: "Are you going to attack my other interests, the Steel Trust, and the others?" Roosevelt's answer was "certainly not, unless we find out that in any case they have done something that we regard as wrong." After the financier had gone, Roosevelt said to Knox: "That is a most illuminating illustration of the Wall Street point of view. Mr. Morgan could not help regarding me as a big rival operator who either intended to ruin all his interests or else could be induced to come to an agreement to ruin none." Roosevelt's anecdotes usually gained something with repetition, and the exchange with Morgan probably had a less symbolic character when it took place. For Roosevelt, who looked on the business world with some suspicion anyway, the larger point that Morgan missed was that the president and the federal government were different in quality and authority from one of the private competitors of the financier.[13]

Roosevelt did not make any public statement about the merger case. To the one letter of criticism regarding his tactics that his papers contained, he responded that he had not failed to give a public warning of what the administration intended to do. The 19 February announcement was the public warning. Using the ties he had established with magazine editors, the president made sure that his rationale for bringing the suit reached a middle-class audience. He asked Albert Shaw, editor of the *American Monthly Review of Reviews*, to come to the White House on 14 March 1902. "I want to tell you some facts about the merger suit business." In the April issue of Shaw's journal, readers were informed of what "the President has remarked in conversation" regarding the case. Roosevelt had concluded that "the natural tendency toward amalgamation had been proceeding too rapidly" and that "the prevalence of overcapitalization" presented "a serious danger." He had decided, therefore, "that methods for governmental regulation ought by rights to proceed step by step with the development of new business conditions." While the president himself was not sure that the Sherman Act applied to railroad consolidations, "nevertheless for the purposes of the President and the Attorney General, the law is what the courts have construed it to be." Shaw's article, and others like it, put the administration's position as forcefully as Roosevelt could have wished.[14]

Winning the public-relations battle was one key phase of the Northern Securities controversy, but the real arena of the contest was the federal court system. When the Supreme Court rejected Minnesota's petition on 25 February, the federal suit became the sole legal action against the merger. However important the case, Knox and the Justice Department were ill equipped institutionally to take on the legal talent of the Northern Securities forces. During 1901 the department had no permanent headquarters in Washington; its members were scattered in hotels and other office space near the White House. "Little more than a series of claim agencies," the Justice Department had no formal division that specialized in antitrust issues. It exercised only weak control over the highly politicized United States attorneys and, more important, over its own financial resources.[15] The department lacked even the rudiments of a modern legal bureaucracy when Philander C. Knox was named attorney general in April 1901.

Because of Knox's background in corporate law, there was fear that he would not enforce the antitrust statutes. In fact, Knox believed that some business practices were illegal and required corrective action. He kept the *Northern Securities* case in his own hands, and he created a team of lawyers to work with him in prosecuting the railroad combination. He hired a special assistant attorney general and set him to gathering information about the defense that the Northern Securities Company would mount. Moving quickly to start the legal proceedings, Knox instructed the federal district attorney in St. Paul to file the government's motion on 10 March 1902, which said that the united railroad companies were "attempting to monopolize, and have monopolized such interstate and foreign trade or commerce, to the great and irreparable damage of the people of the United States," in violation of the Sherman Act.[16]

The actual conduct of the case moved slowly during the rest of 1902. The president and his attorney general explored ways to accelerate the consideration of such suits in the federal courts. Meanwhile, Knox attacked another notorious economic interest when an antitrust suit was filed to curb anticompetitive practices in the meat-packing industry. Such a legal assault on the "Beef Trust" was very popular because of rising meat prices. The press praised the administration when injunctions were sought to restrict the behavior of the meat companies. "It will encourage other efforts to restrain the greed of combinations," noted a Republican editor.[17]

Theodore Roosevelt did not see the Sherman Act as a permanent answer to the problem of corporate consolidation, but he did believe that establishing the government's authority was a crucial first step. In Charleston, South Carolina, on 9 April 1902, he said that the nation must recognize that "after combinations have reached a certain stage it is indispensable to the general welfare that the Nation should exercise over them, cautiously and with self-restraint, but firmly, the power of supervision and regulation." That, he was convinced, was what he and Knox were doing. As he told one of his correspondents in August 1902 who complained about the attorney general, Knox "has done more against trusts and for the enforcement of the antitrust law than any other man we have ever had in public life."[18]

The president's other primary domestic concern during the first half of 1902 was the long session of Congress. The Republicans had firm control of both houses. In the House of Representatives, however, the speaker, David B. Henderson of Iowa, was a somewhat erratic leader, and his Republican members lacked cohesion. In the Senate, Nelson W. Aldrich, Orville H. Platt of Connecticut, William Boyd Allison, and John Coit Spooner of Wisconsin headed the powerful bloc of conservative Republicans.

Later in his presidency, Roosevelt had difficult relations with Congress, but he started out aware that cooperation with Capitol Hill was in his own best interest as a possible candidate in 1904. His conciliatory resolve was tested at the outset when his request for reciprocal tariff concessions for Cuba encountered strong Republican resistance in both houses. The administration had assembled a comprehensive case to support Roosevelt's program of lower duties for the island. In addition to what the president had said in the annual message, the secretary of war and Leonard Wood, governor general of Cuba, appealed for congressional approval of reciprocity. Wood told a group of influential senators that the Cubans needed help for their tobacco and sugar industries.

Opposition to Cuban reciprocity was strongest among those lawmakers whose constituents produced the American sugar crop. There were the cane-sugar growers of Louisiana, while the beet-sugar industry had expanded across the Rocky Mountain, Pacific, and upper midwestern states after 1897. Already protectionist in principle, legislators from these states now had a specific local interest to safeguard. Friends of the reciprocity initiative noted that the Sugar Trust, dominant in the refining of cane sugar, enjoyed influence on Capitol Hill as well.

Behind the Cuban reciprocity issue itself also lurked divisions among the Republicans over the whole tariff question. In 1901, GOP lawmakers from Minnesota and Wisconsin had sought to lower duties on iron and steel, the products of companies that sold them more cheaply overseas than in the United States. The move faced resolute opposition from within their own party. When these same midwestern Republicans were asked to accept lower duties on tobacco and beet sugar, they balked at what James A. Tawney of Minnesota called an "absolutely indefensible" request.[19] All Republicans feared the prospect of a general tariff debate in an election year. It was therefore necessary to be sure that the issue was limited to Cuban reciprocity alone.

Formal consideration of that subject began in mid January in the House Ways and Means Committee, which Sereno E. Payne (R., N.Y.) chaired. Republican opposition led in mid March to the introduction of a reciprocity bill that provided a 20 percent reduction in the duties on Cuban goods, provided that there were commensurate reductions in the duties for American goods imported to the Caribbean island. Payne and his committee reported the bill to the floor with a favorable recommendation at the end of March. The proreciprocity forces agreed that the 20 percent reduction was too small but contended that this was all the House Republican caucus would authorize.

The Payne bill passed the House on 18 April 1902. It removed the differential between unrefined and refined sugar that had protected the American refining industry. This provision attacked the interest of the Sugar Trust, and it was presumed that the Senate would drop it. When the bill reached the upper house, however, it was apparent that the beet-sugar senators, now called the Boxers, had eighteen or nineteen votes against reciprocity. If they were to vote with the thirty-one Democrats, the bill would fail. While the Senate Committee on Relations with Cuba held six weeks of hearings, the White House and the Republican leadership in the Senate looked for a solution.

Senator Orville H. Platt proposed a substitute for the Payne bill; it limited to five years the time that Cuban reciprocity would be in effect and gave the president the power to end the concessions should he conclude that they were helping the Sugar Trust more than Cuban sugar growers. In early May, Roosevelt indicated that he would call Congress back into special session if the lawmakers did not act on the Cuban issue. One protectionist journal said that "the announcement has been accepted by legislators in both Houses as a threat, and they are feeling resentful as a result of it."[20] Roosevelt's action did not move the Senate, and in mid June he had to increase the administration's commitment.

The president sent a special message to Congress on 13 June. He conveyed an appeal from the Cuban president for assistance and asserted that reciprocity with Cuba was "a proposition that stands entirely alone. The reasons for it outweigh those of granting reciprocity with any other nation."[21] Senator Henry M. Teller (D., Colo.) charged that the White House was working with the Sugar Trust and that Leonard Wood had used government money for lobbying in ways that helped the trust. On 16 June, Teller succeeded in passing a resolution of inquiry which showed that Wood had spent his funds to push the bill on Capitol Hill. "The President is having the fight of his life on Cuba," wrote a journalist privately. The beet-sugar senators were capitalizing "on the hostility of other senators who think T.R. too much President, & complain that he doesn't lie down and let senators walk over him."[22]

Senate Republicans caucused on 18 June, and nineteen members came out against the Cuban proposal. Because those senators and the Democrats together could amend the bill as they chose, the leadership had no option but to let the reciprocity legislation die when the session adjourned on 1 July 1902. In this instance the forces of protectionism had given Roosevelt a strong defeat in the short run. That was not, however, the end of the question. The president intended to negotiate a reciprocity treaty with Cuba and to bring it back before Congress during the session that would convene after the congressional elections.

The Cuban-reciprocity battle revealed how deep were the strains among Republicans over the tariff issue. As Roosevelt told a friend, "In each locality there is a strong feeling for a reduction of the tariff on articles not produced in that locality, together with an even stronger feeling against touching those that are so produced."[23] The episode strengthened Roosevelt's conviction that confronting the tariff on its merits was politically unwise. He had to carry through on Cuban reciprocity, but there was no urgency to touch other parts of the protective system.

Cuba was not the only foreign-policy issue that confronted Roosevelt. As the military insurrection in the Philippines subsided, the problem of how to provide a civil government for the inhabitants came before Congress. The future independence of the Philippines, the conduct of the army during the war, and the role of the Roman Catholic Church in the islands—all went to Roosevelt's desk. The president told Senator George Frisbie Hoar (R., Mass.), an opponent of the American presence in the Philippines, that he was trying "to hasten the day when we shall need no more force in the Philippines than is needed in New York."[24]

The tangle of interrelated subjects in the Philippines made Roosevelt's goal hard to achieve. The McKinley administration had launched the process of civil government during the summer of 1901. The capture of the Filipino leader, Emilio Aguinaldo, in March enabled Secretary of War Root to name William Howard Taft as the first civil governor in July. Because of medical problems, Taft had to return to the United States at the end of the year, but he came back to Washington determined to campaign for a structure of civil government that would include a popularly elected assembly in the Philippines and two delegates in Congress to represent the interests of the islands. Because the Supreme Court had ruled in the *Insular Cases* that the Constitution did not extend to the Philippines directly, Congress would have to decide the form of government for the imperial possession. As Taft later told a Senate committee, the proposal included an elected assembly as "the best possible means of educating their educated men in popular government."[25]

Discussions about the Philippine-government bill on Capitol Hill occurred in a volatile atmosphere during the early months of 1902. Opponents of the administration's policy, led by Senator Hoar, asked for a probe into how the war had been conducted. A leading anti-imperialist, Herbert Welsh, had collected stories about alleged atrocities that American troops had perpetrated, including the infamous "water cure." On the basis of these reports and other information that he had received, Hoar introduced an inquiry resolution on 13 January 1902. Instead of being sent to a special committee, the proposal went to the Committee on the Philippines, which Henry Cabot Lodge chaired.

The Senate panel devoted five months to intermittent hearings on what had happened in the Philippines. During the course of the proceedings, documents revealed that American soldiers had used the water cure and other cruel measures against the Filipinos. Events in the islands in April 1902 strengthened the argument of administration critics. Gen. Jacob H. Smith, the commander on the island of Samar, was reported to have said to his officers: "I wish you to kill and burn. The more you kill and burn, the better it will please me." In the end, Smith went on, Samar would become "a howling wilderness." When these remarks and the actions that they encouraged became public, the administration's policy received intense condemnation both from the Democrats in the Senate and from what remained of the anti-imperialist movement among the public.[26]

President Roosevelt did not intend to let his opponents attain the political initiative on the Philippines. Indeed, part of his irritation with General Miles arose from the support that the soldier's remarks gave to Roosevelt's adversaries over the Philippines. To one of his correspondents, the president wrote: "As regards the cruelties in the Philippines, I know I need not tell you that I will be as active in stopping them as any man can be." The White House took public actions to find out what had occurred in the Philippines. On 15 April, Secretary Root ordered the army to conduct "a most thorough, searching, and exhaustive investigation." The president asked that Taft name a commission of three men "to report on the conduct of the military government at the present time towards the natives and as to whether or not any brutalities or indignities are inflicted by the army upon the natives."[27]

Roosevelt took the offensive against his attackers in a Memorial Day speech to veterans at Arlington Cemetery. Senator Lodge had already responded to the charges against the army in a speech on 5 May. Now Roosevelt added his own rebuttal. While "every guilty act committed by one of our troops" in the Philippines was matched by "a hundred acts of far greater atrocity from the enemy," this could not, he said, "be held to excuse any wrongdoers on our side." The president then went on to say that "from time to time there occur in our country, to the deep and lasting shame of our people, lynchings carried on under circumstances of inhuman cruelty and barbarity." These acts, he added, were "worse to the victim, and far more brutalizing to those guilty of it," than what had happened in the Philippines.[28]

The reaction from many southerners to this statement was renewed anger at Roosevelt, similar to the reaction after the Booker T. Washington episode. Roosevelt had used the president's ability to define the terms of public debate to turn the issue against those southern Democrats in Congress who had assailed the administration. As Roosevelt took the lead on the subject, with the effective efforts of Root and Lodge in support, the nation became satisfied that the Philippines were being governed as fairly as possible in difficult circumstances. The conviction of General Smith at a court-martial and his eventual retirement from the service during the summer of 1902 were taken as evidence that the government did not condone the army's conduct. At the same time, neither the president nor the public wanted a general airing of the extent to which American soldiers had committed atrocities in the Philippines.

The goal of the White House remained the enactment of legislation to address the economic problems of the islands and to provide a civil government for their inhabitants. First, a tariff law for the Philippines was passed on 8 March 1902. It gave Filipino products a reduction of 25 percent below the rates of the Dingley Tariff. Friends of the Philippines, such as Taft, had hoped for more concessions, but again the Republican protectionists would do no more. To solve the problem of civil government, Secretary Root drafted a bill, in collaboration with Senator Lodge, Senator Spooner, and Congressman Henry A. Cooper (R., Wis.), which was introduced on 7 January 1902. The measure retained the structure of government that President McKinley had established, with a governor general, an independent judiciary, a stable monetary system, and greater protection of the individual rights of the Filipinos. The centerpiece of the plan, which Taft strongly supported, was the legislative assembly.

Members of the Senate, particularly Henry Cabot Lodge, were not well disposed to the idea of a popular assembly for the Philippines, and the parliamentary situation became quite complex as Congress prepared to adjourn. The Senate bill, as passed on 3 June 1902, did not contain an assembly, but the House bill, which was voted on a few days later, did. The issue would be resolved in a conference committee. By that time, Taft had left Washington, and the burden of preserving the assembly fell on Congressman Cooper, who fought off efforts by Joseph G. Cannon (R., Ill.) to give the Senate the advantage in the conference deliberations. After extended negotiations, the conferees from the Senate gave in. The conference report, which included an elected assembly that would go into effect when the islands were at peace, passed on 1 July 1902, the day before Congress adjourned.

Another issue relating to the Philippines did not come before Congress directly during the spring of 1902. A chief cause of popular discontent in the Philippines—one that had fueled the revolution against Spain in 1896—was the position of the parish priests, or friars, of the Roman Catholic Church. The role of the friars pervaded Filipino society, and their ownership of large amounts of land, their political influence, and their apparent indulgence in secular luxuries and temptations made them a source of political grievances. An obvious solution was for the

United States to buy the estates of the friars and then resell them to the Filipino people. The Treaty of Paris, ending the Spanish-American War, however, had bound the United States to protect existing property rights in the islands. The departure of the offending religious orders was a goal of the Roosevelt administration. Whether the friars were, in fact, as corrupt an element in Philippine life as the United States government thought is still disputed. Nonetheless, Roosevelt and his advisors believed that they were, and that assumption shaped United States policy.

Roosevelt knew that he had to move carefully in dealing with the friars. He had brought to the White House a broad popularity among American Catholics, which he had acquired in New York politics. The president intended to cultivate Catholic votes for 1904, and he consulted both laymen and clergy whenever Catholic feelings might be affected. Most important, Roosevelt made some timely appointments of Catholics to visible posts in the Philippines and in the federal government. Both Archbishop John Ireland of St. Paul, Minnesota, and James Cardinal Gibbons of Maryland were members of the hierarchy with whom Roosevelt regularly corresponded. The president also kept in touch with political representatives of Catholics in the United States.

Any resolution of the friars problem necessarily involved the pope, and the Roosevelt administration had to devise procedures that would bring the two sides together without entailing any sort of official recognition of the Vatican. Were that to occur, Protestant opposition would be aroused. The solution was to send Taft to Rome in June 1902, on his way back to the Philippines. With Taft went a delegation, including two Catholic members, that could negotiate a settlement of the friars and their landholdings. The president had made certain of the support of Ireland and Gibbons in advance, and he anticipated that American Catholics would approve his conciliatory posture toward the church.

The talks in Rome did not produce the solution that Roosevelt and Taft had envisioned. The discussions themselves went forward in an amicable spirit during June 1902. On several issues the Vatican proved cooperative. The friars' lands could be sold, though the price remained to be fixed, and a new apostolic delegate would be chosen to serve in the Philippines. American insistence on the withdrawal of the friars became the point on which agreement could not be reached. Rome was not willing to admit tacitly that the charges against the friars were correct and to remove so large a part of the Philippine clergy from the islands. In mid July the discussions ended over what Taft called the Vatican's "flat-footed refusal" to accept the departure of the friars. Faced with this rebuff and under political fire at home from the Catholic defenders of the friars, Roosevelt concluded that "we should simply sit still and let the friars get along as best they can, treating them exactly as we would treat Protestant preachers whom their parishioners refused to receive."[29]

The two sides were actually more in agreement than was apparent during the summer of 1902, and the groundwork had been laid for a settlement the next year. What worried Roosevelt most was an outbreak of Catholic criticism of the administration in the aftermath of the Vatican's action. The president found the attacks startling in view of his positive stance toward the church. He called on Catholic friends, especially Archbishop Ireland, to come to his defense. The archbishop told the press at the end of July that no president had been "more fair-minded and impartial in religious matters than Theodore Roosevelt."[30] The outcry gradually diminished during the rest of 1902 and into the next year. By the end of 1903 the Vatican representative and William Howard Taft had reached an agreement on the sale of the friars' lands for $7,239,000. Meanwhile, the number of friars in the Philippines decreased, and the pressure for formal removal of them also ebbed.

The Philippine problems that confronted Roosevelt during 1902 were complex and sensitive, but he handled them with the growing confidence that characterized the first full year of his presidency. He devised solutions to these issues that left him in control of the situation in the distant United States possession. "We have had much to do and we are responsible for what has been done," Roosevelt said with his usual vigor, "and we are exceedingly proud of it."[31]

During the spring of 1902, members of Congress faced important choices about the location of a canal across Central America. Their decision would determine whether Nicaragua or Panama would become the focus of United States interest, pressure, and money. After the ratification of the Hay-Pauncefote Treaty in December 1901, Congress appeared likely to opt for a route through Nicaragua. A bill to make that selection, sponsored by William P. Hepburn (R., Iowa), came before the House in early January and achieved easy passage by a vote of 308 to 2. With the support of key senators, including John T. Morgan (D., Ala.), behind it, and with the endorsement of the report of the Isthmian Canal Commission in September 1901, the Nicaraguan plan looked to be a probable winner when the Senate voted on the Hepburn proposal.

Events soon shifted to favor Panama. A significant obstacle to the Panamanian route had been the amount of money that the New Panama Canal Company, a French corporation, wanted for its holdings that remained from the abortive previous attempts to build a canal there. On the basis of engineering estimates, the Panama route was cheaper, but the company's value of $109 million raised the total price well above the cost of the Nicaraguan route. As congressional action on the Hepburn proposal neared, the directors of the French company told the White House that they would sell their property for $40 million. With that concession in hand, Roosevelt moved rapidly to have the Isthmian Canal Commission rethink its recommendation. The commission decided on 18 January that Panama offered "the most practicable and feasible" route for a canal, and Roosevelt sent its findings to Congress two days later.[32]

Senator Spooner offered an amendment to the Hepburn bill on 28 January 1902. Under its terms, Roosevelt would be given the authority to acquire the holdings of the French firm for $40 million and to obtain from Colombia, which then controlled Panama, a zone through which a canal could be built. Spooner was well placed to lead the administration's campaign to transform an existing Senate majority for the Nicaraguan route into a pro-Panama coalition. During February the Senate Committee on Interoceanic Canals held hearings at which members of the canal commission testified that Panama would be a superior location on engineering grounds, once the French company's price had come down. Still, when the hearings ended on 10 March, the Senate committee reported out the Hepburn bill favorably, with a negative report on Spooner's alternative. Without a clear statement of Colombia's willingness to negotiate a treaty, the Nicaraguan route might yet prevail in Congress. Potential supporters of Panama, including Mark Hanna, wanted a definite expression from the directors of the New Panama Canal Company that they would in fact accept a U.S. offer to purchase their holdings.

By mid April, Colombia had presented a draft treaty for a canal, and the New Panama Canal Company had indicated, by the action of its shareholders, its intention to sell. Hanna and his allies now filed a minority report in favor of Panama, along with the document that Morgan put before the Senate on behalf of the Hepburn bill. The Senate took up the canal issue on 4 June 1902, and two weeks of controversial debate followed. Proponents of Panama, including Philippe Jean Bunau-Varilla, capitalized on volcanic eruptions in the Caribbean to remind wavering senators that Nicaragua had volcanoes of its own. The decisive element in the debate, however, was Mark Hanna, who made important speeches, first on 5–6 June and then at the end of the discussion on 18 June. The minority report was substituted for the Morgan version, and then after other restrictions were rejected, the Spooner version received overwhelming support. The way now lay open for Roosevelt to work out with the government of Colombia an agreement for the construction of the Panama Canal.

In 1902, Congress also enacted a significant piece of legislation affecting the nation's natural resources. For two decades, westerners had been seeking federal support for irrigation projects in their arid region. By the end of the 1890s the western bloc on Capitol Hill was advocating that the government construct storage reservoirs that the states would then control in the interest of entrepreneurs. Encountering eastern resistance to appropriations for reservoirs in March 1901, western senators used a filibuster to stalemate the rivers-and-harbors bill as the congressional session ended. At that time, little support existed, either eastern or western, for a bill sponsored by Congressman Francis G. Newlands (D., Nev.) that would use an arid-land reclamation fund as a revolving resource to finance the government's construction of irrigation works. This measure, which strengthened federal power and enhanced the role of government experts, had an obvious appeal to Theodore Roosevelt. The new president saw irrigation as a way of providing the West with an agricultural population and countering the influence of urban life on the national character.

Gifford Pinchot, chief of the Bureau of Forestry in the Department of Agriculture, and Frederick H. Newell, of the United States Geological Survey, visited Roosevelt, shortly after he took office, and urged him to support national legislation for the arid West. Roosevelt did so in his annual message, and then during the winter and spring of 1902 he worked with Newlands on the bill "to prevent it from being made unworkable by an undue insistence upon States' rights."[33] Roosevelt then used his influence to help the Newlands measure reach the House floor and achieve passage by that body. Favorable action from the Senate came before Congress adjourned.

For political reasons the president did not admit that he and the Democrat from Nevada had worked in tandem, but in fact they had. The result was a law that put the government in the business of creating irrigation works in the West to promote agriculture there. The Newlands Act represented the kind of national control over resource policy that characterized the Roosevelt presidency.

When Congress adjourned, Republicans said that its record had been "an ample and creditable one," with the failure over Cuban reciprocity being the most notable exception.[34] Whether the GOP would do well in the congressional elections remained to be determined. Republican politicians were predictably gloomy about their prospects. The congressional committee had difficulty in raising money, in part because of corporate opposition to Roosevelt's trust policy. Working in favor of party success was the popularity of the president, the general prosperity of the nation, symbolized by a bumper corn crop, and the continuing disarray of the Democrats.

Because the White House was being renovated, Roosevelt spent most of his time at Sagamore Hill in Oyster Bay. The machinery of government gathered there for what would become a summer White House. Press representatives who now covered the president's public movements also assembled there. Roosevelt wrote Paul Dana, publisher of the *New York Sun*, that the newsmen often made up "ridiculous stories" about his summer activities and that the *Sun*'s reporter had created tales that had "not a word of truth in them, and they lean toward the ridiculous." The president was "living here with my wife and children just exactly as you are at your home; and there is no more material for a story in one case than in the other."[35] Since the public wanted to know what the chief executive was doing each day, the journalists responded with stories that drew on possibility and speculation rather than on hard news. Roosevelt was learning that the personalized presidency came with a price.

The business of governing went on through the placid summer. Amid the letters on patronage and the tariff debates, Roosevelt made his first nomination to the United States Supreme Court. Justice Horace Gray of Massachusetts resigned because of poor health. The president wanted to pick as the successor someone from the same state who shared Roosevelt's views about upholding the policies of the Republicans. Letters and petitions came in from members of the Massachusetts bar, and Roosevelt consulted with Judge Gray, among others. The decisive figure in these deliberations was Henry Cabot Lodge, who put forward the name of Oliver Wendell Holmes, Jr., chief justice of the Supreme Judicial Court of Massachusetts.

There was much for Roosevelt to admire in the qualifications of Holmes, who had served with distinction in the Union Army and was an eminent legal scholar and a gifted jurist. The president also thought that Holmes had rendered decisions in labor cases that showed him to be a judge who had kept "his broad humanity of feeling and his sympathy for the class from which he has not drawn his clients." Roosevelt believed that it was "eminently desirable" that the Supreme Court should demonstrate "in unmistakable fashion their entire sympathy with all proper effort to secure the most favorable consideration for men who most need that consideration."[36]

Despite some reservation about Holmes's attitude toward partisan issues, Roosevelt was primarily concerned about whether the judge could be counted on to support the foreign policy of the administration on questions such as the *Insular Cases* that might come before the Court. Because a narrow majority had favored the government in that famous case, it was imperative that the president not choose "any man who was not absolutely sane and sound on the great national policies for which we stand in public life."[37] Satisfied, after consultation with Lodge and George F. Hoar, that Holmes met these standards, Roosevelt announced the nomination in August 1902. Although the president and the judge would soon fall out over the *Northern Securities* case, Roosevelt had made his best selection for the Court in Oliver Wendell Holmes.

As Roosevelt looked ahead to the election campaign, he planned a series of speeches on the tariff and the trusts. The idea of a president's taking an active part in an off-year campaign was an innovation, and the White House told reporters that while Roosevelt's remarks would be "along Republican lines, so far as they may relate to politics, they will not be political speeches."[38] Nevertheless, the president's statements were expected to furnish the party's campaign themes.

The issue of protection remained the most volatile that Roosevelt faced within his own party. In Iowa the sentiment to revise duties downward, particularly on products made by trusts, reappeared, as it had in 1901. The renewal of the "Iowa Idea" attracted national attention. One midwestern editor said that Iowa Republicans represented "the voice of the American people, and the critical Republicans would do well to hear and heed it." For Roosevelt, however, his experience with Cuban reciprocity had shown him the "dynamite" that the subject contained. If revision could not be secured through congressional action or by Senate ratification of reciprocity treaties, then the president could not do it alone. "He cannot afford to publicly advocate action and then fail to get it," reported a tariff revisionist who talked with Roosevelt; "he has gone as far on that line as he can be expected to."[39]

In the speeches Roosevelt delivered at the end of August 1902, he said almost nothing about the tariff; rather, he stressed his antitrust policy. At Providence, Rhode Island, on 23 August 1902, he argued that "the great corporations which we have grown to speak of rather loosely as trusts are the creatures of the State, and the State not only has the right to control them, but it is in duty bound to control them wherever the need of such control is shown." As he had before, Roosevelt stressed that the first requirement was "the securing of publicity among all great corporations doing an interstate business" because "daylight is a powerful discourager of evil." He sounded the same themes at Boston and Haverhill, Massachusetts, and at other stops in New England during late August and early September. The *New York Evening Post* called him "a man who is giving the people his honest thoughts, who is not dazzled by wealth or awed by threats, and who stands firmly for what he believes to be true and right."[40]

Roosevelt escaped death on 3 September 1902, during the tour, when a trolley car struck his carriage in Pittsfield, Massachusetts. The president and other passengers were thrown from the horse-drawn landau. A Secret Service agent in the party, William Craig, was killed. Roosevelt suffered assorted injuries to his face and a series of bruises on his left leg. At first Roosevelt said, "My hurts were trivial"; but the injuries were more serious than he or his doctors initially realized. During the three weeks that followed the accident, he developed a small abscess on his left shin. He went to Tennessee, to give a speech to the Brotherhood of Locomotive Firemen, and also made appearances in West Virginia and North Carolina. To the firemen, he proclaimed: "I believe emphatically in organized labor. I believe in organizations of wage-workers." The threat of an anthracite-coal strike was already on the president's mind.[41]

Before that issue could be addressed, however, there was still the matter of what to say about the tariff on his western tour. A conference at Oyster Bay on 16 September 1902 brought together Nelson Aldrich, Mark Hanna, Orville H. Platt, John C. Spooner, William Boyd Allison, and Henry Cabot Lodge to advise Roosevelt. This meeting has come to have some significance in Roosevelt's presidency as the moment when the youthful chief executive allegedly struck a bargain with the party elders. Those who were present agreed, according to this interpretation, "that he should have his head in all things outside economics and finance, and that they should govern his policy in the reserved subjects." The bargain theory assumes that Roosevelt and the senators had disagreements to resolve; in fact, they concurred on how the tariff and trust issues should be handled.[42]

An event that occurred on the same day as the conference reinforced the apprehension that Roosevelt and his guests felt about the tariff issue. Speaker of the House David B. Henderson declined to accept the nomination to an eleventh term in his Iowa district because he did not "truly represent" the views of his reform-minded constituents about lowering the tariff. The surprise public statement of withdrawal unsettled some Republicans and suggested that there was widespread antitariff sentiment in the Middle West. Aware that Henderson was an unstable figure, Roosevelt and the senators decided to play down the incident and to deny again that any connection existed between the tariff and the trusts. The president was warned that the issue "will not down any easier than Banquo's ghost," but Roosevelt stuck to the course that the leadership had set.[43]

At Cincinnati, Ohio, on 20 September, Roosevelt said: "The real evils connected with the trusts cannot be remedied by any change in the tariff laws." The trust problem was "separate and apart from the question of tariff revision." Three days later, at Logansport, Indiana, he warned against "violent and radical changes amounting to the direct upsetting of tariff policies at intervals of every few years." Instead, Roosevelt urged that "a body of experts" make recommendations to Congress about revision in particular schedules as needed. This was an idea that Nelson W. Aldrich had advanced. The senators who had met with Roosevelt were pleased about his comments. Allison called the Logansport remarks "an admirable statement of Republican doctrine" that would "do much to clear the atmosphere and will generally be accepted as sound and wise."[44]

By the time that Roosevelt spoke in Logansport, three weeks after his accident, the abscess had become worse, and an operation was required. He needed emergency treatment in Indiana and again in Washington when he reached home on 24 September. For the next several weeks he had to stay quiet and not move his leg. The effects of the accident and the operation caused some public criticism about the dangers that Roosevelt had faced during his tour. The *Pittsburgh Times* said that the leg injury should serve as "a warning to the president that the strenuous life may sometimes be overdone"; the *New Haven Register* observed that "the president's strenuousness is picturesque but also terrifying."[45]

As he convalesced, the president confronted the first major domestic crisis of his term, the anthracite-coal strike. By late September the miners' walkout in Pennsylvania was raising the possibility, particularly in the Northeast and the Middle West, of a shortage of fuel for home heating as the winter months approached. The price of anthracite coal was rising in the cities of the region. Henry Cabot Lodge warned his friend about the potential political impact on the Republicans of shortages and soaring prices. "By the first week in November if the strike does not stop and coal begins to go down we shall have an overturn." Lodge recognized that Roosevelt's authority to act in a labor dispute was limited, but he asked, "Is there anything we can appear to do?"[46]

Roosevelt had been watching the events of the coal strike since the United Mine Workers and their president, John Mitchell, had pulled the miners off their jobs on 12 May 1902. The dispute in the coal industry was tangled and complex. A strike in 1900 had been resolved through the intercession of Mark Hanna on behalf of William McKinley. The operators of the coal mines had made wage concessions that they resolved not to duplicate in 1902. Mitchell and his union wanted pay hikes, of course, but they also hoped for recognition as a bargaining agent for the industry. That concession the mine owners refused to entertain. When efforts to reach a negotiated settlement broke down in

May, the miners voted to suspend work, and some 125,000 men left the mines in Pennsylvania. Efforts at mediation by Senator Hanna and the National Civic Federation, an organization that professed to promote management-labor concord, failed in June 1902. Pressure soon mounted for Roosevelt to take some action to bring the walkout to a peaceful end.

The requests that came to the White House looked to the appointment of a commission to investigate the issues of the strike. The railroads that owned the coal mines strongly advised against any presidential action. It would, wrote a railroad president, "be prejudicial to the interests of labor and capital, and of the administration as well." Roosevelt did not name a commission. On 8 June he asked the commissioner of labor, Carroll D. Wright, to report to him about the circumstances of the strike. Wright's assessment, submitted two weeks later, stressed the depth of suspicion between management and labor and made some suggestions to promote a settlement. Roosevelt asked Attorney General Knox whether Wright's report should be released to the public. Knox advised against such action on the grounds that the president had no right to interfere with the strike. Roosevelt agreed for the time being, and the report was not given out.[47]

Roosevelt did not regard the shelving of Wright's findings as a long-range answer. He approached Knox again at the end of August about whether the government could proceed "against the coal operators as being engaged in a trust." Knox said that there were still no grounds for the president to act. The signs, as Roosevelt read them, suggested a worsening situation in regard to anthracite coal. The price in the East had soared above fifteen dollars per ton, more than twice the customary cost, and there were reports of potential shortages in the major cities.[48]

The president saw in the coal strike a test of the authority of the presidency. Roosevelt thrived on crises, and here was one in which the American people wanted him to act. By the last days of September 1902, Roosevelt had decided to take direct personal action to bring together the two warring parties in the strike. The governor of Massachusetts, Winthrop Murray Crane, suggested that the president invite miners and mine operators to come to the White House. Roosevelt still thought that he had "as yet no legal or constitutional duty—and therefore no legal or constitutional right—in the matter," but he was equally persuaded that this was not the occasion to "act on the Buchanan principle of striving to find some constitutional reason for inaction." On 1 October he sent out telegrams to the presidents of the railroads that owned the coal mines and to Mitchell, asking them to come to Washington on 3 October. "The failure of the coal supply," he wrote, had "become a matter of vital concern to the whole nation." The president's initiative received general endorsement from the national press, although some conservative papers were critical.[49]

The rival parties assembled in Washington on 3 October. Because of the continuing renovation at the White House, the conference took place at the temporary residence on Jackson Place. Roosevelt addressed the group at the outset with the disclaimer that he had no "right or duty to intervene in this way upon legal grounds or upon any official relation that I bear to the situation." He believed, however, that "the urgency and the terrible nature of the catastrophe impending" demanded that he exert "whatever influence I personally can" to end the strike. He asked for "an immediate resumption of operations in the coal mines in some such way as will, without a day's unnecessary delay, meet the crying needs of the people."[50]

The meeting was tense. The operators regarded themselves as having been summoned to Washington to receive what one called "a semi-ultimatum" to end the strike. When Roosevelt had concluded his remarks, Mitchell expressed his willingness to have the president "name a tribunal which shall determine the issues that have resulted in the strike." If the owners would accept the tribunal's decision, so would the union. Roosevelt then suggested a recess until that afternoon. During those later deliberations, the mine owners accused Mitchell and his men of fomenting violence. "Are you asking us to deal with a set of outlaws?" was how one owner put it. The operators read their statement, asked Roosevelt to dissolve the United Mine Workers as a trust, and urged him to use troops "to at once squelch the anarchistic conditions of affairs existing in the anthracite coal regions by the strong arm of the military at your command."[51]

Mitchell denied the charges that had been made, and Roosevelt asked the operators if they had any further advice to give. The most that the owners would concede was to leave the strike to the courts of Pennsylvania. They still wanted troops to open the mines. The experience left Roosevelt impressed with Mitchell and angry at the mine operators. That evening, after the conference had broken up, Roosevelt wrote to Hanna: "I have tried and failed. I feel downhearted over the result both because of the great misery made necessary for the mass of our people, and because the attitude of the operators will beyond a doubt double the burden on us who stand between them and socialistic action."[52]

The 3 October meeting was a short-run failure, but its long-run significance was great. The president had placed a labor union and the workers it represented on something approaching the same political level as management and capital. Where Grover Cleveland in 1894 had sent soldiers to end the Pullman Strike, Roosevelt had treated union workers as legitimate participants in the bargaining process. This did not mean that Roosevelt was pro-union. He regarded what he had done as simple justice or, as he would come to call it, the Square Deal. He had also established the precedent that the White House should not remain aloof during a domestic economic crisis. The action that Roosevelt took in this phase of the coal strike proved to be one of the most important of his contributions to enhancing the power of the presidency.

During the week that followed the conference at Washington, Roosevelt looked for a mechanism or a procedure that might enable him to end the strike. He received a letter from Grover Cleveland offering advice toward a settlement. The action of the former president strengthened Roosevelt's position and allowed him to tell conservative associates about Cleveland's support. To John Mitchell, Roosevelt offered to name an investigating commission if the miners would return to work, a proposal that Mitchell declined on 8 October 1902. Other parties, including the National Civic Federation and the National Association of Manufacturers, tried without success to find a compromise. By 10 October no resolution had been reached, and Roosevelt told Cleveland that "the calamity now impending over our people may have consequences which without exaggeration are to be called terrible."[53] By the time the letter was written, however, Roosevelt had found the means to bring the crisis to a conclusion.

The president moved on two levels. He began assembling a commission to look into the strike for him; it included such figures as Cleveland, federal judge William R. Day, and members from business and labor who would, as Roosevelt said, do "even handed justice to operator and miner alike." More sweeping was the plan he had devised if a negotiated solution did not occur. Roosevelt had decided that he would employ the United States Army to go into the mining areas of Pennsylvania, open the mines to those who wanted to work, and "dispossess the operators and run the mines as a receiver" until the commission reported to him. He approached a retired army officer, Maj. Gen. John M. Schofield, about undertaking command of the force. Roosevelt also informed Knox and Root of his intentions. "I knew that this action would form an evil precedent, and that it was one which I should take most reluctantly," he wrote Governor Crane after the crisis had passed, but he believed it was the only approach "which would be effective in such an emergency." In his autobiography, Roosevelt asserted that he had been prepared to act under "the Jackson-Lincoln theory of the presidency" because "occasionally great crises arise which call for immediate and vigorous executive action."[54]

Some question remains about whether Roosevelt outlined this military option in full to Elihu Root before the secretary of war made a move that resolved the strike. On 9 October, Root proposed that he come to see J. P. Morgan with a plan to break the deadlock over the coal walkout. Morgan's banking interests gave him leverage with the coal operators. The president knew about Root's initiative and sent him information to give to Morgan. Root later maintained that he did not use the knowledge of Roosevelt's plan for a military receivership to threaten Morgan. Nonetheless, it is likely that Root and Morgan were aware of what Roosevelt could do.

What the secretary of war proposed was that the miners should return to work and that a commission would be named to examine the issues of the dispute and make recommendations that could serve as the basis of a multiyear agreement. Root met with Morgan on 11 October 1902 on the yacht *Corsair*, and they drafted a document to present as an offer from the mine operators to the American public. The lengthy statement of the owners' case allowed them to express their anger against Mitchell and the UMW. Root also made sure that no recognition of the union was conceded. This stroke gave the operators an important victory. Beyond that, the proposed agreement called for the immediate resumption of mining, for the appointment of a commission, and for the findings of the panel to be effective across the anthracite industry for three years. Morgan took Root's draft to the operators, who agreed to it in principle. They insisted that they specify the kinds of men who could serve on the commission. There would be a military officer, a mining engineer, a federal judge from Pennsylvania, a man who was active in the anthracite-coal business, and "a man of prominence eminent as a sociologist." There was no provision for any representative of organized labor.[55]

Roosevelt put the document before Mitchell on 15 October. The labor leader said that he would accept the plan if the president would add two additional commission members of his own selection. That evening, Roosevelt tried to persuade two of Morgan's men, Robert Bacon and George W. Perkins, to agree to the naming of a Catholic prelate and a member of a union. The discussion went nowhere for two hours until Roosevelt had the idea of calling the union member an "eminent sociologist." That device allowed Bacon and Perkins to avoid even an informal recognition of the union movement. They also accepted the designation of the Catholic clergyman. Roosevelt then appointed Edgar

E. Clark, who was grand chief of the Order of Railway Conductors, and Bishop John L. Spalding of Peoria, Illinois. Both sides concurred in this solution, and a few days later, the mine workers decided to return to work on 23 October 1902.

The anthracite-coal commission conducted its deliberations during the next several months and sent its report to President Roosevelt on 18 March 1903. The settlement that they had reached had something for both workers and operators. The miners received a 10 percent increase in their pay, a nine-hour working day, and a system of arbitration for job-related disputes. The commission did not accord recognition to the union on the grounds that such a concession lay outside its mandate. Other coal-industry practices about which the UMW had complained stayed in place. There was a strong denunciation of violence and of the boycotting tactics of the UMW.

The outcome of the strike left mixed results for most of the direct participants and those who had tried to function as mediators. Senator Hanna had worked for a settlement, as he had done in 1900; but the operators did not trust him in 1902, and his role diminished when Roosevelt stepped in. The one clear winner was the president. His intervention, said a Republican newspaper, represented "a great personal triumph." Secretary of Agriculture James Wilson, campaigning in Ohio, told Roosevelt that "the sentiment is widespread that you risked much, and won much, and that the whole is deserving and will be remembered." The events of the autumn, his injury and bravery, and then his part in resolving the strike, wrote a "progressive Republican" in the *North American Review*, "have given the color of romance and knight errantry to the prosaic office and heightened the appeal of his character."[56] To a significant degree, even more than the filing of the *Northern Securities* suit, the coal strike marked the occasion when Roosevelt's personalized presidency first gained national attention. Ten years later he said that he had begun to assert his own policies "by October 1902 when I settled the coal strike, and started the trust control campaign."[57]

The Republican party also felt the political benefits of the strike settlement during the two weeks that passed before the congressional elections. "The apathy we feared seems to be disappeared," noted one party worker, who predicted a GOP margin in the House of between twenty and forty seats. The results of the elections bore out the optimistic predictions of party strategists. Because of redistricting based on the 1900 census, the House of Representatives grew in size. As a result, both parties gained seats: the Republican bloc rose by eleven, to 208; the Democrats gained twenty-seven seats, to 178. The outcome, concluded the British ambassador, "is regarded as very satisfactory by the Republican managers, and is generally considered to be due to the personal popularity of the President, especially in the Western states." Both parties gained two seats in the Senate. As for Roosevelt, he was "well contented with the elections" because they forecast a victory for him in 1904.[58]

After a little more than a year in the presidency, Theodore Roosevelt reveled in an impressive political standing. He had "followed where his sense of justice has led; and the setting and action have been all that the most imaginative could desire." The editors of *World's Work* decided that he "had the confidence of the nation and of a larger number of the people, perhaps than any other President has had in recent times."[59] The verdict grew out of Roosevelt's success in two dramatic public encounters, the *Northern Securities* case and the coal strike. The difficulties with Cuban reciprocity were largely blamed on Congress. Roosevelt was the master of the American political scene on domestic issues. His triumphs on foreign policy during the first term added to the strong political momentum that carried him toward 1904 and his selection as president on his own merits by the American people that he wanted so badly.

4

★ ★ ★ ★ ★

ROOSEVELT AND
THE WORLD, 1902–1904

Theodore Roosevelt is most remembered for foreign-policy actions that have given him a reputation for bravado or bluster. This impression largely rests on actions during his first term: the Venezuelan crisis of 1902, the Alaska Boundary controversy with Canada and Great Britain, and the acquisition of the Panama Canal Zone during 1903/4. The sending of the American fleet around the world from 1907 to 1909 is also often cited as evidence of Roosevelt's temperament. Did the president issue an ultimatum to the Germans about Venezuela? Did he bully the Canadians about Alaska? Did he commit "an act of piracy" by fomenting a revolution in Panama to seize a zone for a canal that Colombia had declined to grant to the United States legally?[1] In short, did Theodore Roosevelt's conduct of foreign policy reveal that the president rarely spoke softly and often wielded a big stick?

Theodore Roosevelt had little patience for the formalities and procedures of diplomacy. While he admired and respected John Hay, he had less regard for the Department of State and for the representatives of the United States in embassies and consulates around the world. Too many of the ambassadors "in stations of real importance," he wrote in 1904, "totally fail to give us real help and real information, and seem to think that the life work of an Ambassador is a kind of glorified pink tea party."[2] To those ambassadors whom he liked and trusted, such as Joseph Hodges Choate and, later, Whitelaw Reid in London, Roosevelt wrote private letters outside the State Department channels. In some cases the president did not use effectively the diplomats he had in the field. United States ministers and, later, ambassadors to Japan did not receive the close attention that he gave to their counterparts in Great Britain. Instead of using the diplomatic corps, Roosevelt reached out to other sources of information, including journalists and personal friends.

Roosevelt also had varying success with the foreign ambassadors in Washington. The French embassy was an asset, especially after Jean Jules Jusserand became ambassador. The two men built a close friendship, and Jusserand concluded that the president "could be in every way likened to radium, for warmth, force and light emanated from him and no spending of it could ever diminish his store." As British ambassador, the president's choice was his friend and best man at his second marriage, Cecil Spring Rice. Unfortunately, Spring Rice was serving in posts in Persia and Russia, and the British government selected Michael Herbert to replace Sir Julian Pauncefote, the long-time envoy, who died in 1902. Herbert died in 1903, and his successor was Sir Mortimer Durand, whom Roosevelt disliked and with whom he could not cooperate effectively. In the case of Germany, the president and Theodore von Holleben were not close, and Roosevelt lobbied for the appointment of his friend Hermann Speck von Sternburg as the kaiser's man in Washington. The Russian ambassador, Count Arturo Cassini, was such a chronic liar that neither Hay nor Roosevelt trusted him.[3]

To get around these obstacles, Roosevelt used his friends as conduits to their governments. Some important messages to the British Foreign Office went first to Spring Rice, who replied in letters addressed to Mrs. Roosevelt but meant for the president. Other letters went to John St. Loe Strachey, editor of the *Spectator*, and to Arthur Lee, a soldier and politician whom Roosevelt had met in Cuba. When Sternburg became ambassador in 1903, Roosevelt had the direct line to the kaiser that he wanted. He did not have as many German friends as he had among the British. During the Russo-Japanese War, the president also cooperated with Baron Kentaro Kaneko, who had been at Harvard with Roosevelt and who served as a special envoy from Tokyo. In these friendships Roosevelt found the kind of diplomacy that he liked. It was confidential, effective, and personal.

No major foreign-policy crisis marked the initial twelve months of Roosevelt's presidency. The broad outlines of United States diplomacy remained what they had been under William McKinley, as the continuity of policy on Cuban reciprocity and civil government for the Philippines indicated. But there was unfinished business: to achieve a zone where a Central American canal could be constructed and to settle the boundary between Canada and Alaska at a time when gold discoveries in the Yukon gave the area an increasing importance. Finally, the president was particularly sensitive to the strategic effect that might arise from the failure of Latin American countries to meet their international obligations. An expansion of the influence of European nations in the Western Hemisphere would confront the United States with a potential or actual challenge to the Monroe Doctrine.

During the administration of Theodore Roosevelt the most likely agent of such a threat seemed to be the Germany of Kaiser William II. Since the Spanish-American War had raised tensions between the two nations over the Philippines, the United States had watched the actions of Germany with a mixture of suspicion and caution. As German trade with Latin America increased and as German settlers appeared in South American countries, policy makers in the United States prepared themselves to respond should the kaiser's government seek any kind of naval base near the Caribbean. Washington also began to feel a greater identity between its foreign-policy interests and those of the British after 1898. Relations with Germany suffered as a consequence.

The Germans hoped to offset the pro-British posture of the United States through a sustained campaign to restore amicable relations. The problem was that German interests did not run parallel with American needs. To the extent that Berlin wanted the United States to follow Germany's anti-British lead, it was asking Washington to foresake traditional noninvolvement for a policy that most Americans opposed. Even the kaiser's attempts to build a personal working relationship with the president were abortive. "I cannot of course follow or take too seriously a man whose policy is one of such violent and often wholly irrational zigzags," Roosevelt wrote about the German ruler in May 1905. As the kaiser pursued a strategy of heavy-handed personal flattery, Roosevelt responded with public politeness and private reserve.[4]

The interplay of German-American relations commenced soon after Roosevelt became president. Long interested in expanding its influence in Venezuela, Germany had loaned the government of Cipriano Castro, Venezuela's dictator, more than seventy million marks, on which Berlin had not been paid any interest. Early in 1901, Castro indicated that he did not intend to pay back any of the loans or the interest. Other European powers experienced similar treatment. By the end of 1901, Germany was considering whether to establish a blockade and by force to collect the money owed. On 11 December 1901, Ambassador Holleben told Secretary Hay about Germany's plans and assured the United States that "under no circumstances do we consider in our proceedings the acquisition or permanent occupation of Venezuelan territory." There was the possibility, however, that Germany "would have to consider the temporary occupation on our part of different Venezuelan harbor places and the levying of duties in these places." The American reply echoed the president's annual message: the United States would object only if a foreign power sought to create a permanent base in the Western Hemisphere.[5]

The Germans postponed further action in January 1902. The brother of the kaiser, Prince Henry, was to make a goodwill visit to the United States during the winter, and military coercion of Venezuela must not interfere with that state occasion and the good will that it might produce. The impression that Henry made in the United States stimulated press comment, especially speculation about a "romance" between the prince and Alice Roosevelt. Although the president told Sternburg that "the coming of Prince Henry had done good and removed causes of friction between the nations," this ceremonial interplay had not changed the basic shape of German-American affairs.[6] Roosevelt used the opportunity to lobby with the prince for the selection of Sternburg as ambassador.

The resolution of the Venezuelan crisis during 1902/3 hinged in part on the decisions that Roosevelt made about the navy around the time that the Germans made known their intention regarding a possible blockade of Venezuela. The president intended that the navy should be brought up to a higher degree of readiness for possible action. The appointment of William H. Moody as secretary of the navy was one sign of Roosevelt's intention. Another was his insistence that naval officers become accustomed to regular sea duty.

Even more directly related to the Venezuelan situation were the navy's movements during the first half of 1902. The navy had not previously conducted peacetime maneuvers in the Caribbean, nor had there been coordinated exercises by the whole fleet of battleships at any time. Early in the year, Rear Adm. Henry C. Taylor was named chief of the Bureau of Navigation. He pressed for annual fleet maneuvers to improve the fighting efficiency of the service. This change represented an important and overdue reform. To naval leaders who were suspicious of German intentions, it also served to marshal American power in case of a crisis. In January the navy asked Congress for money to conduct the drills, and intelligence was gathered about defending Venezuela against a German attack. By June 1902 the future mobilization of the fleet was announced.

Roosevelt also picked Adm. George Dewey, the hero of Manila Bay, as commander of the American flotilla. "It will be a good thing from the professional standpoint," Roosevelt wrote Dewey on 14 June 1902, "and what is more, your standing not only in this nation but abroad, is such that the effect of our presence will be very beneficial outside of the service also." Dewey's earlier confrontations with the Germans in the Philippines gave his selection an added political dimension. The choice would "put pride in the people and arrest the attention of the Kaiser," said the president in September.[7] By mid November the fleet and Dewey were assembling at their advance base on Culebra Island near Puerto Rico. Efforts to acquire the Virgin Islands from Denmark or to establish bases in Cuba had not borne fruit at this time.

During the summer of 1902, Britain and Germany renewed their discussions about possible joint action against Castro and Venezuela. By November the two countries had agreed to move ahead, along with Italy, and to declare a blockade of the Venezuelan coast. On the German side, the aim of the crisis was to rebuild relations with Great Britain that the Boer War had strained and to see to what extent the United States would vigorously defend the Monroe Doctrine.

The events of the blockade and its diplomatic outcome during December 1902 and January 1903 are not in dispute. In November the European powers sent Venezuela their ultimatums, which Castro rejected. After informing the United States of their intentions, a joint Anglo-German force set up a blockade on 9 December 1902. They sank Venezuelan ships, and the Germans landed some troops. On 11 December, Castro agreed to have the dispute arbitrated, an offer that the United States conveyed to London and Berlin on 12 December. Four days later, Secretary Hay renewed the arbitration proposal. The British accepted on the following day, and the Germans did so on 19 December. The two countries asked Roosevelt to serve as arbitrator. He declined to accept on the ground that the matter should be referred to the Permanent Court of Arbitration at The Hague for settlement. By Christmas 1902 it looked as if the international crisis was on its way to being resolved. That judgment was premature, as events would prove in January 1903. For Theodore Roosevelt's role in this episode, however, what took place during December 1902 has received the most intense analysis.

During World War I, thirteen years after the crisis itself, Roosevelt told a biographer of John Hay that there had been another dramatic dimension to the Venezuelan incident. The former president revealed that he had informed the kaiser, through the German ambassador, that if Germany did not agree to arbitrate the dispute, "I would be obliged to order Dewey to take his fleet to the Venezuelan coast and see that the German forces did not take possession of any territory." A week after this interview with the ambassador, when no answer had been received from Berlin, Roosevelt again told Holleben that "Dewey would be ordered to sail twenty four hours in advance of the time I had set." On the next day, Holleben "notified" the president that the kaiser had agreed to Roosevelt as an arbitrator. It was, Roosevelt added later, an example of "how I applied the policy of 'speak softly and carry a big stick.' "[8]

For the past seventy years, scholars have been debating the accuracy of these statements and whether they reflect the reality of what Roosevelt said and did in 1902. The details of this intricate controversy can only be touched on in a general way. Those who accept that Roosevelt did issue a personal ultimatum to Germany make their strongest argument on the basis of Roosevelt's own statements between 1902 and 1915. In private letters and conversations he conveyed to friends the substance of what he discussed more fully later. "I was ready to fight Germany in the winter, but I am not ready at present to fight Russia," he commented to the British ambassador in June 1903. Three years later he told both the diplomat Henry White and Whitelaw Reid what he recalled. Biographers have found other instances before 1915 when Roosevelt mentioned his statements made in 1902.[9]

The problem remains that no confirming contemporary evidence of what Roosevelt said has yet been found. The published United States, British, and German documents make no reference to an ultimatum; and the original sources are also silent. Citing large gaps in the records for all three countries, one scholar has argued that the Germans and the Americans, and to some degree the British, purged their diplomatic archives of the traces of Roosevelt's actions. The kaiser's backing down would thus be preserved from later scrutiny. The absence of evidence thus becomes a support for Roosevelt's statements.[10]

The only recorded occasion when the president saw the German ambassador, however, was on 8 December. Holleben brought the imperial German commissioner to the Louisiana Purchase Exposition to meet Roosevelt. The press carried an account of the meeting with the two Germans the next day. Perhaps Roosevelt and the ambassador spoke privately as well, although it is improbable that such an exchange occurred. It has been proposed that Roosevelt could have met again privately with Holleben on Sunday 14 December to renew an ultimatum delivered a week earlier. The scenario is ingenious, but one problem remains. Throughout this period the Germans never reacted as they would have had the president of the United States threatened them with a war.[11]

Emphasis on Roosevelt's private diplomacy has diverted attention from the effectiveness of his public actions in affecting the international policies of Germany. The administration made a number of diplomatic and military moves during the crucial period in December.[12] Dewey was named commander of the United States fleet on 8 December, and the cabinet closely and publicly tracked events in the Caribbean. More ships were sent to the fleet, and conferences began with congressional leaders. Secretary Hay's interest in arbitration offers was discussed in the press, and further movements of naval vessels closer to the blockade zone were announced on 16 December. These actions brought the German chargé d'affaires, Albert von Quadt, to see Hay on 18 December. The secretary told Quadt that the American public was upset about events in Venezuela and that an aroused Congress would likely consider a resolution upholding the Monroe Doctrine. Quadt wired a report of his talks with Hay to Berlin the same day.

By the time his dispatch from Washington reached Germany, however, the kaiser's government had already decided that arbitration was its preferred solution to the crisis. The German ambassador in London told the British that "action should be taken upon the Venezuelan proposal at once, without waiting until Washington 'exchanged the role of post-office for one of a more active character.' " These discussions occurred on the day that Hay and Quadt met, and it is improbable that events in Washington shaped decisions in Europe. The Germans also said that Roosevelt should serve as an arbitrator, and it has been persuasively contended that an ultimatum to the kaiser would, in German eyes, likely have disqualified Roosevelt for that assignment. [13]

The issue of Roosevelt and Venezuela is not one for which a final word is ever likely to be written. The president had acted forcefully to have the diplomatic and military resources of the United States at the ready when Great Britain and Germany acted. It did not take an ultimatum to induce Berlin to see that challenging the United States in Latin America would imperil good relations with Washington and drive the Americans closer to the British. The Germans had a contradictory policy that involved simultaneous conciliation and confrontation of the United States. This problem worsened as the Roosevelt administration reacted to the intervention.

As for Roosevelt's memory of his warning to Berlin, he remembered, after the passage of years, the fleet he had maneuvered, the public diplomacy he had practiced, and the German acceptance of the arbitration solution. Soon he came to believe that he had in fact delivered a warning. His letters to friends and for posterity embodied what he now believed to be true.

The Venezuelan imbroglio did not come to an easy conclusion during December 1902. On the day that the British and the Germans announced their willingness to see Roosevelt serve as an arbitrator, they also proclaimed a blockade of the Venezuelan coast that had greater standing in international law than their joint action earlier in the month.

This policy kept British and German ships in place off Venezuela, and in mid January 1903, German vessels fired on Venezuelan installations at Puerto Cabello and Fort San Carlos.

By the time this new crisis flared, the Germans had replaced their ambassador in Washington. Holleben had irritated his government for reasons that were unrelated to the situation in the Caribbean, and he had also not done well during the events of December. To replace him the kaiser insisted on sending Sternburg, whose friendship with the president outweighed his American wife, relative lack of experience, and sympathies with the concept of the Monroe Doctrine. "Nice little Baron Speck turned up as the representative from Germany," Roosevelt told his eldest son. A German source also quoted the president as saying: "I hope, the Emperor does not think me stupid enough to be influenced by Specky!"[14]

The German assaults on the Venezuelan positions renewed fears in the United States that the Monroe Doctrine was in jeopardy. The Germans refused to recognize the legitimacy of that policy. Because negotiations had begun between Venezuela—represented by the United States minister, Herbert W. Bowen—and the European powers, these naval moves caused the Roosevelt administration to look again at the readiness of its naval detachment in the region. There were disturbing indications that the United States might not be certain of victory should a confrontation occur. Still, U.S. deployments underlined the risks that the Germans were running in the Western Hemisphere. Public opinion in the United States and in Great Britain became even more hostile to Berlin and its policy. As the British government lost its stomach for the Venezuelan project, the Germans had little choice but to reach a final settlement of the matter in February 1903.

In 1904, Roosevelt put "the Venezuelan business" among the important achievements of his first term because of its positive impact on the Monroe Doctrine. His experience with European nations endeavoring to collect debts from countries in Latin America bothered the president. When Sternburg told Roosevelt in mid March 1903 about an idea of a great-power syndicate to run the finances of Venezuela, the president responded that even with the United States in the lead, public opinion would oppose such an idea. Roosevelt decided that he should assert that no American republic should "come under the control of a European power by any such subterfuge as exercising this control under color of a pretense to the guaranteeing or collecting a debt."[15] Out of these ideas would soon come the Roosevelt corollary to the Monroe Doctrine. This was a concept that Germany disliked even more than the doctrine itself.

Great Britain had been a coparticipant in the European blockade of

Venezuela, but its role, which was criticized in the United States, never aroused the same hostility that the Germans evoked. Relations between London and Washington had been improving since the Spanish-American War. That trend intensified while Theodore Roosevelt was president. He believed that Britain was inherently friendly to the United States. Important issues had to be resolved, however, especially the Canadian boundary question, but Roosevelt saw little chance of an Anglo-American clash of serious dimensions.

World events during 1902 kept the two countries from considering seriously the questions in dispute. Britain still had the Boer War to conclude, and Roosevelt declined to address the issue of the Canadian boundary "because I am friendly to England, and while the South African War is unfinished I don't want to give the American pro-Boers a chance."[16] The war came to an end in May 1902, and the government in London could now take up other matters. King Edward VII had been crowned, and Arthur James Balfour had come in as prime minister of the Conservative government. There had been a brief, intense flurry of press comment regarding the degree of Britain's friendship during the war with Spain, to which both the British and the Germans contributed. Prince Henry's visit had also complicated the situation somewhat. Nonetheless, by the early summer of 1902 there seemed to be the prospect of serious negotiations on a friendly basis to take up the volatile and vexing problem of Canada's boundary with Alaska.

The dispute over the precise boundary between British Columbia and Alaskan territory stretched back to a treaty between Great Britain and Russia in 1825. The United States assumed the Russian rights when it acquired Alaska in 1867. Gold discoveries in the Yukon in 1898 made access to those areas where gold was found the key to domination of the riches of the region. The Canadian-boundary issue was as complex as national feelings and geographic disagreement could make it. Along the southeastern coast of Alaska lay islands and inlets that opened the way to the gold fields. The United States contended that the 1825 treaty gave it control of the Portland Canal in the south and a line of territory along the coast to the north that accorded it the Lynn Canal and the towns of Dyea and Skagway. The British and the Canadians disputed both of these assertions, though the British thought that the Canadian case regarding the Portland Canal was "hopelessly untenable."[17] There was more of an argument to be made about how far inland the United States territory might extend.

The situation in the disputed areas was dangerous because miners on both sides might resort to violence on behalf of their claims and country. Would Canadian territory be seized as an ostensible prelude to

United States occupation and annexation? Would the Canadians move into the towns of Dyea and Skagway by force? An armed clash would produce a crisis that none of the three countries wanted. Roosevelt watched the situation with care, and in late March 1902 he sent American soldiers to southern Alaska, where they could be present "promptly to prevent any possible disturbance along the disputed frontier line."[18]

Theodore Roosevelt had firm views about the merits of the Canadian-boundary controversy. He wrote John Hay in July 1902 that what the Canadians contended for "is an outrage pure and simple." British maps, including one in the cabinet room in London, gave the same boundary that the United States claimed. The Canadians and the British had accepted this line "until the last few years." Canada had no right to expect territory or money from the United States. "To pay them anything where they are entitled to nothing would in a case like this come dangerously near blackmail." The same logic led him to resist arbitration of the dispute. He was willing to have three U.S. commissioners meet three Anglo-Canadian commissioners, but only with the understanding that the representatives of the United States "were not to yield any territory whatsoever, but were as a matter of course to insist upon our entire claim." The only negotiation would be about the precise limits of the United States claim.[19]

Roosevelt never wavered from this basic position. He believed that the Canadians knew that they had a weak case and that they were acting for domestic political reasons. The United States, on the other hand, had an unassailable position from which no appeal was justified. The president did not see himself as being moved by any internal political forces except those that affected the tactical questions of how to mobilize support in Congress for an eventual settlement. He pushed the British and the Canadians very hard during 1902/3 to achieve his foreign-policy goals. The prestige of the United States demanded no less.

The diplomatic deadlock between Canada and the United States over the Alaska question broke during the summer of 1902. The prime minister of Canada, Sir Wilfrid Laurier, was in London for an imperial conference. He first told the British and, later, Henry White at the American embassy that he would agree to have an even-numbered tribunal negotiate the boundary. This act would eliminate the chance of a result that would be adverse to the United States. Second, the Canadians would recognize Dyea and Skagway as American possessions even if the tribunal decided that they were legally Canadian. "I gather that Sir Wilfrid is in a conceding mood," wrote the British colonial secretary.[20]

This change of position, which many in Laurier's own cabinet disliked, may have stemmed from the prime minister's desire to forestall reciprocity-treaty negotiations between the United States and Newfoundland. If that was his strategy, the move did not work. Deliberations on a trade pact went forward between Secretary Hay and Robert Bond of Newfoundland during the autumn of 1902. The treaty, which lowered duties on the products of both countries, was signed on 8 November 1902. When it reached the Senate, Lodge opposed it because of its potential impact on Gloucester fishermen in his son-in-law's congressional district. The treaty did not come to the Senate floor during Roosevelt's first term.

Before the United States and Great Britain could open negotiations for a treaty to embody the concessions that Laurier had made regarding procedures for settling the boundary issues, the two nations had to go through the Venezuelan incident at the end of 1902. The British cooperated with the Germans without fully appreciating the effect their actions might have on Washington. The death of Ambassador Julian Pauncefote contributed to the absence of a consideration of possible American reaction. When the Anglo-German initiative commenced in November 1902, the new ambassador, Sir Michael Herbert, told his superiors: "I wish we were going to punish Venezuela without the aid of Germany, for I am not sure that joint action will be very palatable here."[21]

During the crisis of December 1902–January 1903, the British government responded both to American anger and to the reaction of its own people and sought to limit the damage to Anglo-American relations that the Venezuelan intervention was causing. The British agreed to arbitration by Roosevelt in December, said openly that no British troops would go ashore in Venezuela, and accepted Bowen, the United States minister, as a negotiator for Venezuela. When the naval actions of January 1903 aroused United States and British opinion against the intervention in an even more pronounced manner, the government in London faced a decision. "The time has almost come in American opinion," wrote Ambassador Herbert, "for us to make the choice between the friendship of the United States and that of Germany."[22] The British moved in the way that Washington desired, the Venezuelan intervention ended, and the Balfour government came out publicly for the Monroe Doctrine. The result on the side of Britain was to strengthen relations with Washington, in direct contrast to the outcome for Germany.

While the Venezuelan drama was taking place, Herbert and Hay were in the middle of their negotiations for a pact that would specify the procedures for settling the boundary dispute. Theodore Roosevelt had insisted throughout most of 1902 that any U.S. members of an Alaskan-boundary commission could not yield on any aspect of their country's claim. By December, however, the position of the United States had shifted, in part because of Republican success in the congressional elections and also because of the Venezuelan crisis. Washington now agreed to an even-numbered tribunal that could arrive at a final outcome regarding the Alaska boundary. On 18 December, Hay put before Herbert a draft treaty. It called for a tribunal made up of "six impartial jurists of repute who shall consider judicially the questions submitted to them."[23] Four would be needed for a decision, and the tribunal members would pledge themselves to make an impartial judgment.

The Canadian government did not think much of Hay's draft, and it suggested tribunal members who were not from the affected nations. The United States would have none of that proposal, and the British put a good deal of pressure on Ottawa to accept the treaty. The Canadians reluctantly went along. On 24 January 1903 the Hay-Herbert Treaty was signed in the library of Hay's home. The treaty faced uncertain prospects in the United States Senate because of opposition from a bloc of lawmakers from the Pacific Northwest and the reported unpopularity of Hay himself with members of the upper house. Both the British and the Canadians took seriously the language in the treaty regarding "impartial jurists of repute." Hay indicated to Herbert that members of the United States Supreme Court would likely compose the U.S. delegation.

The president gave some credence to this commitment by asking each member of the Court to serve on the tribunal. After he had received their individual refusals, Roosevelt turned to the problem of the Senate. Lodge told him that he should conciliate some of the senators who "could not agree to having anybody on that tribunal who would yield on the American claim, which they rightly believed to be wholly sound."[24] Lodge informed these wavering lawmakers that Roosevelt intended to select Secretary of War Elihu Root, Lodge himself, and Senator George Turner of Washington, a Democrat who was retiring from the Senate on 4 March 1903. With these assurances in hand, Lodge gained ratification of the treaty on 11 February 1903 in an executive session on a voice vote. On an up-or-down recorded vote the pact might not have been approved.

The British learned of the U.S. tribunal members on 14 February and knew that Canada would hardly agree to three such commissioners. Lodge and Turner were outspoken partisans of the U.S. position, while Root was a member of the administration. London arranged for the king to ratify the treaty on 17 February and then broke the news to the Canadians the following day. The Venezuelan situation, then coming to a climax, undoubtedly played its role in moving the British to such peremptory action. Ratifications were exchanged with the United States on 3 March 1903 in what Laurier later called "a slap in the face for Canada."[25] The Canadian government could do little about what was an accomplished fact.

Several reasons accounted for Roosevelt's decision to name Lodge and Turner. These selections, Lodge believed, were the price of quick Senate ratification. More judicious appointments might well have resulted in defeat of the treaty. Moreover, Roosevelt thought that he had done the British and the Canadians a good turn by agreeing to a tribunal at all. Since Canada had no case, in Roosevelt's mind, the tribunal was a graceful way of allowing them out of an awkward situation.

The Canadians took a contrasting approach in making their selections: their two members of the tribunal, L. A. Jetté and A. B. Aylesworth, were prominent representatives of the legal profession in their country. The British selected Lord R. E. W. Alverstone, the chief justice. The next problem was setting a time when the tribunal would convene in London. According to the treaty itself, the date would be 3 September 1903, six months after the formal exchange of ratifications. As the Canadians prepared their case, they decided that more time would be necessary. In July they requested that the date for beginning the deliberations be pushed back to late in September. A postponement would inconvenience both Root and Lodge, who wanted to be back for the beginning of the congressional session in November. They laid their objections before the president.

Roosevelt readily concurred with the need to stay on the schedule. "I don't want the thing pending during a presidential campaign," he told Hay. Any failure of the British to conclude an agreement, "under any pretense," would be "due to bad faith." They should be informed through Ambassador Joseph Hodges Choate that Roosevelt would, in the absence of a settlement, "bring the matter to the attention of Congress and ask for an appropriation so that we may run the line ourselves."[26] The president was more aggressive on this point than Hay was, and the secretary offered to resign. Roosevelt did not accept, so Hay stayed at his post. When Lodge left for England, he carried with him a letter, signed by Roosevelt, that again threatened to let Congress settle the matter in November if an agreement had not been reached.

Lodge reached London at the end of July, and he conveyed Roosevelt's position forcefully to the ambassador and orally to members of the British government, including Prime Minister Balfour, whom the senator knew personally. Roosevelt did not limit his diplomatic offensive to Lodge. He also wrote to Justice Oliver Wendell Holmes, who was on vacation in England, that "if there is disagreement I wish it distinctly understood, not only that there will be no arbitration of the matter, but that in my message to Congress I shall take a position which shall prevent any possibility of arbitration hereafter."[27] The prospect of any postponement soon faded, and the tribunal began as scheduled.

The key to the result was, of course, the vote of Lord Alverstone, and Roosevelt took almost every possible step to see that the chief justice and the British government were aware of the president's attitude toward the issues in controversy. He wished the British would understand, he wrote Elihu Root on 3 October 1903, "that this is the last chance, and that though it will be unpleasant for us, if they force me to do what I must do in case they fail to take advantage of this chance, it will be a thousandfold more unpleasant for them."[28] With Roosevelt's insistence always in the background, Root, Lodge, and Henry White kept the pressure on the Balfour government and Alverstone for a verdict favorable to the United States. A letter from John Hay to White, arriving in mid October, underlined the danger of the situation to the British. If Roosevelt were compelled to act on his own, it would be very unfortunate for Canada. "And all the labor of the last few years, to bring about a closer friendship between the two governments will have gone for nothing."[29]

These sentiments reached Lord Alverstone by several channels. His vote tipped the balance toward the United States in the decision that was announced on 20 October 1903. The tribunal awarded a strip of land along the coast to the United States and also allocated two small islands near the Portland Canal in the same way. The Canadians received two islands in the area but believed they should have had all four. Lord Alverstone came under a great deal of criticism from the Canadian press for what was called favoritism toward the United States. Roosevelt was "very much pleased" with the outcome. He credited Alverstone's vote for part of the victory, but he also thought "that the clear understanding the British government had as to what would follow a disagreement was very important and probably decisive."[30]

The United States clearly had the better of the case on its merits, and Laurier's concessions in 1902 meant that a result favorable to Washington was always likely. For Roosevelt the evident strength of the U.S. position warranted the strongest possible assertion of his country's claims. Roosevelt then took public credit for what the White House called "far and away the greatest diplomatic success which the United States have gained for a generation." In his annual message he informed Congress that "the result is satisfactory in every way" and would be "of great material advantage to our people in the far Northwest."[31]

Even as dedicated and hardworking a president as Theodore

Roosevelt could not devote the same attention and interest to all aspects of foreign policy that he expended on the Venezuelan crisis and the Canadian-boundary negotiations. While he was aware of the strategic and diplomatic importance to the United States of its Far Eastern policy, he did not become heavily involved with that area of the world until the outbreak of the Russo-Japanese War in 1904. His mediation of that conflict properly belongs to the record of his second term. Nonetheless, relevant background events that occurred between 1901 and 1904 established the context within which Roosevelt would later function.

The fate of three nations—Russia, Japan, and China—largely governed what American policymakers could do in Asia. For each of these countries the United States had evolved contradictory and sometimes inconsistent policies. Washington wanted to preserve China's territorial integrity against the incursions of other countries. If achieved, this goal would safeguard the ability of Americans to compete for trade in what was believed to be a large pool of potential customers. The Open Door policy was most notably associated with its architect, John Hay. While Americans' interest in the destiny of China was pervasive during the first decade of the twentieth century, it did not extend to taking any direct military or political action that might involve U.S. forces in Asian battles.

Theodore Roosevelt did not think much of China as a power in world affairs or of the political and intellectual capacity of the Chinese as a people. The military and diplomatic weakness that the Chinese displayed served as a vivid lesson to Roosevelt of the international dangers that accompanied a lack of national strength and will. He treated China as a kind of object that the greater nations of the world must to some degree guide and direct. In return, he thought the Chinese should be grateful for the concern that the United States expressed regarding their national welfare.

While it behaved as a kind of benevolent, if often impotent, patron of China, the United States acted toward Chinese visitors and immigrants in ways that subverted the ostensible good intentions of the president and his fellow citizens. Sino-American treaties, such as the Gresham-Yang pact of 1894, as well as restrictive congressional enactments of the 1880s and 1890s, gave the Bureau of Immigration sweeping authority to screen Chinese students, diplomats, and workers who were seeking entry and to regulate their lives once they were in the United States. Immigration inspectors insulted Chinese upon their arrival, used medical examinations and grueling interrogations to find a plausible pretext to deny admission, and detained or questioned legal immigrants capriciously and, in some instances, brutally. Legislation that the

Roosevelt administration supported in 1902 tightened the restrictions that the Chinese already faced. The president wanted a stronger exclusion policy, and he supported tougher tests, in the bills that were being considered, than the State Department had recommended. The Bureau of Immigration also made sure that the exclusion laws were stringently enforced. The president's position was very popular on the West Coast, especially in California, where his attitude on Chinese exclusion helped his election prospects in 1904.

The issue that affected Chinese-American relations most directly before 1904 was Manchuria. Long anxious to expand its influence there, Russia had used the Boxer Uprising of 1900 as an occasion to create a military and economic presence. The aim of Chinese diplomacy was to secure a Russian evacuation, while the tsar and his government hoped to delay that action. The United States wanted to preserve its economic stake in northern China and to restrain Russian ambitions. The means of achieving these goals would not be the power of the United States against Russia but, rather, the efforts of China, Great Britain, and Japan, which Washington would encourage and support. Over the next two years, Secretary Hay sought a policy that would ensure, whatever its outcome, that "the United States shall not be placed in any worse position than while the country [Manchuria] was under the unquestioned domination of China."[32]

This approach seemed to work in 1901/2 as the Russians and Chinese negotiated about the terms of a Russian withdrawal. The Anglo-Japanese Alliance of 1902 and the general opposition of the powers to Russia brought about an apparent resolution of the issue in the form of a Russian promise to depart from Manchuria in April 1902. The president congratulated Hay on "your success with Russia."[33] In reality, Hay's policy was ambiguous and flawed. Rather than recognizing Russia's presence in Manchuria and seeking formal concessions to protect American interests, he tried to reconcile what was taking place with the principles of the Open Door. As long as Russia continued its withdrawal during late 1902 and into early 1903, the secretary was content with this situation. At the same time the United States and China began talks that would lead to a revised commercial agreement between the two nations.

In April 1903 the problem of Manchuria heated up again when the Russians announced a slowdown in the pullout of their forces and made renewed demands on China for concessions that would work against American economic interests. Hay told Roosevelt that it was "out of the question" for the administration to take part in "any scheme of concerted action with England and Japan which would seem openly hostile to Russia." Public opinion would oppose such a move. Roosevelt continued to let Hay handle the subject. During a tour of the West in May 1903, the president wrote to the secretary: "As to Manchuria there does not seem to be anything for me to say at present, or any need of my saying anything. We are in no 'entangling alliance'; and things are settling down anyhow."[34]

It looked at first as if the crisis indeed might ease during early May 1903. It soon became evident, however, that Russia was following a duplicitous policy. While assuring the United States that there could be U.S. consulates and treaty ports in Manchuria, the Russians were actually demanding that China not allow these concessions to any nation other than Russia. "Dealing with a government with whom mendacity is a science, is an extremely difficult and delicate matter," the exasperated Hay told Roosevelt on 12 May 1903. Roosevelt echoed Hay's frustration: "The bad feature of the situation from our standpoint," he wrote on 22 May, "is that as yet it seems that we cannot fight to keep Manchuria open. I hate being in the position of seeming to bluster without backing it up."[35]

An issue unrelated to Manchuria but bearing on the general behavior of the Russian people and their government gave Theodore Roosevelt one opportunity to combine diplomatic action with a popular domestic political initiative. In April 1903 a pogrom against the Jews in the Russian city of Kishinev erupted over imaginary actions of the Jewish population that outraged the Christians. Forty-five Jews were killed, more than five hundred were injured, and thousands were left homeless in a wave of anti-Semitic violence. This outbreak of bigotry was not a new problem in Russia and eastern Europe. There had been difficulties with the Russians over the issue in 1902, and the condition of Jews in Rumania had evoked a U.S. diplomatic protest that same year. The atrocities in Kishinev triggered protests in the United States, efforts to help the victims, and pressure on the Roosevelt administration, from such prominent Jews as Jacob H. Schiff and Oscar S. Straus, to enter a formal diplomatic protest with St. Petersburg. Despite the public outcry, Hay and the State Department showed no official reaction during April and May. They asked whether it would be worthwhile "if we should make a protest against these fiendish cruelties and be told it was none of our business?"[36] Then, in the middle of June, with the worsening situation in the Far East, the policy of the administration shifted.

After having kept Jewish groups at arm's length, the president and the secretary of state now met with Jewish leaders and promised support for the campaign to send a protest petition to the Russian government. The administration made sure that the press knew about its new stance. When the Russians indicated that they might not accept the petition, Roosevelt instructed the State Department on 1 July 1903 to issue a release explaining that the government would send the document as soon as all the names had been collected. While "the requirements of official propriety" would be observed, the State Department would "most certainly not hesitate to give expression to the deep sympathy felt not only by the administration but by all the American people for the unfortunate Jews who have been the victims in the recent appalling massacres and outrages."[37]

Two weeks later the petition went off to St. Petersburg, only to have the Russians refuse to accept the document, which they considered to be outside interference with their internal business. The release of the petition to the press and the publication of the names of the signers had the desired impact on Jewish opinion in the United States. "I think we did that business pretty well," Roosevelt told Congressman Lucius N. Littauer (R., N.Y.), who had been involved in the petition drive. "We certainly went to the limit in taking the lead on behalf of humanity."[38] To some degree the president had responded to public pressure, with an eye to the role of Jewish voters in the key state of New York. This action also allowed the administration to do something anti-Russian that did not involve dangerous participation in the unfolding events in Manchuria.

On 14 July 1903 the Russians announced that they did not object to open ports in Manchuria that did not have foreign settlements. United States negotiations with the Chinese then turned to obtaining Peking's agreement to that policy. After an ultimatum from the United States, the Chinese accepted the provision and said that a commercial treaty would be signed on the date the Russians were to withdraw, 8 October 1903. However, in September the Russians proposed new terms for their departure that would have left their troops in place into 1904. The Japanese looked to see how the United States would react. The administration stalled, and this action may have added to Tokyo's conviction that only war could restrain Russian ambition.

The treaty with China was concluded as planned, and the Chinese promptly sought United States support against Russia. Roosevelt declined to have his country act because of relative military weakness and the absence of any popular backing for an aggressive policy in the Far East. Notes and paper protests did not move the Russians. The Japanese, for their part, concluded that they could only rely on their own military power to keep Russia in check. During the last months of 1903 the Russians and the Japanese moved toward the commencement of hostilities. The United States under Roosevelt would be neutral in that conflict, but as the Japanese had been assured, it would be a "very benevolent neutrality."[39]

The foreign-policy record of Theodore Roosevelt with regard to such subjects as Venezuela, the Alaskan boundary, and the Far East is now largely of interest only to scholarly students of his life and presidency. His involvement in the events that led to the creation of the Panama Canal Zone and the construction of the canal remains his most disputed and controversial act. Because of the continuing United States interest in Central America, including the difficulties with the Panamanian leaders who have shared control of the canal since 1979, the circumstances under which Roosevelt gained the right to build a canal across Panama have been examined from strongly partisan viewpoints. Many Americans still believe that in the late 1970s the United States gave away a possession that Theodore Roosevelt had acquired by forceful executive action. Defenders of Roosevelt have asserted that the behavior of Colombia offended the president's moral code and thereby justified his interpretation of events and the response that he made to them. Critics of the president, on the other hand, contend that the case of the Panama Canal shows Roosevelt's dangerous tactics in foreign affairs and his insensitivity to Latin American opinion.

After the passage of the Spooner Act in 1902, the State Department pursued negotiations with Colombia about a canal treaty. Roosevelt believed that the isthmian canal would be "the great bit of work of my administration, and from the material and constructive standpoint one of the greatest bits of work that the twentieth century will see." He asked Hay "to take personal direction" of the talks. In mid July 1902 the secretary reported: "I have got at last a draft embodying all things which are at present possible, and which, if accepted by the other side, will make a very good treaty."[40] It remained for the representative of Colombia to consult with his government during the summer.

The precise nature of the regime that governed Colombia during the Panama crisis seemed very clear in the minds of Theodore Roosevelt and the members of his administration as the negotiations began. To their way of thinking, the remote South American nation was under the control of a virtual dictator in the person of its vice-president, José Marroquín, who had assumed power in a July 1900 coup. Roosevelt later called Marroquín "an irresponsible dictator" who ruled his nation autocratically. Once a treaty had been made with the United States in January 1903, Roosevelt went on, Marroquín "had the absolute power of an unconstitutional dictator to keep his promise or break it."[41] Given this view of the situation, the president believed he had a right to expect that Colombia would live up to its international obligations. He had a moral duty to act in the best interest of the United States if Colombia proved faithless to this trust.

In 1902, Colombia was an impoverished country which civil war had convulsed for the preceding three years. Governmental finances were in chaos, and the political system had broken down in the wake of inflation and social violence. Worse still, the geographic isolation of Bogotá often made diplomatic procedures the hostages of erratic transportation and communication. For Colombians the prospect of a canal across Panama offered the possibility of a dependable source of revenues and the chance to share in the wealth that the United States possessed. At the same time, however, the sovereignty of Colombia must not be diminished in an agreement with Washington. Complicating the problem even more for the Colombians was the persistent sentiment for independence that pervaded Panama and had previously led to sporadic rebellions in that remote province. In quelling such uprisings in the recent past, Bogotá had called on the United States for military assistance under the provisions of an 1846 treaty with the nation then called New Granada. Colombia was in a fragile diplomatic posture as it talked with the Roosevelt administration.

Nor was José Marroquín the dominant political force that John Hay and Roosevelt believed him to be. The endemic factionalism that had brought about civil strife had not disappeared when the fighting between Liberals and Conservatives stopped in November 1902. In a country whose politics often turned on issues relating to sovereignty and nationhood, the aged vice-president was not secure enough to force through a disadvantageous canal agreement with the United States simply by fiat. As he told a friend during the summer of 1902: "Of me history will say that I ruined the isthmus and all of Colombia, not permitted the canal to be opened or that I permitted it to be done, scandalously injuring the rights and reputation of my nation."[42] The risky strategy that Colombia adopted was to play for time, hoping to bolster its negotiating position and perhaps to gain a better financial offer from the New Panama Canal Company or the United States.

What seemed to Colombia's leaders to be in their own national interest appeared to Theodore Roosevelt to be bad faith and international blackmail. William Nelson Cromwell, the lawyer for the New Panama Canal Company, reinforced Roosevelt's attitude. Cromwell cooperated with the Colombian diplomats in the United States in writing a treaty about the canal. He preferred, however, to have his company's payment come from Washington rather than from the uncertain and perhaps grasping hands in Bogotá.

Meanwhile, Philippe Bunau-Varilla was ready to advance his dream of a canal across the isthmus. A French engineer in his early forties who had worked on the abortive Panama canal project of Ferdinand Marie de Lesseps during the 1880s and 1890s, Bunau-Varilla was a balding man with a flowing mustache. He was a passionate, unofficial advocate for the Panama route. From 1901 onward, he campaigned tirelessly in the United States on behalf of his chosen cause. He and Cromwell were unwilling allies, but their joint lobbying efforts were a significant element in the eventual choice of Panama as the site for the canal.

Hay's negotiations with the Colombian minister were still going on when another revolt took place in Panama during September 1902. United States marines went ashore to safeguard the railroad that traversed the region. Similar action had happened during earlier revolts, but in this instance the Americans had not obtained permission from Colombia beforehand. The Colombian minister sent in his resignation in November 1902 in response and was replaced by the chargé d'affaires, Dr. Tomás Herrán. By the time that Herrán had entered the diplomatic maneuvering, the position of his country relative to the United States and the canal was not promising. Hay and Roosevelt had proposed that the United States be granted the right to construct a canal, to control a zone along either side of the canal for one hundred years with police regulations and U.S. courts, and that the rights of the New Panama Canal Company be ceded to the United States without any compensation to Colombia. The only subject that the United States would discuss with Herrán was the recompense that Colombia would receive. The Colombians hoped to achieve a $10 million indemnity and an annual payment of $600,000. Meanwhile, pressure was building in the United States Congress for prompt action, as a statement of Senator Shelby M. Cullom (R., Ill.). revealed. He thought that perhaps Washington should bargain with the New Panama Canal Company to build a canal. On 21 January 1903, Secretary Hay issued an ultimatum to Herrán in which he threatened to negotiate with Nicaragua if Colombia did not accept the treaty as the United States had proposed it. Herrán capitulated, and the Hay-Herrán Treaty was signed the following day. The *Boston Transcript* said: "We have an opportunity that is not likely to knock twice."[43]

The Hay-Herrán pact specified that the rights of the New Panama Canal Company would be sold to the United States. Colombia would receive no compensation from the French company because that would raise the eventual cost to the United States of purchasing the company's property. The resulting canal zone would be six miles in width across Panama. Nominal sovereignty would stay with Colombia, but the United States could create courts and police regulations within the zone.

93

Colombia would be paid $10 million in gold and would receive an annual rental of $250,000. "The Hay-Herrán Treaty, if it erred at all," Theodore Roosevelt wrote in 1913, "erred in being overgenerous toward Colombia."[44]

Ratification of the treaty in the Senate encountered the stubborn resistance of Senator John T. Morgan on behalf of his favored Nicaraguan route. In the end, the upper house gave its consent on 17 March 1903 by a vote of 73 to 5. A week later, Roosevelt was directing members of the Isthmian Canal Commission to visit Panama and determine the status of the work that had already been done. The *New York Sun* spoke for many people in the United States: "The proposed arrangement is too greatly to the advantage of Colombia to make its rejection conceivable."[45]

In Bogotá, however, what were advantageous provisions in U.S. eyes seemed to be violations of Colombian sovereignty. Marroquín put the issue before his Congress in a message of 20 June 1903 that said nothing specific about whether the treaty should be accepted or rejected. The tactic was aimed at his domestic political critics. To Theodore Roosevelt, it became further evidence of the dictator's purpose to sabotage the treaty and hold the United States up for more money. The reports that came from American diplomats in Colombia confirmed Roosevelt and Hay in their negative judgment of the government in Bogotá.

The Colombian Senate debated the treaty for nearly two months. Despite a warning from Hay that "the Colombian Government apparently does not appreciate the gravity of the situation," the lawmakers sought to amend the pact to limit the jurisdiction of the United States over the canal zone, to retain Colombia's power to negotiate with the New Panama Canal Company, and to restrict the authority of the United States in Panama within Colombian sovereignty. The U.S. minister in Bogotá denounced the changes, a move that backfired politically. The Colombian Senate turned down the treaty on 12 August 1903 by a vote of 24 to 0, with two members abstaining and one absent.[46]

On 13 August, with only fragmentary news from Colombia, Roosevelt was "totally in the dark as to what the outcome in the isthmus will be." By the next day, word of Colombia's proposed amendments reached the president. He met with Senator Cullom, who told reporters that "we might make another treaty, not with Colombia, but with Panama." On 16 August the State Department received official reports of the Colombian action, and Hay informed Roosevelt that "there is nothing to be done for the moment." It would be necessary, the secretary went on, to decide between "the simple and easy Nicaragua solution, or the far more difficult and multifurcate scheme of building the Panama Canal *malgré* Bogotá."[47] The president told Hay that he preferred a Panama canal on engineering grounds and did not believe that "the Bogotá lot of jack rabbits should be allowed permanently to bar one of the future highways of civilization." Roosevelt did not intend to return to the Nicaraguan option. That would have meant asking Congress to reverse itself again and would have compelled the administration to negotiate with Nicaragua, which a brutal dictator then ruled.[48]

The administration signaled its intentions through the press. After a Hay-Roosevelt conference on 28 August at Oyster Bay, the *New York Herald* told its readers that the White House planned either to use its rights under the treaty of 1846 with New Grenada (the predecessor of Colombia) to build a canal on its own or to see what Colombia might now do in light of U.S. intentions. The Nicaraguan approach was not given much weight. The president had received a memorandum from a student of international law, a former State Department official named John Bassett Moore, who argued that the United States had the right under the 1846 pact to go ahead with the canal. This thesis appealed to Roosevelt's broad concept of executive power, but Hay continued to advise caution and patience. By early September 1903, the United States government was in a public posture of carefully considering its alternatives. Action was postponed until the president returned from his summer stay on Long Island at the beginning of October.

The possibility that a separatist revolution might erupt in Panama and solve the Colombia problem was often in the minds of U.S. officials throughout the summer. William Nelson Cromwell had planted a story in the *New York World* in mid June that asserted: "The state of Panama, which embraces all the proposed Canal Zone, stands ready to secede from Colombia and enter into a canal treaty with the United States."[49] In July the prospective Panamanian insurgents commenced their preparations to launch an uprising. Initial attempts to establish communications with Cromwell and the New Panama Canal Company collapsed when the Colombian government learned of the initiative. During the last week of September 1903, Philippe Bunau-Varilla and the Panamanian rebels began talking about the precise arrangements for their attack. The Frenchman now decided that it was time to discuss his plans with Theodore Roosevelt in person.

In a meeting arranged by an assistant secretary of state, Francis B. Loomis, the two men met at the White House on 10 October 1903. As Bunau-Varilla recalled the incident ten years later, the president asked him: "Well, what do you think is going to be the outcome of the present situation?" After a brief pause, Bunau-Varilla replied: "Mr. President, a

Revolution." Roosevelt seemed surprised: "A Revolution! Would it be possible? But if it became a reality, what would become of the plan we had thought of?" Roosevelt said nothing that could be construed as having encouraged a revolution. The administration was careful to maintain a posture that rejected any attempt "to foment the secession of Panama." As Roosevelt wrote to editor Albert Shaw, the United States "cannot go into the securing by such underhand means, the secession." Of course, he added to Shaw, he would privately "be delighted if Panama were an independent State, or if it made itself so at this moment; but for me to say so publicly would amount to an instigation of a revolt, and therefore I cannot say it."[50]

After the revolt had taken place, Roosevelt wrote that it was Bunau-Varilla's "business to find out what he thought our Government would do. I have no doubt that he was able to make a very accurate guess, and to advise his people accordingly. In fact, he would have been a very dull man had he been unable to make such a guess."[51] The specific actions of the United States in the following weeks helped Bunau-Varilla to grasp what Washington would do if Panama were to rebel. On 15 October the commander of the Pacific Squadron received orders to move his forces toward Acapulco, Mexico, a week later and await further instructions. Other ships were directed to move toward the Caribbean and the Pacific coast of Central America.

Meanwhile, on 16 October the president met with two army officers who had just come back from an intelligence survey of Venezuela and Colombia. They had stopped in Panama on their journey homeward, and they told Roosevelt about their conviction that "a revolutionary party was in the course of organization having for its object the separation of the State of Panama from Colombia." On the same day that this meeting occurred, Hay saw Bunau-Varilla at the former's home. Hay said to his guest: "But we shall not be caught napping. Orders have been given to naval forces on the Pacific to sail towards the Isthmus." Other instructions, sent out on 2 November to the naval officers, told them, in the words of the Treaty of 1846, to "maintain free and uninterrupted transit" across the isthmus and to prevent the landing of any armed force, whether Colombian or Panamanian.[52]

The revolt in Panama began on 3 November 1903 and was over within two days. Success was achieved with little bloodshed. A cable from the U.S. consul in the area arrived shortly before noon on 6 November at the State Department. It announced that "Isthmian movement has obtained so far success" and described the situation. The rebels had performed the initial task of stopping the Colombian forces. The presence of the gunboat USS *Nashville* persuaded some Colombians not to shell the city of Colón. The subsequent arrival of more U.S. ships during the succeeding week ensured the survival of the new Panamanian nation. The State Department also moved quickly when it had the news of the apparent rebel victory. Within an hour of receiving the consul's cable, the United States granted de facto, or limited, recognition to the new government in Panama whose people had "by an apparently unanimous movement" broken away from Colombia and "resumed their independence."[53]

Hay told the American people, in a statement that drew heavily on the wording of the Treaty of 1846, that the president had "no plainer duty" than "to preserve, for the benefit of all, free transit over the isthmus and to do all that lay in his power to bring a permanent peace to its people."[54] Formal recognition came on 13 November, when Roosevelt accepted Bunau-Varilla's credentials as minister plenipotentiary of Panama. By this time, most of the European powers and such Latin American nations as Peru and Costa Rica had accorded recognition to the new country. Work also began on a treaty between Panama and the United States to accomplish what the Hay-Herrán Treaty had failed to do. John Hay knew that he could operate with Bunau-Varilla from a much stronger diplomatic position than even had been the case in dealing with Colombia.

Using amendments that Senator Morgan had proposed to the Hay-Herrán document during the ratification debate, Hay inserted language to give the United States a perpetual grant to the Canal Zone, broader rights over the canal itself, and a zone that was ten miles wide instead of six. Other provisions of what Hay advanced put Panama at a further disadvantage relative to the United States. In the version that was put before Bunau-Varilla on 15 November 1903, Washington proposed to guarantee Panamanian independence but did not speak to Panama's sovereignty over the zone. Bunau-Varilla would later claim personal credit for what became the Hay–Bunau-Varilla Convention, but modern scholarship has revealed Hay's decisive part in the actual drafting of the document.[55]

What the Frenchman did was to put back in the $10 million payment that Hay had deleted and to make other changes that favored Panama on points of detail. Most important, he diminished Panamanian sovereignty by granting to the United States "all the rights, power and authority . . . which [it] would possess and exercise if it were the sovereign of the territory . . . to the entire exclusion of the exercise by the Republic of Panama of any such sovereignty, power and authority." Bunau-Varilla and Hay both knew that such language would be very helpful when the Senate debated whether the treaty should be ratified.[56]

After some additional rewriting, the treaty was signed on 18 November 1903. Both men wanted to move rapidly before a Panamanian delegation arrived in Washington and took over the negotiations from Bunau-Varilla. The Frenchman put his name on the document at Hay's home and then met his sometime countrymen at the railroad station a few hours later. "The Republic of Panama is henceforth under the protection of the United States," he told them: "I have signed the Canal Treaty."[57] Despite some reservations about what had been done in its name, the Panamanian government agreed to the convention on 2 December 1903. Panama received $10 million immediately and an annual rent of $250,000 that would begin in nine years. The New Panama Canal Company obtained $40 million from the United States. The language about Panama's sovereignty became a key issue in the later arguments about the treaty during the twentieth century. Colombia was left on the sidelines, defeated and empty-handed.

For Theodore Roosevelt the actions of the United States toward Panama had created an intense public controversy with which the president had to grapple as 1903 ended. While most Americans applauded the likelihood that a canal would be built, there was pervasive disagreement about how Roosevelt and his administration had used presidential authority and military muscle to accomplish the objectives of the United States. "This mad plunge of ours is simply and solely a vulgar and mercenary venture, without a rag to cover its sordidness and shame," asserted the *New York Evening Post*.[58]

Theodore Roosevelt had no doubt about the rightness of his conduct toward Colombia. "The Colombia people proved absolutely impossible to deal with," he informed Cecil Spring Rice. "They are not merely corrupt. They are governmentally utterly incompetent." When the Colombians said on 6 November that they would put the Hay-Herrán Treaty into effect if the United States would help quell the Panamanian revolt, they simply reinforced Roosevelt's faith in the morality of the United States position. He set forth his own rationale at length in the annual message that went to Congress on 7 December 1903. Colombia had forced the United States "to take decisive steps to bring to an end a condition of affairs which had become intolerable." When these comments did not quiet the political controversy, he sent the lawmakers a second special message on 4 January 1904. That statement reviewed his actions in detail and denied that anyone in the government had had "any part in preparing, inciting, or encouraging the late revolution on the Isthmus of Panama."[59]

The Roosevelt administration won the short-run political battle. Although some Democrats, led by Arthur Pue Gorman of Maryland, tried

to defeat the Hay–Bunau-Varilla pact in the Senate, the public approval
of Roosevelt's conduct was so widespread that the opposition party
could not act cohesively when the final vote came in late February 1904.
Roosevelt believed, as he wrote in February 1904, that the United States
had acted toward Colombia and other nations in the region "on the
theory that it is our duty, when it becomes absolutely inevitable, to
police these countries in the interest of order and civilization."[60] He
never wavered in his conviction about the justice of his actions throughout the subsequent controversies regarding Panama that dotted his life.
In 1904 his immediate thought was to turn to the work of building the
Panama Canal.

Accomplishment was the dominant theme of Roosevelt's foreign
policy during his first term. Alaska and Panama were successes he could
enjoy at the time and later. Because of its anti-German aspect, Venezuela grew in significance when the First World War began. To some
extent the practice of foreign affairs was still relatively simple in
Roosevelt's time. The volume of business that the president dealt with
was still manageable. No power threatened the United States and its
supremacy in the Western Hemisphere. It was fun for Roosevelt to be
his own secretary of state and to impress the kaiser, outmaneuver the
Canadians, and overawe the Colombians. Asia was more frustrating,
because United States power was so limited in the context of world
rivalries. Roosevelt earned his diplomatic victories, but they were
neither expensive nor dangerous. With easy triumphs and no losses,
Roosevelt gained a popular acclaim that added to his political standing.
In foreign affairs, Theodore Roosevelt had to his credit the tangible
expansion of the nation's power and influence when he faced the voters
in 1904.

5

★ ★ ★ ★ ★

THE SQUARE DEAL,
1903–1904

Despite his foreign-policy successes, Theodore Roosevelt had to overcome an array of domestic problems as the 1904 presidential election neared. The range of issues that he confronted was growing, and he showed himself willing to expand the agenda still more. From the role of his family and the physical condition of the White House, to the issues of tariffs, trusts, and banking, and ending with the military reform of both the army and the navy, the president engaged these subjects with the energy and vitality he was making famous. The process produced a compelling slogan. Roosevelt announced that he was providing the nation with a Square Deal.

Roosevelt understood that the American people had an increasing fascination with the occupant of the White House and his family. During the first term what the president did even in casual moments became news for the country. Accordingly, Roosevelt employed his family as a means of placing his personal social values before his fellow citizens. Edith Roosevelt set in motion trends that would affect future first ladies. At the same time, Alice Roosevelt emerged as a celebrity presidential daughter. This broadened use of the first family was a key component of Roosevelt's personalized presidency.

The Roosevelts came to an executive mansion that showed the cumulative effects of a century of presidential life. The eight Roosevelts and their frequent guests pushed the family quarters to their limits, while the formal offices were cramped and inefficient. There were also fears about the soundness of the walls and the rooms under the constant wear that they received. The deteriorating condition of the structure persuaded the Roosevelts to set about an ambitious and speedy renovation campaign during the spring of 1902.

Edith Roosevelt invited the prominent New York architect Charles F. McKim to advise about needed repairs. There was a bill before Congress to appropriate $16,000 for this work. McKim reported on 15 April 1902 that much more money would be needed to make effective changes in the building. He then met with Charles A. Moore, an aide to the powerful Senator James S. McMillan (R., Mich.), who chaired the District of Columbia Committee. Moore brought McMillan into the meeting, and the senator listened to McKim's list of needed renovations. McMillan convinced his committee on the spot to increase the appropriation for the White House and the executive offices to $130,000.

Theodore Roosevelt and McKim met on 19 April 1902 in New York City, and the architect's firm agreed to renovate the White House. As McKim became more involved in the work, the cost rose. A final sum of $475,445 went into an appropriation bill that became law on 28 June 1902. The president also specified that the changes must be completed by the time Congress convened in December. That deadline was met. The Roosevelts moved back in on 4 November 1902, the cabinet convened for its first meeting there two days later, and all work ended on 18 December. The changes in the White House were substantial. There were new executive offices in what came to be called the West Wing. The East Wing was thereafter reserved for the social events. Roosevelt liked what had been done. "The changes in the White House have transformed it from a shabby likeness to the ground floor of the Astor House into a simple and dignified dwelling for the head of a great republic."[1] The speed on which Roosevelt had insisted proved costly over the long term. Parts of the structure were still weak, and in their haste the workmen left materials that should have been removed. In 1902, however, McKim's alterations made the White House a better place in which to conduct the business of the presidency.

The wife of the president had not traditionally been an important visible part of her husband's tenure in the White House before 1900. Since the era of Dolley Madison, only a few ladies—such as Mary Todd Lincoln, Lucy Hayes, and Frances Cleveland—had attracted popular attention. In the case of Ida McKinley, illness had made her a recluse. Edith Kermit Roosevelt saw herself as an appropriate cultural symbol for the people of the United States. She wanted to make the White House "the recognized leader of Washington official society," to establish it as a "factor" in the "moral social life of America." She introduced a number of innovations in the role of the first lady. In 1902 she named Isabelle

("Belle") Hagner of Washington as her social secretary, to deal with the mail and invitations and to coordinate social activities. The statuesque Hagner became a fixture in the Roosevelt White House. In 1908, Roosevelt's military aide, Archie Butt, reported that "her sphere has broadened until it is sort of head aide, general manager, and superintendent."[2]

The first lady pursued an ambitious cultural agenda. She met with cabinet wives each week, sometimes as a group. As a result, the "several wise little reformations" in social practices avoided some embarrassments for the administration. Mrs. Roosevelt held elaborate teas on Friday afternoons for well-connected visitors to Washington. At these events, the Marine Band played, cabinet wives greeted the guests, and daughters of the president and cabinet secretaries served the tea. Another innovation was a series of regular evening musicales where concert artists, including the young Pablo Casals, appeared.[3]

To the public, Mrs. Roosevelt was careful to appear as the nonpolitical helpmate. Even when writing to a family friend such as Cecil Spring Rice, she adopted the position that in those moments when men at the White House discussed serious issues, she and other women would "meekly listen as becomes our sex and position." In fact the first lady served as an intermediary through which a diplomat such as Spring Rice might send unofficial letters for the president's eyes. Each day she and her husband walked in the White House gardens, and their conversations often turned to matters of state. She had a good deal of influence on appointments, and many friends of Theodore Roosevelt believed that Edith's judgment was better than his on issues of character. Edith Roosevelt played an important and as yet largely unmeasured part in the administration.[4]

The presence of four sons and two daughters, ranging in age from seventeen down to four in 1901, was another novel aspect of this presidency. The four boys, Theodore, Jr., Archie, Kermit, and Quentin, delighted the nation with their robust antics. Quentin and his schoolmates formed the "White House Gang" which rollicked through the mansion. The ailing Archie became healthier when Quentin used the White House elevator to bring his 350-pound calico pony, Algonquin, to Archie's second-floor sickroom. The president's residence housed a virtual zoo —from Archie's Josiah the Badger to Alice's snake, Emily Spinach, named after the first lady's maiden sister. The president often acted as the largest child in Mrs. Roosevelt's brood. When "the two small persons in pink tommies" saw him come in before a dinner for the diplomatic corps in January 1903, "they instantly raced for the bed and threw themselves on it with ecstatic conviction that a romp was going to begin." Their father "did not have the heart to disappoint them," and he had to put on a new shirt before descending to the meal.[5]

The president had two daughters. Ethel, who was born in 1891, grew up outside the public eye. During the summer of 1903 she undertook, her proud father wrote to his sister Corinne, "the summer education of Archie in music, and of Quentin in everything. She is a little trump."[6] Alice Lee Roosevelt, his daughter by his first wife, would turn eighteen in February 1902. She made her debut at the White House early in January. This was the beginning of four years of ceaseless publicity as "Princess Alice," the celebrity daughter of the first family. When she christened Prince Henry's yacht, the *Meteor*, in March 1902, the *New York Tribune* commented: "In a day she has become one of the most regarded women in the world, replacing the young Queen of Holland in popular favor." Soon there were songs about her, including "Alice Blue Gown" and "Alice, Where Art Thou?" The president both gained from her notoriety and worried about the effect on her of "the life of social excitement," which he did not "regard as healthy from the standpoint of permanence."[7]

To the American people the Roosevelt family seemed to embody the virtues and tolerable foibles that the nation expected of a father, a mother, and their children. It was widely believed that Theodore Roosevelt had said: "I can be President of the United States, or I can attend to Alice. I can't do both."[8] In private there were strains and difficulties between the president and Alice and between Alice and her stepmother. The presidency's long-range effect on the other children was also uncertain. In addition, Mrs. Roosevelt had two miscarriages during the first term.[9]

As Roosevelt prepared to send in his second annual message to Congress in December 1902, he told Kermit: "I am of course in a perfect whirl of work and have every kind of worry and trouble—but that's what I am here for and down at bottom I enjoy it after all."[10] He had already made the White House into a place where an invitation to luncheon or dinner meant the chance to meet poets, scientists, cowboys, and writers, as well as politicians and cabinet officers. Roosevelt's vast reading and those who told him about authors informed him regarding people across the nation whom he then invited to be his guests. Indicative of Roosevelt's impact was the national reaction to his hunting trip to Mississippi in November 1902. When a small bear was provided for him to shoot, he refused to kill the animal. A cartoon depicted the incident, toy makers created the "Teddy bear," and an enduring fad was born.[11]

The popular attention that his family aroused was an important political asset for Roosevelt. He knew, however, that lasting electoral success depended on his actual record as a policy maker. The congressional session in December 1902 offered him another opportunity to enact his legislative program. In a shorter annual message on 2 December, he came to the main theme at the outset: "Corporations, and especially combinations of corporations, should be managed under public regulation." He drew the line "against misconduct, not against wealth"; but "no more important subject can come before the Congress than this of the regulation of interstate business."[12] He urged lawmakers, under their power to supervise interstate commerce, to enact a stronger antitrust law in order to test its constitutionality. If an unfavorable court ruling were to make an amendment necessary, "we should not shrink from amending the Constitution so as to secure beyond peradventure the power sought." Later he advocated the creation of a department of commerce, which would have "large powers" to oversee "the whole subject of the great corporations doing an interstate business."[13]

On the tariff issues and on the connection between high rates and the trusts, Roosevelt stuck to the themes of the campaign of 1902. "The question of regulation of the trusts stands apart from the question of tariff revision."[14] He discussed reciprocity treaties as a means of adjusting the tariff and called cautiously for their adoption. Once again he suggested using tariff experts to offer advice to Congress about proper rates. Finally, Roosevelt did ask for a lowering of the tariff on monopoly products, and he urged that anthracite coal be put on the free list. He informed the legislators that he would soon submit a reciprocity treaty with Cuba.

The main thrust of the administration's program during the second session of the Fifty-seventh Congress was for trust-related actions. Attorney General Philander C. Knox defined the objectives in a letter to Senator George F. Hoar on 3 January 1903. Knox reviewed the status of antitrust law; then he suggested to Hoar's judiciary committee that the panel make it illegal for railroads to give or receive rebates. Second, Knox advocated the creation of a commission that would "make diligent investigation into the operations and conduct of all corporations, combinations, and concerns engaged in interstate or foreign commerce." He also asked for an antitrust law "aimed at what we certainly know to be unreasonable practices directly restrictive of freedom of commerce." His last recommendation was for a measure that would expedite the judicial consideration of antitrust cases and provide the government with a rapid appeal process to the Supreme Court.[15]

Knox also wanted increased appropriations for his department, as well as more personnel to enforce the antitrust laws. This request was well received on Capitol Hill, and the bill passed within a month. The Antitrust Division of the Justice Department was the outgrowth of this legislation. Knox now had half a million dollars to expend in prosecuting antitrust cases.

There was little opposition in Congress to the bill that Senator Stephen B. Elkins (R., W.Va.) sponsored to outlaw rebating. The railroad companies themselves supported this legislation, because it removed a competitive weapon that shippers had employed to achieve lower rates. "No respectable railroad or respectable shipping business can openly object to the rebate bill," Roosevelt wrote in February 1903.[16] Few railroads complained because the Elkins law did not deal with the regulatory issues that formed the background for the Hepburn Act of 1906. Both houses easily approved the Elkins law in mid February.

The actual trust sections of the Roosevelt-Knox program took more time to achieve. The president had already concluded that antitrust suits alone were a clumsy way to achieve regulation. He preferred a system of government publicity to induce corporations to behave in the national interest. The best available means would be a department of commerce, within which would be located a commission or bureau to investigate corporations. Roosevelt turned to a friend whose advice on corporate matters he trusted, the New York associate of J. P. Morgan, George W. Perkins. The president asked Perkins on 26 December to get "whatever influence you can bear on Speaker [D. B.] Henderson" on behalf of the Department of Commerce measure.[17]

Roosevelt's attitude toward corporate regulation was not inherently antibusiness, as his recruitment of Perkins disclosed. Perkins sent William C. Beer, a seasoned political operative, to Capitol Hill. Timothy E. Byrnes, a railroad lobbyist, joined Beer and George B. Cortelyou in the work of influence and persuasion. They reminded key Republicans where previous campaign contributions had originated. For example, the Speaker, who would be retiring at the end of the session, was told that "if he gets a move on and puts this thing through quickly," he could then expect some help from Perkins in setting up in private business.[18]

The Senate passed the bill creating the Department of Commerce and Labor in late January 1903. It contained no language that specified any kind of agency or bureau to investigate and publicize corporations. The House version included a section that established a bureau of corporations "to gather, compile, publish, and supply useful information" about corporations engaged in interstate commerce. That bill cleared the House on 17 January 1903. In a conference committee, a new amendment, drafted by Senator Knute Nelson (R., Minn.), was included. It changed the wording on a bureau of corporations so as to authorize the new commissioner of corporations to assemble data that would allow the president to make recommendations to Congress. The bureau would "report such data to the President from time to time as he shall require; and the information so obtained or as much as the President may direct shall be made public." This language gave Roosevelt the executive discretion that he sought.[19]

Roosevelt added some personal pressure of his own to the quiet lobbying efforts of Perkins, Beer, and others. He warned legislators that he would summon them back into special session in March 1903 "if we failed to get such a vote before adjournment." On 3 February he said that "the Nelson amendment and the bill to expedite legislation, to both of which there have been the most violent opposition, have now been rather sullenly acquiesced in." The president overstated the opposition to these proposals, but in his mind the Department of Commerce and Labor bill and its Nelson amendment demanded even more presidential pressure a few days later.[20]

During the day on 7 February 1903, reporters learned "from the White House or from persons whose relations with the President are so close as to give their statements the form of semi-official utterances" about a lobbying campaign against the bill. According to these reports, John D. Rockefeller of Standard Oil had "sent telegrams to nine Senators urging them to kill the Nelson publicity amendment."[21] The report caused a temporary sensation. The actual messages were not from the oil magnate himself but from John D. Rockefeller, Jr., and perhaps another Standard Oil executive. The wires themselves had almost no impact on the legislative process, but they did give Roosevelt a superb opportunity for a public-relations triumph that undercut any potential Democratic grumbling about the substance of the administration's program. The press was informed that Roosevelt "thought that the publicity given to this alleged interference had made certain the enactment of judicious laws for the regulation of combinations of capital."[22]

By the president's standards, a more sweeping antitrust bill that Congressman Charles E. Littlefield (R., Me.) had sponsored did not qualify as a "judicious" approach to the trusts. The bill specified that a corporation that failed to comply with its reporting provisions could be barred from doing business in interstate commerce. The president may have used the Littlefield legislation as a lever against those who opposed the Department of Commerce and Labor bill and the Nelson amendment. When that important measure moved through Congress on 10/11 February 1903, Roosevelt lost interest in the Littlefield option. Although the latter bill had passed the House without opposition on 7 February

1903, the Senate twice refused to consider it, so it died. A Republican newspaper said of the Roosevelt trust program: "The Republican party has redeemed itself, the President is a winner, and the Democrats have lost their most effective war-cry."[23]

As head of the new Department of Commerce and Labor, Roosevelt appointed his secretary, George B. Cortelyou. In the White House the efficient Cortelyou had been recognized as perhaps "the best president's secretary in the history of the Government." After the renovation of the White House had been completed, Cortelyou had worked out new rules under which the daily business of the presidency would be carried out. His pamphlet "White House and Executive Office: Organization and Rules" set out the precise duties of the clerks and the secretaries, specified the hours and procedures when the White House would be open, and instructed employees regarding the style of documents and the appearance of their desks. In his service with McKinley and Roosevelt, Cortelyou had been an important force in setting up the institutional framework for the modern presidency.[24]

James R. Garfield was named to the position of commissioner of corporations. His service on the Civil Service Commission had impressed Roosevelt with Garfield's "ability to deal with men & questions." His legal training and sponsorship of a corrupt-practices law in Ohio added to his appeal. Garfield became a fixture in the Roosevelt administration as a prominent member of the "Tennis Cabinet" of the second term. The selection of Cortelyou and Garfield showed Roosevelt's capacity to identify men of talent and to place them in important governmental positions.[25]

While the trust program moved forward, the administration had less success in tariff policy. Late in 1902 the economy of the Philippines was still in difficulty, and Governor General William Howard Taft asked Roosevelt to push legislation creating a reformed monetary system for the islands and lowering American tariff duties on Filipino products. Eventually a law that dealt with the currency of the Philippines was approved. On 18 December 1902 the House passed a bill that reduced the customs rates on Philippine goods by 50 percent. The legislation then languished in the Senate. Protectionist Republicans allied with Democrats from the Rocky Mountain states to mount a "determined resistance" to the proposed concessions that would have opened markets to Philippine sugar and tobacco. Roosevelt warned Nelson Aldrich that Congress would take "the gravest responsibility" if it did not pass the Philippine bill, but the president did not throw his own prestige behind the proposal. The tariff bill died in the upper house.[26]

More central to Roosevelt's priorities was Cuban reciprocity, on which Congress had failed to act in 1902. During the summer and fall the State Department negotiated a trade treaty with the newly independent Cuban government. After extensive discussions, a treaty was signed in Havana on 11 December 1902. Six days later the pact went to the Senate, where it rested during January and into February as the protectionist forces asserted themselves again. By early 1903, prospects for reciprocity improved. The Sugar Trust had acquired some of the beet sugar companies, and the legislators from the sugar-beet regions were no longer an obstructive force. Foreign customers for Cuban sugar appeared in Europe, which made Cuban reciprocity more advantageous to the United States. Still, the Senate had not acted upon the treaty by 4 March 1903. Roosevelt therefore called them back into special session to deal with Cuba as well as the Hay-Herrán Treaty with Panama. On 19 March, senators approved the Cuban agreement by a vote of 50 to 16. They added language that allowed the treaty to take effect only if both houses of Congress approved it at the next session. This deference to the House meant that Roosevelt would probably have to call another special session during the autumn to complete work on Cuban trade policy.

The short session of Congress had been very productive for the Roosevelt administration, but not all the divisive issues that came before Congress had been resolved. Led by a coalition of Republicans and Democrats, an attempt to obtain the admission of the territories of Arizona and New Mexico ran into the determined opposition of Senator Aldrich and the Republican leadership. For Aldrich himself the session also brought defeat for a banking bill that he sponsored. The currency issue that the Aldrich bill represented would claim much of the president's time during the rest of 1903 as he negotiated with the Republican congressional elders about the timing of a special session. Overall, however, Roosevelt had good reason to write Speaker Henderson with some understandable exaggeration on 4 March 1903: "Taken as a whole, no other Congress of recent years has to its credit a record of more substantial achievement for the public good than this over the lower house of which you presided."[27]

This session of Congress showed that Roosevelt was becoming more comfortable with the instruments that a president could use to work his will. The episode of the Rockefeller telegram during the debate over the Department of Commerce and Labor bill demonstrated that he understood how well-timed public actions could undercut his political rivals. The rapport between the president and the people that Roosevelt established during 1902/3 would be one of the chief assets of his adminis-

109

tration. He employed the devices of publicity in a manner that foreshadowed the techniques of his successors in the modern presidential office.

The retirement of Henderson added to the Washington political scene a new player with whom Roosevelt would have to contend for the rest of his presidency. Joseph G. Cannon, or "Uncle Joe," as he liked his colleagues in the House to call him, had been in Congress since 1872. At the age of sixty-seven he saw no reason to abandon the values of the rural district in Illinois that he represented or to question the economic principles that had made him a successful banker in Danville, Illinois. Cannon was elected Speaker in part because House Republicans wanted a leader who would compete for the attention and power that senators wielded. Cannon affected a rustic appearance; his affinity for vulgar language and his use of the spittoon were notorious. He was also an intelligent and crafty political operator.

Because of the congressional sessions and his accident during the fall of 1902, Theodore Roosevelt had not traveled much during the first eighteen months in office. The hunting trip to Mississippi in November 1902 was disappointing. The attendant newspaper coverage for that trip made him wonder if he should attempt another hunting expedition in 1903. By the late winter, however, he had arranged to combine some speeches on his way westward for a hunting expedition at Yellowstone Park in Wyoming with the naturalist John Burroughs. Roosevelt added plans to go on to the West Coast, to Yosemite, where he would meet another conservation advocate, John Muir. In the end, the trip took the president away from Washington for two months. At that simpler time, the president could still embark with a hunting expedition into the wilderness, away from the intense press coverage that followed when he spoke publicly during the trip.

As he went west, Roosevelt made a number of speeches. At Chicago on 2 April 1903 he spoke on the Monroe Doctrine: "There is a homely old adage which runs: 'Speak softly and carry a big stick; you will go far.' If the American nation will speak softly, and yet build, and keep at a pitch of the highest training, a thoroughly efficient navy, the Monroe Doctrine will go far." He talked about the tariff in Minneapolis on 4 April. If the Dingley Tariff was functioning well, he argued, "it may be better to endure some inconveniences and inequalities for a time than by making changes to risk causing disturbance and perhaps paralysis in the industries and business of the country."[28]

The issue of the conservation of natural resources often arose as Roosevelt traveled across the West. At a reception in Yellowstone Park on 24 April he said: "The creation and preservation of such a natural playground in the midst of our people, as a whole, is a credit to the nation, but above all a credit to Montana, Wyoming, and Idaho." He sounded a similar theme at Boise, Idaho: "We must handle the water, the wood, the grasses, so that we will hand them on to our children and children's children in better and not worse shape than we got them."[29]

The conservation goals that Roosevelt proclaimed commanded general support from the American people in principle. As Roosevelt and Pinchot defined it, however, conservation involved the wise use and orderly management of natural resources under the watchful supervision of the federal government. That precept meant a reduction in the role of state and local governments in how the forests, streams, and minerals would be developed. The resulting reaction of western politicians to these edicts meant that serious differences emerged when the specifics of conservation came to be implemented. The passage of legislation regarding natural resources through Congress would not be an easy matter politically. Achievements such as the Newlands Act would be hard for the Roosevelt administration to duplicate during its first term.

Executive action under the provisions of existing law or the implied authority of the presidency served as the major weapons of Roosevelt's resource policy. On 14 March 1903, for example, he established a federal wildlife refuge on Pelican Island in Florida to protect endangered birds there. Ornithologists had asked him to do so, and Roosevelt inquired: "Is there any law that will prevent me from declaring Pelican Island a Federal Bird Reservation?" Informed that the island belonged to the federal government, he said: "Very well, then I so declare it."[30] Roosevelt also took the important first steps in 1902 toward the preservation of the few remaining buffalo in the United States. During his first term, he added Crater Lake in Oregon to the roster of the country's national parks. By 1904 he used an executive order to set up fifty-one national bird reserves in Alaska, Puerto Rico, Hawaii, and seventeen states, as well as the Breton Wildlife Refuge in the Louisiana marshlands.

When it came to policy decisions that affected the public domain and resource questions in a more general sense, Roosevelt moved purposefully but rather cautiously during his first term. The institutional obstacles that he faced were substantial. Jurisdiction over conservation topics belonged both to the Department of Agriculture, under James Wilson, and to the Interior Department, under Ethan Allen Hitchcock. Within the Interior Department the General Land Office had a long history of deference to western land developers; its commissioner of public lands, Binger Hermann, would be a participant in pervasive land frauds in Oregon and the Pacific Northwest. As a result, Roosevelt wrote in 1912, "throughout the early part of my administration the public-land policy was chiefly directed to the defense of the public lands against fraud and theft."[31]

The Oregon land scandals illustrated the depth of the problem that Roosevelt faced. In that state, prominent politicians, including Senator John H. Mitchell, had conspired with mining and lumber companies to obtain large tracts of forest land in Oregon and California by fraudulent means. Roosevelt named a special investigator, Francis J. Heney, to gather evidence about the crimes. William A. Richards, a former governor of Wyoming, succeeded Hermann at the General Land Office. While in Oregon in May 1903, Roosevelt ordered Richards to look into the general handling of forest reserves there. The extent of the Oregon land scandal would grow over the next several years as a kind of background theme to the larger story of conservation.

To address the issue of how the federal government might best foster conservation, Roosevelt sought to place in positions of importance men who thought as he and Pinchot did. Jurisdictional changes were also pursued. Pinchot wanted to have the General Land Office, the U.S. Geological Survey, and the Bureau of Forestry all combined within the Forestry Bureau, which was in the Agriculture Department. Pinchot pursued that goal in part through the Public Lands Commission, which Roosevelt appointed in 1903. The commission, composed of Pinchot, Richards, and Frederick H. Newell, was instructed to make a prompt report on the condition and operation of the existing land laws and to recommend public-land policy. In the two interim reports that it filed in 1904, the commission recommended greater governmental supervision over the public domain. Its findings proved less significant than did the cooperation it fostered among those in government who favored Pinchot's ideas and the help it afforded to the movement for transferring authority to the Bureau of Forestry. Legislation on behalf of the transfer gathered momentum in Congress during 1903/4, but it would not succeed until after Roosevelt was elected in 1904.

In executing its conservation policies, the Roosevelt administration relied on the support of the major lumber companies and cattle corporations. That decision enabled Pinchot and the White House to develop procedures that allowed for sustained-yield forestry practices and for grazing that made maximum use of the national forests. It failed to please those conservationists, such as John Muir, who wanted to have natural beauty preserved. More important in political terms, the Roosevelt-Pinchot approach to conservation angered the smaller stockmen and lumber operators in the West. These conflicts became bitter during the second term. Up to 1904, Roosevelt's own popularity in the West overshadowed tension on specific conservation issues.

The *Literary Digest* observed in September 1903 that "Few imagined, when President Roosevelt took the oath of office, that one of the slogans of the next campaign might be 'Turn the rascals out!'" Government scandals of varying proportions marked the second full year of Roosevelt's presidency. The Democratic press suggested that "if the Republican party shall remain in possession of the Government for another four years, corruption will be intrenched in every department."[32] In fact, Theodore Roosevelt moved vigorously and for the most part with effect to remove the corruption in the federal government that had preceded his administration.

The most sensational of these examples of official misconduct were the Post Office Department scandals that became public knowledge before Roosevelt departed on his western trip in April 1903. There had long been rumors that corruption pervaded the Post Office Department; these included abuses of civil-service rules, fraud in official accounts, and political favoritism. Henry Clay Payne, the postmaster general, set in motion an investigation late in 1902 when he quietly asked Congress to set aside several thousand dollars for a probe. News of the inquiry broke when the superintendent of the Division of Salary and Allowance, George W. Beavers, resigned under a cloud in March 1903. Because Roosevelt was on his western tour and because Payne was away for reasons of health, newspaper coverage of the disclosures went on without a response from the administration. Before the president left Washington, however, he had named the fourth assistant postmaster general, Joseph L. Bristow, to look into the scandal. Roosevelt told Bristow "that I wished nothing but the truth and that I wished the whole truth and cared not a rap who is hit."[33]

For the moment, matters worsened. The assistant attorney general who was assigned to the Post Office Department, John N. Tyner, resigned in April amid well-founded charges that he had removed and destroyed crucial documents in the case. Payne's handling of the scandal was defensible; but his treatment of the press was inept. He tried to minimize the amount of damaging information that the newspapers received. Then a post-office employee charged that the postmaster general in McKinley's cabinet, Charles Emory Smith, and the first assistant postmaster general, Perry S. Heath, had used the department for political ends. Payne told reporters that the allegations contained "hot air." The controversy that the statement provoked led Roosevelt to advise Payne "against your issuing any further statements whatever. I do not think it well to let the answers and statements go out piecemeal."[34]

Upon Roosevelt's return to Washington, the pace of the official response quickened. Bristow submitted a preliminary report on 17 June, suggesting that the charges against Smith and Heath had substance. Seven days later, the attorney general, at the president's request, named Charles J. Bonaparte and another lawyer as special assistants in the Justice Department to aid in the post-office probe. By July 1903 the removals in the Post Office Department had dealt with much of the problem. Roosevelt told Payne that he was "gratified" at the "evident thoroughness" of the inquiry, which sought "to get at all the facts and to punish any wrongdoer who can be reached whether within or without the service."[35] Later in the autumn of 1903, when more evidence developed against Perry Heath, Roosevelt pressed for his indictment. Bristow's final report on the case, issued to the public in December 1903, was very critical of Heath and Smith. Nonetheless, Heath escaped prosecution for lack of evidence, and Smith put up a vigorous defense of his own record.

Roosevelt publicly praised Payne in late February 1904 for what he called "a signal triumph for the cause of popular government." Payne's critics were less impressed with his handling of the scandal. One journal called him "the miracle of incompetence."[36] He was very useful politically in the president's rivalry against Mark Hanna. Despite Payne's health problems and weak grasp on the department, he stayed in office until his death on 4 October 1904. Payne had absorbed much of the blame for the way the Post Office Department issue had been addressed; otherwise, that blame might have gone toward the president. Roosevelt had, however, demonstrated his capacity to move vigorously when confronted with a damaging problem and to contain its negative impact on both sound government and his political prospects.

The other scandals that entranced reporters during midsummer 1903 did not reveal much substance or staying power. In the Indian Territory there were some misdeeds that Roosevelt dealt with promptly through Francis E. Leupp, a special investigator. Tales of indiscretions in the Agriculture Department and in the administration of the Philippines also came to little. By August the Democrats were reduced to assailing Roosevelt for having traveled across the West in a special train that the railroads provided and for having used a naval yacht in connection with a review off Oyster Bay. "I know that I have done exactly what President McKinley did," Roosevelt wrote Cortelyou. "Is it not also true that I did exactly what President Cleveland did?" Soon "a friend of the President" assured the public that the special trains were not for Roosevelt personally but for the person who happened to be president at the time. The to-do over Roosevelt's travels and naval reviews, along with the renovation of the White House, would recur from time to time in 1904 but would not emerge as a major liability for him.[37]

Roosevelt returned from the western trip in good spirits. "His journey has been a political triumph," wrote the British ambassador, "and his nomination next year is practically certain." Roosevelt stayed in Washington for most of June before heading to the coolness of Oyster Bay, where he could escape the presidency and "live as any family of gentlefolk of small means should live."[38] There domestic issues competed for his attention with the situation in Manchuria and the fate of the Hay-Herrán Treaty in Colombia.

During the middle of July a new problem involving organized labor came before Roosevelt in a way that called into question the apparent pro-union position he had won as a result of the coal strike. In the Government Printing Office an employee, William A. Miller, had been discharged from his position as a foreman. The chief of the office, Frank W. Palmer, had fired Miller because the International Brotherhood of Bookbinders had expelled Miller from their ranks. The union's grievances against Miller arose from the criticisms he had made regarding practices in the GPO based in part on the brotherhood's control of hiring in what was a union shop. Miller appealed his firing to the Civil Service Commission on the grounds that he was being dismissed for his refusal to stay in the union and submit to its flawed procedures. The commission decided that it was wrong to make union membership a condition for government employment and ordered that Miller be reinstated. The case came to Roosevelt from Secretary of Commerce and Labor Cortelyou. In letters of 13 and 14 July 1903, the president asserted that there was "no objection to the employees of the Government Printing Office constituting themselves into a union if they so desire." That union could not, however, override the laws of the United States, "which it is my sworn duty to enforce."[39]

Roosevelt immediately recognized the political risks and opportunities in his action. He did not want to enter "a needless conflict with a labor union, especially in the year before a presidential election." He disagreed with the principle of the closed shop, and he thought that what the brotherhood was advocating represented "intolerable tyranny, and I will not submit to it." Since the business community regarded him as too prolabor because of his role in the anthracite coal strike and the *Northern Securities* case, he saw the Government Printing Office episode as a chance to show the public that "my business is to see fair play among all men, capitalists or wage workers, whether they conduct their private business as individuals or as members of organizations."[40]

The brotherhood had handed Roosevelt the kind of issue that suited his personal views and political situation during the summer of 1903. Still apprehensive about a challenge from Mark Hanna and worried about the softness in the economy, he now had the occasion to underscore his conservative credentials. "The labor unions shall have a square deal, and the corporations shall have a square deal, and in addition all private citizens shall have a square deal." It was a philosophical formulation on which Theodore Roosevelt would rely during the rest of his first term. In August he issued an executive order that established the open shop in each of the executive departments.[41]

The public response among middle-class Americans was favorable. "The United States can brook no divided authority and no divided allegiance on the part of its employees," said the *New York Tribune*. It was, stated the *Wall Street Journal*, "a question of simple morality." Organized labor was, of course, very angry over the president's rulings, but it was in this instance a subordinate element in his calculations. The unions were, he wrote, "very arrogant and domineering, because they did not believe I would face the music." It had become necessary "to give them a good jolt" to make them see that "I would not tolerate anything in the nature of tyranny on their part."[42]

Roosevelt did act to limit the damage that the Miller case caused among unions. He kept his lines open to other unions and made sure that the public saw the issue as one of fairness to capital and labor. In late September the president met at the White House with Samuel Gompers, John Mitchell, and others on the executive committee of the American Federation of Labor. Roosevelt did not change his position, but he said that he only espoused the open shop within the federal government. The pardon of a jailed union leader who was in federal custody helped to improve the mood of the labor leaders as well. The controversy dragged on into 1904 before a final decision was announced that Miller would remain a governmental employee.

The whole incident was a political windfall for Theodore Roosevelt. He could now combine the coal strike and the Miller case to show his evenhanded posture on all labor issues. His actions toward the Government Printing Office were stressed in his 1904 campaign literature. In addition, the inquiries into the actual workings of the printing office that the case produced became important forerunners of the administrative reforms that Roosevelt pursued within the federal government after 1904.

Another domestic issue that intruded frequently into the quiet of Roosevelt's summer in 1903 was banking-and-currency legislation. Roosevelt told a Republican member of the House Ways and Means Committee on 21 July 1903 that "nothing is giving me more anxiety now than this financial question."[43] After several years of prosperity, stock prices fell during mid 1903 in what some called the "Rich man's" panic. New York banks that held industrial securities in their portfolios, found that the downturn diminished their ability to meet the demands of interior banks for cash owed to them. The ensuing financial stringency had immediate implications for the 1904 elections and Roosevelt's chances.

Secretary of the Treasury Leslie M. Shaw had already tried to promote a more elastic currency and to overcome the limitations of the National Bank Act (1863), which governed the nation's policy. These measures included accepting the uncontested bonds of cities and states as security for deposits in national banks. This practice made government bonds, the basis of the currency, more available. Shaw allowed banks that held government deposits not to maintain reserves against the public funds in their possession. This ruling freed additional bonds for circulation. Finally, during the summer of 1903, Shaw had internal-revenue receipts returned to depository banks. Shaw's actions were innovative and of somewhat dubious legality. Wall Street bankers applauded; midwestern Republicans and Democrats were less enthusiastic.[44]

The problem for Roosevelt was whether action on banking should occur during a special congressional session in November or even earlier. Republicans in the East, as well as members of the banking community there, wanted to see Senator Aldrich's bill pushed at the special session. His measure would have given clear authority for what Shaw had done and would have expanded the secretary's ability to place governmental deposits in banks that held city and state bonds. It also would have broadened the powers of the secretary through the use of customs receipts to the advantage of eastern banks. Tied to the tariff as it became, the Aldrich bill had encountered fatal opposition among Democratic and midwestern Republican lawmakers during the preceding short session of Congress. For that reason, suspicions about the measure persisted.

A significant obstacle to an agreement on behalf of the Aldrich bill was Speaker Cannon. "There seemed to be plenty of money in the country for business needs," he told the press. Leading members of the Senate Finance Committee met with Aldrich at his Rhode Island home on 6 August 1903 "to consider financial matters." They reported to the president a week later but could not do more than endorse the principles of the Aldrich bill. Roosevelt wrote to Cannon on behalf of "some legislation, not of a radical or revolutionary sort, which will provide a certain amount of elasticity; that is, will provide not merely for expansion in time of stringency, but for contraction when the stringency is over."[45]

Cannon remained unpersuaded. By the end of the summer of 1903, GOP congressional leaders had decided that the safest course was to avoid an early special session devoted to banking and to leave the whole topic alone. Any airing of the issue might allow for consideration of more radical solutions that the rank and file of Republicans would oppose. Leaving the matter as it was came to be the favored option for the party as September opened. After Shaw took some further steps, including the establishment of a relief fund of $40 million for the banking system, the whole crisis eased. "The Wall Street situation is greatly improved," Roosevelt told Lodge; "the chance of a panic seems to be pretty well over." The basic weakness in the structure of banking remained, as Roosevelt would discover at some political cost during the Panic of 1907. For the time being, however, economic prospects looked good for Roosevelt and the Republicans as the election year approached.[46]

Theodore Roosevelt enjoyed writing letters to Americans in all stations of life. Many of these missives became public and served to spread the president's views to the nation at large. During his active summer of 1903, he read how the governor of Indiana, Winfield T. Durbin, had acted to end a race riot in Evansville, Indiana, that lasted for three days in July. The president praised the governor "for the admirable way in which you have vindicated the majesty of the law by your recent action in reference to lynching." Roosevelt used the letter, copies of which were sent to the newspapers, to spell out his judgment on lynching as a social problem. While he felt "the gravest alarm over the growth of lynching in this country," he warned black Americans that they must see that black criminals were legally punished so that lynching would not be necessary. "The slightest lack of vigor either in denunciation of the crime or in bringing the criminal to justice is itself unpardonable." He concluded his long letter with the argument that "where we permit the law to be defied or evaded, whether by rich man or poor man, by black man or white, we are by just so much weakening the bonds of our civilization and increasing the chances of its overthrow and of the substitution of a system in which there shall be violent alternations of anarchy and tyranny."[47]

The problem of race relations, which had first appeared at the time of the Booker T. Washington episode, was a constant problem for Theodore Roosevelt. Two cases during his first term revealed the difficulties that the issue presented. Both the decision to close the post office in Indianola, Mississippi, and the struggle to confirm the appointment of Dr. William D. Crum in South Carolina gave Roosevelt opportunities to set out his position on what he called "the negro problem."[48]

For Roosevelt the question of race had an overriding political impli-
cation. He wanted to ensure that the southern states would support his
candidacy and not Senator Hanna's possible ambitions. At the same
time, Roosevelt looked to Booker T. Washington to assist him in finding
suitable blacks for government service. While Roosevelt also aimed to
reduce the total number of black appointees, he was not in sympathy
with the movement among white Republicans in the South to exclude
blacks from party affairs in the future.

The Indianola Post Office episode occurred because of Roosevelt's
efforts to reshape Republican politics in the South. In Mississippi the
agent of the president's program was Edgar S. Wilson, a Gold Democrat
who became marshal of the state's southern district in January 1902.
Booker T. Washington strongly supported Wilson's selection and agreed
with Roosevelt's decision not to reward James Hill, a prominent black
Republican. The white community in Indianola, seeing a white receive
preference over a black in Roosevelt's political calculations, decided to
move against their black postmistress, Mrs. Minnie M. Cox. By the fall of
1902 there were petitions for her removal and public meetings to demand her ouster. Under the threat of harassment and in some physical
danger, Mrs. Cox resigned on 4 December 1902.

Roosevelt discussed the event with Postmaster General Payne, who
recommended the use of force if necessary to keep Mrs. Cox in place and
the post office open. Roosevelt decided instead to close the post office on
2 January 1903. Mrs. Cox stayed in office and received her salary. Mail
for Indianola was routed to Greenville, some thirty miles distant. The
president was the object of strident criticism from Mississippi politicians. Gubernatorial candidate James K. Vardaman called Roosevelt "a
political boll weevil pregnant with evil" and rode that rhetoric to the
Democratic nomination. Roosevelt kept the post office closed until Mrs.
Cox's term had expired. The facility was reopened in 1904, with a white
appointee who had helped Mrs. Cox during her troubles. The post office
itself became a fourth-class one that gave lesser services than before the
Cox controversy. In this case, as in others, Roosevelt believed that it was
his responsibility "not to join with those who strive to thrust the negro
down instead of endeavoring cautiously, temperately, and sanely, to
raise him up."[49]

The selection of Dr. William D. Crum as collector of the port at
Charleston, South Carolina, posed the problem of black appointments
in the South in a manner that had more lasting consequences than the
plight of Mrs. Cox. In the region, white Republicans had during 1902
responded to Roosevelt's designation of whites such as Edgar S. Wilson
and others by pushing the "lily-white" cause to exclude blacks from

party activities. By the end of 1902, Roosevelt, Henry Clay Payne, and James S. Clarkson, Roosevelt's link with southern Republicans, had decided to check the lily-white movement. In North Carolina and Alabama, Roosevelt revealed his disagreement with lily-whitism. While it would be wrong, he wrote to Clarkson, to name an unqualified man because he was black or to gain black votes, it would be equally bad "to exclude a proper man from an office or as a delegate because he is a Negro. I shall never knowingly consent to either doctrine."[50]

The case of Dr. William D. Crum became an exacting test of Roosevelt's commitment to this position. In South Carolina the Republican party was divided into warring "lily-white" and "black-and-tan" factions in 1901. President McKinley and Senator Hanna had generally favored the lily-whites and had tried to woo Democratic Senator John L. McLaurin over to the GOP. After Roosevelt took office, McLaurin's influence waned because of his closeness to Hanna. Two white candidates that McLaurin suggested for the post of revenue collector at Charleston proved to be a drunkard and a lyncher respectively. Roosevelt named a Gold Democrat and former Rough Rider to the position and sought to find a black Republican whom he might name to another patronage opening. When the president visited Charleston during April 1902, he asked white Democrats for advice and information about Crum. They said that Crum was qualified for a subsidiary post, but they urged Roosevelt "not to appoint any negro to an important office in the South."[51]

When the incumbent collector of customs in Charleston died in September 1902, Crum's name came up at once as a possible successor. A resident of Charleston and a physician, he had long been active in Republican politics in the state and had served regularly as a delegate to the GOP national conventions. He was moderate in his views within the oppressive context of the time. "All we ask is the God-given right to earn an honest living," he said, "and the privilege of enjoying the fruits thereof, unmolested by the lyncher with his shotgun and rope." Crum overcame two rivals for the party's endorsement as collector, and the president announced that Crum would be selected during the early days of November 1902.[52]

The news of Crum's designation brought angry protests from the leaders of Charleston's white community who believed that Roosevelt had given assurances that a white would be named. Being black was enough "to bar him from the office," wrote a local editor; "as a Negro he could represent nothing but his race and his color." Roosevelt responded to his critics with an "Open Letter," dated 26 November 1902, that was quickly released to the newspapers. He denied charges that he had promised not to appoint a black, and he noted that whites made up the majority of his appointees in the state and across the South. Roosevelt added that he "could not consent to take the position that the door of hope, the door of opportunity—is to be shut upon any man, no matter how worthy, purely upon the grounds of race or color. Such an attitude would, according to my convictions, be fundamentally wrong."[53]

The appointment of Crum marked the beginning of a long battle in the Senate to achieve his confirmation. Democrats, led by Benjamin R. ("Pitchfork Ben") Tillman of South Carolina, were united against Crum, and the Republicans were divided. Roosevelt was compelled to make three recess appointments while the upper house was not in session to keep the nomination alive until 1905 when Crum was finally approved. For Roosevelt this matter became a test of his prestige and honor as the president, and he saw it through to a successful conclusion. The experience did not sharpen his zeal for further such confrontations.

The effect of these two episodes was to solidify Roosevelt's reputation as a friend of black Americans during his first term. He had shown himself to be "such a stalwart friend of ours," wrote one black politician, while another proclaimed, "Hurrah for Teddy!"[54] In reality, Roosevelt's patronage policies produced far fewer black appointees in the South than had earlier been the case. When it came to efforts to extend suffrage to more blacks in the South or to punish the region for denying blacks the right to vote, Roosevelt declined to lend presidential support to these initiatives.

The president liked to think of himself as the heir of Abraham Lincoln. In several ways Roosevelt did act in the interest of African-Americans. The administration prosecuted several cases involving peonage in the South; the practice of debt servitude fell with particular harshness on blacks in the region. The disclosures about the conditions of these workers left Roosevelt outraged. Moreover, Roosevelt never indulged in the race baiting and hatred of African-Americans that marked the public language of many southern Democrats. In that sense, he held open the door of hope rather than nailing it shut.

Could he have done more? Like William McKinley, William Howard Taft, and Woodrow Wilson, Theodore Roosevelt accepted the racial mores of his time. "All reflecting men of both races are united in feeling that race purity must be maintained," the president said in 1905. Even if he had doubted the conventional stereotypes about black people, assailing racism would have required a high order of political courage and would probably have impeded his effectiveness as president. Since Roosevelt wished to be judged by the highest standards for presidential conduct, it must be said that he failed to believe in and work for a future when racial equality and justice would be possible in the United States.[55]

If race was a problem that Roosevelt engaged reluctantly and in which his performance often fell short, military reform offered a subject that attracted his martial temperament and personal concern about the nation's welfare. In the case of the navy, the question was how well American ships would fare when it came to shooting at their enemies. For the army the problem was greater efficiency and modern leadership, which brought Roosevelt first to the fate of Gen. Nelson A. Miles.

On 8 August 1903, Miles reached the mandatory retirement age of sixty-four, and his military career ended. Theodore Roosevelt had waited impatiently for this action during 1903. When the general stepped down, he went into private life without the presidential letter of commendation that was usually sent to a retiring senior officer. Democrats criticized the apparent slight, but Roosevelt was unrepentant. He would not have lauded "the most insidious enemy which the army has had during my term of public life." Miles had been disloyal and unscrupulous, and he had opposed the administration's policy in the Philippines. "Nothing will hire me to praise him," Roosevelt told Lodge.[56]

Writing about Miles's departure, one newspaper said that it "signalizes the abandonment of an outworn and obsolete army system." Theodore Roosevelt was interested in making both the army and the navy more efficient instruments of national defense and foreign policy. During his first term he endeavored to make both services responsive to the possible demands that warfare in the new century might place upon them. In his first annual message he had stressed the need to make changes in how the armed services functioned. He returned to that theme in December 1902 when he urged Congress to pass "a bill providing for a general staff" and for the reorganization of the supply department that Secretary of War Elihu Root had proposed in late 1901.[57]

As a result of his experiences with the War Department during the McKinley administration, Root had called for reforms in the organization of the army and in the relationship between the National Guard and the regular army. Under the authority of his office, he set up the Army War College in 1901. More sweeping changes would require congressional approval, and General Miles had strong influence on Capitol Hill. The general's opposition helped to block Root's proposal for a general staff in the spring of 1902. Later in the year, Miles embarked on a world tour which removed him as a disturbing element when Congress again took up Root's measure in December 1902. White House lobbying, press support, and the endorsement of reform-minded officers helped the general-staff law clear the legislative process on 14 February 1903. The law granted the secretary much, if not all, that he had sought: the new post of chief of staff, a general staff, and a reduced role for the adjutant general in the running of the army. The existing supply arrangements were not disturbed. Root had achieved changes that were "at least potentially radical."[58]

The short session also brought Root another accomplishment in the Dick Militia Act of 1903, which established a greater range of federal supervision over the militia units of the National Guard. The link between guard units and state politics was as politically potent as it was militarily inefficient. Root moved with a high degree of political skill between 1901 and 1903 to persuade the National Guard Association to accept a larger participation by the regular army in the Guard's affairs in return for larger federal subsidies to the states. Root did not achieve the National Reserve Force that he wanted, but he did limit the role of the guard in a future military crisis. The Root reforms did not end all the organizational difficulties of the army; these would plague Presidents Taft and Wilson. There was much that was accurate in the letter that Roosevelt sent to Root when the latter tendered his resignation from the cabinet in August 1903. The president praised the departing secretary for "signal and striking triumphs in the administration and reform of the military branch of the Government," as well as his achievements in the Philippines and elsewhere. The contrast with how the president had treated Miles was noted in the opposition press.[59]

Theodore Roosevelt was even more interested in the future of the navy than he was in the structure and reform of the army. The navy would be necessary at once in the event of hostilities. "It is impossible after the outbreak of war to improvise either the ships or the men of a navy," he said in August 1902.[60] While the president watched over naval affairs closely, he did not give the service as effective direction as he might have. During his two terms, six men held the post of secretary of the navy, and Roosevelt seems to have seen the position as a convenient place for political rewards to regions or factions within the Republican party. The president wanted to be his own secretary of the navy, to be sure, and the arrangement allowed him to be involved on many subjects ranging from ship design to personnel policies.

The major goal of Roosevelt and William H. Moody between 1902 and 1904 was to increase the size of the United States fleet. Congress authorized thirty-one new ships, including ten battleships. Moody established the United States Battle Fleet during the Caribbean maneuvers of 1902. He also asked Congress to create a larger officer corps and to increase the number of enlisted men in the service. Moody was not as successful as Root had been with reform. Congress took no action on Moody's recommendation that a general staff be set up for the navy. By 1903 the secretary was reportedly ready to leave the Navy Department, in part because of the frustrations of working with the chairman of the Senate Naval Affairs Committee, the crusty Eugene Hale of Maine.[61]

In one key area, naval gunnery, Roosevelt himself promoted constructive change. Lt. William S. Sims had for several years been a critic, within the navy, of the quality of American marksmanship at sea. Failing to accomplish positive results with the reports he sent through channels, he decided to write the president directly. In November 1901 Sims informed Roosevelt of "the extreme danger of the present very inefficient condition of the Navy, considered as a fighting force." Sims laid particular stress on the deficient protection and armament of the navy's modern battleships and the marksmanship, which he described as being "crushingly inferior" to that of the Japanese. Roosevelt regarded Sims as a "preposterous alarmist," but he took the information seriously.[62] He instructed the navy to circulate the Sims reports to all of its officers. This exertion of presidential influence started the process that enabled Sims and other reformers of gunfire practices, such as Bradley A. Fiske, to change the way in which the navy fought and shot.

The cumulative impact of Roosevelt's administrative style during his first term was largely positive in regard to the armed services. He gave Root the authority to move ahead with useful changes, and he encouraged a man such as Sims who spoke out. Roosevelt imparted to the military much of his energy and resolve. The entrenched power of General Miles and the lawmakers in Congress, not to mention the influence of the National Guard and bodies of private citizens, placed limits on what he could achieve. Moreover, Roosevelt did not create an institutional framework that could sustain his policies, as the revolving door in the Navy Department showed. All in all, however, Theodore Roosevelt had legitimate reason to be proud of how he had handled civil/military relations during the early years of his presidency.

The long summer respite at Oyster Bay ended in late September 1903, and the president returned to Washington to resume his work. The Panama crisis, the impending election of 1904, and the Alaska-boundary problem, made it a busy autumn. The off-year elections went reasonably well for the Republicans. Strong victories in Ohio, where Hanna was returned to the Senate, and in Pennsylvania, along with successes elsewhere, overshadowed Republican defeats in New York City and in Maryland. Editor Albert Shaw called it "a remarkable tribute" to the administration that in state campaigns before a presidential contest, "the party in power should have been so strongly supported."[63]

The Congress that convened in special session on 9 November 1903 finally brought the long struggle for the Cuban reciprocity treaty to a happy conclusion. The House acted favorably on 19 November, and the Senate did so a month later. Senator Shelby M. Cullom of Illinois argued that the victory would not have been won "had it not been for the determined, vigorous fight made by President Roosevelt for its ratification."[64]

In mid December 1903 the Republican National Committee assembled in Washington to select Chicago as the site for the 1904 national convention and to fix 21 June 1904 as the date when the conclave would open. The consensus was that Theodore Roosevelt's nomination was assured. "Mr. Roosevelt is so popular that it is not probable that anyone could rob him of the nomination," said one newspaper.[65] The standing of the president owed a great deal to the manner in which he had dealt with trusts, organized labor, conservation, and scandal during 1903. He had governed effectively, and that proved to be good politics too. Of course, while he had conducted the public business, he had also taken care to see that his own nomination would succeed. That endeavor involved a long and intricate test of will with Senator Mark Hanna, the only Republican who had any chance of denying Roosevelt the election in his own right that he coveted so fervently after 1901.

6

★ ★ ★ ★ ★

"HOW THEY ARE
VOTING FOR ME!"

On election night in 1904 the returns showed a decisive victory for Theodore Roosevelt and the Republicans. As the White House clerks brought the news of his triumph, Roosevelt "strode up and down the room exclaiming, 'How they are voting for me! How they are voting for me!'" Roosevelt's landslide over Alton B. Parker and the Democrats marked the electoral high point of his political career. Election to the presidency with an overwhelming mandate capped off three years of effort. In that campaign, Roosevelt used his political skills and the instruments of the personalized presidency to create a gratifying success.[1]

The political scene had not been so promising when Roosevelt succeeded William McKinley. The assassination took place just two months after McKinley had turned aside pleas that he run for a third term. Within the Republican party, it was still early to mount a serious campaign for the next presidential race. Nonetheless, the immediate precedents seemed to be against Roosevelt. The vice-presidency had not been a route to the nomination for those such as John Tyler, Millard Fillmore, Andrew Johnson, and Chester Alan Arthur who had become president after the death of an incumbent. There were as well a number of Republicans who were looking at 1904, including Leslie M. Shaw of Iowa, Senator Charles W. Fairbanks of Indiana, and perhaps Senator Marcus A. Hanna of Ohio.

On paper these men represented formidable adversaries, but the reality was far more favorable to Roosevelt even before he assumed the presidency. Shaw was little known outside of Iowa, and Fairbanks

lacked decisiveness and popular appeal. Hanna had an imposing reputation as a Republican boss, but it was not clear how much that depended on his friendship with McKinley. None of these Republicans
approached Roosevelt in personal popularity and national standing.

Roosevelt assembled the elements of an organization to support his
candidacy during the summer of 1901. He had the backing of Thomas C.
Platt in New York, William Allen White of Kansas, and both wings of the
Republicans in Illinois. If the sentiment for Roosevelt could be maintained and "(very gently and without very much show of design) organized and agitated, the situation can be held as it is until 1904," White
wrote in mid August 1901.[2] Roosevelt, on his own merits, had a reasonable chance to succeed McKinley as September 1901 opened.

Accession to the presidency gave Roosevelt the advantages of in-
cumbency. The president took a close interest in patronage matters, and
he was sensitive to the claims of Republican factions and ethnic groups
in all of the states. The Washington observer and historian Henry
Adams noted in January 1902 that Roosevelt was "devoured by small
personal details," including "appointments or removals of fourth-rate
officials in remote mountains under cow-boy influence." For a chief
executive who was seeking the GOP nomination from a party that was
still uncertain about his reliability, the minutiae of patronage could not
be ignored.[3]

Roosevelt enlisted advisors who acted as an informal campaign task
force. Henry Clay Payne's links to the business community and his
expertise about the South made him an important asset. During the
spring of 1902, Roosevelt named James S. Clarkson to be the surveyor of
the port of New York. An Iowan with deep roots in the midwestern
GOP and strong ties to the South, Clarkson enhanced Roosevelt's appeal to ethnic groups in New York, including Hungarian-Americans and
Jews, and shored up the president's position in Dixie. For Roosevelt
these achievements outweighed criticism of Clarkson's reputation as
a spoilsman. Joseph B. Bishop of the *New York Commercial Advertiser*
tracked opinion in his state, as did Nicholas Murray Butler, president of
Columbia University. After George B. Cortelyou joined the cabinet early
in 1903, William Loeb, Jr., became the president's secretary. He
functioned as a conduit of information and advice to the president about
the progress of the nomination campaign.

Throughout 1902 the president's prospects steadily brightened.
Prospective rivals fell away. The appointment of Leslie Shaw to the
treasury portfolio preempted that potential opponent. Senator Fairbanks was a colorless challenger in comparison to Roosevelt. Delegates

to thirteen Republican state conventions in 1902 endorsed Roosevelt for the nomination. These states would send 286 delegates to the convention, which meant that the president was well on his way toward the 498 delegates he needed to win. The work that Roosevelt was doing with Booker T. Washington, as well as the twists and turns of his southern policy, were serving his political interests effectively throughout 1902 and 1903.

Amid all of these positive signs there was one continuing source of apprehension for Theodore Roosevelt which dotted his mail in 1902. "Senator Hanna is *making ready* to run for the presidency," one of his correspondents told Roosevelt in March 1902. The question of Hanna's intentions was one that obsessed Roosevelt and fascinated Washington. Hanna informed a friend that "the President is always at him for a pledge to support his nomination in 1904." The senator's reply that only Roosevelt could defeat his own nomination was not all that reassuring. With Hanna's public endorsement in hand, the nomination would belong to Roosevelt. Without a statement from the party leader, the older Republicans, whom Hanna seemed to represent, might snatch the prize away before Roosevelt could claim it.[4]

During 1902 and 1903, Roosevelt conducted an intense intraparty battle with Hanna for control of the Republican organization. A Roosevelt biographer has called this contest "his happiest campaign."[5] How difficult in fact was it for Roosevelt to win? Answering that question depends first upon an accurate evaluation of Hanna's place within the Republican party in 1901. The senator was very popular with the party regulars, and he had close ties with the business and financial community across the country. Judgments that he was a "boss" or the dominant leader of the GOP were exaggerated. Hanna's standing with the party rested on the presumed influence that flowed from his friendship with William McKinley. When the president was killed, Hanna's direct power in the party receded. The senator remained a force among Republicans, but he was not an unchallenged master of GOP affairs.

Nor had Hanna created a national political organization of loyal lieutenants in individual states to support his ambitions for higher office. The states in which Hanna men were supposed to dominate—Colorado, Missouri, and Kansas—were fragile examples of the senator's ostensible power. In Colorado, the leading faction, headed by Senator Edward O. Wolcott, had been loyal to McKinley, not to his friend. Similarly, in Kansas, the Hanna faction, to the degree that there was one, was losing ground to intraparty rivals. Missouri Republicans were inclined to support Fairbanks rather than Hanna. In a presidential nominating contest, Hanna could not even count on his home state. There Senator Joseph B. Foraker was ready to exploit any opportunity to weaken his long-time adversary.[6]

Hanna was hardly powerless. He had made many friends in the party since 1895, and the business community respected him as a sane spokesman for their interests. Had he opposed Roosevelt, he could have waged a competitive fight. At the same time, the senator could have been vulnerable as the embodiment of corporate power. His candidacy would have been premised on the judgment that Theodore Roosevelt was a political and policy failure as president. As Senator Albert J. Beveridge (R., Ind.) put it in May 1902: "How could we make a campaign at all if we should turn down the man upon whose record and upon whose administration the campaign must be made."[7]

Theodore Roosevelt saw Hanna's power within the GOP as formidable; he also regarded any opposition to his own plans as more cohesive and conspiratorial than it often was in fact. When the president received gossip and rumor about Hanna's activities, he gave such information a good deal of weight. Some friends of the president, as well as politicians who wanted to court favor with him, perceived that if they warned Roosevelt about Hanna, he would listen to them attentively.

Where did Hanna himself stand? The senator left few direct statements about his predicament. His health was not good, and he probably did not want to be president. He knew that the public saw him as the champion of big business. To be chosen as the nominee after Roosevelt had been rejected and to be the national symbol of corporate power could make the Republican nomination an empty prize. The life of a senator suited Hanna's temperament, and he had work to do toward improved business-labor relations with the National Civic Federation. Hanna was probably sincere in August 1902 when he told a fellow conservative: "I am not a candidate and will not be a candidate."

An endorsement of Roosevelt might have seemed a logical next step, but it was a move that Hanna declined to make. In the same letter in which he said he was not a candidate, he also maintained that it was "out of place to permit so much discussion about the future selection of the candidate for the Republican party."[8] Still chairman of the Republican National Committee in 1902, the sixty-five-year-old Hanna contended that his position required him to be neutral. Since Hanna had pressed for early endorsements of McKinley in 1896, his concern for propriety during 1902/3 seemed a little disingenuous to the men around Roosevelt. If Hanna was not a candidate and was not trying to upset the president's bandwagon, he should say so publicly by making an endorsement of Roosevelt.

The two men managed to get along reasonably well during 1902. In April, Hanna sent the president a magazine article by Charles Emory Smith that said the senator had "no idea of being himself a candidate." Hanna assured Roosevelt that "a man like Smith can *see* things outside the area of *smoke*." They cooperated in the settlement of the anthracite coal strike, and the Ohioan gave the administration's legislative program his support. As 1903 began, however, the White House heard about "lots of Hanna talk" in New York and the Middle West. Doubts about Hanna's intentions persisted as the president left on his trip across the West. Roosevelt was planning to attend the wedding of Hanna's daughter in June 1903. Friends of both men hoped that the tension could be resolved at that time.[9]

The situation reached a climax before a meeting could be held. The Ohio Republican State Convention would meet in early June 1903. Friends of Hanna declared in May that the Ohio party would refrain from endorsing Roosevelt a year early and would focus on state matters and the senator's race for reelection. There were reports that Hanna had promised conservative Republicans in the Northeast that he would not come out for Roosevelt and thereby end any chance of a challenge to the president.

Joseph B. Foraker saw his opening. He could underline his support for Roosevelt and also embarrass his Republican enemy. Reporters were informed that the president was "the best known and the most popular man in the United States." Foraker added that Ohio Republicans would "be very much disappointed" if the state convention did not declare for Roosevelt. This action of capitalizing on Roosevelt's popularity placed Hanna in an awkward position which the president would be able to exploit. Roosevelt and Foraker may not have consulted about this maneuver, but it served their mutual interests.[10]

Hanna tried to wriggle out of his predicament. He issued a public statement and sent Roosevelt a telegram that said the endorsement question was premature and should not be forced on him or the state convention. Hanna attributed Foraker's action to political jealousy. "When you know all the facts," he informed the president, "I am sure that you will approve my course." Roosevelt was on the West Coast when he shot back an answer to Hanna and released a statement to reporters on 25 May 1903. The question of an endorsement "was bound to arise." Now that it had, "those who favor my Administration and nomination will endorse them, and those who do not will oppose them."[11]

Once the issue had been put in that context, Hanna could not do anything but back down. "In view of all this," he said to the press, "I shall not oppose such action by the convention, and I have telegraphed the President to that effect." The Hanna men felt some resentment over the way their leader had been treated. Still the political effect of Foraker's ploy and Roosevelt's response was clear. Orville H. Platt wrote that Hanna had performed a "back-action-double spring feat" which left little doubt about the Republican nominee for 1904. [12]

While Roosevelt was pleased because the result had "simplified things all around," he still did not have what he most wanted, a personal endorsement from Senator Hanna. [13] When the two men met in June at the wedding, Roosevelt thought that a promise to do exactly that had been made. He wanted Hanna to agree that he would again serve as the chairman of the Republican National Committee during the 1904 contest. Hanna did not regard himself as obligated to take that step during the summer of 1903, and relations between the two men worsened. When the stock-market panic took place in mid 1903, fears about Roosevelt's unreliability were renewed on Wall Street. The nomination of Leonard Wood for military promotion aroused Hanna's opposition in the Senate. Finally, the senator's victory in his race for reelection in Ohio rekindled speculation that he might become a presidential candidate. For Roosevelt there remained the nagging point that Hanna had not yet agreed to be the chairman of the national committee in 1904.

The senator was being importuned to help an anti-Roosevelt drive. "If we renominate Roosevelt, it means defeat," wrote Nathan B. Scott of West Virginia. Hanna refused to authorize a campaign on his own behalf. The most he would allow was an assurance to J. P. Morgan and others that "he would not advocate the nomination of Roosevelt before the convention, thus giving them the opportunity to get another candidate." The president would not have regarded this as a helpful position, but in fact it was. The possibility of Hanna's making the race prevented any other potential anti-Roosevelt alternative from emerging before the national convention. [14]

Within the White House, however, patience with Hanna was running out. The president and his men wanted an outright declaration of support. Endorsements were assembled from prominent Republicans and released to the press. In January 1904 the Roosevelt camp put together "a little organization to combat some of the work that is being done against the President." When William Jennings Bryan and William Randolph Hearst gave well-publicized radical speeches, it reminded conservative Republicans that there were unacceptable alternatives to Roosevelt. By the end of the month, Roosevelt had learned from a friend in New York that "the anti-Roosevelt-Morgan-Hanna-N.Y. Sun house of stacked cards has been caving in, & some of the financial house cats are crawling out of the ruins as fast as possible."[15]

Hanna's death on 15 February 1904 rendered these organizational initiatives superfluous. During Hanna's last illness, the president and the senator put aside their differences. After Hanna died, Roosevelt told Root that his erstwhile rival had been "a big man in every way and as forceful a personality as we have seen in public life in our generation." Roosevelt also recognized that "the point had been passed where he could either harm or hurt me to any appreciable extent."[16]

Such serenity came to Roosevelt only after Hanna's death. The underground struggle that they had conducted was not an even contest. Hanna did not pose a substantial challenge to Roosevelt, and there was no real doubt about the presidential nomination. The factional warfare that grew out of the encounter persisted in several states and spilled over into Roosevelt's second term. The nomination process also disclosed some of Roosevelt's liabilities as a party manager because the Hanna problem did not merit the energy that he devoted to it.

During 1903, partially in response to the potential threat from Hanna, Roosevelt sought to reassure the GOP about his conservative leanings. After the legislative flurry in regard to the trusts early in the year, the administration played down the regulation of business until after 1904. On the protective tariff, Roosevelt sought early in 1903 to persuade Iowa Republicans to soften their commitment to lower duties on the products that trusts made. He succeeded in having the "Iowa Idea" put on the shelf. The president was convinced that the tariff issue was "one of expediency and not of morality," and he shaped his strategy to accommodate the protectionist majority within the GOP.[17]

The short-run gains for Roosevelt from this approach were evident in the election of 1904 when the Republicans said little about the tariff beyond generalities. The president preferred such a strategy because he found the tariff tedious. Allowing the protectionists to dominate the issue made sense because other foreign and domestic issues absorbed him. In the long term, Roosevelt's evasion had negative consequences. Protection was the core doctrine of the Republicans. Unresolved discord about the merits of the tariff ate away at Republican unity. To have the issue fester, adding to the tensions it caused within the GOP, meant a lessening of harmony inside the party. Roosevelt did not want to examine the details of the tariff question or to work out what his own position was. The consequences for the GOP would emerge after Roosevelt's administration ended.

Political events during the first half of 1904 bolstered Roosevelt's chances for election. Approval of the Hay–Bunau-Varilla Treaty by the

Senate confirmed the president's greatest foreign-policy success. On 15 March 1904, after Congress had failed to act, Roosevelt had the Pension Bureau issue an order lowering to sixty-two the age at which Union veterans could receive benefits. The rationale for the change made sense. "The average toiler, the average wage-worker, whose work is physical," Roosevelt wrote, "has at 62 lost half of his capacity to do his work." What the president did not say was that the veterans also represented a powerful group of Republican voters, which the Democrats lost no time in pointing out.[18]

The Supreme Court handed down its decision in the *Northern Securities* case in March 1904. The government had won in the circuit court in April 1903, and the case had quickly moved on appeal to the Supreme Court because of the Expediting Act. The 5-to-4 ruling sustained the position of the federal government that the railroad combination violated the Sherman Antitrust Act. While the majority opinion of Justice John M. Harlan suited the president, the dissent of Justice Oliver Wendell Holmes, Jr., did not. The friendship of the jurist and the president ended because, as Holmes later put it, Roosevelt "couldn't forgive anyone who stood in his way." That personal by-play did not affect the public's seeing the decision as a clear success for the Roosevelt antitrust policy.[19]

As the Republican National Convention neared, the president sent further signals that he intended to emphasize conservatism. On the party platform he wanted to reaffirm the existing tariff policy while leaving open the possibility of future action to revise duties. The document, he maintained, should praise what the administration had accomplished and should say relatively little about future initiatives. The Republicans should "*attack* the do-nothings and the barren critics," he informed Elihu Root, adding that "honestly I do not see that we have anything to defend."[20]

Replacing Hanna as the national chairman proved to be a prolonged process, but it became one that Roosevelt employed to stress his party regularity. He approached Winthrop Murray Crane, Elihu Root, and Cornelius N. Bliss, a wealthy New Yorker who had served in McKinley's cabinet. These names reassured nervous conservatives. After much discussion and refusals from those whom he approached, the president came to the man he had wanted all along, George B. Cortelyou. The secretary of commerce and labor had "the requisite capacity and integrity to make him direct a strong, square campaign."[21] The selection of Cortelyou caused some party regulars to grumble because they perceived correctly that Roosevelt wanted to be his own campaign manager. Roosevelt's insistence carried the day.

Cortelyou's departure necessitated one of Roosevelt's periodic shuffles of the cabinet. When Root left at the end of 1903, William Howard Taft came back from the Philippines to take over as secretary of war. To succeed Cortelyou, Roosevelt chose Victor H. Metcalf, a congressman from California whom he intended to move to the Navy Department or the War Department after the election. The appointment was also designed to help with West Coast voters. Attorney General Knox resigned when he was elected to the Senate from Pennsylvania. To his place at the Justice Department, Roosevelt moved William H. Moody from the Navy Department. For the navy slot, the president chose railroad executive Paul Morton. Adding a businessman to the cabinet was another timely stroke. After the election, further changes were planned so that Cortelyou could rejoin the official family.

The vice-presidency did not assume a large part in Roosevelt's political considerations. The choice of the party was Senator Fairbanks, whose middle-western background would supply a traditional balance for Roosevelt and New York. The president expressed a mild preference for Congressman Robert R. Hitt of Illinois. "If I should be elected," Roosevelt told his eldest son, "he would be of all men the pleasantest to work with." Party leaders preferred Fairbanks as a way of relieving "the general feeling of distrust" that lingered "among those conservative men of property who have heretofore been pillars of party support." By the time the Republicans met in Chicago, Fairbanks was the vice-presidential front runner.[22]

Management of party affairs required the president's close scrutiny on the eve of the convention. Roosevelt did not offer much encouragement to those within the GOP who were quarreling with the Republican leadership in individual states. In Illinois, for example, the White House backed the faction identified with Chicago boss William Lorimer. The situation in Wisconsin reflected the warfare between the reform-minded governor, Robert M. La Follette, and his conservative enemies, led by Senator John C. Spooner. Roosevelt did not delve into the rights and wrongs of the case. "For Heaven's sake," he wrote to Henry Cabot Lodge, "make the Wisconsin people settle their differences without dragging in the National Convention, to the certain detriment of the ticket." Reform and political probity weighed less with Roosevelt in 1904 than did his own success at the polls.[23]

The Republican National Convention, held at Chicago from 21 to 23 June 1904, lacked excitement for the 994 delegates and their alternates. The president's nomination was made unanimously. Fairbanks was placed in nomination for vice-president, whereupon the Illinois delegation announced that Hitt had withdrawn as a candidate. The Indiana

135

senator was then named on a voice vote. James R. Garfield looked at the outcome and concluded that "the people have compelled the old political leaders to come into line."[24]

The assemblage did have one moment of genuine and spontaneous emotion: on 22 June the permanent chairman, Joseph G. Cannon, instructed the clerk to read aloud a news bulletin from Washington. It reported that the State Department had sent a message to the United States consul in Morocco which stated: "We want either Perdicaris alive or Raisuli dead." The delegates erupted in cheers. As the *New York Times* put it, "Roosevelt and Hay at last had succeeded in creating artificial respiration and heart action in the convention through saline treatment." Who was Perdicaris, and why did the Republican convention concern itself with his fate?[25]

The episode began in Morocco on 18 May 1904 when Ion Perdicaris and his stepson were kidnapped from their home by a bandit known as the Raisuli. Because Perdicaris was believed to be a citizen of the United States, there were protests in the press against what had taken place. Theodore Roosevelt shared the public anger; he decided that U.S. warships that were already on their way to Europe should be sent to Tangier to support the diplomatic protest. The incident offered the president a chance to demonstrate the broader role that he envisioned for the navy on the world scene. As negotiations for the release of Perdicaris dragged on, more United States ships were sent to the region. By mid June, as the Raisuli increased his demands regarding the ransom for the release of Perdicaris, Roosevelt told Hay that "our position must now be to demand the death of those that harm him if he is harmed."[26]

Within the next week, the possibility of landing United States marines to seize the customhouse at Tangier was discussed on the scene and in Washington. As that prospect loomed, the U.S. naval commander in Tangier drew back from such a course. The telegram that was read to the convention was designed to pressure the government of Morocco toward a peaceful solution. It had no effect on the Raisuli's decision to release Perdicaris on 24 June. Hay wrote in his diary that the disclosure of the message was "a concise impropriety" that pleased the public. The long-range importance of this case was Roosevelt's willingness to project United States power into a European diplomatic issue. In that same summer the president used the fleet to pressure the Turkish Empire and thus "gave Europeans notice that the United States was a world power in the fullest sense."[27]

With his own nomination in hand, Roosevelt awaited the selection of his Democratic opponent. The prospects for the other party were not bright in 1904. The president's popularity remained high, and the economy was prosperous. In addition, the tensions within the Democratic organization over the party's future had not yet been resolved, as its national convention would demonstrate. Roosevelt could hardly have asked for a weaker political adversary than the Democrats had become.

After the defeat of William Jennings Bryan in 1900, the conservative wing of the Democracy dominated the race for the 1904 nomination. Bryan stood aside, and the candidacy of the maverick publisher William Randolph Hearst never attained much credibility. For a brief moment the possibility of a third term for Grover Cleveland came up. Bryan's opposition and memories of Cleveland's record during the 1890s ended that boom quickly. The Democrats needed a fresh face and a candidate who had not been wounded during their fratricidal battles of the 1890s.

The conservative Democrats thought that they had found their champion in Judge Alton Brooks Parker of New York. Fifty-two years old in 1904, Parker held several attractions for the beleaguered Democrats. He could carry his home state, they believed, as he had proved during his race for the New York Court of Appeals in 1897. Given the solid hold the party had in the South, New York's electoral votes would bring the party close to victory. If Parker could add New Jersey and Connecticut to his total, he would be on the edge of election. As a sitting judge, Parker had not been compelled to take positions on the issues that had divided the Democrats, beyond voting for Bryan in 1896 and 1900. Unlike Roosevelt, the conservative Parker was "no roving comet seeking change and adventure through the corners of the universe."[28]

Parker and his managers pursued a strategy of silence as the key to his nomination. When a reporter asked for a statement of his opinions, the jurist replied: "You may be right in thinking that an expression of my views is necessary to secure the nomination. If so, let the nomination go."[29] Silence represented the best politics for Parker during the preconvention period.

The nomination came to Parker easily when the Democrats gathered in St. Louis in July. Other aspects of the convention illustrated the problems that the Democrats faced. The platform was conservative, which aroused Bryan's ire. He fought for a stronger antitrust plank and for a commitment to tariff reform. The issue of whether or not to mention the currency question proved more difficult to settle. Finally, Bryan decided that he had to accept that the subject would be left out of the platform completely.

After Parker was selected on the first ballot on 9 July 1904, the convention reconvened in the afternoon to vote on its vice-presidential choice. The roll call was beginning when news came that Parker had sent the convention a telegram asserting his monetary views. The convention adjourned until an evening session while deliberations began about the meaning of what was called Parker's "gold telegram." The nominee had stated that in his opinion the gold standard was "firmly and irrevocably established." That would be his position as president. If the delegates did not concur, he would not run.[30]

An intense debate erupted, with Bryan, the champion of free silver, as a leader. Finally, the convention responded to its nominee that "the monetary standard" was not "a possible issue in the campaign," as the platform's silence confirmed. Parker could take whatever position he liked. This answer did not please Bryan, but there was not much he could do about it. To run with Parker, the convention chose eighty-two-year-old Henry Gassaway Davis of West Virginia. Davis had ample personal wealth, which his backers hoped could in part bankroll the Democratic campaign. Roosevelt said that Parker's action was "most adroit, and he is entitled to hearty praise, from the standpoint of a clever politician, for what he has done."[31]

The Democrats came out of St. Louis with a certain amount of optimism regarding Parker's chances. They needed 239 electoral votes to win, and they could count on 150 from the Democratic South. Presuming that Parker could carry New York, New Jersey, and Connecticut, the addition of three border states—Delaware, West Virginia, and Maryland—would leave the party close to success. The Democrats hoped that their organization in Indiana would supply the remaining votes they needed in order to achieve 239 electoral votes and the presidency. They counted on money from Davis and other eastern conservatives, and they saw Parker as a sane and calm alternative to Roosevelt. The choice would lie between "the hair trigger man and the judicial mind."[32]

Theodore Roosevelt faced the election race in a state of some personal frustration. Long-standing political custom said that an incumbent president should not campaign openly for votes, so a formal speaking tour was out of the question. Roosevelt would deliver one speech accepting the Republican nomination, and he would also issue a letter of acceptance that would set out his own views on the campaign ahead. Beyond those two public acts, he was expected to remain subdued until election day had passed. Republican party workers and surrogates for the president would do the campaigning for him. "I wish I were where I could fight more offensively," he told Henry Cabot Lodge on 14 July 1904; "I always like to do my fighting in the adversary's corner."[33]

The speech of acceptance and his lengthy letter of acceptance reflected the intensity that Roosevelt had to keep in check otherwise. He wrote, in his acceptance letter to Joseph G. Cannon on 12 September 1904: "We base our appeal upon what we have done and are doing, upon our record of administration and legislation during the last seven years in which we have had complete control of the Government. We intend in the future to carry on the Government in the same way that we have carried it on in the past."

In the president's mind, that position justified a vigorous defense of his record in Panama, on the Alaskan boundary, and in the use of the navy to protect a citizen such as Perdicaris. Roosevelt rebutted the Democratic assaults on his pension order and accused the opposition of evasion regarding his antitrust policy and the settlement of the coal strike. On the tariff he wrote an extended defense of the protective policy. If the Dingley law ever needed modification, it would be done "with the utmost care and conservatism" and ought to be undertaken "by the friends and not the enemies of the protective system." He was equally critical of the Democrats for promising independence to the Philippines. Throughout the lengthy document, he countered opposition charges that he had exercised presidential power unwisely. "There is not a policy, foreign or domestic, which we are now carrying out, which it would not be disastrous to reverse or abandon." Having "striven both for civic righteousness and for national greatness," he was confident of support from "all who feel love of country and trust in the uplifting of mankind."[34]

The Democratic campaign began in August in a manner that gave the Republicans further reasons for electoral confidence. Parker delivered his acceptance speech at his home in Esopus, New York, on 10 August. Those who had seen the "gold telegram" as a preview of an aggressive candidate were soon disappointed. He spoke out for self-government in the Philippines and said that the common law supplied all the weapons that the states would require in order to regulate the trusts. The rest of his remarks ran through the usual Democratic positions in a stale way. "It does not appear to me," wrote the British ambassador, "that Mr. Parker's speech has done much to animate his party."[35]

Parker's style of campaigning did not disclose much energy either. He wanted to model his canvass on McKinley's front-porch campaign of 1896; but Esopus was hard to visit, and the voters stayed away. The Democratic National Committee had money at its disposal, but it was notably inefficient in the execution of campaign activities. Little was done to mobilize regular Democrats or to offset Republican penetration into such usually reliable voting blocs as Irish Catholics. "Judging from

the character of the campaign the boys on the other side are putting up,"
concluded Senator Jonathan P. Dolliver, an Iowa Republican, "I should
say that we will carry every Northern state."[36]

The Democrats had miscalculated in their assumptions about the
election. When they presented themselves as the more conservative of
the two major parties, they enabled Roosevelt and the GOP to dominate
the middle and left of the political spectrum without challenge. The
emphasis that the Democrats placed on Roosevelt's personal character
also backfired. By attacking the president, his opposition allowed the
GOP to unite on that basis without having to address any divisive issues. In any case, making the campaign turn on Roosevelt himself
meant that the Democrats had to overcome his personal popularity directly. The American people regarded Roosevelt as courageous, not
dangerous. Compared to the charisma of the president, Parker seemed
dull and empty, offering, in the words of the New York Sun, "to the
inquiring vision all the salient qualities of a sphere."[37]

Cortelyou and the Republicans, on the other hand, had a superb
presidential candidate and a mastery of the techniques of modern political campaigning. The process of reaching American voters was shifting
from the mass rallies and spectacular politics of the Gilded Age to the
advertising and merchandising style that would become characteristic
during the twentieth century. George B. Cortelyou was well suited to
this method of campaigning. The organizational ability that he had refined in the White House and at the Department of Commerce and
Labor easily transferred to the managerial task of directing the Republican canvass. He oversaw the dissemination of hundreds of thousands of
pamphlets, and he directed a corps of party writers who furnished information to Republican newspapers "upon any subject connected with
the campaign."[38]

One key to the GOP effort was an elaborate appeal to ethnic,
economic, and religious groups. Republican canvassers were instructed
to record if voters were "of German or Irish birth," and campaign
documents and organizations were shaped accordingly. There were
French Canadians for Roosevelt in Rhode Island, the Independent
Roosevelt Committee for Jewish voters, and the National Roosevelt
League for German-Americans. Black voters were warned of the dangers of Democratic rule, while veterans learned again about the impact
on their lives of Roosevelt's decisions about the age of pensioners.[39]

The Republicans worked particularly hard to enlist religious bodies
in the Roosevelt coalition. "All Jews, whatever their origin, glory in the
President's sympathy for our people in Russia," wrote a Jewish spokesman in New York. The campaign devoted a good deal of time to the

Protestant denominations as well, but it was among Catholics that Roosevelt pursued his ethnocultural strategy in the most concerted way. The initiatives regarding the Philippines and the friars, along with the judicious selection of Catholics to key patronage positions, resulted in a strong movement toward the president. For the first time in the party's history, noted one newspaper, Roosevelt's "tolerance, democracy, and contemptuous disregard of lines of wealth, race and color" brought "a majority of the Irish vote to the Republican side."[40]

Despite all the signs that pointed to an overwhelming success for his candidacy and his party, Theodore Roosevelt could not shake some apprehension. "Unless we throw it away ourselves, we have the victory," he wrote in early September, "and it would be a wicked thing to throw it away." A particular source of concern was the state of New York, with its thirty-nine electoral votes. During the summer the president tried to persuade Elihu Root to be the Republican candidate for governor there. When that initiative failed, Roosevelt attempted to draft Nicholas Murray Butler for the race. The eventual Republican choice, Frank W. Higgins, was "an admirable man" who did not allay the president's worries. Roosevelt tried to have John Hay speak in the state. He also approached E. H. Harriman, the railroad magnate, about more campaign funds "in view of the trouble over the State ticket in New York."[41]

Most observers found the 1904 race dull and listless. "Our canvass is going on with amazing quietude," John Hay wrote, and an informed journalist concluded that "the country exhibits only the most languid interest" in how the campaign was proceeding. Some of the relative calm grew out of the conclusion that the election was almost decided before it began. Parker did not recover from the fiasco of his acceptance speech. "He lacks both sense and sanity in his canvass," was Senator William Boyd Allison's verdict.[42]

The 1904 election also grew out of longer trends in the nation's political history. The partisanship that had characterized the late nineteenth century was beginning to ebb away. Buttons, rallies, and overt displays of party allegiance were becoming less common. The race between Parker and Roosevelt was less a contest of two rival political parties than a referendum on the merits of the individual candidates. By making the major appeal to independent votes, the new campaign styles spent less time trying to involve the voters in the election. As a result, the turnout and participation in the 1904 election showed a marked decline from the results of the preceding decade.

Another new element in the 1904 presidential contest was the extent to which it represented a personal referendum on Theodore Roosevelt rather than a contest between opposing political parties. Roosevelt's policies during his first term had not diverged all that much from what William McKinley had done. In his approach to the presidency, however, Roosevelt had made his personality, his temperament, his family, and his character central elements of his national appeal. The modern presidency, as Roosevelt practiced it, derived its major strength from an emphasis on his unique personal qualities. When it came time to face the voters, the president's allure and celebrity helped him win out over his colorless rival.

The campaign finally came to life during its closing weeks. Needing to find an issue that would hurt Roosevelt, Parker charged that the Republican campaign had been raising money from the large corporations that the president had earlier attacked. Armed with information that Cortelyou had obtained as secretary of commerce and labor, the GOP was using that knowledge to induce the trusts to finance Roosevelt's election, or so the Democrats claimed. Party newspapers had been making this allegation throughout most of October 1904. Now Parker took up the theme as part of his brief campaign swing through the Northeast. The trusts, he said, "were being allowed to buy protection."[43]

In addition to the charges that the press carried, wealthy Democrats had told Parker that Roosevelt had asked prominent businessmen to contribute to Republican coffers. No details were given to Parker, and his informants swore the candidate to secrecy. One participant at the alleged meeting with the president said of Roosevelt years later: "He got down on his knees to us. We bought the son of a bitch and then he did not stay bought." The image of Roosevelt as a supplicant is an entrancing one, but the anecdote overdramatizes the events that took place during the autumn of 1904.[44]

The president was, as usual, worried about his chances for victory as November neared. No amount of favorable indicators could quiet his apprehension. On 10 October he asked E. H. Harriman to come see him at the White House to discuss politics in New York. The railroad leader subsequently said that Roosevelt had made certain promises in return for a donation of $250,000 to the Republicans. Roosevelt denied that the arrangement had taken place. At the same time, Cortelyou and the campaign treasurer, Cornelius N. Bliss, were accepting contributions from large corporations. The Republicans received a check for $100,000 from the Standard Oil Company. Roosevelt was probably unaware of what the campaign officials were doing, but he also did not make much of an effort to learn how the money was being raised on his behalf.[45]

The charges that Parker leveled brought an angry response from the president. "I used to think Parker only a fool," he informed Cortelyou, "but I guess he is as much of a knave as his associates." Roosevelt instructed his campaign manager to return the money to Standard Oil. The controversy stirred Roosevelt to a flurry of action. To Cortelyou the president sent telegrams and letters asserting his probity. Standard Oil could "count upon being treated exactly as well by the Administration, exactly as fairly, as if we had accepted the contribution." Meanwhile, he warned Cortelyou to "say nothing" and to avoid campaign meetings where the press might raise questions about Parker's allegations.[46]

By the beginning of November, Roosevelt feared that the Democratic assaults had had "a certain influence." He began to consider whether he should release a statement responding to Parker. On 3 November the Democratic candidate said that Cortelyou was engaged in "organized importunity." That remark made up the president's mind. A statement was issued from the White House on Roosevelt's behalf on 4 November; it appeared in newspapers the next day. Parker's charge was "unqualifiedly and atrociously false." In office, Roosevelt would be "unhampered by any pledge" and would "see to it that every man has a square deal, no less and no more." Roosevelt's personal intervention in the campaign put the burden of proof back on Parker.[47]

The Democrat had his chance to support his charges during a speech to an audience in Brooklyn, New York, on 4 November. Parker kept his promise to the source of his information; he confined himself to vague statements in his address. This did not impress his expectant audience or the skeptical press. The event, wrote editor Albert Shaw, "undoubtedly contributed not a little to the all completeness of his defeat."[48] While the interchange about campaign funds did not help Parker's cause to any marked degree, it was a signal of a new issue that would surface during Roosevelt's second term. Public apprehension regarding the prevalence of corruption and the impact of business on political life was growing, and the sentiment that Parker appealed to would show itself to be more powerful and influential during 1905/6.

On 8 November, Roosevelt traveled to Oyster Bay to cast his vote; then he returned to Washington to await the results. It did not take long for the trend to become apparent. Parker had the electoral votes of the Solid South, but the rest of the nation was going overwhelmingly for Theodore Roosevelt. Judge Parker sent his congratulations to the president, and the victor wired his son Kermit: "Am elected by overwhelming majority, about as great as that of McKinley four years ago."[49]

With victory assured, the president decided to see reporters in his private office in the Executive Office Building, across the street from the White House. The newsmen were "ranged in a semi-circle" around

Roosevelt as he read a statement. He expressed his appreciation for the confidence the American people had placed in him. He then went on to say that the time he had been in the presidency "constituted my first term. The wise custom which limits the President to two terms regards the substance and not the form. Under no circumstances will I be a candidate for or accept another nomination."[50]

Roosevelt did not act in haste or without considering the consequences in making this crucial announcement. He had discussed the merits of the statement with Winthrop Murray Crane and probably his wife, among others. It is likely that Roosevelt recalled the popular approval that followed McKinley's statement about a third term during the summer of 1901. Making the declaration when he did also undercut potential Democratic claims that he had dictatorial aspirations.

Despite this thought and preparation, the anti-third-term pledge was a political mistake in timing and substance. By removing any suspense about his future as a presidential candidate, it had the practical effect of rendering him a lame-duck executive during the latter years of his second term. His influence with Congress steadily decreased as March 1909 neared. He would have served his own cause better had he made the declaration at some later point in his presidency.

Roosevelt remained true to his commitment during his presidency; he reaffirmed it whenever the issue arose until he left office. These renewed pledges neither convinced his friends nor allayed the fears of his enemies. While the president did not intend to be a candidate himself, he was equally intent that the Republicans should choose a successor who would carry on the policies that he favored. He would continue to be the dominant presence in Republican deliberations about who the next nominee would be.

In 1904, of course, the important consideration in Roosevelt's mind was the breathtaking size of his election triumph. "The election results are really astounding," he wrote, "and I am overwhelmed by them."[51] Roosevelt won 7,628,875 votes, or 56.4 percent of the total; Parker received 5,084,442, or 37.6 percent. The Socialist candidate, Eugene V. Debs, had around 402,000 votes; and the Prohibitionist party garnered 258,000. The president had won 336 electoral votes, the most any candidate had won up to that time. He had carried thirty-three of the forty-five states. The Republicans won Missouri, then classified as a southern state, in a break with the Democrats' electoral lock in Dixie.

In the North, Roosevelt showed impressive strength. The majorities in normally Republican states such as Ohio and Pennsylvania were overpowering. He outdistanced Parker easily in New York and thrashed the Democrats in Connecticut and New Jersey. Outside its southern base, the Democratic electoral strategy worked not at all. The Republican ethnocultural appeal operated impressively. The president made a good showing in the Democratic areas of such cities as Milwaukee, La Crosse, and Madison, Wisconsin. He ran well among the Poles, Italians, Swedes, Jews, and Germans of Chicago. The vote for Roosevelt also showed, said *World's Work*, that he "is the most popular man that has come into public life within recent times. The people like his energy, his frankness, his robust ways."[52]

So successful had the campaign and election been that the Republicans now had to answer the question that one of them posed: "What are we going to do with our victory?" Roosevelt did not address that question precisely in those terms, but some of his private thoughts were apparent in a letter he wrote to Philander C. Knox about what the former attorney general should emphasize as a new United States senator. Roosevelt "most earnestly" hoped that Knox would "make the problem of labor as thoroughly yours as you have made the problem of capital." The GOP could not become simply the party that opposed labor and its goals. "We must not only do justice, but be able to show the wage workers that we are doing justice."[53]

Roosevelt believed that it would be "a dreadful calamity" if the country were to become "divided into two parties, one containing the bulk of the property owners and conservative people, the other the bulk of the wage workers and the less prosperous people generally." The defenders of property must realize, Roosevelt warned, "that the surest way to provide an explosion of wrong and injustice is to be shortsighted, narrow-minded, greedy and arrogant." The president had touched on a problem that many in his party were viewing with concern during late 1904. Some Republicans thought that a realignment of parties was possible, with conservatism on one side and what one senator called "populism, socialism, rheumatism, etc." on the other.[54]

Roosevelt's acute diagnosis of the potential dangers to the nation that he was leading had not shown up in the campaign of 1904. The contest had turned "on the personal characteristics of the President— one might even say, on his personal manner." That strategy, in addition to the weakness of Parker, brought about the Roosevelt landslide. If the election represented a mandate at all, it was for four more years of the presidency as Theodore Roosevelt had personalized it.[55]

The 1904 election was a final showing of the forces that had brought the Republicans to national power during the 1890s. The keynotes of the GOP appeal were the protective tariff, economic prosperity, an expansive foreign policy, and a posture of ethnic inclusiveness. The major focus of national politics, however, was shifting. The issue of promoting economic growth, which had dominated the nineteenth century, was fading. Now the question was to what extent the federal government should intervene to regulate and supervise an industrial society. At the same time, public suspicion of partisan political methods was intensifying. It would be up to Theodore Roosevelt—now president, as he said, in his own right—to respond to and to manage the social forces that were shaping the United States in the progressive era.

7

ROOSEVELT AND
REGULATION, 1905–1906

Theodore Roosevelt's pleasure in his electoral success soon yielded to the need to formulate policies for the second term. Advocates of change in the protective tariff and of the greater regulation of railroads made their preferences known to the president and to Congress when the lawmakers assembled for the last session of the Fifty-eighth Congress in December 1904. During the two years that followed, Roosevelt led the Republicans toward a greater use of national power to address social and economic issues. The results were important legislative accomplishments and also division within the GOP over the reach and extent of Roosevelt's regulatory program.

Pressure for revision of the tariff was the most immediate problem. The president's friends, including Nicholas Murray Butler and Elihu Root, urged him to take prompt action to lower rates. They even suggested that he call a special session of Congress in March 1905 that would focus on the tariff and be "unhampered and undelayed by the performance of any other duty whatever." Across the Republican Middle West, there were numerous party members in Iowa, Minnesota, and Wisconsin who believed, in the words of an Indiana man, that "the people are as much opposed to a tariff for monopoly as they are to a tariff for revenue only."[1]

At the outset, Roosevelt seemed to share this general view. In his upcoming annual message, he drafted language that addressed the tariff question. "I am aware that there are dangers in the attempt to revise it," he told an industrialist, "but I am convinced that there are more dangers

147

if we do not attempt to revise it." This mood of resolve did not last. Senator Orville H. Platt saw Roosevelt on 18 November 1904 and made the case against tariff revision and a special session. On the following day, press reports said that there would be a special message on the tariff. The White House promptly issued a release declaring that the president "will not discuss tariff revision or reciprocity in his annual message."[2]

The best alternative strategy that Roosevelt devised was contained in a letter to Speaker of the House Joseph G. Cannon on 30 November 1904, to whom Roosevelt sent a draft of a special message about the tariff that offered a cautious argument for revision: "It would be far better to keep the present tariff unaltered than to upset business by sweeping and radical alterations in it." Further along, Roosevelt conceded that "there may be some schedules that are too high or which, for one reason or another, should be changed." He proposed that Congress create a joint committee of senators and representatives to investigate the tariff question and report back on its merits to a special session to be convened "as early as possible."[3]

When the idea became public, it aroused immediate opposition among protariff Republicans. "This is no time to meddle with our Tariff system," argued the American Protective Tariff League in January 1905.[4] The possibility of meaningful revision or a special session soon faded. The president met with Cannon and other congressional leaders early in 1905. At that point they decided that tariff revision should wait until the following autumn.

These maneuverings ended any chance of changes in the Dingley Tariff during the rest of Roosevelt's second term. By the summer of 1905 the idea of a special session was quietly interred. With little prospect that the Republicans would allow a tariff battle during the election years of 1906 or 1908, the problem would be left to the president's successor. Roosevelt preferred to reap the short-range political benefits of caution on the tariff and to pursue topics, such as railroad regulation, in which he had a greater interest. "On the interstate commerce business, which I regard as a matter of principle, I shall fight," he observed in January 1905; "on the tariff, which I regard as a matter of expediency, I shall endeavor to get the best result I can, but I shall not break with my party."[5]

The discussion of the tariff occurred when relations between the president and Congress were already strained. The leaders of the GOP had thought that they could "go slow now for awhile." Instead, Roosevelt pressed them for action. He took more interest in the allocation of the patronage, and his annual message advanced a number of proposals regarding social problems. One notable suggestion involved corporal punishment for those who beat their wives in the District of Columbia. There was a sense among conservatives that the president intended "to force his views, instead of his recommendations, on Congress."[6]

An example of this senatorial suspicion emerged in February 1905 when the upper house debated a series of ten identical arbitration treaties that the United States had signed with nine European powers and Mexico. The issue became one of the extent of executive power. Senators asserted that the treaties contained language that gave to the president the right to conclude a "special agreement" when the United States and another power were about to enter the arbitration process. Lawmakers argued that the Senate had to insert language replacing the word "agreement" and putting in its place the word "treaty." Senator Shelby M. Cullom, chairman of the Senate Foreign Relations Committee, contended that the Senate must "assert and uphold its rights as part of the treaty-making power."[7]

Roosevelt responded that such amendments would reduce the arbitration process to "a sham." He wrote Cullom a letter on 10 February 1905 that described what the Senate had proposed as "a slight step backward." Unpersuaded, the Senate voted 50 to 9 the following day to go ahead with the offending language. Roosevelt's friend Henry Cabot Lodge joined the majority. The president then declined to proceed with the treaties on that basis. The episode left Roosevelt with bad feelings. "I do not much admire the Senate," he told Joseph B. Bishop, "because it is such a helpless body when efficient work for good is to be done." The lawmakers reciprocated Roosevelt's ill will. "Unless some restraint can be placed on the White House," wrote Jacob H. Gallinger (R., N.H.), "the Republican party will be divided into hostile camps before 1906."[8]

The regulation of railroads had the potential to promote such a division. Roosevelt brought up the subject during his annual message in a manner that posed the issue of governmental regulation directly. "The government must in increasing degree supervise and regulate the workings of the railways engaged in interstate commerce," he argued. Only in that way could the nation avoid "an increase of the present evils on the one hand or a still more radical policy on the other." The danger of governmental ownership and socialism were not far from the president's mind throughout the struggle over the Hepburn Act.[9]

Roosevelt had decided that railroad regulation was necessary because governmental agencies had informed him regarding the practices and abuses of the major rail companies. The Interstate Commerce Commission (ICC) had sent him evidence about how the railroads used private freight cars to give advantages to favored shippers such as the meat packers. The problem, wrote ICC Commissioner Charles A. Prouty, "seems to demand legislative and perhaps legal action." Also, some information arising from the probe of the beef trust convinced the president that it was necessary to give the ICC "additional power of an effective kind" to regulate railroad rates.[10] He had begun discussing the issues with members of his cabinet, including Navy Secretary Paul Morton, a former railroad executive himself, as well as Elihu Root and Philander C. Knox.

While the internal workings of his administration moved Roosevelt to act on the railroad issue, he was also aware that public sentiment favored regulation. The Middle West and the South strongly supported giving the ICC greater authority over the railroads. There was no better topic on which to focus the Square Deal that the president had announced. In his message, sent to Congress on 6 December 1904, Roosevelt requested that the ICC be given the power, when a railroad rate was in dispute and had been "found to be unreasonable, to decide, subject to judicial review, what shall be a reasonable rate to take its place." According to the president's proposal, the rate that the ICC set would go into effect immediately and would remain in place until a federal court issued a ruling about it. That stance put the president among those who believed that the burden of challenging an ICC decision about rates should fall on the railroads, rather than on the shippers.[11]

Theodore Roosevelt did not create the movement to increase the power of the ICC and to limit the rate-making autonomy of the railroads themselves. The campaign had been gathering force for several years among shippers in the South and the Middle West. The Elkins Act of 1903 had addressed rebates but had left alone the problem of the rates themselves and the resultant discrimination against and among localities. Edward P. Bacon and his Interstate Commerce Law Convention embodied this sentiment among midwestern shippers by the end of 1904. In Iowa, Minnesota, and Wisconsin the sentiment for regulation mounted after Roosevelt's election. Similar constituent pressure brought Democratic lawmakers in the South into the regulatory coalition. The ICC had a jurisdictional concern with seeing its own authority enhanced, and its members spoke out for what Roosevelt advocated.

The agitation about the railroads in 1904/5 reflected a pervasive concern about the future of society. More than any other industry of the day, the railroads symbolized the popular apprehension regarding the impact of business consolidation on the nation. At a time of increasing consumer prices, fears about inflation associated higher railroad rates with a rising cost of living. As an issue of public policy, however, the railroad question was a struggle among competing economic forces about the price of using the rail lines and whether the management of the roads was fair. The opponents of the railroads contended that the rates were rising from an already exorbitant level. Even more vexing was the practice of using a rate structure that favored one locality or city over another. Finally, it seemed manifestly unjust that the railroads themselves should be the final judge of the merits of a rate dispute.

The railroads countered that their critics were mistaken on all points. Rates needed to be higher so as to bear the cost of doing business and raising capital. Discrimination among geographical areas was inherent in the railroad itself. The assault on the railroads, moreover, was far from disinterested in the eyes of the spokesmen for the lines. The effort to broaden the power of the ICC had as its real aim, one of them wrote, "to enable some Government tribunal to assume the affirmative direction and rearrangement of the railroad policies of the country."[12]

The controversy about the railroads was not a simple issue of right and wrong. By 1904 the industry had changed from its reckless and often speculative habits during the late nineteenth century. The structure of rates had stabilized and was not confiscatory for shippers. Economic forces had as much to do with how the railroads operated as did impulses of greed and power. The traveling and shipping public received services that were of high quality. There was some merit to the view that the railroads were being caricatured. They had a legitimate case when they claimed the need for a rate structure that would bring them enough revenues to enable them to raise funds for needed expansion.

Critics of the railroads, on the other hand, argued that ample evidence existed to justify a more effective ICC. Continued rebating and discriminatory tactics hurt the Middle West and the South. They maintained that when a rate was disputed, it was unfair to have it stay in force "until the case has run the gamut of three federal courts, and has finally been settled by the Supreme Court of the United States." It was time for the federal government to create a tribunal that was "at once impartial and powerful enough to do justice between the Railroad and the Citizen."[13]

Despite the odds against passing important legislation through the postelection session that would end by law on 4 March 1905, the administration and the president put "the full power" of the White House behind a regulatory bill in the House during the weeks after Roosevelt's message was submitted. The measure came under fire and was amended. A House committee approved the compromise bill on 31

January 1905. Known as the Esch-Townsend bill after the two midwestern Republicans who had sponsored it, its key provision was its grant of power to the ICC to set railroad rates that would be just and reasonable and that would go into effect in sixty days. The decisions of the commission would then be subject to review by a commerce court. The bill received decisive approval from the House on 9 February 1905 by a vote of 326 to 17.[14]

Reflecting his confidence that election on his own had built, Roosevelt added his personal prestige to the regulatory campaign. On 30 January 1905 he told the conservative Union League Club of Philadelphia that the country would not "permanently tolerate the use of vast power conferred by vast wealth, and especially by wealth in its corporate form, without lodging somewhere in the Government the still higher power of seeing that this power, in addition to being used in the interest of individual or individuals possessing it, is also used for and not against the interest of the people as a whole." The press concluded that a "serious conflict" existed between the White House and Congress "and that the President has decided to force the fighting."[15]

The advantage for the moment lay with those in Congress who opposed Roosevelt. The Republican leaders of the Senate, especially Nelson W. Aldrich, saw no reason to hurry. With the end of the session in sight and with the arbitration treaties and other issues taking up time, the conservatives contended that it would be wrong for the Senate "to simply pass that bill without discussions." The upper house did allow its Interstate Commerce Committee to conduct hearings on the Esch-Townsend bill and other regulatory ideas during the months when Congress was not in session.[16]

Roosevelt's maneuvers at this time have been linked to the earlier negotiations regarding a possible special session on the tariff. Had he used the threat of tariff revision as a way of prompting Congress to act on the railroads? The president knew that he could wage only one large legislative battle during the next session of Congress. From his perspective the tariff was less important than the railroads, and he was always more likely to put aside tariff revision rather than railways. Making so much of the tariff in late 1904 probably pushed some lawmakers to turn to the popular problem of the railroads with relief.

The key point was that attacking the railroad companies was something that pleased Americans during early 1905. Had Speaker Cannon, the target of a presumed tariff bluff, held up the railroad bill in the House, he would have been swept aside. Roosevelt did not need to use the tariff to have the issue of railroad regulation considered. That would have occurred no matter what he did.

Congress adjourned in early March 1905 as Washington prepared to inaugurate Theodore Roosevelt. The president was the preeminent figure in national politics. He started his full term "with the good wishes of all the people and with the hearty applause of most of them." The country was prosperous and at peace. Roosevelt told an English friend that he "greatly enjoyed inauguration day, and indeed I have thoroughly enjoyed being President." The issues that the United States faced, as he saw them, lay more in the domestic area than in foreign policy. It was necessary to devise "methods of controlling the big corporations without paralyzing the energies of the business community." At the same time he was intent on "preventing any tyranny on the part of the labor unions while cordially assisting in every proper effort made by the wageworkers to better themselves by combinations." Abroad, he believed that the country was "learning to take its position more seriously."[17]

By 1905, Theodore Roosevelt had settled himself comfortably into a White House routine that characterized the rest of his presidency. He rose at 8:00 A.M. and went to a family breakfast with his children. After that boisterous interlude, he often walked with Mrs. Roosevelt or a relative around the White House garden. His daily appointments began at 9:00, when William Loeb, Jr., admitted visitors to his office. Those who saw Roosevelt mentioned how quickly he grasped their business and gave them an answer. Newsmen frequently saw the president when he was being shaved daily at 12:40, before lunch. The writer Lincoln Steffens waited until the barber moved to Roosevelt's lower lip. "Then I had a second chance to get in a word to hold or turn the flood of his monologue." At lunch, Roosevelt had the usual assortment of diverse guests. In these conversations he often impressed foreign visitors as being "amazingly indiscreet, amusing and interesting." During the afternoons there was more work, then horseback riding or vigorous hiking in the Washington area.[18]

By the time of his second term, Roosevelt had developed several effective methods of managing the news that flowed from the White House. In addition to the techniques that George B. Cortelyou and Loeb had set up during the first term, the president sought new ways to get his message across to the American people. "When do I get the ear of the public?" he asked Edward W. Bok of the *Ladies Home Journal* during 1905. Roosevelt lamented that his words were read by the citizenry "only in its busiest moments" and rarely by women. Bok suggested that his magazine create a department called "The President," which would convey Roosevelt's views "on those national questions which affect the vital interests of the home." Robert L. O'Brien of the *Boston Transcript* served as the conduit for the president's thoughts, and the page ran successfully for a year.[19]

On several occasions during his second term, Roosevelt tried to put in place more direct measures to supervise the flow of news. After a cabinet meeting in mid October 1905, the president informed the major press associations "that hereafter no information will be given to anyone about anything that has occurred at a Cabinet meeting." The White House also reminded cabinet members that they had "a moral obligation" not to talk about their deliberations or to be induced by "weakness or good nature" into leaking tidbits about what the cabinet might have decided.[20]

A few months later a Washington correspondent complained that the White House was sitting on all kinds of news that might be unfavorable and was passing out news that it wanted the public to know. "It is becoming more difficult to get uncolored news; yet the press agency feature of the executive departments was never so active." At the same time, correspondents recognized that "you must not print news objectionable to or censorious of the administration, especially from the White House, or you will get disliked, and will probably suffer for it."[21]

In Roosevelt's press relations, one feature of the second term was the full emergence of what the reporters and the president called the Ananias Club. A journalist who betrayed Roosevelt's trust or who contradicted the president's version of events was relegated to this informal organization, named after a liar of biblical times. In some instances, newspapers and reporters could be barred from the White House altogether. Membership in the club was not limited to reporters, but they found their way to its roster most often. The majority of journalists took the president's tactics as a necessary part of the assignment of covering the White House; they enjoyed the excitement and interest that Roosevelt generated among their readers. The combination of pressure and allure that Roosevelt exerted on reporters, along with the sheer volume of news that came from his administration, ensured that the press coverage was strongly favorable throughout most of his second term.

The cabinet was for the moment stable, but it would undergo numerous changes during the full elected term. These began when Cortelyou rejoined the administration as the postmaster general in 1905, and Elihu Root replaced John Hay in July 1905, when the incumbent secretary of state died from the heart disease and other ailments that had bothered him for years. Events on the railroad issue would soon prompt another shift in the ever-changing portfolio of the Navy Department. On the whole, Roosevelt gave his cabinet members a good deal of latitude to express their own policy views. Leslie M. Shaw at the Treasury spoke out for high tariff protection in ringing terms, often at the cost of some embarrassment to the White House. The president said of his official family, as he did of his administration's appointees in general: "We have never before had a finer grade of men, men more capable, more zealous, fearless and disinterested."[22]

A month after his inauguration, Theodore Roosevelt left Washington for a hunting trip in Oklahoma and Texas. "As regards internal affairs," he wrote to the ailing John Hay, "there is no reason why I should not be gone for the six weeks." The nation was outwardly calm during the spring of 1905, but evidence was gathering that the public mind had mounting worries regarding the relationship between large corporations and the future of society. "Corporation morals and Senatorial morals," wrote the editors of World's Work at this time, "these are the subjects that are going to suffer an increasing intensity of public attention."[23]

During the ensuing year a new political attitude emerged that was very critical of corporate practices. This progressive spirit formed the setting within which Theodore Roosevelt pursued his campaign for railroad regulation. The episode that initiated this process was a probe of gas and insurance companies in New York, led by Charles Evans Hughes, a young attorney. The inquiry revealed a pattern of corporate crimes that included bribery, payoffs to politicians, and extensive campaign contributions. The revelations spread across the country, and political reactions rapidly followed. There was an upsurge of criminal actions filed against public officials, some of whom went to jail for their crimes.

Popular anxiety about the problem of corporate influence also mounted during this period because of a wave of magazine disclosures about how business affected public affairs. In the widely read periodicals such as McClure's Magazine, World's Work, and Collier's, reporters exposed corruption in the cities, revealed that unsafe products and diseased food threatened the public's health, and uncovered how the fortunes of millionaires had been acquired. The names of Lincoln Steffens, Samuel Hopkins Adams, and Ida M. Tarbell became well known to the middle-class audience that eagerly read these magazines each month.

Another powerful force during the second half of Theodore Roosevelt's presidency was a rising level of consumer prices. The effects of inflation that had been so welcome between 1897 and 1902 now began to irritate the electorate. "They say we can live comfortably on our present wages," remarked a longshoreman in New York in 1907. "My answer is this: 'I used to pay 6 dollars a month rent; now I pay 13 dollars. We pay a cent a piece for potatoes. We paid half that price a few years ago.' " The higher cost of living added weight to the Democratic criticism of the Republicans on the tariff issue.[24]

The shifting political atmosphere after 1905 had its greatest impact on the Republicans as the party in power. Factional alignments rose to the surface after eight years of relative calm. Across the country, from California and Oregon, on the West Coast, to Kansas, South Dakota, Iowa, and Wisconsin, in the Middle West, and to New Hampshire and New Jersey in the East, the GOP plunged into bitter struggles between regular Republican organizations and rebellious and ambitious younger members of the party. Grievances centered on the railroad issue, tariff policy, and campaign practices. The progressive Republicans, as they began to call themselves, said that there should be direct primaries to choose candidates and there should be a reduction of "boss rule" in the party itself.

Among the political leaders of the new Republican spirit were Albert B. Cummins, the low-tariff, antirailroad governor of Iowa, and Robert M. La Follette of Wisconsin, who had fought against the rail companies in his own state. La Follette moved on to the Senate in 1906, where Cummins joined him two years later. They maintained that the Republican party "must be dominated by the spirit of progress," as Cummins phrased it in 1906.[25]

The emergence of La Follette, Cummins, and other progressive Republicans from 1905 onward presented Theodore Roosevelt with delicate political choices. He did not share some of the policy positions of the reformers. His view of the trust issue was more accepting of bigness and consolidation than were the midwesterners. They believed in the enforcement of the Sherman Act in simple terms as the president no longer did. Their skepticism about the tariff was not a passion that he shared. They could all collaborate on the railroad problem, although even in that instance, Roosevelt operated in a less punitive spirit than La Follette did. The progressives and the president had some potential enemies in common in Speaker Cannon, Senator Aldrich, and the wing of the Republicans that they represented. From that mutual antipathy toward the conservatives flowed some cooperation during Roosevelt's second term.

The railroad issue became the dominant topic of American politics before Congress resumed its deliberations in December 1905. The railroads themselves began a concerted "campaign of instruction and defense" to change popular attitudes toward them. They came before the Senate Interstate Commerce Committee, chaired by Stephen B. Elkins of West Virginia, and contended that no change in existing law was required. One railroad executive said that giving power over rates to the

ICC carried with it the risk of "imminent and widespread danger to every commercial interest." An expensive lobbying effort was mounted to influence editorial writers and the public. So obvious was the campaign that it backfired and stirred up more negative feeling against the railroads.[26]

Theodore Roosevelt kept the heat on the railroads through the weapons of publicity that he used with even more vigor as a strong president during his second term. On his way back from the hunting trip in May, he spoke in Denver and Chicago. "Personally, I believe that the Federal Government must take an increasing control over corporations," he told the audience at the Iroquois Club in Chicago on 10 May 1905. Power to do this must exist, Roosevelt went on, and "the power must be lodged in the representatives of the people." He conceded that the potential for abuse existed, but that was not an argument "against placing it where we shall have a right to expect that it will be used fairly toward all."[27]

Meanwhile, Attorney General William H. Moody was telling the Senate Interstate Commerce Committee, in a letter, that what Roosevelt proposed about the ICC was constitutional and proper. At the end of the 1890s, the Supreme Court had limited the commission's power over railroad rates in substantial ways. Now Moody argued that rate making was "purely a legislative function" and that Congress had the right "to avail itself of the aid of an administrative body for the execution in detail of general rules which have been enacted into law."[28]

When it came to his own cabinet, there were limits on how far Roosevelt wanted to pursue a campaign against the railroads. Secretary of the Navy Paul Morton had come to the government from the railroad industry. "Very few Presidents," he told a friend in July 1904, "would have had the courage to ask a railroad man into his Cabinet." Investigations of the way in which the Atchison, Topeka, and Santa Fe Railroad treated its favored shippers revealed a pattern of rebating at a time when Morton, in Roosevelt's words, "was vice-president of the road and nominally directed the department which covered the action in question." The lawyers who looked into the issue for the Justice Department recommended that the government proceed against officers of the Santa Fe, including Morton. That was a step that Roosevelt declined to take. He defended Morton and his own judgment in several public letters. The secretary, however, decided to resign from the cabinet and pursue business opportunities.[29]

The public campaign by the White House on behalf of railroad regulation continued. While the Senate Interstate Commerce Committee was meeting during the middle of May, the administration indicated that it would use cheaper foreign supplies, rather than protected U.S. products, in the building of the Panama Canal. The order was withdrawn three days later, when high-tariff men protested, but the episode linked possible action on the tariff with the railroads. Behind the scenes, the president used cooperative journalists to set out the case against the railroads in middle-class periodicals. Roosevelt spoke himself for his program when he toured the South during October 1905.

The president knew that his railroad bill would have to satisfy both Congress and the courts. He did not like the Esch-Townsend bill, because it gave the ICC authority to fix a rate. Roosevelt believed that the commission should set a maximum rate to be charged in a disputed case. "It will speedily become impossible," he maintained, "thus to favor any shipper save in altogether exceptional cases." He adhered to that position throughout October and November 1905, and he held conferences with such proregulation Republicans as Jonathan P. Dolliver of Iowa, Shelby M. Cullom of Illinois, and Moses E. Clapp of Minnesota about how to get an administration measure out of the Interstate Commerce Committee. After reading a draft of Roosevelt's annual message in late November, Henry Cabot Lodge conceded that "it is impossible to hope for a moment to prevent a bill which gives to the Commission a measure of power to fix rates."[30]

In the annual message that was read to Congress on 5 December 1905, Roosevelt renewed his plea for regulatory legislation. He asked the lawmakers to give the government the power to exercise "such supervision and regulation of the rates charged by the railroads of the country engaged in interstate traffic as shall summarily and effectively prevent the imposition of unjust or unreasonable rates." To that end he wanted an administrative agency to have the capacity "to fix a given maximum rate, which rate, after the lapse of a reasonable time, goes into full effect, subject to review by the courts." Roosevelt had modified his stance a little since the ICC decision would not go into effect at once. Nonetheless, the proposal of the president represented a substantial step toward more effective regulation.[31]

Railroads were not the only subject involving expanded governmental power that Roosevelt mentioned in his message. He asked that the Department of Commerce and Labor investigate the problem of child labor, he advocated an employers' liability law for the District of Columbia, and he endorsed pure-food-and-drug legislation, along with governmental supervision of insurance companies. A Democratic newspaper said that Roosevelt's initiatives constituted "the most amazing program of centralization that any President of the United States has ever recommended." This broadening of the national agenda, together with the strengthening of presidential authority that it implied, formed the context in which the railroad battle was waged.[32]

The major priority of the White House during the early stages of the session was the railroad bill. The House posed few obstacles for the president. The Republicans had a 114-seat margin over the Democrats after the 1904 election, and most House members of both parties were likely to support the curbing of railroad power. The situation in the Senate also favored the Republicans, with their 57 senators to 33 for the Democrats. Yet, many GOP senators were cool to both railroad regulation and Theodore Roosevelt.

The first step was to unite behind a railroad bill that had a reasonable chance to gain a Senate majority. During the two weeks after the annual message, Senator Dolliver brought forward legislation that Roosevelt wanted. The senator introduced his bill on 19 December 1905. At the same time the administration filed more antirebating suits against offending railroads. Information was also supplied to reporters about the excesses of the rail lines and their efforts to sway the public.

Dolliver collaborated with Congressman William P. Hepburn (R., Iowa) of the House Interstate Commerce Committee to work out a joint strategy. What the press called the Dolliver-Hepburn bill was formally introduced on 24 January 1906. The measure was favorably reported to the full House three days later. Hepburn's bill received the overwhelming support of both parties in the lower house on 8 February 1906: there were only seven dissenting votes.

The fate of railroad regulation was now in the hands of the Senate. The Dolliver version had been bottled up in the Interstate Commerce Committee during December 1905 and January 1906. The Iowan was reaching out to the Democrats on the panel to see that the bill was reported out for full debate. By late January, Dolliver wrote: "It is now up to the Senate to beat it if they can. I do not think they can."[33]

Dolliver and the White House discovered the lengths to which Nelson Aldrich and his allies were prepared to go during February 1906 when the Senate committee dealt with the Dolliver-Hepburn bills. Between 9 and 23 February 1906 the alliance of proregulation senators of both parties beat back amendments to dilute the measure. The climax to committee consideration came on 23 February, when the lawmakers took up the essence of the Dolliver bill. Senator Cullom had been ill and was convalescing in Florida. Dolliver had Cullom's proxy and his instructions about how to vote it.

With three Republican votes in hand and five Democrats also in favor of regulation, Dolliver was able to win an eight-to-five triumph for his side. At this point, Senator Aldrich used his influence with several of the Democrats to deny Dolliver the right to report the bill to the Senate. The two men had clashed in years past, and Aldrich saw a chance to help his own cause and to spite a rival. The honor of having charge of the bill went instead to Senator Benjamin R. ("Pitchfork Ben") Tillman, a South Carolina Democrat. The administration's legislation would be in the hands of the political opposition. A bitter Dolliver said: "If the rail-road fellows had employed a pack of d——d fools to make the worst possible mess of their case they could not have improved upon the present situation."[34]

The selection of Tillman posed personal problems for Roosevelt, as Aldrich well knew. The president and Tillman had clashed over a number of personal and social issues; they were not speaking to each other during early 1906. It would take some time for Roosevelt to ac-commodate to the reality of having Tillman sponsor the bill. In any case, the South Carolinian reported the bill to the Senate on 26 February, and general debate opened two days later.

Protracted discussion focused on what the role of the courts would be, once the bill had been passed. The opponents of regulation, not wishing to take the unpopular stance of being prorailroad, concentrated on how much power the judiciary would have in interpreting the rulings of the ICC in rate cases. Those who were in favor of the bill wanted the courts to have only a "narrow review" that would address questions of procedural fairness. Aldrich and his followers endorsed a "broad re-view" that would allow judges to decide whether the rulings of the commission were fair on their merits as public policy.

As Dolliver had drafted the bill, it was silent on the court issue. Because "a properly constituted Commission is the best tribunal before which these matters can be presented," Dolliver argued, his bill made no provision "for transferring the dispute from the Commission to the courts." The course of the Senate debate during March revealed that the president did not have the necessary votes to put the bill in that form through the Senate if he relied only on Republicans. A newsman close to the White House said toward the end of the month that Roosevelt "will not treat with the railroad Senators on the Rate bill. They have had their day at the White House." Still, as the month ended, it was apparent that the bill would have to contain some explicit language regarding the scope of what the courts might review.[35]

On 31 March 1906, Roosevelt met with a group of senators, includ-ing Dolliver and William Boyd Allison, and they agreed on an amend-ment that Senator Chester I. Long of Kansas introduced on 2 April. The proposed change would have limited the courts' review power to decid-ing "whether the order complained of was beyond the authority of the

Commission or in violation of the rights of the carrier secured by the Constitution." In the days that followed, other amendments were discussed. One included wording to limit the power of the courts to issue orders that would suspend rates that the ICC had set; another would have put the money in controversy between shipper and railroads in escrow until the lawsuits had been decided.[36]

These amendments offered Roosevelt the mechanism to achieve a compromise. He still needed to obtain forty-six Senate votes to secure passage. He adopted a strategy of bipartisan compromise that would link Democrats and Republicans. Roosevelt was trying to have the bill pass "in the form I want by the aid of some fifteen or twenty Republicans added to most of the Democrats." To make the plan work, he needed to reach Tillman personally. On the suggestion of a newspaperman, Roosevelt turned to a former Republican senator, William E. Chandler of New Hampshire, as an intermediary. Chandler and Tillman had been friends since their days in the Senate, and Chandler hated the railroads because their opposition had cost him reelection in 1900.[37]

On 31 March, Roosevelt asked Chandler to visit him at the White House. He reported to Chandler that the bill would pass if Tillman could deliver twenty-six Democratic votes to the coalition. The president indicated that he could count on the votes of twenty Republicans. Chandler went to see Tillman that same evening to put the plan into motion. For the first half of April, vigorous consultation among Roosevelt, Chandler, and the Democrats went forward to frame the language about judicial power upon which all sides could agree.[38]

As the days passed, however, questions arose regarding Tillman's ability to supply twenty-six votes from the Democratic side of the aisle. The Tillman coalition seemed to be several votes below that key number. By 12 April, after reviewing his options, the president was telling Allison that "the easy way will be to come right back to the bill as it passed the House, and with very few unimportant amendments to pass it as it stands."[39]

Roosevelt decided to rally public support for his position and to woo the Senate Republicans simultaneously, in a speech that he gave during ceremonies for laying the cornerstone of a new office building for the House of Representatives on 14 April. The speech became famous instead for the president's attack on the crusading journalists whom the public was then avidly following. Roosevelt was engaged in a characteristic act of political balancing. One of the most sensational examples of the literature of exposure was a series of articles entitled "The Treason of the Senate," written by David Graham Phillips, the first of which appeared in the March 1906 issue of *Cosmopolitan*. Phillips suggested that a general pattern of corruption and illegal relationships permeated the upper house. However sympathetic Roosevelt may have been privately with attacks on his conservative opponents in the Senate, he knew that he needed their votes for the Hepburn bill. He also knew that Phillips's series was far more irritating to the conservative bloc in the Senate than any previous journalistic assault had been. He decided to criticize the reporters while at the same time moving ahead with his own more advanced regulatory program. Conservatives in the Senate would have sympathy; progressive Republicans and Democrats would have substance.

The president tried out his themes at a Gridiron Club dinner, where he first labeled the reporters as "muckrakers," using an image from John Bunyan's *Pilgrim's Progress*. In his 14 April speech, Roosevelt warned more publicly about "the man who never does anything else, who never thinks or speaks or writes, save of his feats with the muck-rake." Roosevelt argued that pursuing such tactics made these reporters "not a help to society, not an incitement to good, but one of the most potent forces for evil."[40]

Roosevelt's assault on reporters such as Phillips and Ray Stannard Baker overshadowed two other parts of the speech which were designed to take regulation to another level of discussion. Roosevelt called for an inheritance tax on fortunes "swollen beyond all healthy limits." The president also advocated governmental "supervision over corporations engaged in interstate business"; this would permit the nation "to deal with the far-reaching evils of overcapitalization." He made it clear that railroad regulation represented the beginning of an expanded federal role in this area.[41]

The "muck-rake" speech caused an uproar because of the president's apparent break with journalists whom he had previously encouraged. To the extent that the speech was designed to influence either conservative Republicans or wavering Democrats in the Senate, it failed to achieve that goal. On 18 April the Senate Democrats caucused, and it was evident that Tillman and his ally Joseph Weldon Bailey of Texas could only rely on twenty-five votes at best. Seven or eight of their colleagues did not want to give the federal government the power that Roosevelt sought, or they agreed with the economic and constitutional principles of Aldrich and his allies.

With his bipartisan coalition short of a majority, the only place for Roosevelt to go in April 1906 was back toward the Republicans. Aldrich and Allison had drafted an amendment that gave the courts authority over cases resulting from the Hepburn Act but that did not specify precisely how far such jurisdiction would extend. This vague language satisfied conservative Republicans, who called it "the broadest kind of court review." It pleased Roosevelt because it ensured that the bill he wanted would be passed. "The Hepburn bill with the Allison amendment," he later wrote, "contains practically exactly what I have both originally and always since asked for."[42]

There remained the embarrassing connection with Tillman and the need to explain Roosevelt's adoption of what was becoming known as the Allison amendment. On 4 May 1906, Roosevelt announced that he would see the press corps. He informed the thirty-nine journalists who were present for his twenty-minute discussion that he endorsed what Aldrich and Allison had worked out and that it was "just what he had wanted all the time." Skeptical reporters concluded that "he has failed in his effort to lick the United States Senate." When the Democrats heard this news, they felt that they had been betrayed. Roosevelt had sought their support when his own party had failed him, and now he was trying to shift the credit for railroad regulation back to the Republicans in an election year. "Let us have no more talk in the Senate and in the country about this 'iron man,'" said Senator Bailey; "he is clay, and very common clay at that."[43]

Roosevelt's change of position led to an acrimonious public row with Tillman and Chandler about the extent to which they had been allied with the president. In letters to Allison and Lodge that became public, Roosevelt denied that he had been openly critical of Senate Republicans who had opposed the bill. Newspaper reports from the White House also said that Roosevelt had not referred negatively to men such as Senators Spooner, Foraker, and Knox. Roosevelt's disclaimers left members of the press unconvinced. His statement to Allison, one wrote, "sounds more like the foxy Root and the amiable Taft than the impetuous Roosevelt." The controversy did no lasting damage because the public regarded it as only another example of Roosevelt's personal vigor and energy in office.[44]

The agreement on the Allison amendment opened the way for passage of the Hepburn bill. On 18 May 1906 the bill was approved by a vote of seventy-one to three. Senator Foraker was the only Republican who voted against it. The legislation went to conference, and both houses agreed to it in June 1906. Who deserved the credit for the enactment of serious railroad legislation? That question was much discussed during the summer of 1906, along with the related topic of whether the president or the Senate had prevailed in the struggle about court review.

Roosevelt had no doubts. The bill was "a fine piece of constructive legislation, and all that has been done tends toward carrying out the principles I have been preaching." Others were less sure that the president had won that much. The issue of court jurisdiction had been left so vague that, as Senator Beveridge wrote, the " 'railroad senators' won out in the fight for broad review." John C. Spooner, a leader of the conservatives, agreed. The Senate bill was "as nearly constitutional as we could make it," he wrote. The victory for the prorailroad forces on this point proved only symbolic. When the Supreme Court ruled on the question four years later, it took a position close to what the advocates of narrow review had sought as far as the power of the ICC was concerned.[45]

A railroad-regulation bill had become law in 1906, and its provisions strengthened the power of the ICC. The act covered both express and sleeping-car rail companies, and it contained a broader definition of what constituted transportation as a subject of governmental regulation. When a shipper filed a complaint, the ICC could now set "just and reasonable maximum rates" that became effective in thirty days. There were also important provisions regarding the authority to review and publicize railroad-company accounts, to supervise oil pipelines, and to scrutinize other railway practices. In some respects the measure did not go as far as the midwestern progressive senators wanted. For example, Robert La Follette did not obtain his pet scheme for the physical valuation of railroad assets as a basis for rates. In fact, his idea was less practical than he believed. Overall, the Hepburn Act represented the major domestic legislation of Theodore Roosevelt's presidency, and the credit clearly belonged to the president. "If it had not been for Theodore Roosevelt," Senator Beveridge wrote, "there would not have been any railroad legislation of any kind."[46]

The battle over the Hepburn Act demonstrated how Roosevelt functioned as a chief legislator in the White House. Much of the language of the bill was framed in the Department of Justice. Roosevelt provided the policy initiative for railroad regulation in his annual messages of 1904 and 1905. Presidential speeches during 1905 put the issue at the top of the public agenda. His moves on the tariff, while not decisive in shaping congressional willingness to regulate the railroads, reminded lawmakers where their attention should be focused. Antirebating suits underscored the president's commitment and kept the railroads off balance. When the bill came to the Senate, Roosevelt acted as a kind of co-senator who functioned as a go-between for the various factions. In the Tillman strategy and after its demise, Roosevelt showed a high degree of flexibility and adroitness. The passage of the Hepburn Act culminated two years of effective and purposeful presidential leadership.

Historical scholarship during the 1960s questioned whether the Hepburn Act was a regulatory law at all, or only a sham measure that the railroads themselves used in order to escape state regulation or more punitive federal action. This view rests on a reading of the evidence that is at best selective and in some places highly misleading. The railroads accepted the Hepburn Act because they had no alternative, but they did not like what Roosevelt had done to them. By the 1970s the opposite charge was leveled. The Hepburn Act had, according to this theory, been part of a policy of overregulation that had denied the railroads between 1906 and 1917 the rate increases they needed in order to respond to inflation. While the law itself had positive aspects, it became in time an antirailroad weapon that did more damage than good to the nation's transportation system. In general, the second thesis has more merit than the first, but its view of the regulatory process has more relevance to what happened after 1906 than to Roosevelt's original purposes in pushing for the law. He thought a more powerful ICC should be fair rather than harmful. It did not turn out that way, but the fault was not the president's.[47]

While the Hepburn Act was making its way on Capitol Hill, two other regulatory issues emerged, at the end of the session, into the spotlight of public attention—pure-food-and-drug legislation and the issue of the quality and cleanliness of the meat that Americans consumed. These two related problems were added to the regulatory agenda of this important congressional session, and they increased Roosevelt's commitment to expand the supervisory power of the federal government.

Pure-food-and-drug legislation was not in itself a new issue. In his annual message of December 1905, Roosevelt had recommended the passage of legislation "to regulate interstate commerce in misbranded and adulterated foods, drinks, and drugs" in order "to secure the health and welfare of the consuming public."[48] The campaign to oversee the purity and quality of the nation's food and drugs had been before the Congress for more than a decade. Since the mid 1890s there had been attempts to pass laws to safeguard the consumer from adulterated or impure food. Harvey W. Wiley, chief of the Bureau of Chemistry in the Agriculture Department, had dramatized the issue with his "Poison Squad" of young men who conducted tests on themselves with suspected additives and chemicals. The power of the members of the food industry that made such products was strong enough on Capitol Hill to frustrate these regulatory endeavors. Up to the end of 1903, legislation on the pure-food problem had been stalled.

The prospects for congressional action changed during 1904 and 1905. Popular fears grew about the ingredients that patent medicines contained. The American Medical Association (AMA) and such popular periodicals as the *Ladies Home Journal* revealed that alcohol and other drugs were primary elements in the "vegetable compounds" and "soothing syrups" that many Americans used for treating their ailments and tensions. The campaign that the muckraking periodicals waged against these nostrums reached a peak during the second half of 1905. A series of articles written by Samuel Hopkins Adams appeared in *Collier's* from early October 1905 onward. Roosevelt received a number of requests to mention the subject in his 1905 message, including letters from the Consumers League and the AMA. The day after the message was read, Senator Weldon B. Heyburn (R., Idaho) introduced a pure-food-and-drug bill. He reported the measure back to his colleagues eight days later, on 14 December 1905.

Senate debate on the pure-food bill took place at intervals during January and February 1906. Opposition to the regulation of food and drugs came from such groups as the Proprietary Association of America, the National Wholesale Liquor Dealers Association, and those members of the National Food Manufacturers' Association who relied on preservatives and cheapeners in their products. Some industry leaders, such as H. J. Heinz and Frederick Pabst, favored regulation as a way of making their business "respectable and trusted."[49] By the third week of February 1906, Senator Aldrich had decided to let the pure-food bill come before the Senate. Knowing the popular support behind the legislation, the Republican leader in the Senate saw no reason to have his colleagues attacked for obstructionism. In any event, there was a good chance that the House would not act on the bill during that session. Whatever the reason, the Senate passed the pure-food bill on 21 February by a vote of sixty-three to four.

In the House, another version of the law had also been introduced during December 1905. Because of the attention devoted to railroads, hearings on the bill that Congressman Hepburn offered did not begin in his Interstate and Foreign Commerce Committee until mid February 1906. After the hearings had finished, James R. Mann (R., Ill.) worked out a substitute bill with Harvey W. Wiley. It was reported to the House on 7 March 1906. The new measure took action against patent medicines. Now it was necessary for the House to vote on the bill. As the weeks passed, however, consideration of the pure-food question kept being postponed. The feeling grew in Congress that Speaker of the House Joseph G. Cannon did not want the bill to be considered. The Speaker claimed that there was not a majority for the House bill unless it had additional amendments. With the end of the session in sight, a disappointed Wiley told a friend, "I do not see any chance that it will not go over" until the next session of Congress.[50]

At that point, events gave the cause of pure food some unexpected assistance. Earlier in the year a novel had been published that described conditions in the nation's meat-packing industry. In vivid and often shocking prose, Upton Sinclair's *The Jungle* told how meat was processed on its way to the consumer. Sinclair's book was not the first publication to address how the meat packers conducted themselves. Articles had appeared in *Everybody's* magazine and in the British medical journal *Lancet*. These exposés did not have the immediate impact that Sinclair achieved with his riveting treatment of the filth and disease that accompanied meat packing in Chicago. Senator Albert J. Beveridge read the book and sent a copy to Roosevelt, who also heard about the subject from Sinclair himself. Roosevelt instructed his secretary of agriculture, James Wilson, to start preparing for a thorough probe of the industry. "It is evident," Roosevelt wrote, "that we do not want any merely perfunctory investigation at this time."[51]

Roosevelt appointed two men, Charles P. Neill of the Department of Labor and James B. Reynolds of New York, to conduct an investigation of the Chicago stockyards. They reported back to the president, in Roosevelt's words, that "the stockyards and packing houses are not kept even reasonably clean, and that the method of handling and preparing food products is uncleanly and dangerous to health." After Neill and Reynolds made their findings, Senator Beveridge worked with them and the Department of Agriculture to prepare a meat-inspection law that he offered in the Senate on 21 May 1906. The measure called for the inspection of all meat that was purchased in interstate commerce, mandated that such meat products be inspected and dated, and gave the Agriculture Department the power to oversee the conditions in the packing houses themselves. The cost would be borne through a fee that the packers would pay for each animal processed. Beveridge proudly told Albert Shaw that the proposed law represented "The most pronounced extension of federal power in every direction ever enacted, including even the rate bill itself."[52]

For the time being, however, Roosevelt did not wish to make public the report of his investigators. Beveridge added to the pressure on the packers on 25 May 1906 when he made his bill an amendment to the agricultural appropriation bill that the Senate was then considering. Using the threat of the public disclosure of the packing-house report, the president and Beveridge saw the Senate approve the amendment without opposition. Roosevelt turned his attention to the House and warned that he would not release the report "provided we can have the meat inspection amendment that has been put on in the Senate in substance enacted into law."[53]

That would not be easy to do. The meat packers had not made a fight in the Senate, but they had effective political allies in the House. The most influential was James W. Wadsworth (R., N.Y.), who chaired the Agriculture Committee. He was himself a stock raiser in upstate New York and was close to the industry leaders. The antiregulation forces could assemble a substantial number of votes from those members who represented western cattle raisers and from other conservatives who opposed Roosevelt's ideas on constitutional principles.

The president's strategy of using the Neill-Reynolds report as a threat to Congress did not work. Wadsworth devised amendments of his own to what Beveridge had offered and sent them to the White House in late May. The changes diluted the authority of the Department of Agriculture over the inspection process and put the burden of paying for the new procedures on the government, rather than on the meat packers themselves. Roosevelt told Wadsworth "that each change is for the worse and that in the aggregate they are ruinous." On 4 June 1906, Roosevelt sent the Neill-Reynolds report to Capitol Hill. "The conditions shown by even this short inspection to exist in the Chicago stock yards are revolting." he wrote; "it is imperatively necessary in the interest of health and of decency that they shall be radically changed." He asked the lawmakers to specify that a fee should be paid when "each animal" was slaughtered. Otherwise a future Congress could cut the appropriation for the program and render it worthless. The unwillingness to leave the issue to future action indicated something about the real extent of congressional and Republican enthusiasm for meat inspection during 1906.[54]

The publicity approach of the White House caused an outcry from the voters but left the opponents of inspection unmoved. The bill that Wadsworth's committee reported on 14 June 1906 did not use the fee approach; rather, it made a very limited appropriation for a federal inspection service during its first year. The issue of judicial review came up again in the bill. The committee provided broad court jurisdiction which would, if retained, according to the president, "nullify the major part of the good which can be expected from the enactment of this law."[55]

Despite Roosevelt's objections to the bill on these and other grounds, the House committee reaffirmed its position on 15 June 1906. The president, Speaker Cannon, and Congressman Henry C. Adams (R., Wis.) worked out a compromise during the next four days. The inspection-fee proposal was put aside, and the appropriation for the service was increased to $3 million a year. The provision for court review was dropped in return for removal of the language that gave "final and conclusive" authority to the secretary of agriculture. Roosevelt accepted these changes because, as he told Beveridge, "I am concerned with getting the result, not with the verbiage." A relieved Adams wrote that "a fight which would have had disastrous effects to the republican party has been disposed of."[56]

The compromise bill was reported to the House on 19 June 1906, and it passed quickly. Senator Beveridge made a determined stand in the Senate on the issue of an inspection fee and on a provision to mandate a label with a specific date when meat had been put into a can. His colleagues agreed, and the matter went to a conference committee. The House would not yield on the fee question and on whether the can should have a dated label. If Beveridge and the Senate had held out, the end of the session would likely have rendered all his hard work useless. He decided to give in, and he told his fellow senators to accept the House version. The measure passed rapidly, and Roosevelt signed the agricultural appropriation law on 30 June 1906. The president sent Beveridge the pen that he had used to approve the bill. As passed, Roosevelt wrote, the amendment "will enable us to put a complete stop to the wrongdoing complained of."[57]

The pressure for meat inspection also freed the pure-food-and-drug bill from its immobility in the House. In late May, Roosevelt told Speaker Cannon that he wanted the bill considered along with legislation on immigration and naturalization issues; he also reminded Cannon about White House concern a few days later. House members now said that the issue would come up before the session closed. The bill emerged from the Rules Committee on 20 June, and debate opened on the next day. After amendments were considered, the bill passed the House 241 to 17, with another 118 members present or not voting, on 23 June. The conference committee made the bill stronger than either the House or the Senate version. Like the meat-inspection law, the Pure Food and Drug Act was signed into law on 30 June 1906.

"It has been a great session," a pleased Theodore Roosevelt wrote on 3 July 1906. The three major pieces of legislation that had been passed, he told a friend, were "the railroad rate bill, meat inspection bill & pure food bill." Their combined impact seemed significant to the president. "Taken together," Roosevelt contended, they marked "a noteworthy advance in the policy of securing Federal supervision and control over corporations." One commentator in the press concluded that these policies disclosed "a marked tendency toward the centralization of power in the United States and a corresponding decrease in the old time sovereignty of the states, or of the individual."[58]

The 1905/6 session of Congress also addressed a number of other policy questions. On some of these the White House prevailed; on others the president was defeated. A bill to remove the Dingley tariff rates on Philippine products, except for residual duties on tobacco and sugar, easily passed the House and then was bottled up in the Senate committee. Roosevelt did obtain an employers' liability act for the District of Columbia. Congress also approved a measure to grant joint admission to the Union to the western territories of Arizona and New Mexico, as well as to Indian Territory and Oklahoma. Oklahoma became a state in 1907; Arizona and New Mexico turned down the congressional arrangement. There were also laws to reform the consular service, to lift the tax on alcohol imported for artistic use, and the Naturalization Act, which tightened procedures for becoming a United States citizen.

Despite these accomplishments, Roosevelt had more issues that he wanted to take up during the remainder of his second term. He hoped to persuade legislators to limit the power of corporations to make campaign contributions, and he still thought that a Philippine tariff bill might be achieved. He was already contemplating how to pass an inheritance tax and an income tax in the future.

Roosevelt's relative success during the 1906 session attested to his increasing readiness to make forceful use of the weapons of the strong presidency. The battles over railroads, meat inspection, and pure food had seen an adroit mix of publicity, administrative actions, and quiet negotiations. The president had not achieved all that he had wanted on these subjects, and their actual enforcement would test his abilities and resolve. In the area of the presidency that dealt with legislation, Theodore Roosevelt had demonstrated in 1906 that the incumbent of the White House would be a participant with Congress in the future. William McKinley had done this quietly before 1901. Theodore Roosevelt put the process on the nation's front pages and raised expectations that his successors would have to emulate.

These triumphs had been achieved at some cost to Republican-party unity in 1905/6. Congressional Democrats argued, with some justice, that they had been better friends of Roosevelt's programs than had members of his own party. "At this moment," said a New York Democrat in May 1906, "the only support in either House of Congress which Mr. Roosevelt can depend on with certainty is the Democratic vote."[59] The president's regulatory program and his forceful public advocacy of it was forcing Republicans to confront a new issue of how active they wished the government to be in pursuing the control of corporate power.

One important element in Roosevelt's personal success as a legislative leader was his standing as a world figure. The early months of his second term brought his mediation of the Russo-Japanese War, followed by his role in the Algeciras Conference of 1906. As he moved trium- phantly on the international stage, his domestic prestige increased. Americans watched with admiration as their president worked for peace among kings and emperors. As long as international involvement brought gain to the United States at little cost, Roosevelt's foreign policy enjoyed their support. The president knew, however, that he could only ask so much. The diplomacy of his second term mixed participation and restraint in a way that showed Roosevelt's capacity in foreign affairs even as the struggle over regulation had revealed his ability in the domestic arena.

8

★ ★ ★ ★ ★

PRESIDENT OF
A GREAT NATION

Theodore Roosevelt's election victory in 1904 allowed him to use presidential power in foreign policy in a manner that reflected his prodigious energies. "This country cannot count upon any ally to do its work," he told George von Lengerke Meyer in late December 1904. "We must stand upon our own feet and try to look into the future as clearly as may be." The world as Roosevelt saw it in 1904/5 seemed on the surface to hold few immediate threats to national security, but he wanted his fellow citizens to be aware of the duties that went with his country's new standing. "We have become a great nation," he said in his Inaugural Address on 4 March 1905, "forced by the fact of its greatness into relations with the other nations of the earth, and we must behave as beseems a people with such responsibilities."[1]

To the president the nation's obligations went beyond the relations with the Latin American nations that had dominated his first term and would carry over into his second four years. The United States had a larger duty "to help on, with cordial good-will, every movement which will tend to bring us into more friendly relations with the rest of mankind." Beyond the arbitration treaties that he sent to the Senate during early 1905, this obligation meant promoting the balance of power and the Open Door in Asia through the settlement of the Russo-Japanese War. In Europe, it required American actions to reduce, where possible, tensions among such powers as Great Britain, France, and Germany.[2]

Roosevelt found the practice of foreign policy to be a rewarding exercise of personal presidential power. There the supremacy of the executive was evident. The interplay of character and policy on the world scene suited Roosevelt's penchant for intimate exchanges at the highest level. He could move with secrecy and quiet to shape events, letting only a few close friends know even a portion of the larger picture. The president did not believe that the American people would support all that he wished to do in foreign policy, and so without their knowledge he prepared to act in what he took to be their best interests.

An important change in Roosevelt's foreign-policy operation took place as the second term began. The illness that had been troubling John Hay for some time worsened, and the secretary of state became less and less involved in events. He sought relief in a European visit during the spring of 1905, returned home in mid June, and died on 1 July 1905. For some time, Theodore Roosevelt had been acting as his own secretary of state, and so Hay's departure did not disrupt the continuity of policy.

For a successor, Roosevelt turned naturally to Elihu Root, who would, the president predicted, "make in my judgment at least as good a Secretary of State as we have ever had." Root was one of the best appointments that Roosevelt made. Sixty years old in 1905, Root had become a tested public official after service in two administrations as secretary of war. He and the president collaborated effectively because Root shared the views that Roosevelt brought to foreign affairs. As he said about his chief, Root himself "was never indifferent to the broader aspects of the country's international relations or to the effects upon the prosperity and morale of the United States which might come in the future as results of the immediate present'treatment of situations arising in those relations."[3]

Root was a cautious diplomat who preferred formal routines and bureaucratic organization. In the area of Latin American relations, he displayed an acute sensitivity to the feelings of these nations and did much to restore good will toward the United States across the region. The largest role for Root lay in Latin American affairs, but he also contributed to the improving relationship with Great Britain. His participation was less significant during 1905/6 for policy in the Far East, because the president had established an ascendancy there before Root had rejoined the cabinet. After 1906, however, Root's role in Asian policy became more evident.

Roosevelt's penchant for informal diplomacy did not slacken while Root was in office. Although the president continued to make use of private channels, Root endeavored to impart more of a sense of order to his department's practices. Root supported reform of the consular service to make it more professional and less political. He also introduced changes that brought standardized procedures and greater flexibility in the way that diplomatic records were maintained. At the suggestion of an assistant secretary, Huntington Wilson, the Far Eastern Division was set up in March 1908, in what became the first of the State Department's system of geographic divisions. These actions helped to make Root an important figure in the institutional evolution of United States diplomacy.[4]

The first two years of Roosevelt's second term produced an expansion in the nation's overseas involvement in both theoretical and actual ways. One of the president's doctrinal innovations was what became known as the Roosevelt Corollary to the Monroe Doctrine. The most widely recognized expression of the president's position occurred in his annual message of December 1904. Writing about the relations of the United States with Latin American nations that did not pay their debts to European powers, Roosevelt told Congress that "chronic wrong-doing, or an impotence which results in a general loosening of the ties of civilized society," might require "intervention by some civilized nation." In the case of the United States and Latin America, the existence of the Monroe Doctrine might "force the United States, however reluctantly, in flagrant cases of such wrong-doing or impotence, to the exercise of an international police power." Roosevelt cited Cuba under the Platt amendment as a positive example of a country that was moving toward "stable and just civilization." If other countries "washed by the Caribbean Seas" would emulate Cuba, "all question of interference by this nation with their affairs would be at an end."[5]

The Roosevelt Corollary grew out of the Venezuelan controversy and the Panamanian revolution. It received its first public expression in a letter that the president gave to Elihu Root to read at an anniversary dinner for the Cuban Republic on 20 May 1904. The language of the letter anticipated exactly what Roosevelt would say in a more expanded form later. Since the Roosevelt Corollary was first applied to the Dominican Republic in early 1905, the situation of that unhappy state was part of the background for the announcement of the policy. Roosevelt had evolved the corollary out of his experience with Cuba, Panama, and Venezuela during 1902/3. As he put it to Root in June 1904, if the United States sought "to say 'Hands off' to the powers of Europe, then sooner or later we must keep order ourselves."[6]

When Roosevelt enunciated his principle during the spring of 1904, he knew about the financial problems in the Dominican Republic, which included more than $32 million in debts, primarily to European investors. At the end of 1903 and into 1904, reports reached Washington that the plight of the Dominican economy was worsening. Rumors of German interest once again appeared in the press. The government of the island sent its foreign minister to ask for American aid. Roosevelt was cautious about a large commitment. "I want to do nothing but what a policeman has to do in Santo Domingo," he wrote in February 1904. "As for annexing the island, I have about the same desire to annex it as a gorged boa constrictor might have to swallow a porcupine wrong-end-to."[7]

Roosevelt's attitude shaped administration policy in 1904. Governmental officials wrote in newspapers and periodicals about how the Dominican situation might result in "foreign attention in a way somewhat similar to the Venezuelan affair." By the end of March, however, the president had decided not "to take part in the pacification of the Republic." If he had the support of the American people, he might act in "the spirit of altruistic humanitarian duty" and "take partial possession" of the island at once. Knowing that he did not command such backing and being aware of his own election hopes, he decided to wait and watch. Meanwhile the financial predicament of that republic deteriorated during the summer of 1904. In mid July an international arbitral commission ruled about how money that was owed to the United States for payment to foreign creditors should be handled.[8]

After Roosevelt was elected in November 1904, foreign governments became more importunate about the failure of the Dominican government to meet its claims. The Italians were particularly forceful. The president's annual message was a signal of the administration's concern about conditions on the island. Root's remarks in a speech on 22 December underlined Roosevelt's fears: "What we will not permit the great Powers of Europe to do, we will not permit any American republic to make it necessary for the great Powers of Europe to do."[9]

Eight days later the United States minister in the Dominican Republic was ordered to determine whether that government was ready to ask Washington "to take charge of the collection of duties" and to arrange for their equitable distribution to the powers. On 5 January 1905 a naval officer was sent to assist with the negotiations. An agreement was signed two weeks later to have the United States deal with the foreign debt of the Dominican Republic to "restore the credit, preserve the order, increase the efficiency of the civil administration, and advance [the] material progress and welfare of the Republic."[10]

At first the administration regarded this document as one that did not require Senate action. Hostile reaction from Democrats soon convinced Roosevelt that the Senate could not be by-passed. On 25 January 1905 he said that either a protocol or a treaty would go before the Senate. With the treaties about international arbitration already causing difficulties in the Senate, Roosevelt knew that he could not afford to alienate

Capitol Hill again. As events proved, a confrontation with the Senate over the United States role in the Dominican Republic could not be avoided.

The administration concluded the formal protocol with the Dominican government on 7 February 1905. Roosevelt sent the document to the Senate on 15 February 1905. Faced with the conditions that existed in Santo Domingo, Roosevelt contended that "either we must submit to the likelihood of infringement of the Monroe doctrine or we must ourselves agree to some such arrangement" as the one he was sending to the Senate. The protocol, he concluded, "affords a practical test of the efficiency of the United States Government in maintaining the Monroe Doctrine."[11]

The response of the Senate suggested that the United States was not likely to earn a passing grade. Roosevelt had miscalculated about the willingness of the lawmakers to approve his foreign-policy leadership and his expansive view of the president's power. When the news came out about the prospective protocol in late January, the Democrats reacted angrily. "The President has no more right and no more authority to bind the people of the United States by such an agreement than I have as a member of this body," said Henry M. Teller, a Colorado Democrat.[12] After the protocol was submitted as a treaty in February, the opposition outcry continued. Conservative Republicans were also unenthusiastic about Roosevelt's actions. As 4 March 1905 approached, the date when Congress would have to adjourn, the treaty was short of the necessary two-thirds majority.

Roosevelt then brought the Senate back into a special session that ran for two weeks. He believed that it would be "an infamy if a minority of the Senate, from purely partisan reasons," were to turn down the treaty. The chairman of the Committee on Foreign Relations, Shelby M. Cullom, had the treaty voted out of his committee on 10 March 1905 with numerous Democratic amendments. Even in that form, the pact encountered difficulty in obtaining a simple majority, much less a two-thirds vote. Rather than have the protocol defeated, the administration let the Senate adjourn without taking any action. The Democrats stood united against the president's policy, along with several Republicans. "The Democrats killed the treaty," said one of Roosevelt's Republican supporters.[13]

The irate president complained: "The Senate adjourns. I am then left to shoulder all the responsibility due to their failure." The situation in the Dominican Republic remained worrisome. When an Italian cruiser went to the island on 14 March to insist on payment of the debt, the government of the republic, which was "under pressure from foreign creditors and domestic peril," asked the United States for a modus vivendi until the Senate could vote. The proposed arrangement would do the same things as the protocol. The United States would nominate officials to collect Dominican customs, the money would go into a U.S. bank, and it would then be distributed to creditors once the Senate had approved the treaty. Roosevelt consulted with Senate Republican leaders who "heartily agreed that it was necessary for [him] to take this action."[14]

After Roosevelt left the White House, he maintained that he had acted under implied presidential authority. He did not advance this expansive view in March 1905. The modus vivendi was depicted as a temporary proposal that would last until Congress reconvened in December. The president's bold stroke and the efficiency of his plan defused potential critics during the remainder of 1905. In late March he sent a confidential agent to examine claims against the Dominican Republic, including the notorious Santo Domingo Improvement Company. The administration also emphasized that no revolution against the existing government would be tolerated. On 4 September 1905 the president told the secretary of the navy to instruct the naval commander in the area "to stop any revolution. I intend to keep the island *in statu quo* until the Senate has had time to act on the treaty, and I shall treat any revolutionary movement as an effort to upset the *modus vivendi*."[15]

Roosevelt and the Senate Republicans expected a storm of Democratic criticism when the next session of Congress began. The opposition made its case intensely but without the passion that had been there during early 1905. The spokesmen for the president in the Senate, such as John C. Spooner of Wisconsin, advanced a broad view of executive power to counter the Democratic assaults. Spooner and Henry Cabot Lodge contended that the president had "the absolute power" to conduct negotiations regarding treaties.[16] The modus vivendi was an extension of that executive prerogative, and the Senate should stay out of the process.

Despite their lack of passion, Democrats used a party caucus to remain united over the Dominican treaty. A two-thirds vote of the caucus forced other opposition senators to vote against the treaty. Again, the pact was not brought to a vote during the long congressional session because of its likely defeat. The modus vivendi continued in place throughout 1906. By this time, Elihu Root began to change minds in the Senate on the issue, but more time had to pass before his conciliatory actions took effect.

Under Root's leadership, the administration changed the agreement with the Dominican Republic to reflect congressional criticism and to address the sensitivities of the Dominican government. In early February 1907 a new pact was concluded; it omitted references to the Monroe Doctrine and was less intrusive in Dominican affairs. The Senate quickly approved the pact when a few Democrats joined the Republican majority. Roosevelt called the action "another step toward the gradual introduction of order in the West Indies."[17]

The long battle over the proper role of the United States had ended in a limited victory for Roosevelt. The president had assisted the Caribbean nation with its finances and had articulated a more expansive vision of the Monroe Doctrine. In practice the policy that he followed was not the prelude to a United States protectorate. Yet there were lasting negative results. As an idea, the Roosevelt Corollary suggested that the United States had a greater innate political capacity than did its Latin neighbors, and it did so in the context of a strong assertion of presidential power. The episode served as another grievance about the imperialistic tendencies of the United States, one that even Elihu Root's measured approach could not entirely counteract. The nuances of Roosevelt's position were eventually forgotten, but the impression of bluster that the Roosevelt Corollary conveyed would endure.

While the Dominican Republic received a due share of Roosevelt's attention as his second term began, his main concern was with the ongoing war between Russia and Japan. "The situation in the far East is one which needs careful watching," he wrote in late December 1904.[18] The president had followed the conflict since the Japanese attacked the Russians in February 1904. The rivalry between the two warring powers offered opportunities and perils to the United States and its role in Asia. The president did not wish to see either Russia or Japan emerge as the dominant power in the Far East. A rough balance of power would best ensure the United States presence in the area and the Open Door in China.

When the fighting began, Roosevelt's sympathies lay with Tokyo. Two years of dealing with the Russian style of diplomacy and watching that country's policy in Asia had convinced Roosevelt where his nation's interest resided. "The Japs have played our game," he informed Hay in July 1904, "because they have played the game of civilized mankind." He had little more than contempt for the tsar of Russia, Nicholas II, and his government. "For years Russia has pursued a policy of consistent opposition to us in the East, and of literally fathomless mendacity," he observed in late 1904. While the United States was officially neutral, Roosevelt privately let the Japanese know of his sympathies and those of his countrymen.[19]

The president hoped to be a mediator between the combatants

when the time arrived for peace negotiations. He sought to achieve a rough balance between Japan and Russia. He wanted the Japanese to succeed but not permanently to cripple the power of Russia in Asia. He also feared that if he did not act as an intermediary, peacemaking would go forward at China's expense. There were risks for Roosevelt in such an approach. If mediation were to fail, his international standing would suffer. Yet the potential gains for U.S. prestige and national interest seemed attractive. And there were few other potential mediators who could be as appealing to both sides as was the leader of the United States.

An early opportunity to show his desire to be a peacemaker came at the beginning of the war. Roosevelt assumed the leadership of an international effort to preserve the neutrality of China and its territorial integrity. Acting at the suggestion of the kaiser, the administration sent out a diplomatic note asking Russia and Japan to see that during their military operations "the neutrality of China and in all practicable ways her administrative entity shall be respected by both parties." The area of fighting should be restricted so that "undue excitement and disturbance" of the Chinese would be avoided and, at the same time, "the least possible loss to the commerce of the world and peaceful intercourse" would occur. The policy reflected Roosevelt's hope "that the area of the war will be as limited as possible, and that it will be brought to a close with as little loss to either combatant as is possible."[20]

After that initiative during the early days of the war, 1904 proved to be a year of marking time for Roosevelt's plans to mediate. The Japanese were winning victories on the battlefield, so they were unwilling to talk about a negotiated settlement. Despite these reverses, the tsar and his government, expecting an eventual triumph, saw no reason to give a signal of weakness. Each of the major European powers had its own reasons for allowing the fighting to continue because of its impact on their structure of diplomatic alliances. As the fighting persisted, Roosevelt's attitude gradually shifted in response to the continued Japanese successes on the Asian mainland. In mid June 1904 he lunched at the White House with the Japanese minister to the United States, Kogoro Takahira, and with Kentaro Kaneko, a spokesman for Japan who had known Roosevelt at Harvard. The president warned his guests that "their chief danger was lest Japan might get the 'big head' and enter into a general career of insolence and aggression."[21]

These statements and others that Roosevelt made during 1904 did not signal an end to his pro-Japanese views on the war itself. They indicated that he was becoming aware that the interest of the United States might also be at risk if the Japanese were to win too great a military success. Roosevelt also worried that Japan, as its national pride expanded, might not distinguish among western nations that were friendly to it and those that were not. The president and the Japanese had some difficult moments during the second half of 1904. The treatment of U.S. war correspondents by the Japanese army was restrictive and caused complaints to Roosevelt. The seizure of a Russian ship that had taken refuge in Chinese waters also produced some diplomatic strain against Japan in Washington. By the end of the year, Roosevelt had concluded that it was not likely that "Tokyo will show itself a particle more altruistic than St. Petersburg, or for the matter of that, Berlin."[22]

Early in January 1905 the Russian fortress of Port Arthur fell to the Japanese. This major defeat for the Russians produced a round of diplomatic activity looking toward a negotiated settlement. Roosevelt gave renewed attention to how the war might be resolved. Again, the United States took the lead in asking the neutrals not to pursue concessions from China arising out of any eventual peace talks. The State Department sent out a diplomatic circular to that effect on 13 January 1905. In general, the president believed that the Japanese should retain Port Arthur and should exercise a dominant influence over Korea. The powers should guarantee Manchuria as a neutral area under Chinese control. The Japanese agreed generally on the first two points but did not accept the third as a useful solution to the future status of Manchuria.

Roosevelt devoted himself energetically to a mediating role during early 1905. He now had George Meyer in place as his trusted representative in St. Petersburg. During February, Roosevelt met unofficially with his good friend Cecil Spring Rice to work out a joint approach with London toward possible peace terms. No formal alliance resulted, but there was, as Spring Rice put it, "a general community of interest and communion of ideas."[23] Until the situation on the battlefield changed, however, Roosevelt's initiatives as a mediator did not prosper. The Russians had no interest in peace talks while they were losing, and the Japanese did not wish to make an initial step that would be seen as weak.

The diplomatic situation shifted slowly toward peace after military developments that ended during early March 1905. The battle of Mukden brought Japan a tactical victory and the realization among its military leaders that they would soon exhaust their capacity to wage war. Tokyo still wanted to have the Russians ask for peace first, a point on which the Japanese foreign minister, Komura Jutaro, remained adamant throughout March. For Roosevelt there seemed to be every reason to proceed with his long-planned western hunting trip during April and

May 1905. The day before he left, he said to the ailing Hay: "Did you ever know anything more pitiable than the condition of the Russian despotism in this year of grace? The Czar is a preposterous little creature as the absolute autocrat of 150,000,000 people. He has been unable to make war, and he is now unable to make peace."[24]

For the Japanese, however, April was a time when they decided even more strongly that they would have to seek a negotiated peace through the mediating offices of Theodore Roosevelt. The leaders of Japan worked out the important terms they would pursue: these included a free hand with Korea, territorial concessions involving Port Arthur, and the "mutual military evacuation of Manchuria." Having reached that judgment, it was now necessary to have Roosevelt's help in arranging for peace talks.[25]

The Japanese approach began on 18 April 1905 with a report on French efforts to start negotiations. In the course of the note, the Japanese foreign minister observed that "it is not unlikely that the friendly good offices of some Power might be necessary." His government would not "close the door to friendly offices exerted purely for the purpose of bringing the belligerents together." After further exchanges of messages with Roosevelt on his western tour, the president understood that the Japanese were asking him to assist in launching the negotiations. He ended his hunting excursion a week early and returned home. After he was back at the White House, he observed that "just at the moment Russia is riding a high horse and will not talk peace." The Japanese, however, were ready to negotiate, which represented tangible progress.[26]

The Russians hoped that their Baltic Fleet, making its way around the world to Japan, might win a naval victory that would change the war. By May 1905 the world knew that the Russian vessels were approaching Japan. In a battle in the Sea of Japan on 27/28 May, the Russians were smashed. "Neither Trafalgar nor the defeat of the Spanish Armada was as complete—as overwhelming," the president wrote to Kaneko. The Japanese moved promptly to line up Roosevelt's good offices. The president received a message on 21 May in which Tokyo hoped that "the Government of St. Petersburg will now turn its attention to the question of peace." The Japanese wanted Roosevelt "directly and entirely of his own motion and initiative to invite the two belligerents to come together for the purpose of direct negotiation." Roosevelt would thus start the process as the Japanese desired but Tokyo would still not seem to be asking for peace.[27]

While Roosevelt had reservations about the exact terms of the Japanese, his immediate problem was to bring the Russians to the conference table. He believed that "the present contest is absolutely hopeless and that to continue it can only result in the loss of all Russia's possessions in East Asia." The pressure on Tsar Nicholas to agree to peace talks grew during June 1905. The kaiser urged a settlement, and he suggested to Nicholas that Roosevelt might persuade Japan to soften its terms. The president, for his part, did not wish "to be asked to squeeze out of Japan favorable terms to Russia."[28]

On 5 June 1905, Roosevelt cabled Ambassador Meyer to tell the tsar that Russian and Japanese representatives should meet directly "to see if it is not possible for them to agree as to terms of peace." It would be preferable, he added, for the countries involved to talk about peace themselves; an "outside Power" should only "endeavor to arrange the meeting." On the following day, before the statement from the United States had arrived, the tsar decided in a general way, after meeting with his military chiefs, to pursue peace.[29]

Ambassador Meyer met with Nicholas the next day. After a long discussion, the tsar accepted what Roosevelt had proposed. No Russian territory was as yet under Japanese control, Nicholas noted, but enemy forces might yet assault the Russian-owned Sakhalin Island. The time to make peace was before that attack could take place and thus make further fighting necessary. Meyer wired Roosevelt on 7 June 1905 with the good news. The next day the president issued his official offer to the warring powers to "open direct negotiations for peace with one another." The two countries should meet directly, but Roosevelt, while not being part of the talks officially, would be glad to help "in arranging the preliminaries as to the time and place of meeting." A pleased president received back the formal acceptances of Russia and Japan within four days, and the news was made public. Roosevelt wrote Hay: "It really begins to look as if I have got Japan and Russia so that they will be willing to discuss the terms of peace."[30]

"Mr. Roosevelt's success has amazed everybody," wrote a London newspaper after the announcement. The president informed his son Kermit that this achievement had required "infinite labor" as well as "the exercise of a good deal of tact and judgment." Roosevelt's assessment of his deeds was accurate. He had persevered with his peacemaking campaign until the circumstances of the war allowed him to intervene effectively. He had done so with the characteristic secrecy that he brought to diplomacy, and he reaped the benefits of a favorable public reaction. Having arranged for a possible meeting, the president now had to see that peace actually came.[31]

The task proved to be a difficult one. The Russians and the Japanese maneuvered to secure every advantage in the wording of their acceptances and the location of the talks. Weeks elapsed before they agreed to talk at the navy yard in Portsmouth, New Hampshire. The time of the conference was set for early August 1905, and the two delegations began their long journeys to the United States. As June ended, the president exclaimed in a letter to Whitelaw Reid: "Oh Lord! I have been growing nearly mad in an effort to get Russia and Japan together."[32]

Asian policy was on Roosevelt's mind during the summer of 1905. What the attitude of the United States should be toward the victorious Japanese and their ambitions was one concern. Meanwhile in China there was a spreading discontent regarding the treatment of Chinese immigrants and visitors during their sojourns in America. The response in China included a boycott against American goods and coolness toward railroad development within China from entrepreneurs in the United States. With Hay's death and with Elihu Root not yet in place as secretary of state, Roosevelt had to deal with these issues as he grappled with the Russo-Japanese settlement.

The boycott against the United States arose from the continual humiliations that Chinese were subjected to when they came to American territory. The legitimacy of their business did not matter to the heavy-handed exclusionary policy of the Immigration Bureau. Chinese students, even those with letters of introduction from prominent Americans, were photographed, interrogated, and compelled to swear, often after physical or verbal harassment, that they would not compete with domestic laborers. As the prospect of a boycott in China against United States products mounted during the spring and summer of 1905, the president acted to remove part of the irritant to the Chinese. He told the secretary of commerce and labor, Victor Metcalf, that "we will no more tolerate discourtesy or harsh treatment" of Chinese students and travelers than of any other nationality. As a Californian, Metcalf briefly resisted this directive but then agreed to the policy.[33]

Despite Roosevelt's actions, the boycott began on 1 August 1905. As protests poured in from U.S. merchants and those who traded with China, the president indicated his displeasure. "I intend to do the Chinese justice," he informed W. W. Rockhill, the United States minister in Peking, "and am taking a far stiffer tone with my own people than any President has ever yet taken." The predicament left Roosevelt "very much dissatisfied with the Chinese attitude." He agreed that Chinese workers, like the Japanese, should be excluded, but he told a California senator that other Chinese in the United States must have their rights "scrupulously guarded" during their visits or working stays in the country. At the same time, the administration was exploring what its options would be if the boycott continued. Roosevelt hoped that these actions would calm Chinese anxieties and allow him to concentrate on the more pressing problems of Japanese-American relations that were occurring as the peace negotiations between Russia and Japan neared.[34]

Because of the Russo-Japanese situation, the relations of the United States with Japan had a higher priority in Roosevelt's foreign policy than did the feelings of the Chinese or other weak Asian countries. This hard fact determined the fate of the isolated nation of Korea during the summer of 1905. In 1882 the United States and the Hermit Kingdom of Korea had signed a treaty in which Washington agreed to use its "good offices" if another nation should treat Korea "unjustly or oppressively." For the Korean government of Roosevelt's time, that language became a firm U.S. guarantee of their sovereignty against the aggressive Japanese. To Theodore Roosevelt the prospect of war with Japan over Korea was incredible folly. "We can not possibly interfere for the Koreans against Japan," he wrote in late January 1905. "They couldn't strike one blow in their own defence."[35]

Because domination of Korea was a major goal of Japanese diplomacy, Roosevelt believed that the United States had to accept this Japanese intention or Tokyo could turn toward the Philippines, Hawaii, or American interests in China. By 1905 he was aware of the popular sentiment on the Pacific Coast to exclude Japanese immigrants as a potential source of trouble between the two nations. In this context, the independence of Korea carried very little weight in Washington.

An opportunity to confirm this policy with Japan arose in late July 1905. Secretary of War William Howard Taft, on his way to the Philippines, was in Japan, with a party that included the president's daughter Alice. On 27 July the secretary met with the prime minister, Taro Katsura. They reviewed the state of future Japanese-American relations, and Taft then sent a lengthy telegram to Roosevelt. The Japanese leader understood that a formal alliance among the United States, Great Britain, and Japan was not possible, but he hoped for "an alliance in practice if not in name." Taft responded that the president could not make an actual agreement without the Senate's consent. The people of his country shared the views of Japan and Britain about what would bring lasting peace to Asia. If the occasion occurred, Japan could expect "appropriate action" from the United States in a spirit that would be equivalent to a treaty obligation.

What the Japanese really wanted to know was how the United States stood on their presence in Korea. Tokyo deemed it "a matter of absolute importance" that it be allowed to achieve "a complete solution of the peninsula question" once the war with Russia was over. Taft responded that Japanese mastery of Korea would be "the logical result of the present war and would directly contribute to permanent peace in the East." He expected Roosevelt to agree with him. Taft could make the gesture because he knew Roosevelt's views and also because Katsura had told Taft that Japan did not "harbor any aggressive designs whatever on the Philippines."[36]

The two men prepared a memorandum of their talk, which Taft telegraphed to Secretary of State Root on 29 July. Roosevelt received the message himself and wired back that Taft's conversation was "absolutely correct in every respect." He confirmed what Taft had said as a statement of the American position. When the substance of the episode leaked out in Japan a few months later, Roosevelt again said that Taft had accurately stated his position. The Taft-Katsura Agreement, as it became known during the 1920s, was not a clandestine treaty. There was no bargain as such. The Japanese and the Americans had simply reasserted their positions in temporary partnership as the peacemaking process opened formally in New Hampshire during early August 1905.[37]

The Russian and Japanese delegations stayed first in New York City. They went separately on 5 August to Oyster Bay to have a ceremonial luncheon on the presidential yacht, *Mayflower*. Roosevelt handled the delicate diplomatic occasion with a high degree of "admirable tact" and discretion. He arranged for the delegates to drink a joint toast, while standing, "to the welfare and prosperity of the sovereigns and peoples of the two great nations, whose representatives have met one another on this ship." The Russians and their Japanese counterparts then went off in separate vessels to Portsmouth.[38]

The Russians were led by Count Sergei Yulyevich Witte, a reluctant choice of the tsar's because of Witte's well-known opposition to the war. Komura Jutaro headed the Japanese contingent. The issue that promised to give the two sides the most difficulty was whether, as the price of a settlement, Russia should pay Japan an indemnity for the cost of the conflict. Almost as sensitive was the status of Sakhalin Island, which the Japanese occupied and whose fate they wished to control. Other less-contentious problems were easily worked out during the early stages of the negotiations. "I do hope that Russia will make peace," Roosevelt wrote a few days before the deliberations opened.[39]

The president now had a large stake in the conference, and he followed the talks closely. Believing that Russia was defeated and should make the best peace possible, he somewhat underestimated the tenacity of Tsar Nicholas. Roosevelt also thought that the Japanese insistence on an indemnity was misguided. It would be wrong to pursue further fighting for monetary reasons. During the negotiation he was not aware of the desperate financial and military predicament of the Japanese and their need for a settlement. Overall he still hoped for a result that would preserve the balance of power in Asia. He watched the first ten days of the conference as the two sides reduced the number of unresolved issues and the indemnity problem assumed a greater importance. There the talks stalled, and the possibility of a deadlock seemed real by 18 August 1905.

Roosevelt sought to work out an acceptable settlement himself. He spoke to Kaneko about a compromise involving the cession of Sakhalin to Japan and an arbitration of the indemnity problem. That idea was quickly overshadowed by a proposal that Witte and Komura developed but Russia rejected. By 21 August, matters were as deadlocked as they had been earlier. On that day Roosevelt again acted. Through George Meyer, the president sent the tsar a long cable, which offered Japanese cession of the northern half of Sakhalin and Russian payment for the release of prisoners and the return of that part of the island. Roosevelt's initiative came at a propitious moment. The Russian government had sent Witte instructions to end its participation in the conference. With Roosevelt's message to the tsar, Witte had good reason to disobey these orders and keep the talks in motion. In that sense, Roosevelt's part in the peace conference proved decisive.

The president had less to do with the actual outcome of the Portsmouth Conference that came a week later, on 29 August 1905. In the end the Japanese believed that peace was more in their interest than was a continuation of the fighting. They decided to return the northern half of Sakhalin and to give up any demand for a monetary indemnity. For his part, Witte acted on his own to accept these terms, despite the willingness of Tsar Nicholas to fight on. Roosevelt was "overjoyed at the news" and concluded that "the Japanese government has acted most wisely."[40] The treaty was signed on 2 September 1905.

The leaders of both Russia and Japan viewed with some skepticism the peace that they had made. In Tokyo crowds rioted against the treaty. Within Russia the tsar and other national leaders still had illusions that victory could have been achieved in the end. Elsewhere the world recognized that the settlement was in the interest of both sides. Congratulations poured in to Oyster Bay, and the press praised the president's mediating role. The editors of *Outlook* said that Roosevelt had "typified to the world American courage and daring," and these qualities had allowed him "to bring these two warring nations to agree."[41]

In 1906, Roosevelt received the Nobel Peace Prize for his efforts. He naturally enjoyed the acclaim that came to him, some of it from people who rarely praised his presidency. "Just at the moment people are

187

speaking altogether too well of me," he told a friend, and he expected a shift in the public reaction.[42] The president attributed much of his success to his personal style, which had put aside the usual diplomatic techniques in the pursuit of a settlement. Equally important had been the circumstances that had made him a logical mediator once the two sides had seen that they could not force a decision on the battlefield. Roosevelt's information about the war situation was not always accurate. He overestimated the Japanese position and underrated the determination of the tsar and his government to hold out even in a seemingly hopeless diplomatic predicament. Roosevelt was the vital force in keeping the negotiations going at several key points in the process. While the Russians and the Japanese might have found a way to make peace without Roosevelt's aid, it is clear that he provided the means for the two nations to end a war that neither could fight for much longer. The Russians were beset with popular displeasure about the costs of the conflict. The Japanese government knew that it could neither sustain the war effort nor pay for it with the nation's financial resources. In that context, Roosevelt's services as an honest broker were vital to the peaceful outcome.

The end of the Russo-Japanese War had unhappy results for one of the countries in the region. In the Portsmouth Treaty, Russia recognized Japan's predominance in Korea. The Japanese then moved during the autumn of 1905 to establish their protectorate to achieve practical control over Korea. The Koreans relied on the 1882 treaty and sought to have the United States intervene to save them from the Japanese. Roosevelt and Root declined to act during November 1905 because in practical terms the administration had no choice. There was no way to help the Koreans short of a dangerous U.S. confrontation with Japan, a policy that had no appeal for Theodore Roosevelt.

At the same time the issue of China and the boycott against American goods continued to cause concern. There were riots against missionaries in Canton at the end of October. Roosevelt took steps to move navy units into position along the Chinese coast "as speedily as possible." In the president's mind, "the Chinese are not showing a good spirit." Roosevelt also renewed his efforts to eliminate some of the cause of the Chinese irritation. He told leaders of the anti-Chinese protest on the West Coast that the United States must be able to say that "all just cause of complaint by the Chinese against us has been removed." He repeated this theme in his annual message several weeks later.[43]

Continued violence against foreigners in China during December led Roosevelt to send more troops to the Philippines during January 1906. He urged Taft to be sure to dispatch enough men: "We ought not to take any chances. We cannot afford a disaster." Combined with Roosevelt's diplomatic pressure, the policy brought some Chinese concessions and a gradual decline in the boycott by the spring of 1906. The problem of the attitude of the people of the United States, especially on the West Coast, toward Oriental immigration had not been solved. It would soon flare up again, as far as Japanese in the United States were concerned, and force the president to face once again the difficulties of the nation's policy toward Asia.[44]

As for Russian-American relations, the end of the war with Japan and the onset of the revolution of 1905 made diplomacy between the two countries less intense than it had been. The issue of persecution of the Jews in Russia still troubled Jewish citizens in the United States, and the Białystok massacre in June 1906 led to American inquiries about these events. The Russians responded with their standard assertion that it was an internal affair with which Washington was not concerned. Meanwhile, the Japanese and the Russians drew closer together, to the disadvantage of American interests in Manchuria and the maintenance of the Open Door in China.

The Russo-Japanese War and the issue of the United States role in the Far East was not the only area in world politics that engaged Roosevelt's attention during the opening years of his second term. Beginning in 1905 and continuing for more than a year, culminating in the Algeciras Conference of 1906, he played a key role in the international tensions between France, Germany, and Great Britain that were shaping European affairs in the decade before the First World War.

The Algeciras Conference grew out of Franco-German rivalry regarding Morocco which flared up in 1905. Morocco had little intrinsic international interest, but it was the setting for a confrontation between Paris and Berlin that reflected the more profound differences between the two European powers. France and Great Britain had entered into the Entente Cordiale in 1904, and France then moved to assert itself in Morocco. The Germans decided that they should oppose France and test the cohesion of the entente. The symbolic gesture that triggered the international crisis took place when the kaiser stopped off at Tangier on 31 March 1905, spoke out for Moroccan independence, and called for an international meeting about the issue. The Germans' move was based in part on the idea that their nation might secure U.S. support against Britain and France. In the process, Theodore Roosevelt was drawn into the machinations of international diplomacy.

The Germans laid the groundwork for their anti-French campaign with an approach to the president during the late winter and early spring of 1905. The German foreign office remembered the Perdicaris episode of 1904, and it also thought that the cooperation of their two countries in support of the Open Door in China at this time could serve as the basis of additional joint action. These elements, as well as a confidence in the apparent closeness between Ambassador Hermann Speck von Sternburg and Roosevelt, led the Germans to attempt to enlist the president in their campaign against the French position in Morocco. The initiative began in late February 1905, but a key opening event was a meeting between Sternburg and Roosevelt on 6 March 1905. The German envoy conveyed a message from the kaiser, asking the United States to support Germany's position toward Morocco, even to the possible extent of military action. Roosevelt responded with the statement that "I did not see my way clear to interfere in the matter, for I did not think that our interests were sufficiently great."[45]

After the kaiser's visit to Tangier in late March, the Germans came back to Roosevelt with a renewed request to endorse their conference idea. The message arrived during Roosevelt's western hunting trip, and he told Taft that the United States had "other fish to fry and we have no real interest in Morocco." That kind of talk did not quell the German desire to enlist Roosevelt on their side, and in mid April 1905 they made another proposal that he inform England of the American desire for a conference.[46] Throughout the rest of the month and into May the Germans asked Roosevelt several times to press London on this point. While Roosevelt had reservations about the direction and quality of British diplomacy at this time, he had little intention of allowing himself to be used against Britain in the interest of Germany. He was also becoming more and more inclined to favor France in the Moroccan dispute.

By early June 1905, with Roosevelt back from his trip, the European situation had reached a crisis. The French foreign minister, Théophile Delcassé, resigned because of his anti-German stance. Relations between France and Germany worsened to the point of a possible war. By this time, Roosevelt had moved even closer to the French position. Recalling his feelings a year later, he said: "I desired to do anything I legitimately could for France; because I like France, and I thought her in this instance to be in the right." Despite the removal of the French leader, the crisis continued during June. On 11 June the kaiser sent another message to Roosevelt, which warned of a possible conflict and again sought Roosevelt's influence to "prevent England from joining a Franco-German war, started by the aggressive policy of France in Morocco."[47]

With war a possibility, Roosevelt approached France and argued that a conference was in its interest. He told Ambassador Jean Jules

Jusserand that, if it was required, he would adopt "very strong grounds against any attitude of Germany which seemed to be unjust and unfair" during U.S. participation in any talks.[48] Roosevelt's sympathy for France, in addition to the close personal relationship he had already formed with Jusserand, would be an important consideration in persuading the French to trust him during the negotiations that followed.

The French did not want to have a conference, but they also did not wish to fight Germany over Morocco. They decided to accept a conference at the same time that Roosevelt was urging them to adopt that course. It took more time to shape the precise wording of an agreement. Roosevelt confided in Jusserand and flattered Sternburg about the kaiser in order to move matters along. The president produced language that allowed both sides to participate but that accorded France much of what it sought.

Ambassador Sternburg was not a skillful diplomat, and he did not always report accurately what Roosevelt told him. His blunder about Algeciras, however, arose because of his need to maintain his access to the president. To be sure that Roosevelt would see him and not shunt him off to the secretary of state, Sternburg usually treated the dispatches he received as direct messages from the kaiser as if they were aimed for the eyes of the president. Thus, when he received instructions from his government in late June, he transformed them into a commitment from his nation's leader. Berlin told Sternburg to inform Roosevelt that should problems arise in negotiations for the conference with France, Germany would accept "the same decisions as President Roosevelt will commend as practical and fair." Sternburg had it read as if the kaiser, "in every case, will be ready to back up the decision which you [Roosevelt] should consider to be the most fair and the most practical" during the conference itself. Roosevelt called this latter statement "extraordinary," and it was singular to receive what amounted to a diplomatic line of credit. The president informed the French that he possessed the means to influence the Germans decisively if he wished to do so.[49]

By early July 1905, Germany and France had achieved an understanding in regard to a Moroccan conference. The rest of the year was taken up with bringing all the concerned nations together. The site for the meeting was Algeciras, Spain. The United States was formally invited to participate in the conference when the sultan of Morocco asked nations to attend on 31 July 1905. Roosevelt first asked Joseph Hodges Choate to head the United States delegation. The president told the veteran diplomat-lawyer: "We have no interest in the matter, save the interest of trying to keep matters on an even keel in Europe." Choate turned the appointment down, and Roosevelt selected instead Henry

White, then ambassador to Italy. The informal instructions that the delegation received in 1905 stressed the importance of "the continued Entente Cordiale between France and England" as a key element.[50]

The United States involvement in European affairs had remained out of the public eye. The disclosure of imminent participation in the conference prompted senatorial critics to press for information about the role of the United States in this European meeting. Senator A. O. Bacon (D., Ga.) introduced a resolution that asked for the documents about the conference and for the administration's intentions. The senator contended that involvement beyond strictly commercial issues would violate "the settled policy of this Government since its foundation to abstain from taking part in such political controversies between European nations."[51]

The Senate debated this question into February 1906. The administration told the lawmakers that U.S. delegates would only listen, not vote. Large portions of the documents and instructions to the diplomats were released. Root went before the Senate Foreign Relations Committee in mid January to minimize the political issues and to stress the nation's interest in upholding the Open Door for trade in Morocco. On the Senate floor, John C. Spooner and Henry Cabot Lodge offered broad defenses of the president's power in foreign policy. In February 1906 the debate wound down without any action on Bacon's resolution. There remained the problem of Senate acceptance of any treaty that emerged from the deliberations at Algeciras.

The conference itself convened on 16 January 1906. Henry White played a central part in the informal discussions where the real work was done. The United States did not take part in all the subjects that the conference covered. Its representatives focused on the problem of how Morocco would be policed under general French supervision. Here the Germans once again operated at a disadvantage in seeking American help because of Roosevelt's pro-French leanings and his closeness to Jusserand.

When the meeting reached a crisis in mid February and talk of war revived, the United States acted to end the stalemate. Roosevelt put forward to the Germans a proposal designed to move negotiations forward. The plan was strongly weighted toward France on the issue of police, who would be trained and managed by French and Spanish officers. The Germans and the kaiser accepted some parts of Roosevelt's draft, but they balked at the key provision. Yet, Berlin knew that its diplomatic situation was weak and that it could not fight a war over Morocco. The United States was not yet aware of Germany's predicament. Roosevelt decided, after hearing from Henry White about the possibility of an impasse, to redeem the apparent promise that the kaiser had made to him in late June 1905.

On 7 March 1906, Roosevelt informed the kaiser about what the earlier dispatch had said; Roosevelt also reiterated the administration's backing for his initiative. The Germans were naturally surprised at what Sternburg had done, but there was little they could do about it. Roosevelt also told Jusserand that he had held the kaiser to the pledge, and this news persuaded the French to hold out for more concessions.

By now the Germans were in retreat because of their unwillingness to challenge France on the Moroccan problem and because of Roosevelt's possession of Sternburg's promise, which the president was willing to publish if necessary. Issues of language over the police problem still had to be worked out, but the elements of an arrangement favorable to France were in place by March 1906. The treaty that embodied the settlement was signed on 6 April 1906. As far as the United States was concerned directly, the treaty related only to issues of commerce and the rights of its citizens traveling in the area. There was no overt linkage to the European diplomatic implications of the pact. In signing the treaty for the United States, Henry White stated that his government did so "without assuming obligation or responsibility for the enforcement thereof." The language reaffirmed traditional U.S. policy and also helped to reassure doubtful senators who would have to approve the treaty.[52]

The Algeciras Conference represented a serious setback for the Germans, for which President Roosevelt was to a large extent responsible. As he often did with the kaiser, the president buried the bad news under a heavy coating of public flattery. "While I was most suave and pleasant with the Emperor," he later told Whitelaw Reid, "yet when it became necessary at the end I stood him on his head with great decision." That task having been accomplished, Roosevelt did not stint in his expressions of praise. To an audience of German-Americans that he asked Sternburg to assemble at the White House, Roosevelt observed that nowhere else "is there a warmer admiration for Germany and for Germany's exalted ruler, Emperor William, than here in America." He added words of congratulations for Germany's part in the peaceful results of the conference.[53]

None of this could fully mask the range of the diplomatic humiliation that the Germans had experienced. Part of their problem was Sternburg's diplomatic failings. He did not represent the views of his government accurately, nor did he see through Roosevelt's manipulation of him. Sternburg took the visible manifestations of Roosevelt's friendship as the hard coin of genuine collaboration. In contrast, Jusserand was much more deft and assured, and he worked with the president in the larger interest of France. The episode also left Roosevelt more and more convinced that Sir Mortimer Durand was inadequate as the British ambassador, and the president would soon launch a campaign to have Durand replaced.

In diplomatic terms, Roosevelt's intervention in the Moroccan situation had been instrumental in securing agreement to have a conference held, and he had aided the French and strengthened their entente with Great Britain. Roosevelt thought that it would be best for Morocco to be under full French control, no matter how that might bother the Germans. For all the flattery that he pushed toward the kaiser, Roosevelt had added somewhat to the German feeling of being surrounded by hostile powers. A less sweeping defeat in 1906 might have eased the German sense of persecution a little. Nonetheless, the personalized diplomacy of the president had produced short-term benefits for European stability.

The Algeciras Treaty had to go before the Senate for its advice and consent before the end of 1906. Secretary Root submitted the pact on 25 May 1906 and asked the legislators to act promptly. The Democrats postponed action on the treaty during the remainder of that session of Congress because the Republicans lacked the votes to assure passage. Roosevelt tried making personal appeals to key lawmakers. "I am literally unable to understand how any human being can find anything whatever to object to in this treaty," he told Shelby M. Cullom on 26 June. With Bacon in the lead, the Democrats regarded the treaty as an unwise and inappropriate involvement in European affairs.[54]

As the administration prepared to press for approval of the treaty during December 1906, Henry White came back to the United States, at Roosevelt's request, to lobby with undecided senators. In his annual message, the president asserted that the pact "does not entail a single obligation of any kind upon us, and I earnestly hope it may be speedily ratified." The Senate consented to the ratification of the Algeciras Treaty in mid December, after it had appended a significant reservation. This stated the economic and commercial purposes of American approval and asserted that there was no purpose "to depart from the traditional American foreign policy which forbids participation by the United States in the settlement of political questions which are entirely European in their scope." The president did not like the implications of the reservation, but it was the price of getting the treaty approved.[55]

The end of the Algeciras Conference in the spring of 1906 closed out a memorable eighteen months of diplomatic achievement for Roosevelt. The Peace of Portsmouth, the Roosevelt Corollary, and the Algeciras

Conference were high points of Roosevelt's foreign policy. He had fostered international order in the Caribbean, in Asia, and in Europe, as he saw it, through the exercise of effective personal diplomacy. "I do not believe that this country has ever done more for peace than it has done during the last five years," he wrote in September 1906.[56]

Roosevelt's style in foreign affairs had worked well during this stage of his presidency. Because no vital interests of the United States were involved in the Russo-Japanese War or in the Moroccan crisis, he could practice diplomacy at the highest level through his chosen ambassadors without concern for domestic public opinion. He also enjoyed a position as a natural mediating force among the powers involved. Some of his success depended on the good sense of Jusserand and the blunders of Sternburg, but Roosevelt properly received the bulk of the credit. As the restiveness of the Senate revealed, with regard to Morocco and Santo Domingo, the president was approaching the limits of his discretionary authority in foreign policy by the middle of 1906.

The diplomatic issues that Roosevelt faced, like his program for governmental regulation of the economy, did not exhaust his restless energies during his second term. In the administration of his office and of the federal government, he found many problems that required executive action. One of the central aspects of Roosevelt's personalized presidency was his conduct as an administrator, where he set patterns that other presidents would extend after he left the White House.

9

★ ★ ★ ★ ★

ROOSEVELT THE ADMINISTRATOR, 1905–1909

During the spring of 1908 an English writer said that Theodore Roosevelt had "gathered around him a body of public servants who are nowhere surpassed, I question whether they are anywhere equalled, for efficiency, self-sacrifice, and an absolute devotion to their country's interests." Roosevelt was so pleased that he sent copies of the quotation, along with a letter of his own, to the various executive departments. The praise reflected Roosevelt's own view of his administrative style and the values he wanted in his government.[1]

The talents that Roosevelt brought to administration as president have often been noted. Less attention has been devoted to how he functioned as the chief executive officer of the federal government. Freed from the immediate constraints that Congress imposed in legislative matters, the president exercised what he later called the stewardship theory of presidential power. His authority "was limited only by specific restrictions and prohibitions appearing in the Constitution or imposed by the Congress under its constitutional powers." There was no need to wait for "some specific authorization" to take a needed action in the public interest. Instead, the chief executive should act, "unless such action was forbidden by the Constitution or by the laws." As Roosevelt phrased it in his autobiography, "I did not usurp power, but I did greatly broaden the use of executive power."[2]

A central thrust of Roosevelt's administrative style was to select qualified subordinates and let them exercise their own judgment. The policy brought a large number of able men into the government service.

197

The more favored among them became part of the president's "Tennis Cabinet," which came to the White House to join Roosevelt on the mansion's courts and often stayed to discuss affairs of state. Gifford Pinchot, James R. Garfield, Charles P. Neill of the Bureau of Labor, Herbert Knox Smith of the Bureau of Corporations, and others made up this informal group. It existed as much in spirit as in fact, but it was a key component in the high morale among segments of the governmental bureaucracy while Roosevelt was in office.

The designation of particular officials as presidential intimates led to some resentment against those who were called the "Incense Swingers" around Roosevelt. The readiness of junior members of the administration to use their power freely in pursuit of the president's goals was another element in the political resentment that mounted over the course of the second term. One conservative Republican complained that the president and his subordinates were "consciously, or unconsciously, . . . trying to concentrate all power in Washington, to practically wipe out state lines, and to govern the people by commissions and bureaus."[3]

Throughout Roosevelt's second term there was a large component of personal executive discretion that the president deemed appropriate to the task of his administration. The exercise of such presidential power was one of Roosevelt's major contributions to the growth in the authority and influence of his office. While this approach gave him a greater opportunity to do good things for the nation, Roosevelt paid less attention to the constitutional limits within which presidents operated.

A significant administrative problem for any president was to balance the competing imperatives of political patronage and civil-service reform. In his handling of Mark Hanna between 1901 and 1904 and in his support of William Howard Taft's presidential bid during 1907/8, Roosevelt showed himself a master in the subtle art of using offices and appointments to achieve a practical political objective. The president was equally adroit in the day-to-day management of the loaves and the fishes of politics. During late June 1906, for example, he had to mediate a dispute between the two Wisconsin senators, John C. Spooner and Robert M. La Follette, over a contested post-office appointment in that state. Roosevelt also displayed a continuing concern for his old comrades from the Rough Riders. For example, he turned to George Curry of New Mexico, who had been with Roosevelt in Cuba, when scandals were revealed in the territory's government in 1906.

Despite the need to respect the patronage demands of his fellow politicians, President Roosevelt also won the admiration and support of the civil-service reform movement that intently watched all presidents for undue deference to the spoils system. During his presidency, the classified civil service—positions that were subject to competitive examination—grew from just over 46 percent of the total governmental service to 66 percent by the time he stepped down. The number of classified positions increased by more than 116,000, and Roosevelt broadened the number of agencies and bureaus that were under civil-service rules. In general, Roosevelt issued and enforced regulations to curb federal employees from direct involvement in partisan affairs or political campaigns. At the end of his term, for example, he placed fourth-class postmasters, who had been bastions of the patronage system, under the classified rules. Even while supporting Taft's nomination in 1908, Roosevelt asserted that his appointments, while helpful to the Republican candidate, did not violate civil-service procedures. The president's friend William Dudley Foulke said that Roosevelt had been "more consistent and energetic" in pursuing civil-service principles than the other chief executives from Benjamin Harrison to Woodrow Wilson.[4]

Roosevelt did not want an honest and efficient government for its own sake. He believed that the president should pursue policies that benefited the nation with as much vigor as possible. The conservation of natural resources became such a policy because it blended desirable goals with Roosevelt's faith in executive authority. Decision making in conservation belonged to trained experts who worked for the federal government. "It was necessary," Roosevelt wrote, "to use what law was already in existence, and then further to supplement it by Executive action." Such a philosophy well suited Gifford Pinchot, who believed "in the use of the law for the public good, and the construction of it for the public welfare." The instruments of the president would be the experienced professionals whom Pinchot assembled in what became the Forest Service.[5]

Pinchot's power grew out of an administrative change that was authorized early in 1905. In his 1904 annual message the president asked Congress to approve the transfer of responsibility for management of the national forests from the Department of the Interior to the Department of Agriculture, where Pinchot's agency was located. The result would be "a better handling of all forest work," because it would be "under a single head." Two months later, Congress agreed, and the transfer was approved. Roosevelt signed the bill on 1 February 1905. Pinchot changed the name of his unit from the Bureau of Forestry to the Forest Service. "From that time on," Pinchot wrote later, "it was fight, fight, fight."[6]

Gifford Pinchot was approaching his fortieth birthday. A graduate of Yale who had studied forestry in Germany, the young man from a privileged background had made forestry his career during the 1890s. He was named chief forester in the Bureau of Forestry in 1898 and became a pioneer in the field in the United States. Pinchot was a tall, thin man who had an intense stare and a noticeable mustache. The president admired Pinchot's "tireless energy and activity, his fearlessness, his complete disinterestedness, his single-minded devotion to the interests of the plain people, and his extraordinary efficiency." These same qualities often struck Pinchot's enemies as highhandedness and ruthlessness in pursuing his goals. "P. is ambitious," concluded John Muir, "and never hesitates to sacrifice anything or anybody in his way." Pinchot's closeness to Roosevelt, as well as their similar views about resource policy, gave Pinchot a decisive influence within the White House until 1909.[7]

The Transfer Act and other legislation of 1905 gave Pinchot and his colleagues some powerful administrative weapons. The transfer measure created a special fund of money that came from the sale of forest products or the use of forest lands. It was, Pinchot noted, "in a way, the power to make our own appropriations." Eventually the Forest Service also obtained authority over the revenues from grazing rights and water-power leases. From other congressional enactments, Pinchot's agency gained the right "to make arrests for the violation of laws and regulations relating to the forest reserves and national parks." In the hands of a vigorous and forceful executive such as Pinchot, these provisions represented a grant of discretion to implement his vision of how the nation should oversee its natural heritage.[8]

The need for better management of the public lands, forests, mineral rights and grazing areas had become very evident by 1905. The Oregon land scandals, uncovered during Roosevelt's first term, had ensnared additional politicians in that state in a spreading network of corrupt relationships. Senator John H. Mitchell, a Republican, was convicted of accepting money from land companies in return for his political influence. The commissioner of the General Land Office, Binger Hermann, had to resign over his conduct, and several congressmen from Oregon were implicated. So were less-prominent public officials in Oregon. The federal prosecutor in charge of the case, Francis J. Heney, became a public figure who handled other notorious graft inquiries for the Roosevelt administration.

Pinchot plunged into the process of creating regulations that would establish the centralized order that he and the president sought for federal policy on resources. Secretary of Agriculture James Wilson was ready to allow Pinchot scope for his energies. The chief forester built morale within his agency by using professional methods while he expanded the range of its supervision. After his election, the president used executive orders to increase the acreage of the nation's forest reserves. During 1905/6 the total of reserve forests went up from almost 86 million acres to about 107 million acres. Sales of timber and grazing fees in the national forests brought in around $800,000 in revenues, nearly equal to the amount that Congress had appropriated for Pinchot's work.

A shrewd political operator, Pinchot set up a publicity bureau that issued press releases when reserves were created or when other policies were adopted. Pinchot called this "educational work" that furthered the mission of the service. Members of the service also attended and sometimes influenced meetings of western livestock associations and other interested groups. Opponents of Pinchot's policies believed that he was trying to manipulate and dominate public opinion. Under Roosevelt the press agentry of the service foreshadowed an expansion of the government's presence in this field.[9]

During the remainder of 1905, Pinchot pushed forward the administration's conservation program. Roosevelt issued a series of proclamations that expanded the forest reserves in Colorado, New Mexico, Utah, California, Arizona, and elsewhere in the West, wherever it seemed, in the language of the law, "that the public good would be promoted by setting apart and reserving said lands as a public reservation." In Colorado, for example, he established eleven new forest reserves that covered almost 8.9 million acres of public land.[10]

In his 1905 annual message, Roosevelt told Congress that "the forest policy of the Administration appears to enjoy the unbroken support of the people. The great users of timber are themselves forwarding the movement for forest preservation."[11] Major timber companies did support what Roosevelt and Pinchot were doing. The forest service and the industry had a shared interest in scientific management of the forests that emphasized a sustained yield of forest products. Elsewhere in the West, however, among the smaller economic interests that used the national forests, unhappiness with Pinchot was mounting.

One focus of protest was the proposal, announced in mid 1905, to charge a fee to western sheep and cattle raisers who grazed their stock in the national forests. Pinchot had obtained legal authority for this new policy with his customary shrewdness. He had posed the question on a matter seemingly unrelated to the real issue, the use of a tract of forest land in Alaska for a "fish saltery, oil, and fertilizer plant." In a letter to Attorney General William H. Moody, Secretary Wilson sought a legal opinion supporting the policy of charging a rental fee for the use of forest land in this way. Pinchot had chosen the Alaska case because "there was nothing to be gained by arousing opposition" through a direct request for grazing fees in national forests. When it seemed that Moody would not respond favorably, Pinchot took the issue to the attorney general and then to the president. Roosevelt agreed with Pinchot, Moody issued the opinion stating that it was legal to obtain "reasonable compensation" for a lease or permit within a national forest, and the program was duly announced, to go into effect on 1 January 1906. The criticism from the West was intense, but Roosevelt endorsed what Pinchot had done.[12]

There was no pause in the administration's conservation initiatives during 1906. Congress passed the National Monuments Act on 8 June 1906, and Roosevelt created four national monuments before the year ended. There would be eighteen during his presidency. Other laws of 1906 established a game preserve in the Grand Canyon and set up regulations for the hunting of wildlife in the District of Columbia. The president's campaign to create national bird reservations also continued.

The possible abuse of public lands that contained potential coal deposits led to further administrative action during 1906. Sixty-six million acres of this part of the public domain was withdrawn from public entry between late July and mid November 1906. The aim of the White House was to secure a rational survey of the coal land and to achieve a price for federal holdings that would reflect the market value of the mineral. On 29 June 1906, Roosevelt asked Secretary of the Interior Hitchcock for a report on coal lands whose value made them candidates for withdrawal from entry. In a special message to Congress on 17 December 1906, Roosevelt sought "vigorous and immediate action to recast the public land laws." The existing coal law put "a premium on fraud" and did not encourage the proper development of profitable coal deposits. An attempt to embody this idea in legislation failed in Congress early in 1907.[13]

During their conservation campaign, Roosevelt and Pinchot continually sought greater institutional cooperation from the departments of agriculture and interior. Secretary Hitchcock of the Interior Department approached the enforcement of the land laws in a spirit of precise adherence to the letter of the law. He did not approve of Pinchot's initiatives such as the leasing of the public domain and commercial ventures in the national parks. The Forest Service and the General Land Office did not cooperate effectively in the execution of the administration's policies. Pinchot and the White House blamed the Land Office for much of the tension.

By the end of 1906, Roosevelt was becoming disenchanted with Hitchcock's performance. In public the secretary asserted that widespread fraud still existed in the land system. Some officials, Hitchcock said, were "bringing reproach upon the public service." He also accused Senator Francis E. Warren (R., Wyo.) of illegal fencing and other misdeeds. Although Warren's practices were illegal, he was an influential westerner who had supported Roosevelt's resource policies. He also chaired the Senate Military Affairs Committee. Because Roosevelt was facing an attack in Congress over his discharge of black soldiers in a shooting incident in Brownsville, Texas, Senator Warren was no one to confront as Hitchcock was doing. By December, Roosevelt had decided that Hitchcock's department had "utterly gone to pieces." The secretary should resign; James R. Garfield of the Bureau of Corporations would succeed him; and a new commissioner of the Land Office would be named. After several candidates declined, Richard A. Ballinger of Washington State was named as commissioner early in March 1907.[14]

As these changes in leadership occurred, the conservation issue moved toward another confrontation on Capitol Hill. In his annual message, Roosevelt commented that "no government policy for the betterment of our internal conditions has been more fruitful of good than this." Several actions indicated the administration's additional purposes. Roosevelt sent in his special message on 17 December 1906, the size of the national forests increased, land-law practices were closely supervised, and the money available to the Forest Service grew. On 8 January 1907, Senator Elmer J. Burkett (R., Nebr.) introduced legislation that would have created a land-leasing system under the control of the Department of Agriculture and, presumably, Gifford Pinchot. The 1907 appropriation bill contained language that also gave the department control over grazing rights on the public domain. Western opponents of Pinchot assailed bureaucrats who "sit within their marble halls and theorize and dream of forests conserved."[15]

The agriculture appropriation bill became the focus for discontent with Pinchot and his policies. A proposed increase in the forester's salary was attacked. Those who opposed Roosevelt "on account of 'centralization'" saw an opportunity "to get their teeth in" the administration's policies. Their vehicle became an amendment that Senator Charles W. Fulton (R., Oreg.) offered to the agriculture measure on 22 February 1907. Unhappy with the prosecution of the land frauds in his state because of his own partial involvement, Fulton proposed to bar, "except by act of Congress," the creation of new forest reserves in Oregon and five other western states. The amendment, which the Senate adopted, directly challenged Roosevelt's authority over land and forest policy.[16]

The president knew that he could not veto such an appropriation bill over the forest-reserve issue. With adjournment scheduled for 4

March 1907, he worked with Pinchot to prepare proclamations that created twenty-one new reserves in the states that the amendment covered. The proclamation was signed on 2 March 1907. "If I did not act," Roosevelt wrote, "reserves which I consider very important for the interests of the United States would be wholly or in part dissipated before Congress has an opportunity again to consider the matter." With a characteristically assertive personal exercise of his official powers, Roosevelt had seized the initiative from his rivals.[17]

Both sides could claim some success from the 1906/7 legislative battles. Pinchot received a salary increase, and the appropriation for the Forest Service went up by a million dollars. The discretionary fund that timber and grazing-rights money had built up was abolished, however, and closer checks were imposed on Pinchot's procedures. Roosevelt's dramatic eleventh-hour creation of the reserves and his other land withdrawals aroused even more intense opposition in the West and stimulated further congressional restraints on the conservation program.

Roosevelt and Pinchot launched a number of conservation-related initiatives during the next two years. On 14 March 1907 the president appointed a commission "to prepare and report a comprehensive plan for the improvement and control of the river systems of the United States." In his letter creating the panel—which consisted of lawmakers, bureaucrats, and a member of the Army Corps of Engineers—Roosevelt argued that it was time to move beyond water projects with "a single purpose" and to develop a plan that would "include all the uses to which streams may be put." The commission should work out procedures that would "bring together and co-ordinate the points of view of all users of water."[18]

The Inland Waterways Commission (IWC) spent the next year analyzing the whole range of waterway issues. Its report to Roosevelt in February 1908 endorsed the multiple-purpose concept that the president favored. The Corps of Engineers opposed the report because of that provision. When legislation to implement the recommendations of the IWC reached Congress early in 1908, its reception was tepid. Senator Francis G. Newlands (D., Nev.) introduced a bill that would have centralized all water-resource problems under a single agency with independent funding. The Corps of Engineers and congressmen who were concerned about pork-barrel priorities did not like that innovative approach. The original Newlands bill died in a Senate committee. In the House, the chair of the IWC, Congressman Theodore E. Burton (R., Ohio), backed a watered-down version of the Newlands plan. That idea cleared the House but was pigeonholed in the Senate.

Roosevelt's flexible and eclectic administrative approach on resource matters also emerged in waterpower where he wanted to have dams on rivers provide revenues for other projects to develop streams. Beginning in late 1907, Roosevelt, probably under Pinchot's influence, concluded that the government should be reimbursed when it granted the right to construct a dam on public lands. The basis for this policy was the language in the General Dam Act of 1906, which allowed the War Department and the Corps of Engineers to set such conditions as were "necessary to protect the present and future interests of the United States." Eager to be free of the constraints of the congressional funding process, Roosevelt said that this language meant that the government could impose charges. Taft and the Corps of Engineers disagreed. [19]

To overcome this bureaucratic opposition, the president designated Pinchot as his spokesman on the issue and insisted that the War Department toe the administration's line. In effect Roosevelt circumvented the department that was legally charged with formulating policy because it differed with him, and he shifted jurisdiction to the more friendly arena of James R. Garfield's Interior Department. The technique demonstrated Roosevelt's adroitness as an administrator. To Secretary of War Taft it became one of the indicators of the legal dangers in Roosevelt's expansive view of the powers of his office.

With Congress unlikely to grant the White House more authority over conservation during 1907 and 1908, Roosevelt and Pinchot relied on a high-profile public-relations strategy to mobilize support for their position at the end of the second term. When the western critics of the administration organized the Public Lands Convention for June 1907 in Denver, the president sent his response with Pinchot, who delivered it to the meeting. In a public letter to Secretary Wilson, Roosevelt said that his policy was "to promote and foster actual settling, actual homemaking on the public lands in every possible way." Major opposition to what the government was doing lay with "the beneficiaries and instigators of, or participators in," land frauds in the West. In a dramatic moment at the meeting, Pinchot faced down his critics in public. The convention delegates adopted some mildly critical language about the government's programs and then dispersed. [20]

Based on their experience with the IWC, the president and Pinchot decided to capitalize on a growing public interest in resource problems and to hold a conference of state governors at the White House. The meeting would provide a public forum to air conservation issues. The Governors Conference deliberated from 13 to 15 May 1908; it was the first time that the governors of the states assembled as a group. From the occasion emerged the National Governors Conference and the greater coordination among the state executives in this century.

Roosevelt told them that conservation was, after morality, "the chief material question that confronts us." He asserted that "all these various uses of our natural resources are so closely connected that they should be co-ordinated and should be treated as part of one coherent plan and not in haphazard and piecemeal fashion."[21]

To avoid dissension over controversial topics, Pinchot kept the proceedings under very close supervision. The conference adopted resolutions that concentrated primarily on a call for a large-scale inventory of the nation's natural resources as a guide for future planning and for the creation of state commissions on conservation. If the aim of the conference was to exert any influence on Congress, then that goal was not achieved. The political obstacles to what Roosevelt and Pinchot wanted to accomplish remained in place. Congress would not provide independent funding for the IWC, and Roosevelt had to act on his own authority to continue the panel in existence for the remainder of his term.

More battles over conservation would be fought during the remainder of Roosevelt's term as president. The positive and negative features of his program had come into clear focus by the spring of 1908. His articulate statements about the need to safeguard natural resources were timely and wise. The United States could not continue to exploit and waste its land, timber, and water with the profligacy that had marked the nineteenth century. Roosevelt's efforts to alert his fellow citizens to the dangers that faced the nation constituted one of his constructive achievements as president.

Roosevelt had less success in shaping a viable conservation program that would have long-range and positive effects. The reliance on bureaucrats and experts whom he and Pinchot favored made their policy vulnerable to congressional attack on the grounds that it did not represent the will of the people whom it affected. At bottom the president was arguing that decisions about natural resources and their management were too complex to be relegated to the whims of the democratic process. Within the federal government there had to be a permanent establishment that would address these problems in a nonpolitical and disinterested way. Roosevelt and Pinchot knew that they would not abuse their power; their critics did not share that certainty. The administration's preference for larger timber companies, cattle grazers, and sheep raisers grew out of its emphasis on rationality and efficiency; but it also suggested that the Roosevelt-Pinchot approach to conservation contained its own political assumptions. The president's conservation campaign merited praise for its general warning about waste and exploitation. Roosevelt's concern for the preservation of wildlife and natural beauty was also salutary. In the practical implementation of resource policy, however, the conservation that Roosevelt and his administration followed would come under increasing criticism as the movement to protect the nation's natural heritage developed during the rest of this century.

The fate of Native Americans in Theodore Roosevelt's day was not as central or as controversial as the conservation problem. Nonetheless, the president's attitude toward the Indian question also reflected his style of governance. He came to the presidency with ideas toward Native Americans that he had worked out from his western experience during his political apprenticeship. "The time has arrived," he said in 1901, "when we should definitely make up our minds to recognize the Indian as an individual and not as a member of a tribe."[22]

The government's census in 1905 indicated that there were 284,000 Native Americans within the continental United States, one-third of whom consisted of the Five Civilized Tribes, located in western Oklahoma Territory. The official national policy was one of assimilating Native Americans into society, rather than preserving the tribal structure and the traditional life style. Church-sponsored schools on and off the reservations sought to prepare Native Americans to take their place in the dominant culture. The major legislative enactment that affected this process was the Dawes Severalty Act of 1887, which allotted some land in trust to Native Americans for a period of twenty-five years and opened the remaining territories to white settlement. The object was to transform the Native Americans into farmers on 160-acre plots or to induce them to become agricultural or industrial laborers. The policy that Roosevelt inherited was paternalistic and exploitative toward those whom it proposed to help, while it was destructive of Native American culture itself.

Roosevelt believed that efforts at assimilation were futile because they did not offer Native Americans a genuine chance to match the achievements of white society. During the mid 1890s, Roosevelt had observed that "to train the average Indian as a lawyer or a doctor is in most cases simply to spoil him." Policy toward Native Americans must recognize the limited capacity of its subjects to develop; it must respect the feelings of whites who lived close to the reservations; and it must not seek to do too much for Native Americans by means of federal power. The situation of the inhabitants of reservations could be ameliorated; Native Americans who were involved in the mainstream of society must rise or fall on their own. Above all, the president was convinced that responsibility for Native Americans should be taken "completely out of the atmosphere of political activity." His administration endeavored to put policy toward Native Americans on a disinterested, efficient, nonpartisan basis so that its subjects could move slowly but eventually toward "ordinary" citizenship. [23]

The main agent of the president's program was the commissioner of Indian affairs, Francis E. Leupp, whom Roosevelt appointed in 1905. Leupp came to his post with experience in the field and through his connections with the reformist Indian Rights Association. "Whatever upbuilds the country in which the Indian lives," Leupp wrote, "upbuilds the Indian with the rest." Like Roosevelt, Leupp did not want to strike at the visible manifestations of the Native American culture. Leupp sought, however, to make it easier for whites to obtain Native American property so that they could instruct the tribes in the wise use of economic resources. Thus the major legislative achievement that occurred during Leupp's tenure was the Burke Act of 1906, named for its sponsor, Charles H. Burke, a South Dakota Republican. The new law changed the provisions of the Dawes Act to give the secretary of the interior the power to shorten the period when land would be held in trust for those Native Americans who, in the secretary's judgment, could manage their own economic affairs. Such designated individuals could in turn sell their land if they so wished. In this way, some Native Americans got money for their land sooner than might otherwise have occurred. Of course, Native American land passed more quickly into white hands as well. [24]

Leupp assumed that Native Americans would, to a large degree, inhabit the outskirts of the economy in a subordinate role. For education the commissioner stressed vocational skills, and he tried to decrease the number of boarding schools away from the reservations, such as the one in Carlisle, Pennsylvania. He also set up an Indian employment bureau to place men in such jobs as the sugar-beet fields of Colorado. As an administrator, Leupp acted forcefully in the Roosevelt mold, and the latter part of Leupp's term saw disputes about his autocratic leadership style with the Indian Rights Association and other defenders of the rights of Native Americans.

Leupp and Roosevelt approached the issue of Native American policy in what seemed to them a kindly and paternalistic manner. Their assessment of the future for these wards of the government was pessimistic. A few talented individuals might become genuine citizens; but most Native Americans could only aspire to a level comparable to African-Americans in the South. The dispersal of Native American lands, the erosion of tribal culture, and the dishonesty and fraud that were often visited upon unwary individuals were lamentable developments, but they also represented the inexorable march of civilization, which should be mitigated but not resisted. Native American affairs under Roosevelt and Leupp were administered with honesty and energy, but both men followed policies that differed little in substance from the assimilationist program that they had criticized. In any event, the long-range effect on the Native Americans was as debilitating and demoralizing as earlier abuses had been.

After he left office, Roosevelt regarded the construction of the Panama Canal as one of the finest accomplishments of his presidency. The Spooner Act of 1902, which had set out an organizational framework for building the waterway, specified that the Isthmian Canal Commission, composed of seven members, would oversee construction. Roosevelt named the panel and gave them their charge at the White House on 8 March 1904. Their assignment was "to be done as expeditiously as possible, and as economically as is consistent with thoroughness." John F. Wallace, a prominent railroad engineer, became the chief engineer of the commission. The president put the panel under the supervision of the War Department on 9 May 1904 and named Maj. Gen. George W. Davis as the first governor of the Canal Zone.[25]

The commission had a flawed organization from the beginning. There was no "centralized administrative organization" or the proper kind of coordination in Panama.[26] The commission mixed the functions of an advisory body to plan the canal and the responsibilities of an executive body to supervise the construction. The first few months of operation did not produce much constructive progress. Wallace proved to be inept, and the confused lines of communication within Panama and back to the United States created bottlenecks in the movement of men and resources. On 13 January 1905, Roosevelt asked Congress to decrease the size of the commission to no more than five members and to expand his authority over it. The House agreed, but the Senate, sensitive about presidential power, refused. The Spooner Act would be in force until Congress reconvened. Meanwhile, Roosevelt shook up the commission during the spring. Its final meeting was held in late March, and then its members resigned at the request of Secretary of War Taft.

Roosevelt established a second canal commission on 1 April 1905. Theodore P. Shonts, a railroad executive, became its president; Charles E. Magoon was named the new governor of the zone; and Wallace stayed on as chief engineer. Despite these changes, the erratic Wallace remained dissatisfied, and he resigned unexpectedly in June 1905 to accept another job. To replace him, Roosevelt selected another railroad man, John F. Stevens. At a meeting at Oyster Bay, the president promised full support to Stevens, who reached Panama in late July and soon demonstrated vigorous leadership. He ended premature excavation and started the necessary preliminary work. A key contribution was the construction of a railroad that could move all the men, supplies, and dirt necessary for efficient operation.

One major problem remained to be resolved. A decision had not yet been made between a sea-level canal and one based on a system of locks. Roosevelt created a board of engineers to advise him on 24 June 1905. At their first meeting with the president at Oyster Bay, he told them: "I expect you to advise me, not what you think I want to hear, but what you think I ought to hear." At that point he seemed to be leaning toward a sea-level canal. The board went to Panama, and on 18 November 1905 it voted eight to five in favor of the sea-level proposal.[27]

The minority report proved to be more convincing to Stevens, to the Isthmian Canal Commission, and, in the end, to Taft and Roosevelt. The president sent the report to Congress on 19 February 1906, with his endorsement of the lock approach as the best method. The Senate Committee on Interoceanic Canals held hearings in which the construction delays and the merits of the two approaches were aired. On 17 May 1906 the committee favored a sea-level canal by a vote of six to five.

Then the momentum shifted toward the lock canal. First, the House voted against the sea-level idea on 15 June 1906. In turn the Senate passed a bill to use the lock method by a five-vote majority on 21 June. The House agreed to that legislation six days later, and Roosevelt signed the law on 29 June 1906. Stevens returned to Panama to push the construction work. With the legislative obstacles cleared, Roosevelt sought prompt action.

For some time the president had wanted to visit Panama to see for himself how the work was going. The historical precedents said that a president should not leave the continental United States during his term of office. Going to Panama, however, appealed to Roosevelt's sense of the dramatic gesture, and he could be innovative at a relatively low level of political risk. His trip would only last about three weeks; he would be going to Puerto Rico, an American possession, and Panama, a foreign nation with a United States zone running through it. He would not be negotiating with foreign leaders, leaving during a time of crisis, or conducting essential business. It was an inspection trip to see the huge project for himself. In late June 1906 the White House announced that the president would make the journey in November, during the rainy season.

Administrative difficulties with the organization of the project still caused Roosevelt concern during the rest of 1906. Within the Canal Zone there was tension among the leaders. Roosevelt was generally pleased with Stevens, whom he called "an admirable man"; but he was worried that the engineer could "render himself worse than valueless in just one way," if he concluded that he was "indispensable." Stevens drafted an executive order to centralize authority in a manner that would give him the power to move ahead with construction of the canal. It would be presented to Roosevelt when he made his visit in November.[28]

The president's tour occurred during three days of heavy rain and abundant mud. Press coverage of Roosevelt was intense while he was inspecting as many facilities and sites as he could reach during the time available to him. In a gesture typical of his personalized presidential style, he climbed into one of the huge Bucyrus shovels and was photographed at its controls in a picture that the American press made world famous at once. He told his son Kermit that "Stevens and his men are changing the face of the continent, are doing the greatest engineering feat of the ages, and the effect of their work will be felt while our civilization lasts."[29]

Roosevelt reported to Congress on 17 December 1906 about his trip. He had already issued an executive order on 17 November, the last day of his visit, which gave Stevens the desired centralized authority. In his message, Roosevelt rejected public criticisms of the way that the canal work was proceeding. He announced that the government would function through private contractors in doing the construction itself, but he left open the possibility that it might be necessary to use governmental power in the end to create the canal.

These arrangements began to unravel soon after the message had been sent. The issue of private contractors and the need to have competitive bidding among these firms aroused tension between Stevens and Shonts as 1906 ended. Then Shonts received an offer to return to private business, and Roosevelt accepted Shonts's resignation, effective March 1907, with a warm letter of thanks. Meanwhile the process of choosing contractors had reached the point of opening bids and assessing the qualifications of the various firms.

The leading contender was a corporation headed by a Tennessee Republican named W. J. Oliver. Stevens believed, with good reason, that Oliver's firm was not well qualified to do the work, so he sent the president a letter that arrived in mid February 1907. It contained what was in effect Stevens's resignation over the issue of private contractors and political interference. Roosevelt responded decisively to what he deemed an ill-tempered and unreasonable action. He was now convinced that he could not rely on private engineers to finish the canal. "I propose now to put it in charge of men who will stay on the job till I get tired of having them there, or till I say they may abandon it," the president announced; "I shall turn it over to the army."[30]

Roosevelt now looked for an army officer to take on the assignment.

Taft recommended Maj. George W. Goethals, a West Point graduate who had had wide experience in building locks and canals on the nation's rivers. On 26 February 1907 the president told Shonts and the Isthmian Canal Commission that he was rejecting all the bids from private firms and was naming Goethals as chief engineer. Roosevelt stressed that "the work of construction is going on well and will continue to do so," and he told his friend Sir Edward Grey that "the Panama Canal is getting along better than I had expected."[31]

Roosevelt had dealt effectively with the various administrative crises that had beset the canal project during its first three years. He had not been farseeing enough to recognize that the structure that Congress had given him was inherently unwieldy. As that liability became evident, Roosevelt learned his lesson and turned to Goethals and the army. Seven years of hard work remained before the canal would open, but Roosevelt's leadership had set this enterprise on a productive course toward eventual completion. The president took pride in what he called "the greatest task of its own kind that has ever been performed in the world at all."[32]

In his autobiography, Theodore Roosevelt said that "one of the vital questions" that confronted him as president "was the attitude of the nation toward the great corporations." During his first term the *Northern Securities* case had established his reputation as a trustbuster. Roosevelt believed that the victory of the government in that case had confirmed its power over corporations but "did not establish the right method of exercising that power."[33] The policy that he preferred to follow as a regulator emerged in its complexity as a central administrative issue of his second term. Roosevelt was convinced that he had devised an approach that represented a middle way between an acceptance of monopoly and a misguided effort to destroy big corporations irrespective of their economic and social contributions. The regulatory policy of the administration between 1905 and 1909 was less clear-cut and straightforward than Roosevelt later remembered. The ambiguities of his relationship with business suggest that the president was not able to develop a program of oversight that fulfilled the promise of his stated position.

The dilemma of Roosevelt's regulatory style lay in the contrasting missions of the Bureau of Corporations under James R. Garfield and the Department of Justice during the second term. Garfield saw his function as the collection of facts regarding business practices so that proper legislation could be developed. In that sense, he did not believe that his agency was an instrument for publicity that should expose corporate wrongdoing to national scrutiny. Based on that premise, he and the president believed that there was every reason to make private agreements in key industries to secure the necessary data that they wanted.

During Roosevelt's first term, Garfield and the bureau reached understandings with the meat-packing industry, with International Harvester, and, to some extent, even with Standard Oil about having information at the agency's disposal. In his 1904 annual message, Roosevelt said that because the bureau's policy was "one of open inquiry into, and not attack upon, business," it had "been able to gain not only the confidence, but, better still, the co-operation of men engaged in legitimate business." The president conceded that these relationships might give the bureau's leader "knowledge of certain business facts" that would have to be kept confidential to prevent "an improper infringement of private rights." This policy would soon complicate the efforts of the Justice Department to enforce the antitrust laws when corporations claimed immunity because of the disclosures they had made to Garfield and his agency.[34]

The connection between the Roosevelt administration and United States Steel Company was a good illustration of how Roosevelt's effort to distinguish between "good" and "bad" trusts worked in practice. The basis for the entente between the steel company and the White House reached back to the time of the *Northern Securities* case and J. P. Morgan's visit to the White House. The connection grew during Roosevelt's first term, as George W. Perkins corresponded with the president and fed him information that reinforced the administration's favorable view of the firm. At the end of 1904, Elbert H. Gary, head of U.S. Steel, told Roosevelt, in the course of a stay at the White House, that if Roosevelt ever believed "that the Steel Corporation should be investigated, you shall have an opportunity to examine the books and records of all our companies." Should the White House or the Bureau of Corporations "find anything in them that you think is wrong, we will convince you that we are right or we will correct the wrong." Roosevelt deemed this offer "to be about the fair thing."[35]

This informal meeting of the minds took on additional importance in January 1905, when a resolution of the House of Representatives asked that the Bureau of Corporations initiate a probe of U.S. Steel. Garfield stalled any action until the fall of 1905 and then spoke with Gary himself. That conversation, in addition to the reluctance of U.S. Steel to cooperate without gaining Roosevelt's approval in advance, led to a White House meeting on 2 November 1905 at which a suitable arrangement was negotiated. Gary told the meeting that he wanted his company "to co-operate with the Government in every possible way" that did not interfere with the rights of his stockholders. The two sides worked out procedures that put the steel company's records at the disposal of the bureau's agents but kept the proceedings confidential. Gary remained a strong supporter of the administration's regulatory policy, and the understanding worked well for all concerned down to the Panic of 1907. The Roosevelt White House put U.S. Steel in the category of socially responsible corporations and treated it accordingly.[36]

The administrative difficulties of Roosevelt's approach, on the other hand, emerged in the ways that the meat-packing industry and Standard Oil were handled, both by the Bureau of Corporations and by the Justice Department. The issue of the beef industry arose first in 1904. A congressional resolution asked Garfield to investigate why meat prices had risen at a time when the returns to western cattle raisers had declined. How much was the notorious "beef trust" responsible for this development? Garfield went out to Chicago and talked with the packers. He promised them that any information provided to the bureau would not be passed on to the Justice Department in any future antitrust action. Even with that pledge, it took months to obtain data from the industry, in part because the bureau was very cautious about using its power to compel disclosures from business records. The packers did not cooperate with Garfield's men until early in 1905 and then only in a grudging way. There was not much time to include the information in the report that the bureau was preparing.

At this time the Department of Justice was pressing its case at the Supreme Court to sustain the injunctions that had been obtained against the meat packers during Roosevelt's first term. The president ordered Garfield to transmit the report on the beef industry to the Justice Department so that indictments could be sought against individual meat packers. The Supreme Court ruled in the government's favor, and Moody prepared to obtain indictments. Despite these steps and the publicity around them, criticism persisted, both in and out of Congress, against the slow pace of the administration's actions. To quiet the uproar, the president instructed the bureau to release the meat-packing report on 3 March 1905.

The lengthy document proved to be a public-relations disaster for the White House. The report generally exonerated the industry from the public charges that it drove up meat prices or gouged undue profits. The press greeted the report with a chorus of criticism that embarrassed the administration. Roosevelt complained to Garfield that the American people "do not understand the report; I want to make it clear to them."[37] Roosevelt asked the bureau to obtain more experienced investigators to look further into industry practices. The president did not consider whether his administration might be following contradictory policies.

As the furor over the report continued, the government obtained grand-jury indictments in Chicago against the six important packing companies and their leaders. Moody told Roosevelt that if "people of the importance of these defendants are convicted and imprisoned, it will be a mighty blow against unscrupulous and predatory wealth."[38] Garfield's tactics in compiling the report left the defendants with an effective legal challenge to the case against them. They contended that since they had little choice but to help the bureau in its inquiry, they were entitled to virtual immunity from prosecution.

During the spring of 1906 the federal judge in the case dropped the indictments against the individual meat packers on the immunity argument. He left in force the charges against the companies themselves. The decision, which occurred while Congress was considering the meat-inspection legislation, represented a legal setback for the White House. A bill was passed to prevent the kind of immunity that the packers had obtained, but the damage to the government had already taken place. The indictments lingered on for seven years and were finally dropped in 1913. Roosevelt's strategy—of conciliation from the Bureau of Corporations combined with coercion from the Justice Department—ended in victory for the industry he was seeking to regulate.

The Roosevelt administration was more unified in its campaign against an inviting corporate target, Standard Oil Company. In 1903 the president had used public distrust of the giant oil firm to obtain enactment of the law creating the Bureau of Corporations. He had also made the gesture of rejecting the company's campaign contributions during the 1904 election. By early 1905, Standard Oil's tactics had again aroused public anger. Independent oil men in newly opened fields in Kansas complained that Standard Oil's monopolistic tactics were forcing down prices and injuring their interests. As it had done with meat packing, Congress directed the bureau to look into the controversy.

Garfield and his men began their inquiry in the midst of criticism regarding the report on meat packing. Perhaps expecting the same gentle treatment that the packers had obtained, Standard Oil cooperated with the bureau and made its records available. Roosevelt did not want a repetition of the mistakes that had surrounded the meat report. He instructed Garfield to go to Kansas and look into conditions in person. The commissioner spent eleven days on the scene, talked with all sides, and asserted that his probe would be nonbiased and objective.

The bureau gathered data during the remainder of 1905 and issued its *Report on the Transportation of Petroleum* on 5 May 1906. Garfield concluded that Standard Oil "has habitually received from the railroads, and is now receiving, secret rates and other unjust and illegal discriminations." He charged that there was a "monopolistic control" that stretched "from the well of the producer to the door step of the consumer."[39] The report reached the president during the debate about the Hepburn Act. Roosevelt sent the bureau's findings to Congress on 4 May 1906 with a message that asked for help with pending railroad legislation. The White House also concluded that an antitrust action against Standard Oil was needed. In June 1906 the Department of Justice declared that it was opening an investigation into the merits of a case involving the oil company.

Meanwhile, Garfield's bureau endeavored to make its own case against Standard Oil. The bureau pursued the issue of rebating while the attorney general looked into the antitrust aspects of the matter. The result was a good deal of friction between the two agencies. By 15 November 1906 the Department of Justice filed motions to dissolve Standard Oil of New Jersey. Garfield proudly told Congress that the bureau had furnished the evidence on which the case was based. He did not say that he had been less willing to publish the other information that the bureau had collected on Standard Oil after his report was issued. Despite the apparent public harmony within the administration, there had been more friction between the bureau and the Justice Department over Standard Oil, and Roosevelt had not tried to resolve it while Moody and Garfield were in their posts.

In late 1906 the president moved Garfield to the Department of the Interior to replace Ethan Allen Hitchcock. Moody was nominated for a vacancy on the Supreme Court, and Charles J. Bonaparte of Maryland became the new attorney general. Garfield had been Roosevelt's kind of administrator. He had carried out his duties efficiently, and he had deferred to presidential directives and policies. His approach to antitrust issues reflected his agreement with Roosevelt that conciliation with industry was more rewarding than confrontation. In the case of the meat packers that posture proved embarrassing, but Garfield redeemed himself with his handling of Standard Oil. Moody's work had also pleased Roosevelt. Moody shared the president's faith in executive discretion and thought it better to use administrative techniques in regulating business than to rely on the Sherman Antitrust Act. While both Garfield and Moody contributed to the fighting between their two departments during the president's second term, the responsibility for the resulting confusion of purpose and action lay with Theodore Roosevelt.

The emphasis that Roosevelt placed on executive discretion as a central element in his decisions about regulation often meant that his personal reaction to an issue or a corporation determined where the White House stood. In the case of the International Harvester Company, one of J. P. Morgan's financial combinations that Roosevelt regarded as a responsible corporation, the presence of George W. Perkins and Elbert H. Gary as spokesmen for the firm helped to sway the president's thinking. During the first term, the administration reached an accord with International Harvester in which the company promised cooperation when any illegal activity on its part was alleged. No other action occurred until, during late 1906, the Senate called for a probe of International Harvester, its domination of the farm-machinery market, and its ties to J. P. Morgan. A month later, Garfield and Herbert Knox Smith conferred with Perkins, Gary, and representatives of the company in New York City. At that meeting an agreement was reached to proceed as had been done with United States Steel. The company would furnish information to a probe, and the government promised confidentiality. No immunity was offered, but there was an assumption on the part of International Harvester that antitrust actions would be deferred.

Once again the bureau and the Department of Justice found themselves at cross-purposes during the handling of the case throughout the rest of 1907. The new attorney general, Charles J. Bonaparte, was sensitive to the public perception that he had come into office less than enthusiastic about the vigorous enforcement of the Sherman Antitrust Act. Early in his tenure he started an investigation of International Harvester, and preparations were made to file suit against the firm. At the end of March 1907 a letter from an official of the company informed Bonaparte about the bureau's parallel inquiry. The letter asked, in light of the arrangement between the government and the company, that the suit not be filed. The attorney general had not been informed about what the bureau was doing, and he did not then believe that the Justice Department should be constrained because such an agreement existed.

During this same period the Justice Department was also conducting an inquiry into the affairs of the American Tobacco Company, which Moody had ordered at the end of 1906. The giant tobacco corporation had achieved its dominant power in its industry by takeovers of smaller competitors and by ruthless tactics toward independent wholesaling and retailing firms. The tobacco company knew about the administration's understanding with J. P. Morgan and his interests, and it sought to obtain a similar deal at the beginning of 1907. The company's approaches to the government did not succeed, but they did give Bonaparte more clues about the extent to which the Bureau of Corporations had entered into informal understandings with important industries. In July 1907 the Justice Department filed a suit against American Tobacco.

That action convinced the leaders of International Harvester that they had better confirm the understanding with the Roosevelt administration. George W. Perkins went to see the president in August 1907. He told Roosevelt about the company's willingness to have its conduct investigated by the Bureau of Corporations and pointed out that the company had agreed in 1904 to stop accepting rebates. The president informed Bonaparte about the bureau's dealings with the company earlier in 1907. Roosevelt told the attorney general: "Please do not file the suit until I hear from you." After discussions with Herbert Knox Smith, who had succeeded Garfield, about what the bureau had done, Bonaparte heard from the White House on 24 September 1907 that the prospective suit against International Harvester should be abandoned. Smith's contention that the Sherman Act was "an economic absurdity and is impossible of general enforcement" bolstered Roosevelt's own thinking and played a large role in the president's decision to terminate the litigation.[40]

The problem of carrying out the antitrust law remained unsettled as Roosevelt began his last two years in office. The case against Standard Oil was still in the courts, and the suit against American Tobacco was also ongoing. The president was now convinced that the Sherman Antitrust Act could not be enforced, and he had little disposition to have the Justice Department pursue such cases. The process of informal agreements with some corporations, using the machinery of the Bureau of Corporations, was a preferable substitute in Roosevelt's mind. The problem was that such private understandings were politically dangerous and difficult to carry out. The administration could not move openly from trustbusting to the tolerance of big business. Some antitrust prosecutions by the Justice Department had to occur. The result was a confused, vague, and often ineffective policy. In the popular mind, Theodore Roosevelt was a foe of the excesses of large corporations, and the business community distrusted him for it. As an administrator, he could not find a viable way of regulating business in a manner that would make the federal government a credible force in the marketplace.

The complexities of Roosevelt's administrative style were equally apparent in the implementation of the Pure Food and Drug Act of 1906. Dr. Harvey Wiley advocated the vigorous enforcement of the statute, which created repercussions among businessmen and politicians. Roosevelt did not appreciate this, so the two men clashed. Once the pure-food law had been passed, the affected industries tried to get governmental regulators to issue rulings that would favor those industries.

Products such as whiskey, chemical preservatives, benzoate of soda, and sulfur dioxide became the subjects of lengthy proceedings and pressure from concerned capitalists. One particular substance was saccharin, then being used, among other things, in the manufacture of catsup. To settle the dispute over the health risks of the product, Roosevelt named a panel of experts to evaluate the merits of the sweetener. At a White House conference with representatives of the catsup makers, Wiley and other scientists, and Congressman James S. Sherman of New York, the issue was joined about whether saccharin was harmful. Wiley asserted confidently that saccharin was "a coal-tar product totally devoid of food value and extremely injurious to health." Based on his own personal experience, Roosevelt at once became angry. His own doctor gave him saccharin daily, and "anybody who says saccharin is injurious to health is an idiot."[41]

The incident persuaded the president to select a board of experts to review Wiley's decision generally, but that move did not end the controversies that arose from the scientist's energetic enforcement of the pure-food law. Roosevelt and Wiley differed over a case involving the purity of French vinegar, which attracted the attention of Ambassador Jules Jusserand. The president reminded Wiley, through the latter's superior, Secretary of Agriculture Wilson, that the law should not favor "dishonest or deleterious business"; but neither should it be carried out "in a nagging, vexatious, foolish or corrupt spirit towards honest business, not conducted so as to be injurious to the public health." Any confidence that Roosevelt still had in Wiley's judgment was vanishing.[42]

Dismissing Wiley would have brought political criticism that might have hurt the Republicans in the presidential campaign of 1908. Roosevelt and the government's scientists continued to work on the regulatory problems associated with the food law down to the end of the administration. Roosevelt wrote in January 1909 that Wiley had been guilty of "gross errors of judgment" and some rulings that were "nonsensical."[43] Still the administration ruled as Wiley wished on a number of products in 1908/9. The real difficulty was that the pure-food law in 1906 was only the first step in the regulatory process. The equally important and subtle task of administering the legislation required as much presidential care and attention as did the maneuvering with Congress. The case of Harvey Wiley indicates that these matters engaged less of Roosevelt's energy as a chief executive. The exercise of presidential discretion did not prove to be the best mechanism for making regulatory policy.

Theodore Roosevelt became aware during his first term that the federal government lacked the efficiency and rigor that he believed was necessary in order to deal with the nation's complex social problems. "The sole justification of any type of government," he told Congress in his first annual message, "lies in its proving itself both honest and efficient." Three years later he remarked that "the cost of doing government business should be regulated with the same rigid scrutiny as the cost of doing a private business." Roosevelt pursued economy and efficiency as a means of justifying and strengthening the power of the executive branch relative to Congress even more than as an abstract principle. The same impulse lay behind his use of governmental commissions, a device that William McKinley had earlier employed. "One of the ways in which by independent action of the Executive we were able to accomplish an immense amount of work for the public was through volunteer unpaid commissions appointed by the President," Roosevelt wrote some years later. These panels were very helpful in achieving conservation goals, and they became one of Roosevelt's favorite devices.[44]

The most celebrated of Roosevelt's commissions addressed the issue of how well the federal government functioned. The Committee on Department Methods, appointed on 2 June 1905, became known as the Keep Commission, after its chair, Charles Hallam Keep. This presidential initiative grew out of Roosevelt's own experiences as governor of New York, where he had reorganized the operation of factory inspections, prisons, and canals. He also encouraged the reform efforts of Root in the army and the work of Pinchot with his Forest Service. During the first term, Pinchot suggested that Roosevelt set up a commission on the organization of government scientific work. The recommendations of that body would have needed congressional action to be implemented, and the lawmakers were not disposed to carry out suggestions that would have shifted functions from one department to another. If Roosevelt wanted to achieve efficiency, he would have to find ways to do it without the intervention of the House and the Senate.

Pinchot and James R. Garfield, of course, shared Roosevelt's goals for the governmental service. They worked on a plan during the early months of 1905 for a committee to scrutinize how the government operated. Their outline for an inquiry into such issues as how decisions were made, what employees should be paid, procedures for supplies, accounting, and paperwork, and the overall coordination of the government's business went to Roosevelt in May 1905. The president responded positively to what two of his favorite subordinates had proposed. He named a five-man committee consisting of Pinchot, Garfield, Keep, Frank H. Hitchcock of the Post Office Department, and Lawrence

O. Murray from the Department of Commerce and Labor. Roosevelt's letter of appointment charged them to learn "what changes are needed to place the conduct of the executive business of the Government in all its branches on the most economical and effective basis in the light of the best modern business practice." He emphasized that they should be rigorous in their evaluation of existing procedures. "In the adoption of methods and the performance of work," he told them, "every step which is not clearly indispensable should be eliminated."[45]

The Keep Commission served Roosevelt in two different ways during the rest of his presidency. In addition to its designated assignment, Roosevelt asked the commission to look into the continuing difficulties of the Government Printing Office in 1905, the extent of waste in governmental publications, and alleged leaks in the crop-reporting procedures of the Department of Agriculture and the monthly crop statistics that the department compiled. Important as the Keep Commission proved to be as an investigating arm of the president, its long-range significance lay in the pioneering work it did in scrutinizing the procedures within the federal government.

Using questionnaires and interviews with cabinet officers and other bureaucrats, as well as specialized subcommittees, the commissioners examined how employees were graded and paid, how the government was organized, and whether there should be a retirement system for federal workers. The commissioners considered how supplies were acquired, the accounting methods that the government used, and the perennial problem of excessive paperwork. Roosevelt himself encouraged the review and publication of historical documents, and he sent recommendations to Congress in February 1909 about a possible building for the National Archives.

The president extended strong public support to the Keep Commission throughout its existence. Speaking to the commissioners and members of their subcommittees at Gifford Pinchot's home on 20 March 1906, he said: "You have literally an unparalleled opportunity for useful work. As far as I am aware there has never before been made in this country, indeed, in any country, such a comprehensive, systematic effort to put the country's housekeeping in order." In his annual messages from 1905 onward, Roosevelt endorsed the work of the Keep Commission. He told Congress that "there is every reason why our executive governmental machinery should be at least as well planned, economical, and efficient as the best machinery of the great business organizations, which at present is not the case." Although he kept Congress informed and although he wanted legislative support, he had also said to Keep and his colleagues: "I shall value the reports that I receive largely, not exclusively at all, but largely in proportion as they do not call for legislation."[46]

That was just as well, because Congress was not receptive to the reforms that the Keep Commission's work embodied. The lawmakers soon recognized that what Roosevelt was trying to do would involve a reduction in their control over appointments and key departments. The reports that the commission issued were published sporadically, and the president's requests for funds to sustain the panel's investigatory work were severely trimmed. In an appropriation bill toward the end of Roosevelt's presidency, the House adopted language that prohibited the payment of public money to "any commission, council, board, or other similar body" without direct congressional approval.[47] The action was an outgrowth of the suspicion about Roosevelt's executive techniques that permeated Congress during his second term. He was not allowed to carry forward a reform of the executive branch without congressional participation.

The Keep Commission did accomplish worthwhile results on its own, and it established an important precedent for future efforts to make the federal government more efficient. The commission saved public money through its exposure of lax practices, it reformed some procedures, and it introduced order into the routine business of the bureaucracy. The panel began an examination into how supplies were acquired, and it raised the question of salaries and pensions for governmental employees. Above all, it asserted the principle that the president should be in control of the management of the executive agencies. In that sense, the Keep Commission was a notable forerunner of the reforms that created the modern structure of the presidency.

Theodore Roosevelt was a gifted and often effective presidential administrator. He usually evoked a high morale from his immediate subordinates, who relished the chance to work for such an inspiring executive. His men admired Roosevelt for his willingness to consult them and for his support when they faced a crisis or criticism. Roosevelt handled a great deal of business each day with speed and thoroughness. His ability to read quickly and his retentive mind enabled him to move through large amounts of information easily. He also possessed the capacity to make up his mind promptly and decisively. He did not spend time reconsidering the actions he had taken. When the president's interest was engaged, his administrative talents were impressive.

Roosevelt had blind spots about men and policies. He was only a mediocre judge of the motives of those with whom he dealt. People who agreed with his goals and methods tended to receive the benefit of the doubt; their advice was valued. The charge that Roosevelt was impetuous was overdrawn. He consulted widely before making a decision. Yet, he did not ordinarily draw on the views of those who might disagree with him. People who consistently differed with the president soon found that their insights were no longer welcome.

As indicated by his handling of the antitrust issue and, to some extent, conservation as well, Roosevelt did not value consistency and order in his administrative style. A personal, improvised, and self-contradictory cast to his regulatory policy accounted for the stops and starts in his treatment of trusts throughout his second term. Political considerations often dictated the frequent cabinet shuffles that disrupted the continuity of his policy initiatives.

Roosevelt believed that flexibility and creativity in office counted for more than a hidebound deference to established procedures and red tape that frustrated presidential actions. He was less sensitive to the legitimate restraints that the law imposed on him. Legal limits to the president were obstacles to be overcome or circumvented as much as they were guidelines for appropriate action. Roosevelt rarely violated the law as an administrator, but he did push its boundaries in the interest of what he deemed to be larger purposes.

The Roosevelt style of administrative leadership revived and invigorated the United States government. Much as Franklin D. Roosevelt would do twenty-five years later, Theodore made it fun and exciting to work in the federal service. He imparted an elan to the conduct of the public business that drew men such as Root, Taft, Garfield, and Pinchot to his side. To an impressive degree, Theodore Roosevelt succeeded, as he said in his autobiography, in making the government that was under his control "the most effective instrument in advancing the interests of the people as a whole, the interests of the average men and women of the United States and of their children."[48] Amid the political storms that marked Roosevelt's second term, he could rightly be proud of that conviction, which was for him a legacy of accomplishment as an administrator.

223

10

★ ★ ★ ★ ★

KEEPING THE LEFT
CENTER TOGETHER

During his second term, Theodore Roosevelt maintained a high level of popularity. The absence of public-opinion polls made judgments about his standing more a matter of impression than of statistical precision. His fellow politicians, even those who opposed him, attested to the loyalty he commanded among the citizenry in general. "With all his faults," wrote a British diplomat in April 1907, "he is unquestionably today the strongest force in the United States and seems likely to remain so." The president's grip on the public was so powerful, said one easterner, "that if five hundred of the first citizens of New York were to make an affidavit that they had seen the President do a certain thing, and he were to deny it the following day, the five hundred affidavits would be as waste paper in the estimation of the country at large."[1]

One key to Roosevelt's appeal was his capacity to keep the nation entertained and involved in his conduct. His family was a ready source of public fascination, and he missed few chances to let the nation see his human side. The president also had a proclivity to become embroiled in what Americans would later call "flaps." His campaigns for simplified spelling and against nature fakers kept newspaper readers enthralled until he left the White House. Personal feuds with Maria and Bellamy Storer, as well as with E. H. Harriman, added a touch of individual conflict to the generally exuberant atmosphere of Roosevelt's later years in the presidency. As one puzzled Republican noted in July 1907, the American people "pay no attention to any mistakes the President may make, but magnify his virtues with joy and gladness."[2]

Although Roosevelt's popularity remained high before he left office, his relationship with his own party grew strained. The president's standing with congressional Republicans worsened as the end of his term neared. Roosevelt became more committed to the ideas of political reform that were being called progressive, while his legislative adversaries retained the conservatism that many older GOP members shared. While these contrasting political philosophies explain much about the Republican discord between 1905 and 1909, some of the responsibility rests with the political actions of Theodore Roosevelt himself. He was not the sole contributor to Republican factionalism, but he represented a significant component of the infighting that was breaking up the party by the time William Howard Taft was inaugurated on 4 March 1909.

Theodore Roosevelt and his family had settled into a comfortable routine of presidential life by his second term. The passing years revealed the changes that took place as the children grew and their lives developed. In March 1905 the president gave the bride away when his niece Eleanor Roosevelt married their distant cousin, Franklin D. Roosevelt, in New York City. A year later, on 17 February 1906, Alice Roosevelt married Congressman Nicholas Longworth in a White House ceremony. Life as the celebrity daughter of Theodore Roosevelt had become more and more difficult for Alice as she emerged as an independent young woman. Despite a fifteen-year age difference, Longworth offered her a way out of that predicament. His reputation as a womanizer and his taste for alcohol indicated the problems that their union would encounter in the future.

The other children were still in school. Theodore, Jr., attended Harvard, from which he graduated in 1908. Kermit followed his older brother to Groton School, while Archibald, Ethel, and Quentin stayed with their parents at the White House. When they became ready for prep school, as in the case of the boys, or the social rounds that Ethel followed, they pursued the same course as their older siblings. Meanwhile, each summer the family went off to Oyster Bay. In late September the Roosevelts returned to Washington and the duties that the president encountered with the return of autumn. "Edith is now putting up the house," Roosevelt wrote in September 1907, "and we feel a little melancholy, as we always do when the summer is over. I suppose I shall have an awful time with Congress this winter. But the summer has been very pleasant and satisfactory for all the children." Despite the many distractions of his office, Roosevelt devoted ample attention to his bevy of children throughout the remaining years of his presidency.[3]

The emotional center of Theodore's personal life was his marriage to Edith Roosevelt. Their regular White House walks gave her the opportunity to influence him on personnel decisions and occasionally to say a word on policy questions. To enable her husband to obtain some rest and quiet, she found him a country retreat in Albemarle County, Virginia, about 125 miles from Washington. The small rustic cabin was named Pine Knot. The president and his wife went there to be alone, away from the intrusive press corps. Mrs. Roosevelt continued her efforts to set a moral tone for the nation; in the words of Archie Butt, the White House military aide, she became "the embodiment of womanly dignity and social culture."[4]

Because Theodore Roosevelt believed that the president and his family should encourage national literature and art, they used their position to call attention to the work of American authors. Kermit Roosevelt told them about the poetry of Edwin Arlington Robinson. His father reviewed Robinson's work in the *Outlook* and gave the poet a federal appointment that allowed him time to write. Guests at the Roosevelt White House during these years included Henry James, John La Farge, and Augustus Saint-Gaudens. As Archie Butt put it in late 1908, "Any man who has done anything worth notice, whether it be in literature, art, or sport, is certain to receive recognition at the White House."[5]

In December 1907, Roosevelt informed Congress that "there should be a national gallery of art established in the capital city of this country." It was a goal that was "important not merely to the artistic but to the material welfare of the country."[6] By the time he sent his thoughts on the subject to Capitol Hill, the president had already demonstrated his own commitment to the artistic legacy of the nation with his key role in acquiring the monumental art collection of Charles L. Freer for the United States during 1905 and 1906. Theodore Roosevelt's vision of the presidency embraced the need to stimulate and encourage the aesthetic aspects of American society.

Freer, a retired Michigan railroad executive who had amassed a superb collection of American and Oriental art, had first thought about donating his collection to the government in 1902, at about the time when he met Theodore Roosevelt in Detroit that September. For more than a year, Freer discussed the possibility with friends in Washington, and negotiations proceeded during early 1904. A formal proposal from the collector was made to the Smithsonian on 3 January 1905. Freer's gift came with restrictions that would have prevented other art from being added to his holdings even after he had died. For most of 1906 a stalemate ensued, with Freer on one side and the Smithsonian trustees on the other. "I doubt very much if we can find a way to harmonize our different views," Freer wrote a friend in March 1905; "still a way out of it may occur.[7]

The decisive element in this instance proved to be Edith Roosevelt. In collaboration with a local Washington art dealer, she persuaded the president to act. He met with Freer on 13 December 1905 and arranged talks between the collector and the leader of the Smithsonian. The result was a new proposal in which Freer restated his original offer in language that was less irritating to the partisans of the Smithsonian. Theodore Roosevelt added his important influence to the process when he wrote a public letter to the Smithsonian trustees that endorsed Freer's gift. Roosevelt called the conditions "proper and reasonable," and he warned that he would "be obliged," if the Smithsonian declined, "to take some other method of endeavoring to prevent the loss to the United States Government" of what he called "one of the most valuable collections which any private individual has ever given to any people." The Smithsonian then accepted the Freer bequest, and the collection was deeded to the United States in May 1906.[8]

The acquisition of the Freer collection was only one example of Theodore Roosevelt's effort to use the presidency in the interest of artistic and aesthetic ends. He turned to such figures as Saint-Gaudens, a sculptor, and Charles F. McKim, an architect, to advise him on artistic questions. Before Roosevelt left office he set up the Fine Arts Council, which was supposed to provide guidance to governmental agencies on aesthetic topics. After he was elected in 1904, Roosevelt wanted to use Saint-Gaudens's talents to improve the nation's coinage, so he asked Secretary of the Treasury Leslie M. Shaw on 27 December 1904: "Would it be possible, without asking permission of Congress, to employ a man like St. Gaudens to give us a coinage that would have some beauty?" A few weeks later the president invited the artist to give him new versions of the penny, the $10 eagle coin, and the $20 double eagle.[9]

The work of artistic creation went on into 1907, with Roosevelt struggling against the opposition of the officials of the mint and the failing health of the artist himself. Saint-Gaudens died in August 1907, and an assistant finished the $10 and $20 coins, which were issued in November 1907. There was disagreement over the artistic merit of the new coinage, but the focus of public controversy became the absence of the motto "In God We Trust" on the coinage. Early in the design work, Roosevelt and Saint-Gaudens had agreed that the words could be omitted for artistic considerations. At a time when Roosevelt was under political attack during his second term, the issue of the religious phrase offered his enemies the chance to accuse him "of acting hastily without due foresight of the consequences." In the end, Congress, bowing to public pressure and political considerations, restored the motto to its legal status in 1908. Roosevelt regarded the legislation as "rot, pure rot," but he did not object to its passage. The episode reflected how much his active presidential style had made any subject that Roosevelt touched a potential source of public clamor. One of his most significant legacies would be the idea that the chief executive should take explicit positions on issues that had not previously been regarded as subjects for presidential concern. [10]

The muckraker Ida Tarbell wrote about Roosevelt: "I felt his clothes might not contain him, he was so steamed up, so ready to go, to attack anything, anywhere." Even Theodore Roosevelt was not that impetuous, but the public perception that he relished a stirring battle with his adversaries contributed to the degree of entertainment value that his presidency possessed. During his second term he practiced "the art of controversy" on numerous occasions. The encounter with his one-time companions Maria and Bellamy Storer was the most notorious of these incidents. [11]

Maria and Bellamy Storer of Cincinnati, Ohio, had been close friends of Theodore and Edith Roosevelt's in the years before the death of William McKinley. Bellamy Storer had been first minister to Belgium and then minister to Spain under McKinley. His ambitious wife wanted her less-than-talented husband to be an ambassador at a major European capital, and she was pleased when Roosevelt sent Storer to Austria-Hungary in 1902. Maria's Roman Catholic faith led her to meddle in church politics, and she wanted most to see Archbishop John Ireland made a cardinal. To that goal she devoted her own abundant energies, and she sought to enlist the influence of the president in her campaign. She did so indirectly at first. By late 1903, however, Mrs. Storer was implying in Europe that Ireland's candidacy came with a presidential endorsement. For Theodore Roosevelt, who was aware of what political effect the administration's proximity to the Vatican might have on Protestant voters, the Storer initiative was dangerous. He instructed Bellamy in December 1903 not to mention the president's views on the subject again, and the president stressed that the government must be neutral on such an issue. [12]

Despite this implied reprimand to her, Maria Storer kept up her pro-Ireland intrigues as the second term got under way. When it became clear in 1905 that Ireland would not be elevated to cardinal, she wrote to Secretary of War Taft and to Edith Roosevelt with messages asking Roosevelt to endorse the American cleric. The president accused Mrs. Storer of placing the administration in a "false and wholly improper position" because of her personal interference. He insisted that the couple return his letters and stop their efforts on behalf of Archbishop Ireland; otherwise, Ambassador Storer would have to leave his post. [13]

229

The president received no answer, so he dismissed Bellamy Storer as the ambassador to Austria-Hungary during early March 1906. There was some press comment when the Storers returned home, but the episode seemed likely to fade away. Because of his wife's prodding, however, Bellamy issued a long explanation of his views, which he leaked to senators and other politicians at the end of the year. The sensational document was published in early December. Roosevelt's letters to "dear Maria" became a source of public comment and editorial amusement. Most papers regarded Mrs. Storer as overzealous and indiscreet. She learned the dangers of challenging a popular president in a public forum where he had the decisive last word. For Roosevelt, the affair offered its "delicious" aspects, but it did little damage to his standing with the American people.[14]

Similar positive results came out of the president's efforts to limit violence in college football. More than forty players died in 1903 while playing, and the toll prompted calls to outlaw the game. In the fall of 1905, Roosevelt summoned coaches and athletic administrators of Harvard, Princeton, and Yale to the White House to discuss how to put football "on a thoroughly clean basis." Out of the conference came an agreement to change the game's rules in the direction of less-dangerous contests. During the summer of 1906, he also attempted to simplify the spelling practices of the United States government. Congress and the Supreme Court proved unreceptive to the changes, and the campaign provided editorial writers with ammunition for dozens of humorous columns that mocked the president's innovations. The president also found time to indict a number of writers about animals and nature who, in his judgment, imputed reasoning powers and emotions to wild creatures. He attacked these authors in a 1907 article that he wrote in collaboration with a Washington correspondent. It was called "Roosevelt and the Nature Fakirs." Another long controversy ensued. To the president's criticism that the objects of his scorn did not "know the heart of wild things," one author replied that "every time Mr. Roosevelt gets near the heart of a wild thing he invariably puts a bullet through it."[15]

While these and other public quarrels diverted the nation throughout Roosevelt's second term, they did not overshadow the president's political leadership of the Republicans or the problems that his regulatory policies aroused within his own party. The dominant political theme of Roosevelt's second administration was the increasing discord among GOP members over where the president was taking the party. While Roosevelt's own popularity remained high, the internal cohesion of the Republicans was eroding during the two years that followed the triumph of 1904.

In addition to the new issues of railroad policy and governmental regulation that came out of the congressional sessions of 1905/6, the protective tariff continued to be a source of intraparty rancor for Roosevelt. The decision not to revise the tariff in late 1904 and early 1905 did not quiet the calls for adjustment and change that even some Republicans now put forward. In May 1905 a party newspaper in Ohio said that the "protection theory has degenerated into a bulwark of trust aggression and extortion." An Iowa Republican warned William Boyd Allison that there was "a revulsion" against the tariff policy "that unless speedily checked will mean revolution and another set of men at the head of the Republican party or a new adjustment of the parties altogether."[16]

The tariff issue bubbled along throughout 1905 as the proponents of revision convened meetings about possible reciprocity agreements with France and Germany. In the Massachusetts State Convention of 1905, the Republicans, including Henry Cabot Lodge, endorsed "the wisdom of a consideration of the tariff for the purpose of revision and readjustment."[17] This shift toward revision helped the Massachusetts GOP win the governorship and defeat the Democratic candidate for lieutenant governor, who favored more sweeping changes in the tariff.

Theodore Roosevelt remained reluctant to see the tariff become a leading partisan issue. He believed that the Senate would not pass any reciprocity treaty that he might negotiate. In the East, sentiment for removal of the tariff on cattle hides was evident, especially among the shoemakers of Massachusetts. Western Republicans, who raised cattle, deplored the proposal. Within the cabinet, Secretary of War Taft generally favored revisions and reductions; Treasury Secretary Leslie M. Shaw was an outspoken advocate of protection. By the end of the year, Roosevelt had concluded that without a change in the legislative situation, "absolutely nothing" could be done about the tariff. He made only a cautious reference to the subject in his 1905 annual message. He raised the possibility of a minimum and a maximum tariff rate as a way of facilitating reciprocity treaties, but he avoided making any call for a general revision of the protective system.[18]

Roosevelt used this language in part because of criticism he had received at the end of 1905 about his equivocal position on reciprocity. The president became embroiled in a squabble with Henry M. Whitney, the defeated Democratic candidate for lieutenant governor in Massachusetts, over whether Roosevelt had or had not endorsed reciprocity with Canada. The annual message did not quiet the attacks on the president or on the protective policy. Critics noted that his recommendations for tariff concessions to the Philippines once again passed the House and then were bottled up in the Senate. All these events reinforced

Roosevelt's lack of zeal about an issue that he regarded as irrelevant. As Congress prepared to adjourn in June 1906, he repeated his firm conviction that "a large part of the scream about the tariff represents simply an effort to draw a red herring across the trail of genuine economic reform within our own borders."[19]

In addition to the agitation over the tariff, the outcome of the congressional session in which the Hepburn Act and other regulatory laws had been passed left the political environment unsettled as the Republicans looked ahead to the 1906 elections. Senator Joseph B. Foraker told a newspaperman in late May 1906 that "the Democrats are buoyant with hope, and planning for victory at the approaching election while the Republicans are at least doubtful and uncertain as to their position and immediate future." During the session the Democrats had endorsed Roosevelt's initiatives with more cohesion than the GOP had shown.[20]

The opposition party had recovered from the 1904 debacle and was on the offensive against the Republicans. William Jennings Bryan was getting ready to make another try at the White House, and he was placing himself to the left of Roosevelt on progressive issues. Bryan asked whether the president had "the courage to be a reformer." Bryan called his party "the defender of property, because it endeavors to draw the line between honest accumulation by honest methods, on the one side, and predatory wealth and immoral methods, on the other." The Democrats expected that these themes would help them to make a substantial reduction in the Republican margins in the House and Senate and to establish a framework for a more competitive race against the Republican nominee in 1908.[21]

A central element in the Democratic electoral calculations was the potential of organized labor to deliver votes against the Republicans. The American Federation of Labor, some 1.7 million strong in 1904, hoped to achieve federal laws that would safeguard the right to strike and would reduce the power of federal judges to issue injunctions against unions. When the Speaker of the House and his Republican colleagues gave a cold reception to labor's ideas during the spring of 1906, it provided a powerful impetus to the AFL's intervention in the 1906 contest. Samuel Gompers, the union's president, urged his members to display their political muscle by defeating Republican candidates "who have been hostile or indifferent to the just demands of labor."[22]

The Republicans expected to have a difficult task in the election. "I shall do what I can to help out the Congressional Committee this fall," Roosevelt told Henry Cabot Lodge in early August, "but there are mighty ugly propositions to be faced in several different States." The most immediate concern was the September election in Maine. There the AFL had targeted Republican Congressman Charles Littlefield for defeat because of his antilabor votes in the House. The president concluded that "the labor people are utterly unreasonable," and he was prepared "to do everything to help" Littlefield that he could. The GOP sent in Secretary of War Taft, Speaker Cannon, and other party stalwarts. Littlefield held his seat, although labor's offensive cut into his usual majority.[23]

Theodore Roosevelt took a prominent role in the Republicans' campaign to retain their majority in the House. He spent much time during the summer of 1906 negotiating with Cannon, as well as others who were in charge of the Republican canvass, about the exact language of the letter he would write for publication. He did not want the document to reflect the "stand pat" sentiment on tariff revision and other issues. Senator Mark Hanna had used the poker term some years earlier as a statement of his political views, and Cannon's allies had adopted the idea that the party should not disrupt the existing prosperity by making additional reforms. Roosevelt believed that the tactic was unwise because "a good deal of the opposition we are experiencing from tariff revisionists is due to the use of unfortunate terms, 'stand pat' being a striking example of them." As he told Elihu Root, "the tariff is of course what will cause us the most trouble."[24]

Roosevelt's letter, which was addressed to Congressman James E. Watson of Indiana, was made public on 18 August 1906. The president praised Congress for having "accomplished a literally phenomenal amount of good work" and said that electing Democrats would disrupt "the present orderly progress along the lines of a carefully thought-out policy." The Hepburn Act had rendered the railroads "fully accountable to the public for the service which to their own profit they render the public." To offset the criticism of the AFL, he pointed out that the lawmakers had "taken important steps in securing to the wageworkers certain great rights," including an employers' liability law. As for the tariff, he promised revision when necessary and again warned that the tariff and the trusts were separate problems. In closing, he told Watson that "you and your colleagues are entitled to the good wishes of all those American citizens" who wanted to see the "real evils in our industrial and economic system" addressed, "not by loose declamation, but by resolute and intelligent legislation and executive action."[25]

The Republican congressional leadership used Roosevelt's letter to refute the charge that the president had displayed "alleged indifference" regarding "Republican success this fall." Yet, political friends of Roosevelt told him: "You are the issue—whoever fights on *that* issue will win; whoever fights on some other issue will lose—and we'll make that clear to the country." In some areas of the nation, Republicans now preferred not to have Speaker Cannon appear as a campaigner because of "his bitter and acrimonious controversy with Samuel Gompers, and his radical antagonism toward organized labor." Many candidates also found that the campaign committee could not help them financially as in years past, because donations from corporate givers had dried up. Efforts to rely on small gifts from Republican "Dollar Clubs" attested to the novel financial plight of the GOP.[26]

Democratic prospects against the Republicans hinged on Bryan's ability to keep the feuding wings of his own party together during the campaign. His return from a world tour in September 1906 led to a much-anticipated speech in New York City, where a more responsible Bryan would presumably be unveiled. Instead, he came out for governmental ownership of interstate railroads in an effort to put himself well to the left of the Republicans. When members of his party and the GOP criticized him for expressing radical ideas, he retreated. "I think he has helped us immensely," the president told Lodge; "down at bottom Bryan is a cheap soul."[27]

The tariff issue remained a source of Republican discord even after Roosevelt's letter to Watson had been published. In early September, Secretary of War Taft told a Maine audience that changes in business conditions made it "wise and just to revise the schedules of the existing tariff." A month later, Senator Albert J. Beveridge informed Republicans in Iowa that "no tariff schedule is immortal. When conditions change the tariff schedule that was adjusted to that condition ought also to change." Speaker Cannon, however, regarded the Dingley Tariff as "the best protective tariff law ever written upon the statute books," and he sounded that theme in the speeches he made for Republican candidates.[28]

Theodore Roosevelt watched all the developments of the campaign with close attention. In the states where he felt that important issues were at stake, he instructed his cabinet officers to make speeches for the party's candidates. William Howard Taft went on a tour of Colorado and Idaho at the president's behest; Taft's appearance in the latter state reflected Roosevelt's concern with labor violence and its alleged practitioners. The Republican governor, Frank R. Gooding, was under political attack by the Western Federation of Miners. Prolonged labor disputes had culminated in the planting of a bomb that killed a former governor, Frank Steunenberg, on 30 December 1905. Eventually, Idaho authorities charged two IWW leaders—William D. ("Big Bill") Haywood and Charles H. Moyers—with complicity in the governor's death. Roosevelt had the Justice Department look into charges that the two men had been taken from Colorado to Idaho unlawfully to face trial. The president became persuaded that Haywood and Moyers had a "black record of wrongdoing" apart from the merits of the case against them. Roosevelt wanted Taft to speak against "those dynamiters and thugs." During the fall of 1906, Roosevelt's goal was a strong Republican victory over what he deemed to be unhealthy social influences.[29]

Roosevelt was happy to have the fall elections become a test of his popular standing and the regulatory policies of his second term. In a speech at Harrisburg, Pennsylvania, in early October, he called for "adequate supervision and control over the business use of the swollen fortunes of to-day," and he asserted that "the government ought not to conduct the business of the country; but it ought to regulate it so that it shall be conducted in the interest of the public." This assertion of the need to wield governmental power for regulatory ends played well in the Middle West. An Iowa editor said that the "Harrisburg address is everywhere accepted as the platform of the republicanism of 1908," on which Roosevelt's Republican successor would either win or lose. On the other hand, "financial circles in New York" were "reported to be very much agitated over the possible recommendations of the President." The fissures in the party widened during the campaign.[30]

Despite all that the president did, the initial phase of the canvass demonstrated the continuing Democratic optimism. Republican leaders worried that the party might do poorly in such pivotal states as New York, Pennsylvania, Iowa, and Ohio, where problems of factionalism lingered. As a key argument against their opponents, the Democrats used government figures showing "that the cost of living is getting higher, and wages are not keeping pace with the advance in retail prices."[31]

In mid October, however, the momentum of the contest moved back toward the Republicans. As the possibility of a Democratic victory grew, the conservatism of the Republicans reasserted itself. The candidacy of James B. Moran for the governorship of Massachusetts was taken as one sign of how extreme the Democrats would be once they gained power. Even more dangerous was the race that William Randolph Hearst waged to be the Democratic governor of New York. To help Charles Evans Hughes, Roosevelt sent in Elihu Root, who linked Hearst to the assassination of William McKinley.

As the end of the campaign neared, Roosevelt also announced some cabinet changes that were designed to help his party's election chances and to carry his administration through until 4 March 1909. At the Treasury Department, George B. Cortelyou replaced Leslie M. Shaw. Shaw's protectionist fervor and administrative laxity were out of step with

Roosevelt's approach. George von Lengerke Meyer came back from Russia to replace Cortelyou as postmaster general. William H. Moody was named to the Supreme Court, and Charles J. Bonaparte was moved over from the Navy Department to the Justice Department. Victor H. Metcalf left the Department of Commerce and Labor to take over the navy portfolio. For some time, Oscar S. Straus, a prominent American Jew, had been Roosevelt's choice to be secretary of commerce and labor, and now his nomination was announced. Finally, James R. Garfield was selected to be the new secretary of the interior, replacing the discredited Ethan Allen Hitchcock. All these shifts were scheduled to take effect on 4 March 1907.

When the voters cast their ballots in November 1906, the outcome pleased the president. "It is very gratifying," he wrote to Alice Longworth, "to have ridden iron-shod over Gompers and the labor agitators, and at the same time to have won the striking victory while the big financiers either stood sullenly aloof or gave furtive aid to the enemy."[32] In fact the Republicans lost twenty-eight seats in the House and saw their majority shrink to fifty-eight. Republican strength in the Senate rose by four seats. In state races, Hughes defeated Hearst, and the GOP won in Ohio and Massachusetts. On the negative side for the Republicans, there were general Democratic gains as the opposition rebounded from its 1904 disaster. The Republican vote had also slipped from the heights it had attained with Roosevelt at the head of the ticket in 1904.

Friends of the president agreed that the Republican success had occurred because of Roosevelt's policies. "Not one of our men would have pulled through had it not been for the appeal to 'stand by Roosevelt,'" wrote Albert J. Beveridge. Roosevelt was convinced that the "victory for civilization" that his party had won in states such as New York and Idaho demonstrated the wisdom of his overall approach. "The corrupt corporations need the knife as much as the corrupt politicians," he told Charles Evans Hughes.[33]

The day before the balloting took place, Theodore Roosevelt issued an order that opened one of the most bitter controversies of his second term. His actions in regard to the "Brownsville Affray" illuminated his position on racial issues and raised questions about how he viewed the powers of his office toward those who were less fortunate and less privileged. For Roosevelt, who left this episode out of his autobiography, the rightness of his course was never in doubt.

What happened at Brownsville, Texas, on 13/14 August 1906 is still not entirely clear. Theodore Roosevelt received information on 15 August, including a wire from Brownsville citizens, alleging that on the previous day, black soldiers of the First Battalion of the United States Twenty-fifth Infantry, stationed at Brownsville, had shot up the community, killing one bartender and wounding a police lieutenant. After he received the news, Roosevelt ordered an investigation and told the army to keep the troops in Brownsville pending the outcome of the probe. On 24 August the army advised him that twelve suspected black soldiers should be moved to San Antonio until the president could act on their case. Roosevelt issued these instructions on the same day; he also directed that the rest of the black detachment be sent to Oklahoma.

During the next several months the army sought to learn which of the black soldiers had done the shooting. The inquiry proceeded on the assumption that the men were guilty and that the only issue was locating proof of their complicity. "That the raiders were soldiers of the Twenty-fifth Infantry can not be doubted" was the verdict of one officer who looked into the case.[34] In fact, there were substantial grounds for reasonable doubt. Eyewitness testimony about the nighttime events was contradictory; the available physical evidence did not support the official version; and the accused soldiers, as well as the members of the three companies themselves, denied any knowledge of what had happened. In fact, the collective denials that the men issued became, in the minds of the investigators, one of the most conclusive indicators of their guilt. The black soldiers, this reasoning went, were engaged in a cover-up of the deeds that some of their comrades had committed.

At no point in the inquiry process did the army or the Roosevelt administration accord the accused soldiers the presumption of innocence or provide them with legal representation. In the United States during the early twentieth century, black Americans had only the rights that the white majority accorded to them. It would have taken a substantial shift in Theodore Roosevelt's attitude for him to have gone beyond the information that the army was sending him. By 1906, moreover, Roosevelt had moved a significant distance away from the relative racial tolerance that he had displayed during his first term. The Brownsville case came, instead, when the president's courtship of the white South was the dominant theme of his policy toward American blacks.

Once the 1904 election was over, Theodore Roosevelt began to make public statements about "the Negro problem" again. In an address to a Lincoln Day dinner of the Republican Club of New York on 13 February 1905, he urged that the question be approached "with the effort to do fair and equal justice among all men," and he said that every man should have "equality of opportunity, equality of treatment before the law." As his speech proceeded, he stressed the responsibilities that black Americans ought to assume over their own condition: "Every vicious, venal, or ignorant colored man is an even greater foe to his own race than to the community as a whole." His most controversial passage asserted: "The colored man who fails to condemn crime in another colored man, who fails to co-operate in all lawful ways in bringing colored criminals to justice, is the worst enemy of his own people, as well as an enemy to all the people."[35] His remarks drew some criticism from black sources, although the newspapers that Booker T. Washington controlled were favorable. The 1904 Republican platform had called for more stringent enforcement of the rights of blacks in the South, but Roosevelt regarded that course as impractical.

Increasingly, the president looked to white southern Democrats for advice on racial subjects. He indicated to them that he would name fewer blacks to governmental posts, and he implicitly repudiated what had been perceived as the problack actions of his first term. Washington continued to be Roosevelt's link to black America, but the influence of the "Wizard" was clearly diminishing. A signal that Roosevelt had gone back to William McKinley's goal of sectional harmony among whites was given clearly during the tour of the South that Roosevelt made during the autumn of 1905.

As he moved across Dixie in October, the president spoke out on many pressing issues. The disenfranchisement of black Americans was not one that he chose to mention. Instead, he emphasized his family's southern roots and his esteem for Confederate heroes. Only at Little Rock, Arkansas, did Roosevelt attack lynching. This occurred after the state's fiery governor, Jefferson Davis, defended the practice because the "only good Negro was a dead Negro." Roosevelt criticized the governor directly and denounced him for his position.[36]

The main statement of Roosevelt's racial philosophy in 1905 came in an address that he gave at the Florida Baptist Academy and at more length at the Tuskegee Institute. There he told the students that "ignorance is the costliest crop that can be raised in any part of this Union." The education of blacks, however, should not aim beyond the industrial and agricultural training that their school provided. Returning to the theme of his Lincoln Day address, he asserted: "You are in honor bound to join hands in favor of law and order and to war against all crime, and especially against all crime by men of your own race; for the heaviest wrong done by the criminal is the wrong to his own race."[37]

Throughout the rest of 1905 and into 1906, Roosevelt's critical view of the ability of blacks persisted. He told his friend Owen Wister of his agreement about the racial inferiority of blacks in April 1906; but Roosevelt defended some of his actions and appointments, including the government's campaign against peonage in the South. Roosevelt conceded, however: "I am not satisfied that I acted wisely in either the Booker Washington dinner or the Crum appointment," although both were justifiable acts. Although these comments were confined to a private letter, they reflected the verdict that the president had reached by 1906. When riots against blacks erupted in Atlanta in September 1906, Roosevelt said and did nothing, and he placed most of the blame on blacks themselves.[38]

Roosevelt thus had scant reason to question the accuracy of what the army said had happened in Brownsville. The report that reached Roosevelt's desk in late October noted the denial of each soldier that he had been involved. The verdict was: "The secretive nature of the race, where crimes charged to members of their color is made, is well known." The president should discharge without honor all the soldiers in the three affected companies. The rationale for this collective penalty was that some of the black soldiers were surely guilty, the others knew who these were, and thus all shared in a conspiracy of silence. The black men, said the army report, "appear to stand together in a determination to resist the detection of guilt; therefore they should stand together when the penalty falls." At this time, none of the soldiers had been formally charged with any crime, nor had they a chance to confront their accusers or rebut the evidence against them.[39]

On 5 November 1906, the day before the fall elections, Roosevelt issued an order that all the soldiers be discharged and barred from holding any future governmental position. Newspapers across the country ran the story on the following day, but it was too late to affect the outcome of the political contest, including the district in which Roosevelt's son-in-law, Nicholas Longworth, was a candidate for Congress. The presidential decree affected 170 men, 6 of whom had been awarded the Medal of Honor. Two days later, on 8 November 1906, Roosevelt left on his inspection tour of Panama.

From the outset of this controversy, Roosevelt never budged from believing that his initial decision had been the correct one. He informed Booker T. Washington about his decision in advance, but the president stood firm against the black leader's request to provide additional information. "You cannot have any information to give me privately to which I could pay heed, my dear Mr. Washington, because the information on which I act is that which came out of the investigation itself." When other supporters of the accused men persuaded Secretary of War Taft to delay execution of the order until Roosevelt came back from Panama, the president wired his cabinet officer that the discharges were "not to be suspended unless there are new facts of such importance as to warrant your cabling me. I care nothing whatever for the yelling of either the politicians or the sentimentalists." The discharges took place between 16 and 26 November 1906.[40]

The displeasure of black Americans and of their vocal but politically weak white allies represented only an annoyance to Roosevelt during November 1906. By the time the president came back from Panama, however, a potentially more formidable adversary within his own party had taken up the cause of the soldiers. Senator Joseph B. Foraker had been a useful ally in the struggle against Mark Hanna during the first term. Foraker had moved away from the administration when the Hepburn Act was being considered; he was the only Senate Republican to vote against the bill. Sixty years old in 1906, the once-fiery campaigner, who became known as "Fire Alarm Joe" on the Ohio hustings, had strong presidential ambitions for 1908 which were well known in Washington. Since William Howard Taft came from the same state, the two men were bound to clash. No doubt Foraker saw in the Brownsville episode a chance to gain support among black Republicans, north and south. As he examined the evidence, however, he also became convinced that the black soldiers were innocent and had not received fair treatment. News of Foraker's attitude reached the White House. When Roosevelt came back to work, he warned Taft: "We must not fail to have a full set of affidavits in the Brownsville matter when Congress meets. *Very important*."[41] The administration prepared to head off a challenge from Foraker when Congress assembled on 3 December 1906.

That action occurred on the first day, when Senator Boies Penrose (R., Pa.), not usually a White House ally, introduced a resolution to have Roosevelt submit information about Brownsville. Foraker immediately moved a substitute resolution, asking for data from the secretary of war. Both motions were then deferred for several days. On 5 December, Roosevelt asked Taft to look into whether the white officers "of the three colored companies who took part in the murderous riot at Brownsville are or are not blamable." The next day the Senate approved both the Penrose and the Foraker resolutions.[42]

Roosevelt responded to the resolutions on 19 December 1906 in a message that made a vigorous and heated defense of his actions. He said he had made the decision "in the exercise of my constitutional power and in pursuance of what, after full consideration, I found to be my constitutional duty as Commander in Chief of the United States Army." Roosevelt maintained that the race of the soldiers was irrelevant. "Precisely the same action would have been taken had the troops been white—indeed the discharge would probably have been made in more summary fashion." The president said that between 9 and "15 or 20 of the colored soldiers" took part in the attack, and they "were the aggressors from start to finish." Their act was "unparalleled for infamy in the annals of the United States Army."

Roosevelt then denounced the soldiers for carrying on "a successful conspiracy of silence for the purpose of shielding those who took part in the original conspiracy of murder." The discharges were, in his view, a punishment, because dismissing them from the service was "utterly inadequate" in that regard. He then cited a number of precedents for the administrative action he had taken. His conclusion returned to the ideas he had so often expressed in his previous statements on racial matters. "If the colored men elect to stand by criminals of their own race because they are of their own race, they assuredly lay up for themselves the most dreadful day of reckoning."[43]

Senator Foraker responded to Roosevelt's message on the following day with the argument that soldiers who were charged with serious crimes deserved a hearing before being punished. Instead of the "scores of eyewitnesses" that the president mentioned, Foraker counted only eight witnesses. On point after point the senator contradicted Roosevelt's claims for the precedents under which he had acted or the executive authority to make the discharges as he had. Foraker contended that there was no evidence to support the belief that a conspiracy of silence existed among the men. One newspaper commented that Foraker had "dissected the President's evidence against the Negro troops." Roosevelt believed that Foraker was insincere and opportunistic in his advocacy of the cause of the soldiers. "I believe you are absolutely right in saying that Foraker has been representing Wall Street in attacking me on this issue," he told one of his correspondents.[44]

The senator's rebuttal was sufficiently damaging that on 14 January 1907 the president sent Congress another special message about Brownsville, to bolster the administration's case. Because of the doubts expressed in the Senate "as to the sufficiency of the evidence," he had sent a member of the Justice Department and one of the army officers who had earlier looked into the issue to Texas to conduct another probe. They came back with affidavits and other physical evidence that, in Roosevelt's mind, showed even more conclusively the guilt of the black troops. The new material also made it "likely that there were very few, if any, of the soldiers dismissed who could have been ignorant of what had occurred." It was now "impossible to question the conclusions upon which my order was based." He did concede that he lacked the authority to bar the men from other governmental service, and he promised to take appropriate action if any of the soldiers "shows to my

241

satisfaction that he is clear of guilt, or of shielding the guilty." Again, the assumption of the black soldiers' complicity in the incident was not to be questioned.[45]

In the Senate the issue over Foraker's resolution became whether Roosevelt had the power as president to issue the discharge order. Faced with resolute Republican opposition to attacking the president's power, Foraker had to back away from a position that challenged Roosevelt's authority, and he had to accept an amendment that left the presidential decree unquestioned as a prerogative of his office. Roosevelt was delighted at this outcome: "There never has been a more complete case of backdown and humiliation than this of Foraker's."[46]

Four days later the two Republicans had a public confrontation over the Brownsville issue. They both attended the annual dinner of the Gridiron Club. The theme of this gathering of reporters and public officials was Roosevelt's relationship with prominent Americans. Under Foraker's picture in the program appeared a poem whose opening lines ran: "All coons look alike to me, J. B. Foraker, says he, says he." The festivities then went forward with songs and skits that elaborated on the evening's theme. Having "roasted" the president during the proceedings, the organizers gave Roosevelt a chance to respond in the jocular spirit of the gathering. Instead, Roosevelt embarked on a detailed summary of his position on railroad regulation and other matters then in controversy, before discussing the question of his presidential power to decide what would be done about the soldiers. The role of the Senate, he remarked, was an "academic" one as far as the discharge ruling was concerned, and he added the statement "All coons look alike to me."[47]

The toastmaster then accorded Foraker the privilege of making a rebuttal. The senator delivered a powerful address to a receptive audience. "The discussion in the Senate had been more than academic," said one summary of his remarks, "and [he] ventured to predict that the results will prove it." The senator was persuasive and eloquent in defense of the accused men, he accounted for his own motives in coming to their defense, and he asserted that the president should not enjoy a special position when he was in the wrong on a matter of public policy. "No preachments from the White House were essential to the proper performance of his duty as a Senator."[48]

Roosevelt did not appreciate this public scolding, and he made his reply when Foraker sat down. The president said of the black soldiers that some "were bloody butchers," and "the only reason I didn't have them hung" was his inability to learn which men "did the shooting." An obviously angry president remarked that "the only place the Brownsville battalion could get justice was at the White House—the Senate could not mete it out to the discharged negroes, because the power lay with him [Roosevelt], and him alone." An excited crowd left the dinner talking about what they had witnessed.[49]

Ordinarily the Gridiron Dinner was an off-the-record affair at which no hard news was made. For the president and a senator to quarrel publicly became the stuff of instant Washington gossip. The verdict among politicians was that Roosevelt had fared badly, and Foraker enjoyed a brief moment of local popularity. Otherwise, the incident did nothing to injure Roosevelt's position with the American people. There were long-range consequences, however; it marked the end of any personal relations between Foraker and the president. Roosevelt resolved to break the senator's power in Ohio politics. That could best be done by supporting the presidential candidacy of Secretary of War Taft. Swinging the patronage from Foraker to Taft would be a visible sign of Roosevelt's attitude, and that occurred in mid March 1907, when he instructed members of his cabinet to give Taft a decisive voice in the allocation of patronage in Ohio.

The Senate hearings on the Brownsville incident opened in early February 1907 and ran in two phases for the ensuing thirteen months. The Military Affairs Committee issued its reports soon after the testimony concluded in March 1908. Four Republicans and five Democrats contended that the soldiers were guilty and that Roosevelt's allegations were correct. Foraker and three Republican colleagues submitted two minority verdicts. Foraker and a colleague deemed the men innocent; two others said that there was not enough evidence to sustain the charge. The Senate then considered an administration proposal, contained in a presidential message, to allow soldiers to reenlist if they could establish their innocence. Foraker contended that taking an oath of innocence should be enough for reenlistment. On 14 April 1908 the Ohio senator laid his case before his colleagues and concluded that the soldiers "ask no favors because they are Negroes, but only for justice because they are men."[50]

The Brownsville episode was far from over. Foraker and the White House would spar over the guilt of the soldiers during the rest of 1908. On the substance of the charges, the president never shifted his position. He had made up his mind that the soldiers had done what he had repeatedly warned blacks against doing. They had failed to cooperate with white superiors to punish criminals in their midst. Believing that he had the best interests of black Americans at heart, the president could not rise above the racial values of his own time. He did not question the accuracy of the information that he received from the army, and he refused to admit at any time that he might have erred in the conclusions he had reached. The result was a serious miscarriage of justice.

In addition to the arguments about Brownsville, the short session of Congress that began in December 1906 produced squabbling between Capitol Hill and the White House over conservation, naval appropriations, immigration in general and Japanese immigration in particular, and the president's regulatory program. Since he had been so helpful to Republican candidates during the fall elections, Roosevelt expected a certain degree of cooperation. He was disappointed. "I do wish, however," he wrote in December, "that the same men who get elected on the issue of standing by me would not at once turn and try to thwart me."[51]

By the end of 1906, however, the Republican majority in Congress, aware that Roosevelt's presidency was running down, had lost most of their patience with his presidential activism and his policy of enhanced governmental power. When he sent them five special messages during a single week in December, the lawmakers expressed "annoyance over such unwonted activity." The personal tone contained in his messages grated on the sensibilities of congressmen and senators who resented being held up to presidential criticism before the American people. The innovative techniques that had worked well during the first term had less effectiveness as Roosevelt's administration moved into its sixth year.[52]

The annual message, sent to Congress on 4 December 1906, addressed a wealth of issues and laid out an ambitious agenda for action by both the legislative and the executive branches. In the process, Roosevelt used his forum to point up a number of moral lessons. He warned the restive business community that "only reckless speculation and disregard of legitimate business methods on the part of the business world" could weaken the nation's economic prosperity. He also assailed the "sinister demagogues and foolish visionaries" who, in his judgment, tried to inflame "a violent class hatred against all men of wealth." There were also "wealthy reactionaries of such obtuse morality" who were opposed to the enforcement of laws and, indeed, "to any movement of which the aim is fearlessly to do exact and even justice to all." The *Pittsburgh* (Pa.) *Press* said of Roosevelt that he was "no mere party hack, reciting dreary pothouse platitudes, but a John the Baptist turned statesman, altho he does not wear the sandals and the hair shirt and depend on the ravens to feed him."[53]

Among the president's specific recommendations were a law to bar corporations from making contributions to political parties, legislation to limit the use of injunctions in labor disputes, and a measure to restrict the hours that railroad employees worked. He also called for an employers' liability law and the arbitration of labor disputes. These did not end the matters that received presidential attention: he also asked for national laws on marriage and divorce, reductions in the Philippine tariff, and reform in the banking system. "The horrors incident to the employment of young children in factories or at work anywhere are a blot on our civilization." Therefore, Congress should have a "thorough official investigation of the matter," while "a drastic and thoroughgoing child-labor law should be enacted for the District of Columbia and the Territories."[54]

Sensitive to criticism about his policy in the Brownsville case, Roosevelt denounced the lynching of black Americans and advocated more educational opportunities for their race. He also discussed the need for an inheritance tax and the merits of an income tax to finance governmental programs. The pending legislation to encourage American shipping also won presidential endorsement. The message dealt with the controversial question of Japanese immigration on the West Coast, which was Roosevelt's most pressing foreign-policy problem at that time. A discussion of other foreign-policy issues and a review of the needs of the army and the navy brought to a conclusion Roosevelt's longest annual message up to that time.

The short session produced action on some issues that the president raised, but the general record of Congress fell short of what he desired. A measure to restrict the working hours of railroad employees to no more than sixteen in a row cleared both houses. A cautious bill was passed to have the secretary of commerce and labor investigate the child-labor problem. A Philippine banking bill was enacted, as was a law to broaden the government's right of appeal in criminal cases.

A presidential proposal to aid the beleaguered American shipping industry through governmental payments for mail that crossed the oceans did not fare so well. The concept of shipping subsidies divided Republicans on both coasts, who liked the idea, from middle westerners, who saw it as unwarranted support for special interests and as potentially damaging to the railroads that served their region. A bill to help transoceanic mail, backed by a president's message, got through the House but died in the Senate. The sectional split in the party on this question anticipated later divisions over the tariff and other subjects during 1908/9. The adoption of the amendment to limit the president's power to create forest reserves was more than just a sign of western impatience over conservation policy; it also demonstrated a general congressional dislike for the president's assertion of executive power. For the most part, however, Roosevelt was content with the outcome of the session. "I have succeeded in getting thru some things that I very much wisht, altho not always in the form I most desired," he wrote to Edward Grey on 28 February, in a letter that also showed Roosevelt's desire for simplified spelling. What he had achieved compensated for his failure "to get two or three other things which, tho not necessary, were certainly desirable."[55]

The dominant domestic issue for the remainder of 1907 was the president's relationship with the business community, arising from its suspicion and distrust of his regulatory policies. "Mr. Roosevelt is a bugaboo to Wall Street," noted the editor of *World's Work* in April 1907. "The average trader has an hallucination that the President hates Wall Street and would destroy it if he could." Roosevelt spent much time and energy assuring the financial world that he was not an enemy, but the campaign did not produce tangible reconciliation. The president was puzzled at "this belief in Wall Street that I am a wild-eyed revolutionist. I cannot condone wrong, but I certainly do not intend to do aught save what is beneficial to the man of means who acts squarely and fairly."[56]

Despite the nation's prosperity during the first half of 1907, there was apprehension among railroad men and bankers about the future course of the economy. The leaders of the railroad industry were complaining that state legislation to hold down rates was preventing them from borrowing funds needed in order to serve the demand for their facilities. They wanted Roosevelt to reassure the public that he would treat their companies less stringently in the future. The president met with J. P. Morgan on 11 March 1907, and the financier suggested that he also talk with the executives of four major lines about "what steps might be taken to allay the public anxiety as to the relations between the railroads and the government." On the next day, Roosevelt met with one railroad president who indicated that stronger federal legislation was preferable to numerous and separate state laws regarding railroads.[57]

Roosevelt decided not to meet with the other railroad men as a group, and he told his correspondents from the business world that "not one word of mine; not one act, administrative or legislative, of the National Government" was responsible, he believed, for the condition of the railroads. Despite these reassurances, the president's relations with that industry worsened. In April 1907 the publication of some private letters of E. H. Harriman's raised the issue of Roosevelt's conduct during the campaign of 1904 and the impact that corporate contributions had had on his election. The president released one of his characteristic "history letters," which set out his version of what had taken place with

Harriman. The acrimonious controversy further worried an edgy financial community. A week later there was heated talk about a possible union of John D. Rockefeller and Harriman to nominate a conservative Republican in 1908. A financier in Massachusetts called the president "the most effective planter of the weeds of uninformed socialistic propaganda."[58]

Roosevelt made several attempts to placate his critics during trips that he made throughout the spring and summer of 1907. His most detailed response came when he spoke in Massachusetts on 20 August at the dedication of the Pilgrim Memorial Monument. He contended that the Sherman Antitrust Act had been necessary for the American people to use until they decided to "exercise over the great corporations that thoroughgoing and radical control which it is certain ultimately to find necessary." In time he hoped that the nation might have laws that would "permit such useful combinations as are made with absolute openness and as the representatives of the government may previously approve." He lamented the problems that attended the criminal prosecution of corporate leaders, and he charged that "many men of large wealth have been guilty of conduct which from the moral standpoint is criminal." He assured business at the same time that "No individual, no corporation, obeying the law has anything to fear from this Administration."[59]

In the unsettled economic conditions of the summer and fall of 1907, Roosevelt's words soothed few in the business community. The huge fine of $29 million that was levied against Standard Oil after it was found guilty of rebating, even though it was imposed by a federal judge, was seen as an example of the government's punitive policy. The president's tart phrases also stung in the business world. In his annual message in December 1906 he assailed those who, "in a spirit of greed," sought to "exploit" their fellow citizens "with callous disregard to their welfare of soul and body." At Provincetown, Massachusetts, he spoke about "certain malefactors of great wealth" whom the government was seeking to punish. There were the American people, on one side, and on the other, there were "a few ruthless and domineering men whose wealth makes them peculiarly formidable because they hide behind the breastworks of corporate organization." Within that world, businessmen told each other that the president had a drinking problem and was otherwise unstable.[60]

As the year ended, the American economy showed evidence of strain after the ebullient prosperity that had marked most of Roosevelt's presidency. The inflationary pressure on prices was intense throughout the year, and the money markets struggled to meet the demands for credit worldwide. The nation's banking system was still rickety, and there were individual firms in the industry whose structure was very weak. In mid March 1907 there was a record drop in prices on the New York Stock Exchange that required intervention from the Treasury Department to halt. That action was the work of Cortelyou, the new secretary of the treasury, who had replaced Shaw on 3 March 1907. The secretary's policy helped the markets weather the effects of a modest recession that commenced at this time.

The economy remained relatively calm until the middle of October, when events in the copper market worried bankers. As the market price for copper declined, companies that mined the metal endeavored to keep prices up. Efforts to control the market in copper eventually led one company to dump its holdings. The resulting break in the copper price lessened depositor confidence in the banks and in the trust companies that copper magnates controlled. Rumor linked the Knickerbocker Trust Company with the copper industry, and a run on that company began on 22 October 1907. The Panic of 1907 had begun, and the American banking system seemed to be on the edge of general collapse.

Roosevelt was away from Washington when these financial troubles occurred, but he turned immediately to the banking crisis upon his return on 23 October 1907. He spoke with Root, George von Lengerke Meyer, and Robert Bacon of the State Department—all of whom had close ties to Wall Street—to reassure the business community. Meanwhile, Cortelyou had begun to transfer more than $37 million to the endangered New York banks. As the runs continued, the secretary sent an additional $31 million to six major New York banking firms. Despite these actions, the banks in New York eventually had to suspend making payments to their depositors.

The focus of the problem during the second week of the panic became the Trust Company of America, which required an estimated $25 million to keep its doors open. Simultaneously, there was fear that the imminent failure of the underwriting firm of Moore and Schley would cause a stock-market plunge that would, in turn, render it impossible to raise the funds needed to support the Trust Company of America. The key to saving Moore and Schley rested on the shares of the Tennessee Coal and Iron Corporation, which were the collateral for the loans that the investment firm had made. The answer seemed to be to have United States Steel acquire Tennessee Coal and Iron, thereby providing either cash or a marketable stock to Moore and Schley. The directors of United States Steel finally voted to make an offer for the Tennessee firm, but they also decided to obtain the assurance of the president and the Justice Department that the scheme would not lead to an antitrust prosecution.

On 4 November 1907, Henry Clay Frick and Elbert H. Gary of United States Steel met with Roosevelt for about twenty minutes. They told him about the plight of Moore and Schley, although they did not name the firm itself, and they sketched its relation to Tennessee Coal and Iron. They disclaimed any selfish motive behind the action of United States Steel to obtain the stock of the Tennessee company. They said that they were entering the deal because they believed that it would "be an important factor in preventing a break that might be ruinous." They then said to Roosevelt that "they did not wish to do this if I [Roosevelt] stated that it ought not to be done." The president assured them that he "felt it no public duty of mine to interpose any objection." He immediately dictated a letter to that effect to Attorney General Bonaparte. The public announcement of Roosevelt's position eased tensions in the New York financial markets.[61]

Subsequent disclosures about the episode, made by Roosevelt between 1909 and 1912, revealed that he had too readily trusted the assurances that Frick and Gary had given him about the intentions of U.S. Steel. The acquisition of the Tennessee company gave U.S. Steel a strong competitive advantage in the southern steel market. The merger was accomplished at a bargain price. Roosevelt had not pressed his visitors to learn the details of the transaction that was receiving his tacit endorsement. He went ahead, based on his conviction "that what was done was necessary to save the situation; that the panic would have spread and very great disaster occurred if exactly what was done had not been done." As always, Roosevelt was sincere in his convictions, but the incident showed that his personal style of presidential leadership was never any better than his capacity to grasp the facts of a specific issue.[62]

The financial effects of the panic continued to trouble the White House during November 1907. To stem the flow of funds out of the country and to increase the amount of currency in circulation, the president authorized Cortelyou to issue $50 million in Panama bonds and up to $100 million in $50 government bonds paying 3 percent. The secretary did so in a manner that made it possible for banks to acquire the bonds with only a minimal down payment. The government's policy relieved the financial stringency, bolstered international confidence, and provided vital funds to move crops in the South and West.

As the economic situation improved, there began to be discussion about the causes of the panic and about the degree to which Roosevelt and his policies were to blame. The president was "perfectly certain that in the end the Nation will have to come to my policies, or substantially to my policies, simply because the Republic cannot endure unless its governmental actions are founded on these policies, for they represent nothing whatever but aggressive honesty and fair treatment for all—not make-believe fair treatment, but genuine fair treatment." He made the same argument in his annual message on 4 December 1907. Writing about the currency, he asserted: "No legislation can by any possibility guarantee the business community against the results of speculative folly any more than it can guarantee an individual against the results of his extravagance." The business community was not reassured, and antagonism toward the president ran high among that section of the population in the East. As the British ambassador reported, however, after a visit to Cleveland, Ohio, the president's popularity in that midwestern city and across the region "seems to be undiminished among the merchants, bankers, and manufacturers."[63]

The approaching presidential election made the question of Roosevelt's popularity a central one for the Republicans. Should the party select an heir of the president's policies, or should it resume a more traditional conservatism? Roosevelt's own commitment to greater governmental regulation had wrenched the GOP leftward after 1905, but a substantial minority of the party remained skeptical about the stronger government and more powerful executive that Roosevelt represented. "To use the terminology of Continental politics," he told an English friend, "I am trying to keep the left center together."[64]

Roosevelt also wrote in his 1907 annual message that "in foreign affairs this country's steady policy is to behave toward other nations as a strong and self-respecting man should behave toward the other men with whom he is brought into contact."[65] During the closing years of his administration, Roosevelt faced a series of foreign-policy problems that tested his capacity to lead the nation in world affairs. Political unrest in Cuba compelled the president to order a new U.S. intervention in the island. Relations with Great Britain and Germany felt the effects of the growing international tension within Europe. Most volatile was the crisis with Japan over the issue of how immigrants from that nation would be treated on the West Coast. The successful resolution of these difficulties enabled Roosevelt to close out his diplomatic career as president on a positive and peaceful note.

11

★ ★ ★ ★ ★

"WE WERE
AT ABSOLUTE PEACE"

When writing to William Howard Taft in August 1907 about the Philippines, Theodore Roosevelt noted that in foreign policy "we have continually to accommodate ourselves to conditions as they actually are and not as we would wish them to be." For a president who wished to be an active participant in world affairs during the last several years of his administration, the restraints that circumstances placed upon him determined the issues in foreign affairs where he could wield his influence. After six years in office, Roosevelt had recognized that "it is exceedingly difficult to get this people to take a proper view of any emergency that arises." Accordingly, Roosevelt continued to exercise presidential power with moderation and caution on the world scene.[1]

In the volatile region of Latin America, the main initiative during these years lay with Secretary of State Elihu Root. He made a lengthy visit to South America in 1906, where he said in Brazil: "We wish for no victories but those of peace; for no territory except our own; for no sovereignty except the sovereignty over ourselves." Root established friendly personal relations with Latin American leaders and saw to it that the countries of the Western Hemisphere were asked to participate in the peace conference at The Hague in 1907. The secretary also achieved ratification of the Dominican customs treaty, and he negotiated pacts designed to foster peace in Central America. Finally, Root pursued better ties with Colombia in order to reduce some of the residual tensions over the Panama Canal. When he left the State Department in

January 1909, Root had substantially improved the nation's ties with Latin America.[2]

There was one crisis in the Roosevelt-Root policy toward the region that required careful handling. The secretary of state was in South America, mending diplomatic fences, so the problem of Cuba in 1906 fell to Roosevelt and William Howard Taft to resolve. Cuba had been independent since 1903, but the government of Tomás Estrada Palma had encountered increasing popular discontent since national elections in December 1905. In the summer of 1906, armed insurrection impelled Estrada Palma to seek the intervention of the United States under the Platt Amendment. Simultaneously, the enemies of President Estrada Palma were asking for U.S. troops to help them in their rebellion.

For the Roosevelt administration, this new Cuban crisis was awkwardly timed. Root had said in Rio de Janeiro on 31 August that the United States would interfere with less frequency in the affairs of Latin American nations. While Roosevelt had not renounced the right to intervene, he stressed that the United States should interfere to the least degree necessary. An involvement in Cuba might require thousands of U.S. troops and would not help the Republicans in the approaching congressional elections. "On the one hand we cannot permanently see Cuba a prey to misrule and anarchy," he wrote in early September 1906, "on the other hand I loathe the thought of assuming any control over the island such as we have over Porto Rico and the Philippines."[3]

With both sides in the dispute looking for a U.S. presence, the president found it difficult to avoid some kind of involvement. In late August he allowed the Cuban government to buy ammunition from the War Department, and on 1 September 1906 he agreed to have three army officers survey the situation on the island. A key decision to order two naval vessels to Cuba came seven days later, in response to a request from the Estrada Palma government. Explicit statements from the administration about its reluctance to intervene accompanied these actions. When marines went ashore from one of the United States vessels, Roosevelt ordered them back to the ship on 13 September. The president wrote to the Cuban minister in Washington on 14 September, in a letter meant for Cuba's president and other countrymen, that "all Cuban patriots" should understand "that the only way that they can preserve the independence of their republic is to prevent the necessity of outside interference, by rescuing it from the anarchy of civil war." On that same day, Roosevelt sent Taft and Robert Bacon, an assistant secretary of state, to seek a peaceful settlement.[4]

The two emissaries reached Havana on 19 September, and Taft tried to arrange a compromise. His efforts failed when Cuba's president insisted that he would resign rather than agree to the concessions that Taft proposed. The secretary of war sought Roosevelt's approval for United States troops to be landed. Roosevelt had already stressed to Taft that "it is important from the standpoint of public sentiment here that we shall make it plain that we are exhausting every effort to come to an agreement before we intervene." During the period 25 to 29 September 1906, Taft and Bacon looked for a formula that would keep a working Cuban government in place. Their effort failed. On 28 September, Roosevelt gave permission to "land forces and issue proclamations as suggested in my name." He reminded Taft to say that "the Government you form is only provisional and temporary until Cubans can form one for themselves." The next day, Taft began acting as the provisional governor of Cuba.[5]

Taft remained in place for two weeks until Charles E. Magoon came from Panama to take over. The government held power in Cuba until January 1909, when United States soldiers withdrew and an independent government resumed the direction of the island's affairs. The long-range effects on Cuba of this second intervention remain controversial. Theodore Roosevelt and his administration intervened reluctantly and sought to leave as soon as was politically feasible. The president did not endeavor to reshape Cuban society or to guide the island's political developments into new paths. By 1908/9, Theodore Roosevelt wanted no more expansive imperialism for the United States; he wanted only the orderly management and eventual liquidation of the tutelary duties the nation had assumed a decade earlier.

Relations with the major European powers continued in the directions established before 1906. In the case of Great Britain, rapprochement between the two nations was not as smooth as subsequent analysis has suggested. An irritant for Roosevelt was the British ambassador, Sir Mortimer Durand. Appointed in 1903, Durand disappointed the president. When Roosevelt took him on an outing in Rock Creek Park, the ambassador flunked the "hike test," which enabled those who passed it, such as Jules Jusserand and Speck von Sternburg, to become informal friends of Roosevelt's. The president also found Durand an impossible colleague. "He seems to have a brain of about eight-guinea-pig-power" was the verdict, and Roosevelt wanted London to understand that "it is useless to have a worthy creature of mutton-suet consistency like the good Sir Mortimer."[6]

After the Algeciras Conference, Roosevelt decided that the ambassador had to go. The president mounted a private and extensive campaign to persuade the new Liberal government to accept a change. He hoped they would send his good friend Cecil Spring Rice. Through another British friend, Arthur Lee, the United States ambassador, Whitelaw Reid, and other channels, Roosevelt made his dislike of Durand well known to London. The British government had decided to recall Durand even before Roosevelt launched his campaign, but it balked at naming Spring Rice. The new envoy was James Bryce, whose book *The American Commonwealth* had become an instant authority during the 1880s and 1890s. His appointment represented a partial recognition in Britain that their chief diplomat in the United States had to be more congenial to the leader of an emerging world power.

What troubled Roosevelt most about Durand was the large effect that his inability to communicate with the ambassador had on Anglo-American relations. The British seemed to think that the president was closer to Germany and the kaiser than in fact he was, and Roosevelt hoped to convince London that his attitude was more friendly to them and more skeptical about the German leader. One example that occurred before Durand's ouster was a presidential effort to curb the naval weapons race in which the important European powers were engaged by 1906. During the summer of that year, Roosevelt endeavored to persuade other world figures to agree to place limits on the size of the battleships in their fleets.

Roosevelt's plan was framed in the context of two European developments. In September 1905 the Russian government declared that it would transmit invitations for a second international conference at The Hague in Holland to discuss questions of international law, armaments, and world peace. The president himself had proposed such a gathering in his 1904 annual message, but he graciously allowed the tsar to have the credit for the initiative. Three months later, in his 1905 message, Roosevelt said that the United States "would, as a matter of course, take part in the new conference and endeavor to further its aims," as his nation had done in the first conference in 1899. He took the opportunity to remind his readers about the dangers of reckless disarmament. "So long as the world is as unorganized as now the armies and navies of those people who on the whole stand for justice, offer not only the best, but the only possible, security for a just peace."

At the same time, Roosevelt called for a "surer method than now exists of securing justice as between nations." He looked on with apprehension as the Europeans waged their expensive race for naval supremacy. The president was especially concerned about the *Dreadnought* battleship that the British were constructing. If that design became a world standard, it would render obsolete the battleships that he had persuaded Congress to authorize between 1901 and 1905. On the other hand, if he could head off a scramble to build dreadnoughts, it would be very much in the interest of peace and of the United States. The question was whether the Germans, who were trying to catch up with the British, would agree to limitations on their capacity to construct modern warships.[7]

The British tried to induce Roosevelt to join them in a campaign against the naval arms race during August 1906. The president was disposed to go ahead. "I should like to see the British navy kept at its present size," he wrote to Reid, "but only on condition that the Continental and Japanese navies are not built up." A day earlier he had informed Andrew Carnegie that he "sometimes" wished "that we did not have the ironclad custom which forbids a President ever to go abroad." If Roosevelt could consult with the kaiser and other European leaders in person, he felt sure that he "could be of help in this Hague Conference business." Within a few months the president broke with custom by going to Panama and leaving the continental United States. Going to Europe to conduct foreign policy was another matter altogether. Sensitive to his reputation for impulsive gestures, Roosevelt deferred to the implicit proprieties of his office and stretched them in this instance in a manner that pleased public opinion.[8]

The president advanced the arms proposal to the British attaché, Edward Gleichen, in late August; and he asked Gleichen to transmit the idea to his government. "Of course, we should meet with opposition from the Kaiser," the president said, "but that can't be helped." There was a round of discussion in Europe about what Roosevelt had said, but neither Britain nor Germany wanted to make a tangible move that might leave it at a disadvantage in the arms competition. In late October, Roosevelt told a senator about his initiative and concluded: "I see no hope of accomplishing this result." At The Hague conference, Roosevelt did what he could to aid the British, but he took little substantive interest in what took place during the deliberations. "I have not followed things at The Hague," he wrote, once he had decided that the British government would insist, "quite properly, upon maintaining its own great naval superiority."[9]

With Bryce in Washington, Anglo-American relations warmed as the ambassador and Secretary Root dealt with such problems as the North Atlantic fisheries, the international boundary between the United States and Canada, and seal hunting in Arctic waters. The process of "cleaning the slate" contributed to the further reduction of tensions between Great Britain, Canada, and the United States by the time Roosevelt left the presidency. In December 1908 the president informed Arthur Lee that "keeping England and America closer together too" was a cause that he always had "peculiarly at heart." By 1909 the British had begun to understand how friendly Roosevelt had been to their interests.[10]

Relations between the United States and Germany followed a different path during the last phase of Roosevelt's presidency. The clashing national interests of the two countries represented the most stubborn obstacle to the alliance with the United States that Kaiser William and his government vainly pursued. Nonetheless the Germans endeavored to capitalize on the decline in Japanese-American relations from 1906 onward to forge a working partnership with the United States on Asian issues. During the tense moments in the American crisis with Japan, the kaiser would inform the United States ambassador in Berlin about possible Japanese military action in Mexico and elsewhere in Latin America. The president gave little credence to these musings. His policy was one of trying to secure British cooperation in any possible confrontation with Japan. In the process, Roosevelt's doubts about trusting the kaiser intensified.

Late in 1907 the German ruler even tried to assemble an unlikely diplomatic union of his nation, the United States, and China, premised on a defense of the Open Door. Roosevelt was cool to the idea in his talks with Speck von Sternburg and in the written messages that went to Berlin. There was a clear lack of United States interest, which Sternburg often did not convey accurately. The kaiser continued to dream his dreams of an eventual German-American entente. His whimsical and moody personality led to actions that further alienated the president. There was a brief and confusing episode when Roosevelt sought to name a new ambassador, David Jayne Hill, and the kaiser came out against a choice that he had previously endorsed. Equally unsettling was the interview that the kaiser gave in the spring of 1908. In his ramblings in an interview with a *New York Times* reporter, William had denounced the British, forecast an American war with Japan, and said that he did not like William Howard Taft "because he was under Catholic influence." The president persuaded the *Times* not to publish the explosive document. A few months later the kaiser gave a similar sensational interview to a British paper with disastrous diplomatic results that inflamed anti-German opinion in Britain. The *Times* incident convinced Roosevelt that the German ruler could not be trusted.[11]

For the rest of his administration the president continued to flatter the kaiser. When Sternburg died of cancer in August 1908, Roosevelt was "shocked and grieved" at the news about his friend. Later he told the kaiser that he, William, was "the most influential and powerful of living men." The relations between Germany and the United States entered a period of relative calm before the outbreak of World War I, but the tensions that had marked the Roosevelt years had only receded; they had not disappeared. As president, Roosevelt had conducted diplomacy toward Germany with few illusions and with a good sense of the national interest. It was not his fault that the kaiser often deluded himself and that Sternburg was an imperfect transmitter of presidential messages on serious issues. When Roosevelt retired, the Germans had not succeeded in drawing closer to the United States or in halting the progress of the Anglo-American friendship.[12]

The major diplomatic issue that Theodore Roosevelt confronted during the last years of his presidency was his nation's troubled relations with Japan. The conclusion of the Treaty of Portsmouth in 1905 marked a transition between the generally harmonious understanding that had existed with Japan since the mid 1890s and the tensions and war scares that followed from 1906 until 1909. Trade rivalries in the Far East contributed to the problem but were not the primary source of difficulty. The crux of the matter was Japanese immigration to the West Coast of the United States and the resulting hostility to the presence of these Asian newcomers in California and other western states. Anti-Japanese sentiment grew out of the economic competition that the immigrants posed to white laborers, racial feelings against Asians in general, and apprehension about the long-range intentions of Japan toward the United States. Californians explored a number of approaches to reduce Japanese immigration before 1906. The state's long history of anti-Chinese feeling made a campaign against the Japanese a politically potent device that few state leaders in both parties wanted to resist.

A center of anti-Japanese sentiment was San Francisco, and the diplomatic crisis began there on 11 October 1906, when the city's Board of Education directed that Japanese school children be taught in segregated schools. The school board's action provoked a diplomatic crisis. The Japanese reacted with outrage to what was perceived as a racial and cultural slur. The ambassador in Washington was instructed to tell the Roosevelt administration that the segregation order "has produced among all classes of people in Japan a feeling of profound disappointment and sorrow." The Japanese government expected that the decision would be quickly reversed, and Tokyo's response went to the State Department in late October 1906.[13]

Roosevelt's cabinet met on 26 October 1906 to consider what the United States should do. The administration decided to send Victor H. Metcalf, the outgoing secretary of commerce and labor and the future navy secretary, who was himself a native of California, to that state to look into the problem. "I shall exert all the power I have under the Constitution to protect the rights of the Japanese who are here,"

THE PRESIDENCY OF THEODORE ROOSEVELT

Roosevelt wrote to Kentaro Kaneko, "and I shall deal with the subject at length in my message to Congress." The president also asked the navy for an appraisal of United States and Japanese naval strength. In his mind the crisis underscored the need for naval readiness. "I most earnestly feel that we cannot afford to let our navy fall behind," he warned Senator Eugene Hale (R., Me.), chair of the Naval Affairs Committee. The senator proved cool to Roosevelt's argument, but the president intended to press the matter with Congress.[14]

Secretary Metcalf's trip to California did not produce positive results. The school board in San Francisco was not going to amend or discard what it had done. Since the Japanese-American treaty of commerce of 1894 did not contain a general most-favored-nation clause, it was unlikely that the California Supreme Court would rule that the school board's action violated the rights of the Japanese children. Roosevelt was convinced that the only workable solution to the crisis lay in persuading Japan "to prevent all immigration of Japanese laboring men—that is, of the coolie class—into the United States." To do that would require an easing of Japanese unhappiness over the San Francisco case. Because he lacked tangible ways to show that the United States was doing something to assuage Japanese anger, Roosevelt intended to put firm language into his 1906 annual message in order to mollify Tokyo.[15]

The president's statements on 4 December 1906 were strong. He characterized the school board's order as a "wicked absurdity" that represented "a confession of inferiority in our civilization." To the citizens of California, he warned that the government would not sit quietly while the Japanese received mistreatment. "It is only a very small body of our citizens that act badly," he wrote; "where the Federal Government has power it will deal summarily with any such." Roosevelt asked for a naturalization law to apply to Japanese who wished to become citizens, and he also requested that the government be given power "to enforce the rights of aliens under treaties." On the West Coast the reaction to these words was negative. The *Sacramento Union* said that "not even the big stick is big enough to compel the people of California to do a thing which they have a fixt determination not to do."[16]

Roosevelt's message also aroused bad feelings on Capitol Hill. The California delegation was especially angry, and southern Democrats reacted against the contention that the federal government might interfere with a local school system. The president soon retreated from his intense position as he realized the strength of racial feelings in California and the likelihood of a persistent crisis with Japan if immigration from Japan was not reduced. Roosevelt shifted his attention to framing what became known as the Gentlemen's Agreement with Japan. The elements of this informal accord were, first, to have the San Francisco school board withdraw the order that the Japanese found so offensive. The government of Japan, for its part, was not to issue passports to the United States mainland, and Washington elected to pass legislation to restrict immigration from Hawaii, Canada, and Mexico. These arrangements were worked out slowly and with difficulty during the early months of 1907.

The negotiations with Japan revealed that the administration would have to obtain an end to the school board's order before the Japanese would take steps on their side. The president met with the California congressional delegation on 30 January 1907. After a two-hour conference, the congressmen asked the school officials to meet with Roosevelt and Root and also requested that the governor of California defer any legislative action toward the Japanese in that state. News of the secret meeting leaked out, and a brief war scare ensued. Roosevelt may well have capitalized on this moment of popular emotion to help his program of naval appropriations then in Congress.

Still, it seemed as if the basis for an agreement with Japan had been found. For the next several weeks, however, Roosevelt and Root tried vainly to work out a mutual-exclusion treaty with Tokyo. While that futile effort proceeded, the president also met with the San Francisco delegation amid reports of the continuing arrivals of hundreds of Japanese immigrants on the West Coast. It was clear that the Californians would rescind the school board's order only if the administration itself took decisive steps to cut off the influx of Japanese laborers.

Fortunately for the White House, a legislative means to accomplish its part of the process was available. In May 1906, Senator William P. Dillingham (R., Vt.) had introduced a measure to tighten immigration procedures and to impose a literacy test for those over sixteen who were seeking admission to the United States. Roosevelt supported the bill because "we should try only to bring in elements which would be of advantage to our community."[17] He had kept such sentiments muted during the 1904 elections because an overt identification with the restriction of immigration might hurt the Republicans among foreign-born voters. Indeed, Oscar S. Straus later was named secretary of commerce and labor in order to court Jewish immigrant voters for the GOP. In the Senate, where restrictionist sentiment was strong, the bill went through easily with the support of Henry Cabot Lodge and others. Speaker Cannon opposed the bill as written, because its provisions would cut off a supply of cheap labor to manufacturers. Since organized labor supported the measure in order to reduce competition from immigrant

259

workers, Cannon disliked the bill on that account as well. In June 1906 the House rewrote the measure and deleted the literacy test. The bill then went to a conference committee, where it was reposing when the crisis with Japan occurred.

Elihu Root and Lodge devised the idea of amending the immigration bill to address the diplomatic problem by barring laborers from Japan from moving to the West Coast after a stay in Hawaii. To the proposed law, Root and Lodge added an amendment that would give the president the authority to bar entry to an alien with a foreign passport whose admission would be "to the detriment of labor conditions" in the United States. No specific reference to Japan appeared. The price that Cannon extracted for this change was acceptance of the House bill that did not contain a literacy test. The amendment attracted opposition from southern Democrats, but presidential pressure helped put the compromise through the Senate on 15 February 1907. The House acted favorably three days later.[18]

The long-range impact of the 1907 immigration law came from its creation of the Dillingham Commission to probe the issue of immigration restriction as a national policy. The commission's report, published in 1911, lent weight to the movement to close the golden door to immigrants, which culminated during the 1920s. For Roosevelt in 1907 the new immigration statute was another step toward the Gentlemen's Agreement. However, the Japanese government still did not wish to make unilateral concessions. There was no chance that they could achieve the right of their citizens to become naturalized Americans. An informal understanding evolved during late February and early March 1907. Tokyo agreed that the passports it issued would be restricted to Hawaii only and that those documents would be limited to "settled agriculturists" or Japanese who had previously lived in the United States. The president meanwhile pressured the governor of California to prevent the passage of anti-Japanese legislation, and the mayor of San Francisco secured the end of the school board's segregation order. The White House believed that a significant step had been taken toward ending the crisis with Japan and opening the way to diplomatic negotiations that would resolve the immigration question.[19]

The calm that followed the conclusion of the Gentlemen's Agreement lasted until anti-Japanese rioting occurred in San Francisco on 20/21 May 1907. These outbreaks reignited the crisis. "Nothing during my Presidency has given me more concern than these troubles," Roosevelt wrote to his Japanese friend Kentaro Kaneko. While the effects of the riots in San Francisco could be contained through local law-enforcement officials, the international consequences were more unsettling. Newspapers in Japan and in the United States printed sensational stories that led to a serious war scare during June 1907.[20]

The most important consequence of the war scare was the president's decision to send the United States battleship fleet to the Pacific. When Roosevelt went to Oyster Bay for the summer of 1907, he asked the Joint Army and Navy Board to send him their plans in the event of a war with Japan. At a meeting on 27 June 1907, the president indicated that he wanted to have the battleships in the Pacific by October. The explanation would be that the navy was conducting a practice cruise. Word of the fleet's plans soon leaked out. Roosevelt intended from the beginning that the voyage would ultimately become "a practice cruise around the world." He told Lodge that he did not want the navy to be caught unprepared in the event of future hostilities.[21]

The decision to send the fleet to the Pacific stemmed from a number of related causes that changed and evolved as the planning for the voyage proceeded. "My prime purpose was to impress the American people," Roosevelt wrote later. A successful cruise would generate public support for his naval construction program, which had stalled in Congress. At the same time the Japanese, as well as other potential enemies, would be reminded of the naval strength of the United States. The appearance of the ships on the West Coast could also bolster the Republican party there during the presidential elections of 1908. From almost every aspect—its diplomatic effect on the Japanese, the potential political gains for the GOP, military readiness, and personal gratification—dispatching of the fleet fit in with Roosevelt's goals and expectations during the final years of his presidency.[22]

The war scare soon eased after the announcement of the cruise and after the recognition in both Japan and the United States that there was no real reason to fight. The episode persuaded Roosevelt as well that his country could not sustain some of its imperial obligations. "The Philippines form our heel of Achilles," he told Taft in August 1907; "they are all that makes the present situation with Japan dangerous." He recognized that the nation would not "permanently accept the Philippines simply as an unremunerative and indeed expensive duty." It might be necessary to give the islands independence "much sooner than I think advisable from their own standpoint." In October 1907 the president ordered a study of the defense of the Philippines. That inquiry revealed the inadequacy of the projected naval base at Subig Bay. Although for years the navy had urged that an installation of some size be created there, the study shifted the main focus of naval defense to Pearl Harbor. In that sense, Roosevelt's observations represented a gradual reduction in the imperial commitments of the United States.[23]

The issue of immigration from Japan remained unresolved through-out the summer of 1907. The flow of Japanese into the United States continued at an undiminished level, with three thousand immigrants between April and July, and the arrangements previously developed with Japan were not working well. After a conference with Root, Meyer, and Taft on 13 August, it was decided to send the secretary of war to Japan during the course of his visit to the Philippines to open their popular assembly. With that diplomatic move under way, Roosevelt also intended to push in Congress for more battleships.

Taft arrived in Japan on 28 September. The situation had brightened for the United States by that time. Japanese expulsion of Chinese labor-ers from their territory showed that prejudice did not run in just one direction. Anti-Japanese rioting in Vancouver, Canada, during early September embarrassed Tokyo and its ally Britain. Taft had lengthy talks with Japanese leaders. He reported to Washington that a treaty to exclude Oriental laborers was unworkable "but that we can obtain prac-tically the same exclusion by administrative measures." In the end, Taft's approach would prove feasible, but the problem lingered through the autumn of 1907. An initiative from the Japanese ambassador col-lapsed when his government repudiated his efforts and replaced him.[24]

Roosevelt was now anxious to bring the immigration issue to a positive conclusion. With an election year ahead and with the economy in trouble over the Panic of 1907, the administration did not need a running diplomatic crisis with Japan. The White House put pressure on Tokyo over the continuing influx of laborers and warned of the possibil-ity of restrictive legislation during the impending congressional session. As the year ended, Root cautioned Japan "that unless there is a very speedy change in the course of immigration," the administration would not block exclusion laws.[25] The Japanese had already decided that they had to implement the Gentlemen's Agreement more effectively, and the details of the arrangement had been pulled together by late February 1908. The visitors to whom passports were to be issued were specifically delineated, and the Japanese agreed to tighten their procedures for the handling of their emigrants. They also said that they would end the flow of their laborers to the Hawaiian islands. The number of Japanese enter-ing the United States fell substantially from the high levels at the end of 1907.

A parallel aspect of Theodore Roosevelt's treatment of the Japanese problem was an effort to enlist Great Britain's support for the United States position. The British regarded their alliance with Japan as a key to their policy in the Pacific, and they did not wish to offend either Tokyo or Washington. The rioting in Vancouver, however, made the

Canadians potential allies in a North American move about immigration. Roosevelt talked with William Lyon Mackenzie King, a Canadian official who had investigated the Vancouver incident and the immigration issue for his government. The two men held several conversations during late January and early February 1908, and Roosevelt encouraged King to visit London to explain immigration to the British leaders. The president also wrote to King Edward VII and other British friends about his concerns.

Roosevelt's initiatives and King's talks in London did not lead to an Anglo-American coalition to pressure Japan over the immigration issue. There was little chance that the British would risk their connection with the Japanese. The episode did demonstrate to London the depth of United States and Canadian sensitivity over the Japanese presence on the West Coast. That heightened awareness probably increased the perception in Tokyo that restriction of immigration would have to take place. In that sense, Roosevelt had successfully used diplomatic channels to achieve his goals in 1908. "There isn't anything more to do just at the moment," he told Arthur Lee in early April 1908; "but no one can tell when the situation will grow acute."[26]

While all this diplomatic action was occurring, the world cruise of the fleet had begun. The sixteen battleships, resplendent in their white paint, left Hampton Roads, Virginia, on 16 December 1907 as the president, on his yacht, the *Mayflower*, watched the review. "Did you ever see such a fleet and such a day?" Roosevelt asked; "by George, isn't it magnificent?" He told the commander of the fleet to inform the crews that they were going around the world. The ships were on their way, with an ample complement of reporters to record what took place. The president was intent on using publicity about the great white fleet's progress as a part of his personal campaign for increased naval appropriations.[27]

The drive in Congress for more battleships grew out of Roosevelt's conviction that the nation could not afford to fall behind in the international race to build dreadnoughts. The president had hoped that The Hague conference might limit arms, but that had not occurred. The navy told him that four new battleships would maintain the fleet at a level comparable to potential rivals. Roosevelt included a request for these vessels in the 1907 annual message. Because "it would be most unwise for us to stop the upbuilding of our navy," he contended, "in my judgment, we should this year provide for four battleships." The departure of the fleet two weeks later thus reinforced the point that Roosevelt was trying to make on Capitol Hill.[28]

Roosevelt's proposal faced a difficult process in Congress, where major figures of both houses were unsympathetic to additional naval construction. Senator Hale was opposed, and key House members concurred. The president's relatively low standing among lawmakers added to the problems for the navy's building program. Internal disputes within the navy added to the obstacles that confronted Roosevelt during early 1908.

Five days after the fleet had sailed, an article appeared in *McClure's Magazine* that outlined "The Needs of Our Navy." Written by Henry Reuterdahl, a well-informed commentator on naval issues, the essay advanced many of the criticisms about the organization of the navy and its system of separate bureaus, criticisms that reformers such as William S. Sims had long been advancing. The article owed much to Sims's ideas. Reuterdahl's analysis also indicated that there were serious design flaws in the new battleships that had been added to the fleet. Armor belts were under water, the powder magazines were dangerous, and the ships would have difficulty in a sea battle. Personnel policies, particularly the advanced age of high-ranking officers, also came under attack. As the nation read about these charges, a public squabble occurred between Roosevelt and Adm. Willard H. Brownson over the president's decision to assign a medical officer to command a hospital ship. Roosevelt's rebuke of Brownson, after the latter's resignation, contributed to the surge of interest in naval matters during January 1908.

Senator Hale had his Naval Affairs Committee conduct an investigation of the criticisms of the service during February 1908. The proceedings had scant objectivity, as Hale and the naval hierarchy sought to muzzle and refute the opponents of the bureau system and their attacks on the existing battleships. Despite these hurdles, the reformers put some of their message before the public. As a result, the hearings ended in mid passage, with no action taken on any of the issues discussed. The naval "insurgents" had hoped to bring Roosevelt to their side. While he sympathized with what Sims and his allies were saying, the president did not like the publicity tactics that were used. He was also aware that a bitter fight over naval organization would not help the congressional prospects for naval construction. Roosevelt believed that four new battleships were the vital point during the spring of 1908. What would happen if he took up the cause of reform, he feared, would be "a perfect explosion in the Congress, among the people, *and in the navy.*"[29]

The campaign for Roosevelt's four battleships had not begun well during the winter of 1908. He had written to congressional leaders to push larger funds for fortifications and ships, and he had met with House Democrats on the Naval Affairs Committee to enlist their support. Despite all this executive lobbying, the House panel had decided to authorize two battleships when it voted in late February. Meanwhile the House trimmed the administration's request for money for fortifications from more than $38 million to less than $15 million. Lawmakers did agree to another appropriation to fund a base at Pearl Harbor.

After the Senate hearings on the navy had ended and debate had opened on the battleship issue in the House, Roosevelt sent Congress a message on 14 April. He said that the nation should "build a navy commensurate with its powers and needs, because I feel that such a navy will be the surest guaranty and safeguard of peace." The president added that "the most vital and immediate need is that of the four battle ships." The message, though far from inflammatory, did not change many minds in the House when a vote was taken on 15 April. By a vote of 83 to 199 the lawmakers turned back an amendment that would have specified four ships. They also rejected a proposal to fund only one battleship. Except in their refusal of the single-battleship alternative, wrote Roosevelt, members of the House had shown "an infinite capacity to go wrong."[30]

The Senate would be the critical arena for Roosevelt's naval policy. In the upper house the Republican leadership was bitter toward the president, and his legislative program had been generally received with overt hostility. The supremacy of Nelson Aldrich and the Republicans was under attack from a group of progressive senators that included Albert J. Beveridge, Jonathan P. Dolliver, and Robert M. La Follette. Beveridge had agreed to manage the president's proposal on the Senate floor, to the displeasure of the leadership. The battleship issue became a way for Senate Republicans to air their growing differences over the direction of their party under Roosevelt.

From the beginning, there was little question that two battleships would be approved. The struggle centered on an amendment that called for four ships. The president wrote to the sponsor of the amendment that "it will be a damage and a discredit to us as a nation if we fail at this session to get these four battleships." Roosevelt even pressed Henry Cabot Lodge to support the administration. Senate consideration began on 24 April, with discussion about whether Roosevelt had the authority to send the fleet on its cruise. As debate became heated, the key vote was set for Monday 27 April.[31]

The results of the weekend's bargaining pleased the White House. Although the amendment favoring four ships lost by a vote of twenty-three to fifty, Senate leaders assured the president and the public that they would fund the construction of two battleships a year into the future. The process of appropriation "was not a battleship fight at all but a fight against Theodore Roosevelt." The president had won. He turned aside suggestions that he should veto the naval appropriations bill as being inadequate. "Congress will not stand for the four battleships," he told Henry White. "To be frank, I did not suppose that they would; but I knew that I would not get thru two and have those two hurried up unless I made a violent fight for four."[32]

The internal struggle of the navy still festered after the battleship episode was concluded. The insurgents continued with their criticisms of battleship design and the organization of the service. The new battleship *North Dakota* was identified as flawed and dangerous, and a letter to that effect reached Roosevelt in mid June 1908, thanks to the access that his naval aide, William S. Sims, enjoyed. Using Sims's letter to him as a draft, Roosevelt asked the secretary of the navy to call a conference of naval officers to look into the charges about the *North Dakota* and battleship design in general.

The meeting took place at the Naval War College in Newport, Rhode Island, on 22 July 1908. The president spoke to the assembled officers, and he informed them that "no fight was ever won yet except by hitting, and the unforgivable offense in any man is to hit soft." He also urged that changes take place in the bureau system and said that "existing methods must be revised if the maximum of constructive efficiency is to be obtained in building our warships." Despite the president's plea and the efforts of Sims and his allies, the Newport Conference did not adopt the position of the insurgents on the design of the battleships. The "conservatives" in the conference conceded that defects existed, but they remained committed to the designs that had shaped the *North Dakota*. That outcome did not please Roosevelt. The officers who were designing the new ships "seem to have limited themselves to the desire not to lag far behind other nations instead of doing what they of course ought to have done; that is, tried to lead other nations."[33]

During August 1908, Sims suggested that Roosevelt appoint a commission to look at the organization of the navy. After receiving his aide's initial proposal, Roosevelt took no action until after the presidential election. On 1 December, Secretary Metcalf stepped down, and Roosevelt named the assistant secretary, Truman H. Newberry, to hold the post until the end of his presidency. Newberry quickly launched a reorganization plan of his own. In his last annual message in December 1908, Roosevelt wrote: "There is literally no excuse whatever for continuing the present bureau organization." Meanwhile, Sims was telling the president that time was running out in which to set up a commission. Sims and his friends sent the president information about the need for a commission. With the Congress debating the 1909 navy bill, Roosevelt brought a group of naval experts to Washington on 16

January. They ratified the reorganization proposals that Secretary New-berry had developed. On 22 January, by a decisive vote, the House acted favorably on the bill to fund two battleships. Five days later, Roosevelt named a commission "to consider certain needs of the navy."[34]

The panel had barely a month to carry out Roosevelt's mandate to look into such issues as the bureau problem, coordination within the department, and how the secretary should be advised. They reported back to him on 25 February, and he sent their document on to the Senate. The proposed reforms were admirable in seeking better advice for the secretary and a diminished role for the bureaus; but there was not enough time to act on them before Roosevelt stepped down on 4 March 1909. Under the Taft administration, however, these reforms provided a constructive blueprint that the new secretary, George Meyer, used in making changes.

The great white fleet returned from its cruise for a presidential re-view at Hampton Roads on 22 February 1909. Twenty-six ships gave the president their twenty-one-gun salutes after their long voyage. When they came into sight, the president exclaimed: "That is the answer to my critics. Another chapter is complete, and I could not ask a finer conclud-ing scene to my administration." Theodore Roosevelt had been a great friend of the navy for seven years. His achievements in building a mod-ern fleet were impressive. During his tenure, direct naval appropriations totaled more than $900 million. The size of the navy itself rose by more than 19,000—to 44,500 enlisted men. The number of battleships in-creased from seventeen to twenty-seven and the nation stood third be-hind Great Britain and Germany in that category. Relative to other pow-ers, the United States position had not kept pace during the Roosevelt presidency because the construction of two battleships a year did not match what the British and the Germans were doing. The fault lay with Congress and its appropriations decisions, not with the president, who had sought an expanded construction program.[35]

On substantive measures, the navy shot better, because Roosevelt had encouraged a man such as Sims; the morale of the service had improved; and its personnel were more effectively trained. The presi-dent had not succeeded in reforming the internal structure of the navy, and his numerous replacements of the secretary of the navy had pre-vented greater administrative continuity from developing. On balance, Roosevelt had reason to be proud that he had made the United States Navy a better fighting force than when he found it.

While the future of the navy was being addressed during 1908, Japanese-American relations had become less intense than during the previous year. The level of Japanese immigration was dropping, and the people of the United States seemed less concerned about a possible Asian conflict. The administration hoped to resolve the differences with Japan over China and Manchuria, and the secretary of state discouraged those in the government who wished to protest Tokyo's economic dominance in Manchuria. The White House was moving toward a rapprochement with Japan during the autumn of 1908. The fleet came to Japan on 18 October 1908 and had a successful and tranquil visit.

A week after the arrival of the fleet, the Japanese government proposed an understanding that would end any remaining tension. Negotiations went on during the ensuing month between Root and Ambassador Kogoro Takahira. The agreement that they concluded through an exchange of notes on 30 November 1908 declared their intention to support peaceful commerce in the Pacific, to defend "the principle of equal opportunity for commerce and industry in China," and to consult whenever Chinese independence and territorial integrity might be jeopardized. The Root-Takahira Agreement signaled that the United States hoped to help China and the Open Door, but not by risking serious danger with Japan. The president wanted to keep the Japanese out of the United States, because American public opinion insisted that he must. In return he preferred not to challenge Japan in Korea or Manchuria.[36]

The Root-Takahira Agreement did not address the anti-Japanese feeling that persisted on the West Coast. That prejudice reasserted itself during the last months of the presidency. The California legislature considered laws against the immigrants, including one that would have required Japanese landowners to sell their holdings because they were not eligible to become citizens. The measures would offend Japanese public opinion, and Roosevelt wrote the governor of California to warn him against enactment of the legislation. There was "no shadow of excuse for action which will simply produce great irritation and may result in upsetting the present arrangement and throwing open the whole situation again." The president increased the pressure when he released the letter to the press on 19 January 1909; he also had Oscar Straus indicate that the Japanese were complying with the Gentlemen's Agreement; and he called publicly for Japan to receive a "square deal."[37]

Roosevelt's actions won some support in California, which he attributed to his refusal to adopt "the strict and limited constitutional, or President Buchanan, view" of the presidency.[38] The situation moved in Roosevelt's direction during the rest of January. The House approved his two-battleship plan on 22 January, and the Senate was expected to do the same. Meanwhile the president and Root informed the governor of California that they would accept an alien land law that treated all aliens alike and preserved their treaty rights. The governor worked successfully to block even a milder version of the original law by 3 February.

Then the sense of crisis was renewed. The Nevada legislature debated a resolution that criticized Roosevelt for coercing California, an action that aroused his anger. On 4 February the California Assembly approved a school segregation law, which the president labeled "the most offensive bill of all." The Speaker of the California Assembly interceded personally to have his colleagues delay further action. Roosevelt then wired the Speaker: "This school bill accomplishes literally nothing whatever in the line of the object aimed at and gives just and grave cause for irritation."[39]

Roosevelt's public strategy worked as it had so often during his presidency. The assembly reconsidered the school bill on 10 February and then voted it down. "All good Americans appreciate what you have done," the president told the governor. Roosevelt informed Theodore, Jr.: "I think I have won out as regards the Japanese-California trouble." Roosevelt summed up his view of relations with Japan in a long letter of 8 February to Philander Knox, the incoming secretary of state. "Our task," he said, was to accommodate the wishes of the American people about immigration, treat Japan courteously to minimize offense, "and at the same time to prepare our fleet in such shape that she [Japan] will feel very cautious about attacking us." Acting on that principle, Roosevelt resisted attempts to have part of the fleet stationed on the West Coast. His last message as president to Taft warned him: "Under no circumstances divide the battleship fleet between the Atlantic and Pacific Oceans prior to the finishing of the Panama Canal."[40]

In his autobiography, Roosevelt wrote of his foreign-policy record on 4 March 1909: "We were at absolute peace, and there was no nation in the world with whom a war cloud threatened, no nation in the world whom we had wronged, or from whom we had anything to fear."[41] The president achieved that position in part because no major crisis confronted the nation in foreign affairs, such as those that faced William McKinley in 1898 and Woodrow Wilson in 1914. Within the quieter setting of his presidency, Theodore Roosevelt conducted his brand of personal diplomacy with skill and positive results. He avoided war with Japan, promoted a rapprochement with Great Britain, and dealt adroitly with Germany. He completed the work that had begun during the Spanish-American War of establishing United States dominance in the Caribbean and constructing an isthmian canal. In the Philippines he showed himself to be as enlightened as the imperial policy allowed.

Roosevelt had performed well on his world stage, as the ending of the Russo-Japanese War and the Algeciras Conference demonstrated. In his trip to Panama, Roosevelt had broadened the power of the president to leave the United States for foreign-policy reasons. He did not, however, travel abroad as a diplomat and assume a role in the international diplomacy of his time in person. That innovation would be left to Woodrow Wilson in 1919. Nonetheless, Roosevelt had demonstrated the capacity of the president to be a world statesman.

12

★ ★ ★ ★ ★

"THERE IS NO ONE
LIKE THEODORE"

When Theodore Roosevelt's last full year as president began, the major question for the Republican party was the selection of its next leader. Some within the GOP still hoped that Roosevelt might renounce his 1904 pledge and run again, but he was determined to keep faith with the American people. Roosevelt enjoyed being president, but he also believed that he had to be true to his word. "I hate for personal reasons to get out of the fight here," he wrote in December 1907, and he conceded: "I have the uncomfortable feeling that I may possibly be shirking a duty."[1] In view of the nation's attitude toward two terms for the president, he was convinced that he could do nothing else than step aside in 1908.

The president's resolve focused political attention on the other Republican candidates. By the end of 1907 the secretary of war, William Howard Taft, was ahead. Taft's status as Roosevelt's designated choice, plus Taft's own organizational ability, gave him a strong advantage among likely delegates to the national convention in Chicago the following June. That positive result for Taft took place because of the support that the president had extended to him.

While Roosevelt was intent on not being a candidate himself, he saw nothing in his 1904 statement that should prevent him from selecting his successor. During his second term, he weighed the qualifications of leading Republican figures to determine who would best carry on his policies. In so doing, he exercised a controlling influence on his party's deliberations about 1908. These decisions cleared the way for Taft to win the nomination.

Roosevelt and Taft had known each other in Washington since the early 1890s, and they had corresponded warmly during the years when each held important governmental posts. The public believed that they were of the same mind politically, and each of them said much the same thing privately. "I agree heartily and earnestly in the policies which have come to be known as the Roosevelt policies," Taft said at the end of 1907. The president expressed the same kind of opinion. "He [Taft] and I view public questions exactly alike," Roosevelt wrote in June 1908. On such major topics as railroad regulation, the need to supervise corporations, and the dangers of socialism, these statements were accurate. On the tariff problem, Taft was even more in favor of revision than Roosevelt was, and on the campaign trail, Taft advocated changes in the Dingley Tariff.[2]

There were aspects of Roosevelt's presidential style on which the two men differed. While Taft admired the goals that Roosevelt pursued, he thought that a president should observe the law strictly and not construe his authority as broadly as Roosevelt had done. The "stewardship" theory that Roosevelt endorsed did not appeal to his potential successor. During the time that they had worked together, the president and his cabinet colleague had few occasions to sit down and go over their contrasting philosophies of the presidency.

Roosevelt also came to Taft in part by a process of elimination. Most of the conservative candidates were easily ruled out. Speaker of the House Joseph G. Cannon was an impossible reactionary, and Senator Philander C. Knox's turn to the right had ended Roosevelt's earlier confidence in Knox's talent. Vice-President Charles W. Fairbanks hoped to parlay control of the Indiana delegation into an eventual nomination, but he had no chance of winning Roosevelt's support because of his standpat views. Any small hopes that Joseph B. Foraker might have had ended with Brownsville. None of these men came close to what Roosevelt was looking for, someone who would "carry out the governmental principles in which I believe with all my heart and soul."[3]

The candidates from the progressive side also failed to win presidential favor. Senator Robert M. La Follette had little support beyond his own state of Wisconsin, and Roosevelt did not trust him. The problem of Charles Evans Hughes, the newly elected governor of New York, was more serious. Because of his defeat of William Randolph Hearst in 1906 and the progressive record he had made in his state by mid 1907, Hughes was soon talked about as a candidate who could carry New York's substantial bloc of electoral votes. Unhappily for Hughes, he did not accept Roosevelt as an informal advisor during early 1907. The two men then fell out over the allocation of patronage in New York. Soon the president was describing Hughes as one of the reactionary foes of the administration.

Inside the cabinet, however, there seemed to be at least two promising hopefuls for 1908. Roosevelt's first choice would probably have been Elihu Root. The president wrote in July 1906 that Root, if elected, "would carry on the contest very much as Taft and I would."[4] The president recognized, however, that Root also had liabilities. He was a man in his sixties whose health was then uncertain. Most important Root's background in corporate law made him an object of suspicion among Republican progressives.

Roosevelt's attention naturally moved to his secretary of war. Fifty years old in 1907, Taft had been a national figure since William McKinley sent him to the Philippines in 1900. During his second term, Roosevelt had used Taft as a diplomatic and political trouble-shooter, and the secretary's success in "sitting on the lid" while the president was traveling had added to his political appeal. "He would be an ideal President," Roosevelt informed William Allen White in August 1906. The president added, however, that "of course I am not going to try to nominate any man."[5]

During the late winter of 1906, Justice Henry B. Brown of the Supreme Court told the president about his intention to resign. Roosevelt first offered the nomination to Philander C. Knox, who declined. He then told Taft that the place could be his. The secretary, who had loved being a federal judge during the 1890s, was tempted, but eventually he declined, at the urging of his wife, Helen, who wanted to see him become president. Roosevelt wrote to his friend on 15 March 1906, while Taft was still making up his mind, to sketch the alternatives. The president said: "So far you are the man who is most likely to receive the Republican Presidential nomination and who is, I think, the best man to receive it." He cautioned Taft that "the shadow of the Presidency falls on no man twice, save in the most exceptional circumstances." Roosevelt ended with a sentence that foreshadowed his later tense relationship with Mrs. Taft: "No one can with wisdom advise you."[6]

It took Taft until August 1906 to reject the appointment to the Supreme Court definitively. Had the chief justiceship been available, the secretary's decision might well have been different, but the sitting chief justice, Melville W. Fuller, was not going to accommodate Theodore Roosevelt on that point. After Taft said no, the president considered a southern Democrat, Horace H. Lurton, but in the end came to William H. Moody, a more ideologically compatible Republican who shared the president's views on regulation. Moody was named in December; he would be Roosevelt's last Supreme Court selection. Bad health forced him to resign in 1910, which further limited Roosevelt's impact on the Court. The chance to reshape the Court came to William Howard Taft during 1910/11.

Despite the closeness of Taft and Roosevelt in 1906 and despite the encouragement that the president gave his colleague, there was not an explicit presidential endorsement of Taft's candidacy. Roosevelt spoke with Mrs. Taft in October and assured her that the secretary of war was "his first choice." If Charles Evans Hughes beat Hearst in New York, however, that might make him a credible candidate who could challenge Taft. A brief misunderstanding ensued. Helen Taft was, as always, suspicious of Roosevelt's motives. Her husband accurately believed that Roosevelt was urging that he "not be too entirely aloof." By the end of the year, Taft issued a guarded public indication that he would accept the Republican nomination if it came to him.[7]

Still the White House had not accorded Taft an official blessing. The Roosevelt-Foraker encounter over Brownsville at the Gridiron Club tipped the balance in favor of Taft during the winter of 1907. Supporting Taft openly would be a sign of the president's displeasure with Foraker. By mid March, Roosevelt was instructing his cabinet officers that he felt "a peculiar regard" for Taft's judgment that should be followed "in any appointments of importance in Ohio." During the summer, Roosevelt and William Loeb were "looking after the whole of the South" for Taft. Roosevelt had now concluded that Taft stood "above any other man who has yet been named."[8]

Roosevelt's support helped Taft during 1907. The secretary of war was out of the country in November and December when George B. Cortelyou's success in handling the Panic of 1907 aroused presidential talk regarding the secretary of the treasury. Reverses in the Ohio elections also cooled off Taft's candidacy for a moment. James R. Garfield wrote that Cortelyou's boom was causing "possible complications with Taft. The danger is that if our friends are divided Hughes is a possibility." On 12 December 1907 the White House issued a statement that reaffirmed Roosevelt's 1904 declaration. The practical impact of this move was to end any further talk of a third term and to underline the White House support of Taft. Cortelyou's candidacy faded, and the way became clear for Taft to win the nomination.[9]

Theodore Roosevelt's position on the issues was also evolving as 1908 began. His increasing assertion of presidential power and regulatory action intensified the tensions among Republicans. His annual message in 1907 had asserted that more reform proposals should receive congressional action. He advocated a national incorporation law and "additional legislation looking to the proper control of great business concerns engaged in interstate business." He also supported income and inheritance taxes, limits on the use of injunctions in labor disputes, an employers' liability law for industrial accidents, an eight-hour law for all governmental workers, a postal-savings-bank law, and control of campaign expenses. In a letter of January 1908, Roosevelt stated his regulatory creed: "We seek to control law-defying wealth, in the first place to prevent its doing evil, and in the next place to avoid the vindictive and dreadful radicalism which if left uncontrolled it is certain in the end to arouse."[10]

The president was even more progressive in the special message that Congress received on 31 January 1908. The document had both short-run political consequences and longer-range implications for Roosevelt and the GOP. The timing of the message related in part to an upsurge of Hughes strength in New York. To cut off this boomlet, the Roosevelt-Taft men agreed to allow Hughes to control the large New York delegation. When the governor scheduled a major address on national issues for 31 January, Roosevelt acted to preempt the spotlight from Hughes. The message to Congress won the headlines, and the governor's speech was overshadowed. A delighted Roosevelt remarked: "If Hughes is going to play the game, he must learn the tricks."[11]

If the timing of the message grew out of tactics, its substance was an indication of Roosevelt's dismay about the response that the judiciary and the business community offered to his regulatory policies. On 6 January 1908 the Supreme Court, in the *Employers Liability* cases, struck down the 1906 federal law that Roosevelt had advocated as a way of putting "the national government in its proper place as regards such legislation." The Court argued that the law affected workers "engaged wholly in intrastate commerce," as well as those in interstate commerce. In response, in impassioned terms, Roosevelt restated for Congress and the nation his convictions on proper regulatory policy, and he assailed his critics.[12]

His substantive recommendations tracked what he had earlier endorsed. He asked for a national employers' liability law that would meet the Supreme Court's criteria; he also sought a workmen's compensation law for governmental employees and private workers, and the regulation of injunctions in labor disputes. He recommended other labor legislation and sought more power over railroad rates for the Interstate Commerce Commission, including the physical valuation of railroad properties. Finally, he again said that there should be changes in the Sherman Antitrust Act to recognize the differences between combinations that were "useful to the country" and those "huge combinations which are both noxious and illegal."[13]

The greater part of the message was a free-swinging attack on Roosevelt's conservative critics. He referred to "the corrupt men of wealth" who worked through "the purchased politician" and "the purchased newspaper." A judge who failed "to do his duty by the public in dealing with lawbreaking corporations, lawbreaking men of wealth," should "expect to feel the weight of public opinion." Roosevelt charged that "corrupt business and corrupt politics act and react with ever increasing debasement, one on the other." To those who opposed an employers' liability law, he contended that it was "hypocritical baseness" to say that a young girl who was working in a dangerous factory had the "'right' freely to contract to expose herself to dangers to life and limb." The new conditions of an industrial society "make it necessary to shackle cunning as in the past we have shackled force." Finally, alluding to the Panic of 1907, he concluded that "if it were true that to cut out rottenness from the body politic meant a momentary check to an unhealthy seeming prosperity, I should not for one moment hesitate to put the knife to the corruption."[14]

The moralistic tone and the sweeping policy initiatives of the message irritated Roosevelt's conservative opponents. Foraker "found everyone in New York almost bitterly resentful on account of the President's last Message," while in Congress the message "seems to have stirred up both parties." The president himself was "well satisfied" with the document and thought that "it was time to send it in. Of course it caused a great flutter in the dovecote."[15]

The 31 January 1908 message did anticipate the reforms that Roosevelt would advocate after he left the White House, and its substance indicated how far advanced his political thought had become by the end of his presidency. Conscious that "this is well-nigh the last occasion I shall have to speak when all men, however unwilling, must listen," he wanted to set out where his principles of executive stewardship and regulatory policies should lead. Since he also infused the message with his characteristic personal style, the fervor of his argument somewhat obscured the innovative importance of his theme. By now, however, Roosevelt was not trying to persuade but to exhort.[16]

By January 1908, Roosevelt's relations with Capitol Hill were in the last stage of a gradual decline into acrimony and mutual antipathy. "The feeling at the Capitol against anything and everything the President wants, is very bitter," wrote George W. Perkins during that winter. Congress had lost its tolerance for frequent presidential messages, as well as Roosevelt's widely circulated private criticisms of them and their views. "That fellow at the other end of the Avenue," said Joe Cannon, "wants everything, from the birth of Christ to the death of the devil." Roosevelt had his own complaints about the way the lawmakers, especially those in his own party, were treating him and his program. "The ruling clique in the Senate, the House, and the National Committee, seem to regard every concession to decency as merely a matter of bargain and sale with *me*, which *I* must pay for in some way or fashion."[17]

In fact, Roosevelt enjoyed more support in public from the Democratic minority in the House of Representatives than he did from Cannon and his Republican colleagues during the winter and spring of 1908. With an aggressive minority leader in John Sharp Williams of Mississippi and with their numbers increased after the 1906 elections, the Democrats sought to emphasize both their closeness to Roosevelt's policies and the Republican distaste for their own president's recommendations. As a determined Republican partisan, Roosevelt did not succumb to the Democratic temptation to split his own party for the sake of enacting his own program. For all his difficulties with his party, Roosevelt never seriously contemplated crossing partisan lines as a consistent legislative strategy.

The long congressional session of 1907/8 produced sharp battles over such highly charged issues as the tariff, banking, corporate regulation, and naval appropriations. On the subject of currency and banking, which the Panic of 1907 had brought forward, the consensus was that the nation's financial machinery was badly in need of an overhaul. For the moment, both parties endeavored to make the issue work for them in the upcoming presidential contest. The focus for the Republicans became the bill that Senator Nelson W. Aldrich introduced on 7 January 1908. It authorized national banks to issue an emergency currency of up to $250 million upon application to the comptroller of the currency. This money would be based on state and national bonds, as well as municipal and some of the better railroad bonds. The measure, with Aldrich's name on it, aroused intense opposition among southern Democrats and midwestern Republicans. Senator La Follette said that the bill aimed to "provide an emergency fund to meet the speculative needs of Wall Street in a panic."[18]

In the face of this outcry, Aldrich drew back. Railroad bonds were dropped as security for the emergency currency, and the Republican leader announced that the bill contained language calling for a probe of the banking system itself. Nonetheless, it still took ten days of debate and a special message from Roosevelt to get the Aldrich bill through the Senate on 27 March 1908.

The Senate version received a frosty reception in the House. The

House Banking and Currency Committee had already reported a bill developed by Charles N. Fowler, a New Jersey Republican, which combined a currency based on bank assets with the guarantee of bank notes. That aspect of the proposal encountered opposition from many bankers. The Aldrich bill remained unpopular with western Republicans and southern Democrats, who thought it was too friendly to Wall Street. The prospect of a stalemate, with no bill passed before the election, seemed likely. The House committee tabled the Aldrich bill on 18 April 1908 and then took the same action on a substitute proposal that Edward B. Vreeland (R., N.Y.) had offered on 21 April. Roosevelt added his voice with a message to Congress on 27 April that asked for some positive action. A solution to the deadlock was still elusive, but George W. Perkins noted on 7 May that Roosevelt had "made some headway in the last week or ten days, and some of the measures, especially some currency legislation, are now more than likely to go through."[19]

The president and Speaker Cannon met on 5 May 1908 to work out a strategy to push the currency legislation through the House. Their discussion led to a meeting of the Republican party caucus, where members voted to bring up Vreeland's bill. On 13 May 1908 the House approved Vreeland's resolution that took the bill out of committee for a vote. The following day the alternative banking bill was approved by a vote of 185 to 145.

The House and the Senate then insisted on their own bills once again, and the issue went to a conference committee. Both the Senate-backed Aldrich bill and the Vreeland bill from the House enjoyed some backing from segments of the business community and evoked fervent disapproval from others. A stalemate followed for almost two weeks until the two leading legislators compromised, with Aldrich emerging as the closest thing to a victor.

The Aldrich-Vreeland bill, as it became known, allowed for a fairly broad use of bonds to secure the emergency currency in the next crisis. Its most important provision was the creation of the National Monetary Commission; Aldrich later became its chairman. This panel began a process that ultimately led to the Federal Reserve Act in 1913. After an intense three-day filibuster by Senator La Follette, whom Roosevelt called "an entirely worthless Senator," the Aldrich-Vreeland Currency Act was passed on 30 May 1908. The president recognized that the law represented "only a makeshift, an emergency measure," and that the monetary commission would have to recommend "some permanent plan."[20]

The Aldrich-Vreeland Currency Act, despite its flaws, at least represented some positive congressional action on the problems that the

Panic of 1907 had highlighted. A legislative effort to achieve substantive change in the Sherman Antitrust Act during the spring of 1908 ended in failure for the president and his belief that strong executive power was needed in the field of corporate regulation. The battle over this new Hepburn bill also underscored the reservations that had developed on and off Capitol Hill regarding Roosevelt's strong presidency by the end of his administration.

The experience of enforcing the Sherman Act had buttressed Roosevelt's conviction that a more orderly administrative process was needed in order to accommodate business consolidations that served the public interest. He believed that some corporations, such as United States Steel, had cooperated constructively with the White House and that procedures could be worked out to enable them to inform the government in advance of their plans for expansion and growth. Unlike these "good trusts," there were "bad trusts," such as Standard Oil or the railroads of E. H. Harriman, that needed regulation. Oversight of these firms should also be done through administration, not the courts. What he most wanted was "a general scheme to provide for this effective and thoroughgoing supervision by the National Government of all the operations of the big interstate business concerns."[21]

The bill that William P. Hepburn introduced on 23 March 1908 to amend the Sherman Act had passed through many hands before it reached Congress. The National Civic Federation was one notable sponsor because of the interest that its membership of prominent businessmen, lawyers, and academics had in "large-corporate administered markets" that a strong federal government presence would oversee. By early February 1908, in the wake of labor's defeat in the Danbury Hatter's Case (*Loewe* v. *Lawlor*), which applied the Sherman Antitrust Act to union boycotts, the American Federation of Labor wanted Congress to exempt unions from the law's jurisdiction and its sizable potential monetary penalties. One leading member of the National Civic Federation saw a chance to get broad changes in the law, so he urged prompt action: "Let's get everything done at this session that we can."[22]

Circumstances thus gave Theodore Roosevelt the apparent opportunity to achieve the kind of regulatory authority over large corporations that had been one of his evolving aims since the *Northern Securities* case. He had James R. Garfield and the head of the Bureau of Corporations, Herbert Knox Smith, work with Attorney General Bonaparte, Elihu Root, and representatives of the National Civic Federation to pull together a draft bill. Samuel Gompers and other labor leaders were also included in the drafting process. While Roosevelt, by this time in his presidency, understood that getting a bill through would be difficult, he thought that it would be constructive to have a debate over the bill's merits that would set priorities for his presidential successor and promote discussion of the antitrust issue. To achieve that goal, Roosevelt personally played a large part in the shaping of the bill during the first three weeks of March 1908. At a White House meeting on 11 March 1908, he proposed a number of changes in the measure. After the Hepburn bill had been introduced, the president sent in a special message that endorsed the proposal on 25 March 1908. As he wrote privately, "I want full power given to the *Executive* officers in the matter of the Sherman Antitrust Law."[23]

The Hepburn bill provided that corporations engaged in interstate commerce should register with the Bureau of Corporations. They then could submit any contemplated consolidations to the commissioner for his determination of whether they were unreasonable. There were other provisions that granted an amnesty for past violations of the Sherman Act and allowed railroads to register in the same manner as other corporations. For labor, the triple damages of the Sherman Act would have been scaled down to single damages, and there was language to safeguard the right to strike but not the right to boycott. Above all, the bill gave discretion to the president that would, as he put it, "strengthen the hand of the executive in dealing with these matters," which was better than turning them "over to what I regard as the chaos and inefficiency necessarily produced by an effort to use the courts as the prime instrument for administering such a law."[24]

The Hepburn bill encountered a hostile public reaction both on its own merits and because of the strengthening of presidential power that would accompany its enactment. One newspaper called the measure "the President's program for the personal control of the trusts." A New York business paper said that "a powerful weapon of coercion would be placed in the hands of the executive and its use would depend upon the will or judgment of the President and the discretion or honesty of the Commissioner of Corporations." The fragile business-labor coalition that Roosevelt had arrayed behind the bill soon collapsed under the contradictions that it had contained. For labor, the proposal did not do enough to exempt unions from the impact of corporate enemies and their sympathetic judges. From the perspective of business, the bill did far too much to recognize the power of unions. The bill stayed in the Senate committee to which it had been sent until after the 1908 presidential election, and then it received an adverse report. The "movement for corporation control," which the president believed was "essential to the well-being of the country," received extended debate during the spring of 1908, as Roosevelt may well have intended. His policy of broad executive power to regulate big business did not command widespread political support in or out of Congress as his administration wound down.[25]

Roosevelt's relations with Congress had turned sour by the time the lawmakers adjourned at the end of May 1908. The first session of the Sixtieth Congress had passed the Aldrich-Vreeland Currency Act, and an employers' liability law that would meet the Supreme Court's requirements. In the fight that he waged about the navy, Roosevelt had succeeded in obtaining two new battleships. Laws to curb child labor and to outlaw racetrack betting in the District of Columbia had been passed. Other relatively minor achievements went on the credit side of the balance sheet for Congress; but injunctions in labor disputes went unregulated, the Hepburn bill languished, and the president's call for publicity about campaign donations was also lost. Roosevelt was "chagrined that more has not been done," but he was also glad that "we have gone a little ahead and not a little behind."[26]

The theme of executive/legislative tension permeated the congressional deliberations. In the president's favored area of conservation, the lawmakers would not provide money to fund the activities of the Inland Waterways Commission. During the discussions over the appropriations bill, James A. Tawney of Minnesota obtained an amendment that would have restricted the use of Secret Service agents to carry on investigations in other executive departments. Walter I. Smith (R., Iowa), himself the target of a probe, said that the "American government's inspection service and secret service far exceeds that of Russia." Outraged, Roosevelt complained to Speaker Cannon that the administration believed that "this will materially interfere with the administration of justice and will benefit only one class of people—and that is the criminal class." Nonetheless, the amendment stayed in the bill. Roosevelt also had to intervene to have funds restored to the Interstate Commerce Commission, to enable it to monitor the bookkeeping practices of the railroads. What especially frustrated Congress was that their rebukes did not affect Roosevelt's popular standing; if anything, they enhanced it. "In a marked degree," noted one editorial writer, "the President, rather than Congress, possesses the confidence of the people."[27]

Roosevelt's readiness to exercise the powers of his office remained as robust and vigorous as ever during the waning stages of his second term. Late in 1907, responding to the private and official requests of the governor of Nevada, John Sparks, Roosevelt sent army units into the state to maintain order at Goldfield, Nevada, in an anticipated labor dispute with local mine workers. It soon developed that the forecast of possible violence was exaggerated. The president began to retreat, advising Sparks that the troops would be recalled. Roosevelt also sent out a three-man commission to look into the case, and it reported that "there was no warrant whatever for calling upon the President for troops." Two months later the army left the state.[28]

Theodore Roosevelt had little sympathy for socialism as a political or economic doctrine. During his second term he believed that the growth of the Socialist vote in the United States presented a greater danger than the Populist movement of the 1890s. Part of his reform impulse was a desire to preempt the need for the sweeping changes that the Socialists advocated. He had scant patience, however, with newspapers from the Left that attacked his administration and policies. In 1906 he asked the Justice Department to see if charges could be filed against Eugene V. Debs for an article that appeared in *Appeal to Reason*, a major Socialist newspaper published in Kansas. Despite the president's desire for an indictment and for the removal of the paper's postal privileges, no legal action was taken.

An even more striking example of this policy during 1908 was the attempted prosecution and barring from the mails of a New Jersey anarchist newspaper that called for the assassination of police and a general uprising against the established order. An Italian paper, *La question sociale*, came to Roosevelt's attention when the mayor of Paterson, New Jersey, asked for it to be suppressed. On 20 March 1908 the president instructed the Justice Department to see if it would be possible "to prosecute criminally under any section of the law that is available the men that are interested in sending out this anarchistic and murderous publication." The attorney general responded that while the printing and circulation of the paper did not violate an existing federal statute, it was possible for Roosevelt to direct the postmaster general to exclude the periodical from the second-class mail because it contained articles that constituted "a seditious libel" and recommended the commission of "such crimes as murder, arson, riot, and treason." On 9 April 1908, Roosevelt sent Congress a special message, asking for laws to help curb publications that promoted anarchy. Congress did not respond to this initiative.[29]

In the running controversy over the Brownsville episode, the conclusion of the Senate committee's hearings in April 1908 left the president still convinced of the guilt of the black soldiers. If Congress were to pass a bill that Senator Foraker had proposed, which would have allowed the soldiers to reenlist after taking an oath of their innocence, Roosevelt said that "it would be clearly unconstitutional and I should not pay the slightest heed to it." The Foraker proposal was, in his view, "simply to replace murderers in the public armed forces of the United

States on the sole condition that to the crime of murder in the past they add the crime of perjury in the future."[30]

Despite the president's faith in his position, he knew that the government still lacked the tangible and credible proof of the guilt of the soldiers that would destroy his critics. At about this time a Virginia editor and a private detective informed Secretary Taft that they could establish that a conspiracy existed in the shooting. Taft entered into a $5,000 contract with these men and sent them south to bring back their "proof." The methods of these presidential operatives included the manufacture of evidence and the coercion of witnesses. Eventually, they received several thousand dollars for what they had assembled. These paid agents of the White House were being used to obtain evidence to buttress a decision that Theodore Roosevelt had already rendered, based on what official agencies had told him earlier. For the president then to commission private detectives in support of his policies was a broad interpretation of the concept of executive stewardship. The Brownsville matter rumbled on throughout the rest of 1908.[31]

During that final spring, Theodore Roosevelt's thoughts had already turned to what he would do after he left the presidency. In October 1908, as a comparatively young man of fifty in political terms, he rebuffed suggestions that he run for mayor of New York City or represent that state in the Senate. At this stage of his life he did not wish to write his memoirs or to make a round-the-world trip of foreign capitals. By the end of March 1908 he began to consider the possibility of a hunting trip to Africa. "I should like mightily to see the great African fauna," he said, "and to kill one or two rhino or buffalo and some of the big antelopes, with the chance of a shot at a lion." The prospect of the African safari soon filled his correspondence. The trip would take him out of the country during the first year of his successor's term and would thus keep him apart from political events in the United States that might require his comments.[32]

Roosevelt's main political concern was now the nomination and election of Taft. The president spurned all efforts to have delegates elected who favored his own renomination. By late May he was "still actively engaged in getting delegates for Taft" because he believed that the secretary of war was "the best fitted at this time to be President and to carry on the work upon which we have entered during the past six years." The support from the White House made the task of gathering delegates much easier for the Taft campaign as the Republican National Convention approached. How the secretary of war would have fared on his own is, of course, impossible to determine. He evoked some enthusiasm among Republicans, but his biggest asset was Roosevelt's endorsement. Progressive Republicans supported Taft as the president's heir; conservatives backed him to prevent another Roosevelt nomination.[33]

This process had subtle effects on Taft's own presidency. The selection of Taft supporters for federal patronage positions restricted the extent of the new president's power in that area in 1909. Roosevelt also oversold Taft as a friend of progressive reform and created the impression that his successor would carry on the programs of his administration exactly. There were also the ever-present reminders that Taft was the direct beneficiary of Roosevelt's political largesse. The groundwork for future misunderstanding and tension was being laid.

For the moment, all the political signs seemed favorable to Taft. The conservative opposition to him was reduced to contesting the seating of delegates when the Republican National Committee met in early June 1908. After the panel, which the administration controlled, allocated two hundred disputed delegates to Taft, the Fairbanks and Foraker "allies" were out of the race for the nomination. One unhappy supporter of the vice-president wrote that Roosevelt had "placed the seal of approval on the program of driving over everybody who seems to stand in the way." On the eve of the convention, Taft's total of confirmed delegates was above six hundred.[34]

The national convention was more tension-filled than such Republican gatherings had been for at least twelve years. In the Taft camp there was still the unstated fear that the president might at the last moment give in to a third-term boom. On the second day of the convention, a spontaneous demonstration for Roosevelt was quieted when Henry Cabot Lodge announced that "anyone who attempts to use his name as a candidate for the presidency impugns both his sincerity and his good faith."[35] The actual balloting occurred on 18 June 1908. Taft received 702 votes on the first ballot, with the rest scattered. Mrs. Taft wanted the demonstration that took place when her husband's name was placed in nomination to run longer than the earlier one for the president. It was twenty minutes shorter. Even when the news came that Taft had in fact been nominated, his wife retained her suspicions of Roosevelt. At the moment of Taft's selection, the awkward transition from one Republican president to another had begun.

Neither the president nor the new presidential candidate got the vice-presidential running mate that he wanted for the ticket. There was an effort made on behalf of Jonathan P. Dolliver of Iowa, but he would not allow his name to go forward. Charles Evans Hughes turned down Taft's offer of the place, and Albert J. Beveridge declined as well. Since no credible progressive choice had emerged, the party's conservatives obtained the selection of James S. ("Sunny Jim") Sherman, a congressman from New York who was a friend of Cannon and other standpatters.

The two national Republican leaders had somewhat more impact on the party's platform. It supported the further amendment of the Interstate Commerce Act, called for reform in the Sherman Antitrust Act, and advocated a system of postal savings banks. The GOP also came out "unequivocally for a revision of the tariff by a special session of Congress immediately following the inauguration of the next President." The plank reflected the strength of the sentiment for tariff revision in the party. Responding to this pressure, Republicans in the House voted for a revised tariff to be worked on after the election. The House Ways and Means Committee set its experts to work preparing a draft bill for consideration early in 1909. The language of the platform carefully did not specify the direction that tariff revision would take, but the assumption was that its aim would be to lower duties rather than to raise them.[36]

The president and his program fared less well on another controversial subject in the 1908 platform. Roosevelt wanted "a singularly moderate and reasonable provision" to limit the use of injunctions in labor disputes. He did not wish to go as far as Samuel Gompers and the American Federation of Labor, but he hoped to do enough so "that judges shall think before they act." That was more than Cannon and the National Association of Manufacturers would tolerate. The result was a plank that promised to "uphold at all times the authority and integrity of the courts." Progressive language that Senator La Follette offered on other court-reform issues was also rejected. On the whole, Roosevelt was satisfied. He informed a British friend that "the convention is over and Taft is nominated on a platform which I heartily approve."[37]

Although Taft and Roosevelt did not realize it, they had already started on the path that would lead to division and defeat four years later. In the days immediately following Taft's nomination, he remarked to Roosevelt informally that, if elected, "I did not see how I could do anything else but retain all the old members of the Cabinet who had been associated with me." Although the candidate "thought nothing more about it," the president passed the word to each member of his official family, and an implied promise was created. Taft had been careless in making his promise, and Roosevelt had been indiscreet in transmitting the news.[38]

To run against Taft, the Democrats selected William Jennings Bryan to make his third race for the White House. The Democratic party approached the 1908 election with a genuine confidence that had not been seen for more than a decade. They would not be facing the popular Roosevelt again, and the Panic of 1907 made it difficult for the GOP to claim that it was the party of economic prosperity. Gompers and the AFL were now solidly in the Democratic camp. With Taft still something of an unknown element as a presidential campaigner, one reporter noted privately that "this election is not going to be an open-and-shut affair."[39]

The Republican campaign began somewhat slowly. Taft chose Frank H. Hitchcock to run his organization, and the manager's slow pace and cautious approach led to criticism of what seemed to be inactivity as the summer wore on. "I think your decision about Hitchcock wise," Roosevelt assured Taft. The two men worked together on Taft's speech of acceptance. "You are now the leader," Roosevelt said, "and there must be nothing that looks like self-depreciation or undue subordination of yourself." After the speech had been delivered, Roosevelt was pleased. He also praised the way in which Taft had handled the issue of campaign contributions. "I have always said you would be the greatest President, bar only Washington and Lincoln, and I feel mighty inclined to strike out the exceptions!" the president told his friend.[40]

The time for fresh policy initiatives during the Roosevelt administration was running out. Despite the few months that remained, Roosevelt wanted to act in areas of his own special concern. On 10 August 1908 the President's Commission on Country Life was appointed, with Liberty Hyde Bailey as its chairman and with Gifford Pinchot, Walter Hines Page, Henry C. Wallace, and Kenyon L. Butterfield as its other members. In his letter of appointment, Roosevelt told the commissioners that "the social and economic institutions of the open country are not keeping pace with the development of the nation as a whole." He asked the panel to explore ways that "will help to make country life more gainful, more attractive, and fuller of opportunities, pleasures, and rewards for the men, women, and children of the farms."[41]

The Country Life Commission was the offshoot of the efforts of Pinchot and Bailey to place the problems of rural life at the center of the national agenda. For Pinchot the policy goal also included the creation of a new governmental agency to deal with rural issues inside the Department of Agriculture. Presumably the head of the Forest Service would have a large role in the selection of the director of this innovative bureau. When this idea was floated to the secretary of agriculture, James Wilson, he proved to be cool to the change. With that avenue closed, Pinchot turned to the idea of a commission, a device that he and Roosevelt had used frequently by 1908. Pinchot brought Bailey to the White House in

April 1908, where the professor said that he would head the commission once Roosevelt had established it. After the announcement was made in August, Bailey hesitated for a moment but then agreed to serve, under pressure from the president.

The panel was expanded to represent southern farmers and western interests. It was also financed from private sources and with funds from some of its own members. The commission decided not to look into the peonage condition of black farmers in the South, and it generally approached the race issue cautiously. For the most part, however, the idea of the commission was a popular one with the nation. An Ohio woman wrote the president: "It must have been divine inspiration that caused you to try to understand the loneliness of a farmer's life."[42]

Roosevelt was convinced that the social health of his country depended upon the condition of its rural population. He spoke at Michigan Agricultural College (now Michigan State University) in 1907 about "The Man Who Works with His Hands," an address to which Bailey and Pinchot had made significant contributions. Roosevelt also corresponded with the Irish agrarian reformer Sir Horace C. Plunkett in shaping his rural ideas. The president informed his audience that "the permanent greatness of any State must ultimately depend more upon the character of its country population than upon anything else." Roosevelt worried about the movement of country residents to American cities and what the trend might do to the vigor and strength of the nation's population. If farm families were the key to the nation's vitality, a decline in that sector might be as dangerous as the prospect of race suicide if not enough healthy babies were born to parents of native stock. The Country Life Commission was an extension of Roosevelt's thinking that went back to the Newlands Act and the conservation movement in general. Creation of the panel offered him a final chance as president to direct the nation's political priorities in what he deemed to be a productive channel.[43]

As Roosevelt saw it in 1908, the continuation of his political legacy required that Taft be elected. Yet the problems of the Republicans remained imposing as the campaign began. Factional divisions were barely concealed. Speaker Cannon was an object of criticism for GOP congressional candidates in several midwestern states. The prohibition issue hurt the party in Ohio and Indiana, where the Republicans were regarded as advocates of restrictions on personal liberty. There was also bickering about the direction of the party after Roosevelt retired.

Originally the Taft campaign had not intended to have the candidate make much in the way of personal tours. By midsummer, however, calls for Taft to take to the hustings mounted. He went west during the early weeks of September, and he spent time on the road from then until November. Taft proved to be a successful campaigner; the crowds were large and friendly. Continuity was his major theme. What the country needed from a new administration was "not to be spectacular in the enactment of great statutes laying down new codes of morals, or asserting a new standard of business integrity," but to carry on the business of government along the lines that Roosevelt had established.[44]

Roosevelt had broken many precedents during his seven years in office, but he still believed it was wise for him not to make a campaign tour himself as an incumbent president. If he became the center of the canvass, it would divert attention away from Taft. Gradually, the president was drawn into the party battle. He worked hard to have the Republican leaders in New York agree to the renomination of Hughes as governor, so as to help the national ticket in that key state. This task proved difficult, because "Hughes has succeeded in arousing a very bitter feeling against him." In the end, Roosevelt prevailed, and the New York GOP had selected Hughes by September.[45]

The slow pace of the Republican campaign puzzled Roosevelt. He wrote to his son-in-law that he wished "Taft would put more energy and fight into the matter." After a time, the president "decided to put a little vim into the campaign by making a publication of my own." These tactics included public letters that praised Taft and, with somewhat more restraint, the Republican congressional campaign. Taft would, in Roosevelt's view, "protect the just rights of both rich and poor, and he will war relentlessly against lawlessness and injustice whether exercised on behalf of property or labor."[46]

In mid September, William Randolph Hearst made disclosures about links between Standard Oil and Senator Foraker, as well as between the oil company and the treasurer of the Democratic campaign, Charles N. Haskell. This gave Roosevelt the chance to wage his kind of personalized campaign in the press. The revelation that Foraker had represented Standard Oil and had received money while he was a senator proved to Roosevelt that the position Foraker had taken on Brownsville "was merely a pretense." The Ohio lawmaker had really been "the attorney of the corporations, their hired representative in public life." Roosevelt advised Taft not to appear at rallies with Foraker, and Roosevelt said publicly that Taft was "the antithesis of the forces responsible for Mr. Foraker." Taft moved more slowly to distance himself from the Ohio senator, but in the end, Foraker was politically repudiated.[47]

The charges against Haskell, the governor of Oklahoma, afforded

Roosevelt the occasion to aim his fire at the Democrats and their nominee. He attacked Bryan for retaining Haskell in his campaign, and the Democratic candidate replied in a public telegram defending his colleague. As Roosevelt told George Meyer, "Bryan's telegram gave me an opening which I was glad to seize." The president's own public answer to Bryan charged that it was "a scandal and a disgrace that Governor Haskell should be connected with the management of any national campaign." Eventually the public outcry forced Haskell to step down. "How the President does enjoy a fight where there is need of one," James R. Garfield wrote in his diary; "he is a wonderfully wise leader of public opinion & most keen in seeing what proper advantage to take of position."[48]

Roosevelt had succeeded at his goal "to put aggressive life into the campaign." The public letters flowed steadily out of the White House until election day. By the end of October he was "entirely confident of Mr. Taft's election." In fact, for all the assistance of Roosevelt's personal intervention, Taft had shown himself to be a creditable candidate on his own. The combination of Roosevelt's actions and Taft's campaigning, combined with Democratic errors, moved popular sentiment toward the GOP during October. The labor vote did not defect to the Democrats, as Gompers had hoped, and black Republicans did not bolt because of Brownsville. Most of all, Bryan failed to find a winning issue that would give the electorate a reason to reject Taft and the Roosevelt policies.[49]

Election day—3 November 1908—brought a solid victory for Taft and his party. He received 321 electoral votes to Bryan's 162, and he gained almost 50,000 more votes than Roosevelt had received in 1904. Because Bryan's vote surpassed Parker's total, Taft's plurality was trimmed to about half of what Roosevelt's had been four years earlier. The Republicans retained control of both houses of Congress, with only slight losses in the House of Representatives to the Democrats. In five states, however, the Democrats elected governors even though Taft won the electoral votes. The growth of ticket splitting indicated how partisanship had eroded as a basis of voting decisions during Roosevelt's presidency. The White House reaction to Taft's victory was exuberant. The French ambassador, Jules Jusserand, commented that "the president's joy at the result of the election is overflowing." Roosevelt would say periodically to visitors: "We have them beaten to a frazzle."[50]

Roosevelt's pleasure was genuine, but it did not last long. The four months of his presidency that remained would be tumultuous. Behind the public façade of harmony, his friendship with Taft experienced strain. Roosevelt's last session of Congress proved to be a sustained exercise in mutual vituperation. The issue of Panama, which had long seemed settled, also arose to vex him. The transition from one Republican president to another demonstrated how much internal division and potential discord existed within the GOP after seven and a half years of Roosevelt's leadership.

Part of the ensuing problem was the result of the formless nature of the presidential transition process in the early twentieth century. The office was still so small and intimate that the shift was more like a family move than a change from one administration to another. Since Taft and Roosevelt were presumed to be so close, there was little perceived need to work out formal mechanisms to transfer responsibility and to continue policies. As a result, the possibilities for misunderstanding multiplied.

The fissures between Roosevelt and Taft began within days of the election. On 7 November 1908 the president-elect wrote Roosevelt—"the chief agent in working out the present status of affairs"—that "you and my brother Charlie made that possible which in all probability would not have occurred otherwise." Charles P. Taft, a newspaper publisher, had supplied abundant funds to his brother's candidacy, but Roosevelt did not deem that this was comparable to what a Republican president had done. The comment stung. In 1910, Roosevelt observed that it was like saying that "Abraham Lincoln and the bond seller Jay Cooke saved the Union."[51]

Successive events opened the gap between Taft and his predecessor. Charles P. Taft wanted to occupy Foraker's Senate seat, which the Ohio legislature would fill in a few weeks. Roosevelt intervened to make sure that Foraker would lose but did not aid the president's brother. Theodore E. Burton was chosen for the place. Meanwhile, even before 4 March 1909, Mrs. Taft set about the work of shaping the White House as she wanted it. She envisioned "some sweeping changes in her regime," including the use of black liveried servants in place of the existing force of white ushers with whom Mrs. Roosevelt was friendly. The decision distressed the incumbent first lady. The unresolved tension between the presidential wives added to the pressures on their husbands.[52]

The formation of Taft's cabinet was another occasion for presidential misunderstanding. The apparent pledge that Taft had made in June 1908 to keep the Roosevelt men in place soon gave way to the president-elect's determination "to be his own king." He decided not to reappoint James R. Garfield, Oscar S. Straus, and Charles J. Bonaparte; and he delivered the news in awkwardly written letters. The change of mind evoked hard feelings among Roosevelt's friends. Taft thought that keeping James Wilson as secretary of agriculture and naming George Meyer as the secretary of the navy were sufficient gestures in the direction of continuity. To another cabinet officer who had not been reappointed, Roosevelt observed: "Unfortunately you have been too close to me, I fear."[53]

Even relatively minor decisions about patronage caused trouble. Roosevelt wanted to do something for his personal secretary, William Loeb. Roosevelt suggested to Taft that Loeb might be given a cabinet slot briefly. The president-elect did not want to be part of the "manipulation of a Cabinet place for personal reasons," but he did agree to have Loeb become collector of the port of New York. For Roosevelt, who "wisht to see no injury befall him," this place was the best he could do for Loeb. By mid February, Loeb himself said that the president felt "very deeply" that Taft "seems determined to sever all the ties which have bound them together in the past." Another source of irritation in the president's circle was Taft's failure to come to Roosevelt's defense when the president was attacked during these final months. The feuding that Roosevelt did with Capitol Hill was headline news daily, but Taft, in the judgment of the White House, was silent.[54]

In addition to his deteriorating relations with Taft, Roosevelt confronted a session of Congress in which his prerogatives as president and his policies came under persistent assault. His last annual message sounded the familiar theme of enhanced governmental power. "The danger to American democracy lies not in the least in the concentration of administrative power in responsible and accountable hands," he told the legislators; "it lies in having the power insufficiently concentrated, so that no one can be held responsible to the people for its use." He asked for labor legislation, including "a model employers' liability law for the District of Columbia," and for the extension of workmen's compensation. The president strongly criticized judges "who have lagged behind in their understanding of these great and vital changes in the body politic, whose minds have never been opened to the new applications of the old principles made necessary by the new conditions." He wrote about forests, inland waterways, national parks, and other urgent public issues. The message was shorter than some he had submitted, and there were perfunctory passages. The statements about judges received the most attention in the press. "There is altogether too much power in the bench," he wrote privately.[55]

Congress believed that Roosevelt had exercised too much power as president. The lawmakers endeavored to chip away at his authority now that his personal popularity and political muscle would cease to be weapons against them on 4 March 1909. Roosevelt fed the bad feeling on Capitol Hill with the statements regarding Congress and the Secret Service in his message. One argument that was advanced against using the

Secret Service as an investigative arm of the executive, he noted, was that "the congressmen did not themselves wish to be investigated by Secret-Service men."[56]

A branch of the Treasury Department, the Secret Service had made its agents a general investigative force within the federal government by 1900. The chief of the service, John E. Wilkie, fostered a more efficient agency and pushed for probes of cases that attracted public attention. The Roosevelt administration used the service extensively, and Congress reacted during the spring of 1908. It took away the power of the Justice Department to call on the Secret Service for crime detection. Attorney General Bonaparte then turned to miscellaneous funds to pay a detective force made up of former agents. Wilkie called it "a fortunate solution" for agents who would otherwise have been unemployed. The president, the attorney general, and the service's chief—all believed that a cadre of detectives was necessary to achieve what Bonaparte called "a comprehensive investigative service." Out of this small group of detectives emerged, in time, the Federal Bureau of Investigation. For Roosevelt this administrative step led to the strengthening of executive power and to a more efficient means of fighting wrongdoing. In his message he was using his popularity and his command of the national agenda to set up a test of will between himself and Congress on the battleground of legislative/executive relations over which he had fought so often since 1901.[57]

The president clearly had seized the high ground of the argument. Congress could not avoid the imputation that some of its members had something to hide if members opposed the president and sought to limit the scope of the Secret Service. Despite that dilemma, both branches launched proceedings to examine what Roosevelt had written and to ask him to document the charges. The House passed a resolution on 17 December 1908, and the Senate acted a few days later. Roosevelt decided to keep on the offensive, and he directed the cabinet to assemble data so that he could "give comprehensive information to the Senate" about "the employment of special investigators by the different Departments."[58]

The House received a special message on 4 January 1909 in which Roosevelt denied that he had charged anyone with corruption. The main issue, as he framed it, was: "Does Congress desire that the Government shall have at its disposal the most efficient instrument for the detection of criminals and the prevention and punishment of crime, or does it not?" He contended, as he had done before, that "only criminals need fear our detectives," and he cited instances in which members of the

Secret Service had uncovered criminal activity during the course of their duties.[59]

A letter to Senator Eugene Hale the following day added to the intensity of the controversy. Roosevelt explored at length what Secret Service records showed about the efforts of Senator Ben Tillman to profit from land deals in Oregon that involved himself and his family. The case, Roosevelt said, illustrated "in striking fashion" how agents "in the strict line of their duty may develop facts of high importance." The example also allowed Roosevelt to settle a score with Tillman, "one of the foulest and rottenest demagogs in the whole country."[60]

Both houses responded to the president's statements. In the House a resolution was introduced on 8 January to table both the portion of the annual message that dealt with the Secret Service and the special message. The proposal was adopted by a vote of 212 to 36. Cannon thought that the House had struck a major blow against an assertive executive. Tillman answered the charges in a speech that did not do his personal reputation any good. On the whole, Roosevelt came out ahead in the exchange. Public opinion supported him, and "at the White House it is openly said there is not the least concern what either the House or Senate does or says about the President."[61]

Roosevelt saw himself as defending the prerogatives of his office. "I have come out ahead so far," he informed Theodore, Jr., "and I have been full President right up to the end—which hardly any other President ever has been." Roosevelt had a point. Members of Congress had skirted the boundaries of legality, and some had crossed over into criminality. Moreover, Roosevelt was convinced that his motives were above reproach and that his administration would not abuse the investigative power that the detectives represented. In that event, why not centralize detective work in the Department of Justice? Who could object but criminals and their associates? Roosevelt argued that he should be trusted because his intentions were pure and he would not misbehave. In the end, Congress acquiesced, and the investigative reach of the government grew.[62]

The tensions of the session also included two presidential vetoes— of a Census Bureau bill that would have given Congress four thousand patronage slots to allocate and of a measure that would have assigned to a single individual the water-power rights on a Missouri river. Roosevelt rebuffed a Senate committee that sought information about his handling of the Tennessee Coal and Iron episode during 1907. He released only what he wished to disclose, and he suggested that impeachment was the necessary step if they wanted him to do more. On the other hand, when the president transmitted to Congress the report of the Country Life Commission, the lawmakers spurned his request for $25,000 to print the document and ordered the commission to stop its work. They tried as well to restrict his authority to name commissions and panels without their consent.

The Brownsville affair also affected the congressional session. The War Department submitted a report from its two private operatives in December 1908. Roosevelt then sent in another special message, reaffirming his dismissal but allowing any innocent soldiers to be reinstated after a year. Foraker pointed out that payments had been made to the agents. With his public career ending, the Ohio senator had to settle for a compromise measure that left the fate of the black soldiers to an army panel of senior officers. The bill cleared the Senate and the House in late February. Roosevelt signed it on 2 March 1909. After the court met, fourteen men were declared eligible to reenlist. Vindication for the others did not come until 1972. To the end of his presidency and beyond, Roosevelt maintained that he had acted correctly. By 1916 he had reconciled with Foraker. The soldiers vanished into the obscurity of the segregated nation which they had served before their unjust disgrace.

Roosevelt enjoyed this last skirmish in his running warfare with Capitol Hill. When one of Taft's friends commented that there would likely occur "a period of stagnation at Washington" between the election and the inauguration, Roosevelt "felt like wiring him that the period of stagnation continues to rage with uninterrupted violence." Roosevelt's posture of standing up for the rights of his office remained politically popular. "When Roosevelt attacks Congress," said the *San Francisco Bulletin*, "the people feel that he is making their fight."[63]

During the waning weeks of his administration, Theodore Roosevelt wielded the power of his office in order to meet a newspaper challenge to one of the most celebrated acts of his first term. In October the *Indianapolis News* alleged that Roosevelt had erred in his handling of three episodes: the quarrel with E. H. Harriman, the *Tennessee Coal and Iron* case, and the financial aspects of the Panama Canal episode. The last example hit Roosevelt in a sensitive place. The *News* drew its charges about Panama from information that appeared in Joseph Pulitzer's *New York World*. The pro-Democratic *World* claimed that there was evidence to show that William Nelson Cromwell had formed an American syndicate, of which Charles P. Taft and Douglas Robinson, the president's brother-in-law, were members. The syndicate was formed to capitalize on the imminent payment of $40 million to the French bondholders in the New Panama Canal Company. The story went on to allege that the federal government was hiding records that would reveal the nature of the transaction. The issue, as the *News* put it, was "But who got the money?" Roosevelt's political friend in Indiana, William Dudley Foulke, sent him these materials from the *News* during the campaign, but the president did not respond publicly until 1 December 1908. [64]

In an open letter to Foulke, Roosevelt denied all the charges and accused the *News* and the *World* of practicing "every form of mendacity known to man, from the suppression of the truth and the suggestion of the false, to the lie direct." When the presidential blast was printed, the *World* countered with an attack upon the accuracy of what Roosevelt had written. His letter was "full of flagrant untruths, reeking with misstatements," all of which required "that full publicity come at once through the authority and by the action of Congress." [65]

Roosevelt was furious. "I do not know anything about the law of criminal libel, but I should dearly like to have it invoked about Pulitzer, of the *World*," he wrote to Henry L. Stimson, the federal attorney for the Southern District of New York. Unhappily for the president, the capacity of the national government to bring a suit for libel was very much in question. Libel matters were an issue for the courts of the state in which the alleged offense had occurred. There was no federal libel law that the government could use in its prosecution. [66]

On 15 December 1908, Roosevelt sent a special message to Congress in which he sought to refute the charges made by the *World* and the *News*. The allegations were "false in every particular from beginning to end"; they consisted only "of a string of infamous libels." The president concluded that "they are in fact wholly, and in form partly, a libel upon the United States government." Joseph Pulitzer, therefore, "should be prosecuted for libel by the governmental authorities." To support his case, Roosevelt transmitted a mass of papers relating to Panama. [67]

The *World*'s answer addressed the issue that underlay Roosevelt's conduct. "This is the first time a President ever asserted the doctrine of lese-majesty" or proposed to have criminal actions brought against citizens "who criticized the conduct of the Government, or the conduct of individuals who may have had business dealings with the Government." Pulitzer proved to a tough opponent. In Roosevelt's mind, however, the issue was not the First Amendment or freedom of the press. He was responding in kind to what he saw as a personal attack on his character and record. [68]

Two grand juries began hearing testimony in Washington and New York during January 1909. There were delicate legal issues about who was bringing the complaint, what statute was being used, and who the actual defendants were. Indictments were returned in Washington in mid February 1909 against the *World* and the *News*. The New York Grand Jury took similar action during March 1909. In order to establish federal jurisdiction in New York, Stimson relied on an 1898 statute that protected federal installations. The charge was that the libelous newspapers had circulated at governmental facilities in the state.

The actual prosecution of the cases went on after Theodore Roosevelt left the presidency. Both proceedings faltered in the end over the issue of the government's standing to bring the cases or to extradite the defendants to face trial in the District of Columbia. That outcome was the best conclusion to these ill-considered indictments. Theodore Roosevelt had enjoyed unparalleled personal success as president in his press relations. He now labeled vigorous journalistic criticism of his policies intolerable, and he employed the substantive powers of his office to strike back. Coming at the end of his presidency, the libel episode had a comic-opera side that has diminished its historical importance. It merited closer evaluation for what it revealed about the range of Roosevelt's broad conception of executive power.

The waning days of Roosevelt's administration also included moments of characteristic vigor and personal poignancy. Shortly after the election the president issued a public letter in which he denounced the religious bigotry that had been directed against Taft during the campaign because of his Unitarian religion. In late December the president summoned a number of prominent Americans to a White House conference to be held in January 1909 to consider the plight of the nation's dependent children. "Surely nothing ought to interest our people more than the care of the children who are destitute and neglected but not delinquent," the president wrote. He also asked his old friend Ambassador Jules Jusserand to encourage the researches of a Texas author, John A. Lomax, into the origins of cowboy songs. Roosevelt's own personal preoccupation was planning for his African adventure. As his presidency drew to a close, he informed a friend: "I have done my work; I am perfectly content; I have nothing to ask; and I am very grateful to the American people for what they have done for me."[69]

The signs of tension with Taft receded as 4 March 1909 approached. The president-elect sent his Inaugural Address to Roosevelt, whose verdict was: "It is simply fine in every way." The incoming president would confront decisions about the tariff revision that the GOP had promised. He had already decided, with Roosevelt's concurrence, not to oppose Cannon's reelection as Speaker of the House. Responding to the invitation from the Roosevelts, the Tafts accepted the idea of spending the night at the White House on 3 March 1909.[70]

There remained the bittersweet process of saying good-bye to friends and colleagues at the White House. On 1 March the members of the Tennis Cabinet gathered for lunch with the president. When Roosevelt spoke about what they had done together, most of the company were in tears. They gave him a lion in bronze, whereupon Roosevelt said: "You have taken me by surprise. You have caught me napping." Among the other visits of the last days was one that Roosevelt and his wife made to the home of the Lodges. As the president and the first lady departed, Mrs. Lodge said to her husband: "The great and joyous days are over, we shall never have anything like them again—there is no one like Theodore."[71]

The stay of the Tafts on 3/4 March 1909 was awkward and painful for both couples. Conversation at a small dinner was hard to start; the evening went awkwardly. Four years later, Taft referred to it as "that funeral." When inauguration morning came, a severe snowstorm pelted the city. "I knew there would be a blizzard when I went out," Roosevelt said. The inaugural ceremonies were held in the Senate chamber. Taft took the oath as the twenty-seventh president, and he delivered his Inaugural Address. Roosevelt shook his successor's hand and said: "God bless you old man. It is a great state document." The former president then left for the railroad station and private life.[72]

Roosevelt told reporters the next day that he would give no more interviews. He plunged into the preparations for his African adventure. The years in the presidency had exacted their toll, even from a vigorous and active man such as Roosevelt. He had lost the sight of his left eye during a White House boxing match, and he had gained weight from the rich food that he so eagerly consumed. The public knew little about this aspect of Roosevelt. They saw the energetic president who took army officers for a robust hike through Rock Creek Park in November 1908 and waded out into the stream himself. It was to this exciting and popular chief executive, who had personalized his office, that "the requests for autographs, farewell interviews, etc.," came in "by hundreds" during February 1909. Roosevelt now would never stop being famous and celebrated. Mrs. Roosevelt was right when she told Archie Butt, his military aide, that though she wanted her husband "to be the simplest American alive after he leaves the White House," she feared that "he has really forgotten how to be."[73]

Almost a decade as a former president lay ahead for Theodore Roosevelt. There would be moments of great excitement and danger as he hunted animals, explored hitherto unknown rivers, and captivated political audiences. Tragedy also came with declining health and family losses, especially that of his aviator son Quentin, who was shot down during World War I. The postpresidency was lived out in the spotlight of

297

public attention. As a friend wrote in 1916, "At this moment his name, whether in Pekin or Patagonia, or anywhere else in the world means *America*—Americanism, Freedom, the ideals on which the nation has, until lately, been supposed to rest."[74]

In national politics, Roosevelt's regulatory policies and his advocacy of expanded national power contributed to the split that drove the Republicans from the White House in 1912. The Taft-Roosevelt friendship deteriorated between 1909 and late 1911 under the pressure of their divergent perceptions of presidential power and the scope of progressive reform. In early 1912, Roosevelt repudiated his anti-third-term pledge of 1904 and announced his candidacy for the Republican nomination. The bitter personal struggle that followed shook apart the GOP. When he lost the nomination, Roosevelt broke with the Republicans and launched the Progressive party. The split helped to ensure the election of Woodrow Wilson, the Democratic nominee.

Anger at Wilson over the president's neutrality program during World War I had driven Roosevelt back toward the Republicans by 1916, and he campaigned for Charles Evans Hughes during the fall campaign. After the United States entered World War I, Roosevelt asked Wilson for permission to lead a division to France, but the president turned him down. During 1917 and 1918, Roosevelt spoke out on behalf of the war effort while remaining a strong critic of the Wilson administration and its policies. When his life ended on 6 January 1919, Theodore Roosevelt was an old man at sixty. As he had written in September 1918, "we must die soon anyhow—and we have warmed both hands before the fire of life."[75]

The years of the presidency had been the high point of that active and varied life. When he composed his autobiography during 1913, he observed: "Practical efficiency is common, and lofty idealism not uncommon; it is the combination which is necessary, and the combination is rare." He believed that he had possessed those qualities and that he had been a useful president. His achievements were the settlement of the coal strike, "the voyage of the battle fleet around the world," the Panama Canal, Germany and Venezuela, Britain and Alaska, "the irrigation business in the West, and finally, I think, the toning up of the Government service generally." He had, as Gifford Pinchot wrote later, "used the whole Government of the United States consciously, and with the most conspicuous success, as a means of doing good to the people of this country." It was a standard by which Theodore Roosevelt would have liked his presidency to be judged.[76]

Those assessments began coming in even before Roosevelt left office. Former senator William E. Chandler told Henry Cabot Lodge in

January 1909 that Roosevelt had "changed the course of American politics. We can never go back to the position where we were under Hanna." A friendly British writer noted that Roosevelt had "a record of administrative achievement and progress unparalleled in American history." The *World's Work* decided that Roosevelt had been "the happiest man that ever dwelt in the White House," and he had rendered "original and lasting service to the nation." Harry Thurston Peck provided one of the relatively few critical appraisals. "The President really loves justice, yet in practice he has been frequently unjust," Peck observed. "Great power and excessive adulation have had their effect upon a naturally fine and up-right character." Overall the contemporary verdict was warm and positive. "His influence as a moral reformer," wrote the clergyman Lyman Abbott, "will ever remain in the higher ideals and quickened patriotic life of a great people."[77]

During the thirty years after he died, Theodore Roosevelt's reputation as president went into an eclipse. His advocacy of reform seemed quaint throughout the 1920s. There were only the reminiscent biographies of some friends and the two-volume authorized life by Joseph Bucklin Bishop. The first full study to use some of the Roosevelt papers, published by Henry F. Pringle in 1931, treated Roosevelt as a boisterous adolescent. Then another Roosevelt captured the nation's attention and set its agenda during the 1930s and early 1940s. Despite these developments, popular fascination with Theodore Roosevelt persisted.

After the Second World War, interest in Theodore Roosevelt revived. The publication of the eight volumes of his letters brought the president's thoughts to the attention of the historical profession in a convenient way. Out of that editorial endeavor also came John Morton Blum's graceful and incisive examination of *The Republican Roosevelt* in 1954. Blum argued the case for a president who acted like a modern chief executive in all aspects of foreign and domestic policy. At the same time the important contributions of George E. Mowry, William H. Harbaugh, and Howard K. Beale solidified the impression that Roosevelt was a model for the modern presidents of this century. Two decades later the biographies by David McCullough and Edmund Morris captured large audiences and indicated the power that the Roosevelt story had for his fellow Americans.

The writings of these historians and popular biographers commanded agreement because what they said was accurate. Theodore Roosevelt was a strong, effective executive whose policies foreshadowed the welfare state in his domestic programs and who acted like a world leader in foreign policy. He was not, however, a presidential aberration or an institutional innovator who appeared from nowhere. The power of the presidency had been slowly rising since the mid 1870s. His predecessor, William McKinley, had been a modern president in all but the crucial dimension of personalized magnetism that Roosevelt contributed. After March 1909, William Howard Taft made his mark on strengthening the office during a single unhappy term. More important still, Woodrow Wilson built on Roosevelt's legacy and added significant changes of his own. It does not diminish Roosevelt or his achievements to place him within a tradition of growing presidential power between 1897 and 1921.

To that tradition, Roosevelt's personalized presidency added unique qualities and important changes. He wove the office into the fabric of daily life as no previous president had done. Many Americans believed that they knew the friendly man in the White House and his extended family. In his policies and such preachments as the Square Deal, Roosevelt posed some of the right questions about conservation, the control of corporations, the welfare of the average American, and what constituted a just society. As a chief diplomat, he taught the lessons of world power and national obligation.

The prejudices of his own time and the gaps in his sense of justice and fair play set limits on his vision of who should be part of a just society. For African-Americans, Native Americans, Asians, and Socialists, the most the president would accord them was a reluctant tolerance. More often those on the fringes of Roosevelt's consensus faced outright oppression, as in the case of Brownsville. To that extent, Theodore Roosevelt did not transcend the boundaries of his own day, as Roosevelt's favorite president, Abraham Lincoln, had done half a century earlier.

Theodore Roosevelt wanted to be a great president. His administration occurred at a time of relative calm for the nation, compared to the great trials that Lincoln, Woodrow Wilson, Franklin D. Roosevelt, and Harry S. Truman faced. With no crisis to overcome and no war to wage, Roosevelt achieved important legislation and set constructive precedents at home and abroad. He governed with intelligence, energy, and elan.

Roosevelt's vigorous advocacy of the strong presidency also contained potential dangers and troubling implications. The power to do good for the nation carried with it the capacity to prosecute any trusts that the president considered "bad," to discharge black soldiers whom he believed guilty, and to investigate congressmen he deemed to be criminals. Roosevelt accepted the constraints of legality and precedent as necessary conditions of political life during his presidency. He did not view these obstacles as wise provisions that the framers of the Constitution had included as a possible check against either a well-intentioned president gone wrong or a more sinister executive bent on excessive power. One plausible argument against Roosevelt's claims to greatness in the White House rests on those several occasions when he had flirted with an abuse of power.

If Roosevelt fell short of the first rank of presidents, he surely qualified for that ambivalent rating of "near great," conferred upon him in the polls that historians periodically take with each other. As the number of presidents increases and as the relative success of modern chief executives diminishes under the impact of political gridlock and divided government, Theodore Roosevelt's reputation will probably improve, and his rating may climb. His importance to the presidency will endure. He dramatized and personalized the modern form of his office and made it a living reality for Americans of his day and for the generations that followed.

NOTES

Acronyms and short forms used throughout the notes:

Addresses	*Addresses and Presidential Messages of Theodore Roosevelt, 1902–1904.* New York: G. P. Putnam's Sons, 1904.
American Problems	Vol. 16 of *Works*
Autobigraphy	*Theodore Roosevelt: An Autobiography.* Vol. 20 of *Works*
LC	Library of Congress, Washington, D.C.
Letters	*The Letters of Theodore Roosevelt*, selected and edited by Elting E. Morison et al. 8 vols. Cambridge, Mass.: Harvard University Press, 1951–54.
MD	Manuscript Division, Library of Congress
NA	National Archives, Washington, D. C.
RG	Record group
State Papers	*State Papers as Governor and President, 1899–1909.* Vol. 16 of *Works*
TR	Theodore Roosevelt
TRP	Theodore Roosevelt Papers, Manuscript Division, Library of Congress
Works	*The Works of Theodore Roosevelt.* 20 vols. New York: Charles Scribner's Sons, 1926.

CHAPTER 1
"HERE IS THE TASK"

1. For TR's statement see "Theodore Roosevelt," *American Monthly Review of Reviews* 34 (Oct. 1901): 438; the reaction of Senator Nathan B. Scott (R., W.Va.) to this pledge is quoted in *New York Tribune*, 22 Sept. 1901.

2. *New York Tribune,* 21 Sept. 1901.

3. Corinne Roosevelt Robinson, *My Brother Theodore Roosevelt* (New York: Scribner's, 1921), pp. 206–7; Joseph Bucklin Bishop, *Notes and Anecdotes of Many Years* (New York: Scribner's, 1925), pp. 119–20.

4. TR to Henry Cabot Lodge, 23 Sept. 1901, *Letters,* 3:150.

5. David G. McCullough, *Mornings on Horseback* (New York: Simon & Schuster, 1981), p. 186; *American Ideals, The Strenuous Life, Realizable Ideals,* vol. 13 of *Works,* p. 564.

6. McCullough, *Mornings on Horseback,* pp. 69–148, is enlightening on Roosevelt's youth; see also Edmund Morris, *The Rise of Theodore Roosevelt* (New York: Coward, McCann & Geoghegan, 1979), pp. 33–79.

7. McCullough, *Mornings on Horseback,* p. 162.

8. Morris, *Rise of Theodore Roosevelt,* pp. 113, 120.

9. McCullough, *Mornings on Horseback,* p. 220.

10. H. Wayne Morgan, *From Hayes to McKinley: National Party Politics, 1877–1896* (Syracuse, N.Y.: Syracuse University Press, 1969), pp. 201, 233–34; McCullough, *Mornings on Horseback,* pp. 289–315.

11. McCullough, *Mornings on Horseback,* p. 329.

12. Ibid., p. 367.

13. TR to Henry White, 30 Apr. 1897, *Letters,* 1:606; Morris, *Rise of Theodore Roosevelt,* pp. 565–90, exaggerates Roosevelt's influence in the McKinley administration and does not grasp McKinley's capacity as president.

14. TR to George Dewey, 25 Feb. 1898, *Letters,* 2:784–85.

15. TR to Paul Dana, 18 Apr. 1898, ibid., p. 817.

16. Morris, *Rise of Theodore Roosevelt,* pp. 623–24; TR's own account of his experiences in Cuba is in Theodore Roosevelt, *The Rough Riders,* vol. 11 of *Works;* see also Lewis L. Gould, ed., "Theodore Roosevelt and the Spanish-American War: Four Unpublished Letters to President William McKinley," *Theodore Roosevelt Association Journal* 7 (Summer 1981): 17–21.

17. Morris, *Rise of Theodore Roosevelt,* p. 650.

18. G. Wallace Chessman, *Governor Theodore Roosevelt: The Albany Apprenticeship, 1898–1900* (Cambridge, Mass.: Harvard University Press, 1965), is the best source for Roosevelt as governor.

19. Lewis L. Gould, ed., "Charles Warren Fairbanks and the Republican National Convention of 1900: A Memoir," *Indiana Magazine of History* 77 (Dec. 1981): 367–68.

20. Margaret Leech, *In the Days of McKinley* (New York: Harper, 1959), p. 537 (Hanna quotation); Alexander Dana Noyes, *The Market Place: Reminiscences of a Financial Editor* (Boston, Mass.: Little, Brown, 1938), p. 209; Gerard Lowther to Lord Lansdowne, 19 Sept. 1901, FO 5/2548, Public Record Office, London; George H. Lyman to Henry Cabot Lodge, 13 Nov. 1901, Henry Cabot Lodge Papers, Massachusetts Historical Society, Boston.

21. Earle Looker, *The White House Gang* (New York: Fleming H. Revell, 1929), p. 15; William Allen White, *Masks in a Pageant* (New York: Macmillan, 1928), p. 285.

22. Day Allen Willey, "When You Meet the President," *Independent* 56 (30

June 1904): 1487; William Allen White to Cyrus Leland, 19 Dec. 1901, William Allen White Papers, MD, LC.

23. William Dean Howells to TR, 26 Aug. 1906, in William C. Fisher, with Christopher K. Lohmann, eds., *W. D. Howells: Selected Letters*, vol. 5: *1902–1911* (Boston, Mass.: Twayne, 1983), p. 193.

24. Lyman Abbott, in "A Review of President Roosevelt's Administration: IV—Its Influence on Patriotism and Public Service," *Outlook* 91 (27 Feb. 1909): 430, quotes Roosevelt as saying "I have got such a bully pulpit."

25. Entry for 17 Apr. 1908, George von Lengerke Meyer's diary, MD, LC; Mortimer Durand to Edward Grey, 6 Apr. 1906, FO 371/12861, Public Record Office, London; Chauncey M. Depew, *My Memories of Eighty Years* (New York: Scribner's, 1922), p. 169.

26. *Autobiography*, p. 376.

27. Ibid., p. 341 (both quotations).

28. *Addresses*, p. 323.

29. Ibid., p. 124; *Autobiography*, p. 491.

30. William C. Widenor, *Henry Cabot Lodge and the Search for an American Foreign Policy* (Berkeley: University of California Press, 1980), p. 158.

31. Waldon Fawcett, "The President's Business Office," *World's Work* 4 (July 1902): 2310; *The Letters of Archie Butt, Personal Aide to President Roosevelt*, ed. Lawrence F. Abbott (Garden City, N.Y.: Doubleday, Page, 1924), p. 250; White House Permanent Roll and White House Detailed Roll, 16 July 1902, George B. Cortelyou Papers, box 37, MD, LC.

32. George Kennan, "The White House: The Plans for Its Reconstruction," *Outlook 70,* (1 Feb. 1902): 294.

33. Leech, *In the Days of McKinley*, p. 504.

34. Sylvia Jukes Morris, *Edith Kermit Roosevelt: Portrait of a First Lady* (New York: Coward, McCann & Geoghegan, 1980), p. 22; Louis T. Michener to Eugene Ganoe Hay, 21 Oct. 1901, Eugene Ganoe Hay Papers, MD, LC (second quotation); Murat Halstead to Albert Halstead, 7 Oct. 1901, Halstead Family Papers, Cincinnati Historical Society, Cincinnati, Ohio.

CHAPTER 2
THE PERSONALIZED PRESIDENT

1. *New York Tribune*, 4 Dec. 1901; John D. Long to Peirce Long, 5 Dec. 1901, John D. Long Papers, Massachusetts Historical Society, Boston.

2. *Boston Sunday Herald*, 1 Dec. 1901.

3. David S. Barry, *Forty Years in Washington* (Boston, Mass.: Little, Brown, 1924), pp. 267–69.

4. Walter E. Clark to Erastus Brainerd, 26 Jan. 1906, Erastus Brainerd Papers, University of Washington Library, Seattle.

5. "Two Significant Appointments," *Outlook* 69 (19 Oct. 1901): 289.

6. See, e.g., Joel A. Tarr, "President Theodore Roosevelt and Illinois Poli-

tics, 1901–1904," *Journal of the Illinois State Historical Society* 58 (Autumn 1965): 245–64.

7. TR to Alexander P. Doyle, 1 Oct. 1901, *Letters*, 3:156; George B. Cortelyou to Ethan Allen Hitchcock, 15 Nov. 1901, Ethan Allen Hitchcock Papers, RG 316, NA.

8. TR to James Ford Rhodes, 15 Dec. 1904, *Letters*, 4:1072.

9. TR to Booker T. Washington, 14 Sept. 1901, ibid., 3:149.

10. Louis R. Harlan, *Booker T. Washington: The Making of a Black Leader, 1865–1901* (New York: Oxford University Press, 1972), p. 311.

11. The Memphis newspaper is quoted by Pearl Kluger in "Progressive Presidents and Black Americans" (Ph.D. diss., Columbia University, 1974), p. 42; Harlan, *Booker T. Washington*, p. 314, quotes the *Richmond* (Va.) *Times*; Willard B. Gatewood, Jr., *Theodore Roosevelt and the Art of Controversy: Episodes of the White House Years* (Baton Rouge: Louisiana State University Press, 1970), p. 37, has other southern reactions.

12. Harlan, *Booker T. Washington*, p. 305; TR to Owen Wister, 27 Apr. 1906, *Letters*, 5:226; TR to Albion Tourgee, 8 Nov. 1901, ibid., 3:190.

13. Charles S. Olcott, *William McKinley*, 2 vols. (Boston, Mass.: Houghton Mifflin, 1916), 2:382.

14. *Iowa State Register* (Des Moines), 8 Aug. 1901.

15. *Chicago Tribune*, 20 Oct. 1901; Eugene Hale to TR, 22 Oct. 1901, TRP.

16. Joseph Wharton to William Boyd Allison, 30 Oct. 1901, William Boyd Allison Papers, box 345, Iowa State Department of History and Archives, Des Moines; *American Economist*, 8 Nov. 1901 (first quotation); *Chicago Tribune*, 9 Nov. (Hanna) and 10 Nov. 1901 (Lodge).

17. Allison to TR, 2 Nov. 1901, TRP.

18. Aldrich to TR, 15 Nov. 1901, TRP; TR to Aldrich, 18 Nov. 1901, *Letters*, 3:199.

19. *Autobiography*, p. 417.

20. Leslie Hannah, "Mergers," in *Encyclopedia of American Economic History*, ed. Glenn Porter (New York: Scribner's, 1980), p. 641; Mark Sullivan, *Our Times*, vol. 2: *America Finding Herself* (New York: Scribner's Sons, 1927), pp. 351–52.

21. G. Wallace Chessman, *Governor Theodore Roosevelt: The Albany Apprenticeship, 1898–1900* (Cambridge, Mass.: Harvard University Press, 1965), pp. 160, 161.

22. Rita E. Loos, "President Theodore Roosevelt and Eastern Businessmen: A Divergence of Views" (Ph.D. diss., St. John's University, 1971), p. 21, quotes Roosevelt.

23. *Chicago Tribune*, 11 Nov. 1901; TR to Douglas Robinson, 4 Oct. 1901, and TR to Paul Dana, 18 Nov. 1901, *Letters*, 3:160, 200.

24. Albert Shaw to Percy W. Bunting, 30 Nov. 1901, Albert Shaw Papers, New York Public Library.

25. *Addresses*, p. 54.

26. The statistics that follow are taken, unless otherwise indicated, from *The Statistical History of the United States from Colonial Times to the Present* (Stamford, Conn.: Fairfield Publishers, 1975).

27. *Addresses*, pp. 285, 286, 290.

28. Ibid., p. 291.

29. Ibid.

30. Ibid., pp. 292, 293, 294.

31. Ibid., pp. 295, 296.

32. Ibid., p. 297.

33. Ibid., p. 298.

34. Ibid.

35. The quotation is from Beckles Willson, *The New America: A Study of the Imperial Republic* (New York: Dutton, 1903), p. 242. For the figures about the dependence of families on the father's income see David Montgomery, *The Fall of the House of Labor: The Workplace, the State, and American Labor Activism, 1865–1925* (Cambridge, Eng.: Cambridge University Press, 1987), p. 139; for the other reference to studies of income see Harold Underwood Faulkner, *The Quest for Social Justice* (New York: Macmillan, 1931), pp. 22–23.

36. *Addresses*, pp. 299–300.

37. Ibid., p. 301.

38. Maldwyn A. Jones, *The Limits of Liberty: American History, 1607–1980* (New York: Oxford University Press, 1983), p. 321.

39. "The Burden of the New Immigration," *World's Work* 6 (July 1903): 2601.

40. *Addresses*, pp. 301, 302.

41. Ibid., p. 302.

42. Ibid., pp. 302–4.

43. Ibid., pp. 315–16.

44. Ibid., pp. 304–5.

45. Ibid., p. 305.

46. Ibid. Gage is quoted in James Livingston, *Origins of the Federal Reserve System: Money, Class, and Corporate Capitalism, 1890–1913* (Ithaca, N.Y.: Cornell University Press, 1986), p. 153.

47. *Addresses*, p. 306.

48. Ibid.

49. Ibid., pp. 306–7.

50. Ibid.

51. Ibid., p. 308.

52. Ibid., p. 310; Stephen R. Fox, *John Muir and His Legacy: The American Conservation Movement* (Boston, Mass.: Little, Brown, 1981), p. 124.

53. Samuel P. Hays, *Conservation and the Gospel of Efficiency: The Progressive Conservation Movement, 1890–1920* (Cambridge, Mass.: Harvard University Press, 1959), p. 42; *Autobiography*, p. 397.

54. *Addresses*, pp. 308, 309.

55. Ibid., pp. 310, 311, 313.

56. *American Problems*, p. 141.

57. Ibid., pp. 146, 133.

58. *Addresses*, pp. 317, 318.

59. Ibid., p. 320.

60. Ibid., pp. 321, 322.

61. Ibid., pp. 323, 326.

62. Ibid., pp. 326–27, 328.

63. Ibid., pp. 329–30, 332, 333.

64. Ibid., pp. 336–37.

65. Ibid., pp. 344, 345.

66. "The Issues Raised in the President's Message," *Literary Digest* 23 (14 Dec. 1901): 753 (*Post* quotation), 754 (*Chicago Tribune*); the quotation from Mr. Dooley appears in William H. Harbaugh, *The Life and Times of Theodore Roosevelt* (New York: Oxford University Press, 1975), p. 155.

67. E. J. Hill to A. H. Byington, 4 Dec. 1901, E. J. Hill Papers, Sterling Memorial Library, Yale University, New Haven, Conn.

CHAPTER 3
"IMMEDIATE AND VIGOROUS EXECUTIVE ACTION"

1. TR to Joseph Bucklin Bishop, 2 Jan. 1902, *Letters*, 3:215.

2. John D. Long to Peirce Long, 12 Dec. 1901, John D. Long Papers, Massachusetts Historical Society, Boston.

3. "Military Views of the Schley Verdict," *Literary Digest* 23 (28 Dec. 1901): 825.

4. TR to Brander Matthews, 31 Dec. 1901, *Letters*, 3:214.

5. TR To Elihu Root, 18 Feb. and 7 Mar. 1902, ibid., pp. 232, 241.

6. *Autobiography*, p. 417.

7. Hans B. Thorelli, *The Federal Antitrust Policy: Origination of an American Tradition* (Baltimore, Md.: Johns Hopkins University Press, 1955), p. 422 n. 238, quotes Hill.

8. Balthasar Henry Meyer, *A History of the Northern Securities Case* (Madison: Bulletin of the University of Wisconsin, 1906), pp. 242, 243.

9. Samuel R. Van Sant to W. B. Douglas, 19 Nov. 1901 (first quotation), Douglas to James Donovan, 16 Jan. 1902 (second quotation), 44.E.3.9B; and for the statement from Knox see the clipping from *Minneapolis Journal*, 16 Jan. 1902, attached to Douglas to Wayne MacVeagh, 5 Feb. 1902, 44.E.3.10F, Attorney General Correspondence, Division of Archives and Manuscripts, Minnesota Historical Society, St. Paul.

10. Meyer, *History of the Northern Securities Case*, p. 257; William Letwin, *Law and Economic Policy in America: The Evolution of the Sherman Antitrust Act* (New York: Random House, 1965), p. 201 n. 8.

11. Douglas to Philander C. Knox, 15 Feb. 1902, 43.E.3.10F, Attorney General Correspondence, Minnesota Historical Society; TR to Herschel V. Jones, 26 Feb. 1902, *Letters*, 3:236.

12. Knox's statement appears in *New York Tribune*, 20 Feb. 1902; for the reactions in the market and for the quotations see "Investigating the Big Railroad Merger," *Literary Digest* 24 (1 Mar. 1902): 277.

13. For Morgan's visit to the White House see *New York Tribune*, 24 Feb. 1902. Joseph Bucklin Bishop, *Theodore Roosevelt and His Time*, 2 vols. (New York:

Scribner's, 1920), 1:184–85. An earlier version of this episode appears in Judson C. Welliver, "The Epoch of Roosevelt," *American Monthly Review of Reviews* 39 (Mar. 1909): 340–41.

14. TR to Albert Shaw, 4 Mar. 1902, Albert Shaw Papers, New York Public Library; "The Progress of the World," *American Monthly Review of Reviews* 25 (Apr. 1902): 398–99.

15. Thomas Roger Wessel, "Republican Justice: The Department of Justice under Roosevelt and Taft, 1901–1913" (Ph.D. diss., University of Maryland, 1972), pp. 9 (quotation), 10–35. This paragraph is based on Wessel's thorough discussion.

16. *New York Tribune*, 11 Mar. 1902.

17. "Effects of the Beef Trust Injunction," *Literary Digest* 24 (31 May 1902): 727.

18. TR to Frederick Norton Goddard, 14 Aug. 1902, *Letters*, 3:314; *Addresses*, p. 9.

19. James A. Tawney to John C. Crabb, 7 Mar. 1902, James A. Tawney Papers, Minnesota Historical Society, St. Paul.

20. *American Economist*, 16 May 1902, p. 229.

21. Roosevelt is quoted in Richard Cleveland Baker, *The Tariff under Roosevelt and Taft* (Hastings, Nebr.: Democrat Printing Co., 1941), p. 28.

22. George W. Smalley to Moreton Frewen, 16 June 1902, Moreton Frewen Papers, MD, LC.

23. TR to Nicholas Murray Butler, 27 May 1902, *Letters*, 3:266.

24. TR to George Frisbie Hoar, 16 June 1902, ibid., p. 277.

25. Taft's statement is quoted in Oscar M. Alfonso, *Theodore Roosevelt and the Philippines, 1897–1909* (New York: Oriole, 1974), p. 87.

26. John Morgan Gates, *Schoolbooks and Krags: The United States Army in the Philippines, 1898–1902* (Westport, Conn.: Greenwood, 1973), p. 254.

27. TR to Josephine Shaw Lowell, 3 May 1902, and TR to Elihu Root, 9 May 1902, *Letters*, 3:256, 260; Root is quoted in Alfonso, *Theodore Roosevelt and the Philippines*, p. 103.

28. *New York Times*, 31 May 1902.

29. TR to Taft, 31 July 1902, *Letters*, 3:305; Alfonso, *Theodore Roosevelt and the Philippines*, p. 153.

30. Frank T. Reuter, *Catholic Influence on American Colonial Policies, 1898–1904* (Austin: University of Texas Press, 1967), p. 152.

31. George B. Cortelyou to Elihu Root, 29 Sept. 1902, box 25, Elihu Root Papers, MD, LC, quoting Roosevelt.

32. Dwight C. Miner, *The Fight for the Panama Route: The Story of the Spooner Act and the Hay-Herrán Treaty* (New York: Columbia University Press, 1940), p. 121.

33. *Autobiography*, p. 387; William Lilley III and Lewis L. Gould, "The Western Irrigation Movement: 1878–1902: A Reappraisal," in *The American West: A Reorientation*, ed. Gene M. Gressley (Laramie: University of Wyoming, 1966), pp. 73–74.

34. *New York Tribune*, 30 June 1902.

35. TR to Paul Dana, 30 July 1902, *Letters*, 3:303.

36. TR to Henry Cabot Lodge, 10 July 1902, ibid., p. 288.

37. Ibid., p. 289.

38. *New York Tribune*, 24 July 1902.

39. Baker, *The Tariff under Roosevelt and Taft*, p. 31 (first quotation); TR to Nicholas Murray Butler, 12 Aug. 1902, *Letters*, 3:312 (second quotation); George E. Roberts to George D. Perkins, 23 Aug. 1902, George D. Perkins Papers, Iowa State Department of History and Archives, Des Moines.

40. *Addresses*, pp. 15, 17; "Mr. Roosevelt's Trust Policy," *Public Opinion* 33 (4 Sept. 1902): 295.

41. TR to Edward VII, 6 Sept. 1902, *Letters*, 3:325; *Addresses*, p. 54.

42. Nathaniel Wright Stephenson, *Nelson W. Aldrich: A Leader in American Politics* (New York: Scribner's, 1930), p. 196.

43. Baker, *The Tariff under Roosevelt and Taft*, p. 32; James R. Garfield to TR, 17 Sept. 1902, box 155, James R. Garfield Papers, MD, LC.

44. *Addresses*, pp. 69, 70, 77, 79; William Boyd Allison to TR, 24 Sept. 1902, TRP.

45. TR to Orville H. Platt, 2 Oct. 1902, *Letters*, 3:355; "The Perils of a President," *Public Opinion* 33 (2 Oct. 1902): 423.

46. Lodge is quoted in Robert J. Cornell, *The Anthracite Coal Strike of 1902* (Washington, D.C.: Catholic University of American Press, 1957), pp. 174, 175.

47. Thomas P. Fowler to Elihu Root, 5 June 1902, box 26, Root Papers, MD, LC; "The Coal Strike and Government Interference," *Literary Digest* 24 (21 June 1902): 827.

48. TR to Philander C. Knox, 21 Aug. 1902, *Letters*, 3:323. For a more extended treatment of the economic complexities of the coal strike and its ramifications see Robert H. Wiebe, "The Anthracite Coal Strike of 1902: A Record of Confusion," *Mississippi Valley Historical Review* 48 (Sept. 1961): 229–51.

49. TR to John Mitchell, 1 Oct. 1902, TR to Alexander Johnson Cassatt, 1 Oct. 1902, and TR to Winthrop Murray Crane, 22 Oct. 1902, *Letters*, 3:334, 360.

50. There is an account of the conference in TRP.

51. Ibid.; the comments of the mine owners are quoted in Cornell, *Anthracite Coal Strike*, p. 185.

52. TR to Mark Hanna, 3 Oct. 1902, *Letters*, 3:337.

53. TR to Grover Cleveland, 10 Oct. 1902, ibid., p. 347.

54. TR to John D. Kernan, 11 Oct. 1902, and TR to Crane, 22 Oct. 1902, ibid., pp. 348, 362; *Autobiography*, p. 455.

55. *Report to the President on the Anthracite Coal Strike of May–October 1902, by the Anthracite Coal Commission* (Washington, D.C.: Government Printing Office, 1903), p. 11.

56. "The Coal Strike Settlement," *Public Opinion* 33 (23 Oct. 1902): 511; James Wilson to TR, 20 Oct. 1902, TRP; a Progressive Republican, "President Roosevelt's First Year," *North American Review* 175 (Dec. 1902): 729.

57. Mark Sullivan, *Our Times, 1900–1925*, vol. 2: *America Finding Herself* (New York: Scribner's, 1927), p. 446.

58. Henry Casson to Henry C. Adams, 18 Oct. 1902, Henry C. Adams Papers,

State Historical Society of Wisconsin, Madison; Michael Herbert to Lord Lansdowne, 7 Nov. 1902, FO 5/2488, Public Record Office, London; TR to William Emlen Roosevelt, 6 Nov. 1902, *Letters*, 3:373.

59. A Progressive Republican, "President Roosevelt's First Year," p. 729; "The March of Events," *World's Work* 4 (Sept. 1902): 2471.

CHAPTER 4
ROOSEVELT AND THE WORLD, 1902–1904

1. Thomas Boylston Adams, "An Engineering Feat—But It Led to a Social and Political Minefield," *Boston Globe*, 5 June 1983.

2. TR to George von Lengerke Meyer, 26 Dec. 1904, *Letters*, 4:1079.

3. Jean J. Jusserand, "Personal Memories of Theodore Roosevelt," *Journal of American History* 13 (July–Dec. 1919): 321; Stefan H. Rinke, "Between Success and Failure: The Diplomatic Career of Ambassador Hermann Speck von Sternburg and German-American Relations, 1903–1908" (Master's thesis, Bowling Green State University, 1989).

4. TR to Cecil Spring Rice, 13 May 1905, *Letters*, 4:1178.

5. U.S., Department of State, *Papers Relating to the Foreign Relations of the United States, 1901* (Washington, D.C.: Government Printing Office, 1902), p. 194.

6. TR to Hermann Speck von Sternburg, 6 Mar. 1902, *Letters*, 3:240.

7. TR to George Dewey, 14 June 1902, ibid., p. 275; Ronald Spector, *Admiral of the New Empire: The Life and Career of George Dewey* (Baton Rouge: Louisiana State University Press, 1974), p. 141.

8. TR to William R. Thayer, 21 and 23 Aug. 1916, *Letters*, 8:1103 (first three quotations), 1107 (last quotation).

9. Michael Herbert to Marquess of Lansdowne, 19 June 1903, Marquess of Lansdowne Papers, FO 800/144, Public Record Office, London.

10. Frederick W. Marks III, *Velvet on Iron: The Diplomacy of Theodore Roosevelt* (Lincoln: University of Nebraska Press, 1979), pp. 38–47.

11. Edmund Morris, " 'A Few Pregnant Days': Theodore Roosevelt and the Venezuelan Crisis of 1902," *Theodore Roosevelt Association Journal* 15 (Winter 1989): 2–13; Manfred Jonas, *The United States and Germany: A Diplomatic History* (Ithaca, N.Y.: Cornell University Press, 1984), pp. 70–71.

12. Paul S. Holbo, "Perilous Obscurity: Public Diplomacy and the Press in the Venezuelan Crisis, 1902–1903," *Historian* 32 (May 1970): 428–48.

13. Marquess of Lansdowne to Sir Frederick Lascelles, 18 Dec. 1902, in *British Documents on the Origins of the War, 1898–1914*, vol. 2: *The Anglo-Japanese Alliance and the Franco-British Entente*, ed. G. P. Gooch and Harold Temperley (London: His Majesty's Stationery Office, 1927), p. 162; Jonas, *United States and Germany*, p. 72.

14. TR to Theodore Roosevelt, Jr., 1 Feb. 1903, *Letters*, 3:415; Holger H. Herwig, *Germany's Vision of Empire in Venezuela, 1871–1914* (Princeton, N.J.: Princeton University Press, 1986), p. 203.

15. TR to John Hay, 13 Mar. 1903, *Letters*, 3:446 (second quotation); TR to Elihu Root, 2 June 1904, ibid., 4:811 (first quotation).

16. Charles Callan Tansill, *Canadian-American Relations, 1875–1911* (New Haven, Conn.: Yale University Press, 1943), p. 223.

17. Charles S. Campbell, Jr., *Anglo-American Understanding, 1898–1903* (Baltimore, Md.: Johns Hopkins Press, 1957), p. 69.

18. Tansill, *Canadian-American Relations*, p. 224.

19. TR to John Hay, 10 July 1902, *Letters*, 3:287–88.

20. John A. Munro, ed., *The Alaska Boundary Dispute* (Toronto: Copp-Clark, 1970), p. 38.

21. Campbell, *Anglo-American Understanding*, p. 276.

22. Herbert to Lansdowne, 7 Feb. 1903, *British Documents on the Origins of the War*, p. 172.

23. Campbell, *Anglo-American Understanding*, p. 303.

24. Munro, *Alaska Boundary Dispute*, p. 39.

25. Lord Minto to Joseph Chamberlain, 8 Mar. 1903, in *Lord Minto's Canadian Papers: A Selection of the Public and Private Papers of the Fourth Earl of Minto, 1898–1904*, ed. Paul Stevens and John T. Saywell (Toronto: Champlain Society, 1983), p. 272.

26. TR to Hay, 29 June 1903, *Letters*, 3:507.

27. TR to Oliver Wendell Holmes, Jr., 25 July 1903, ibid., p. 530.

28. TR to Elihu Root, 3 Oct. 1903, ibid., p. 613.

29. Campbell, *Anglo-American Understanding*, p. 333.

30. TR to Theodore Roosevelt, Jr., 20 Oct. 1903, *Letters*, 3:635.

31. Munro, *Alaska Boundary Dispute*, p. 86; *Addresses*, p. 394.

32. Raymond A. Esthus, *Theodore Roosevelt and Japan* (Seattle: University of Washington Press, 1966), p. 8.

33. TR to Hay, 14 July 1902, *Letters*, 3:293.

34. A. Gregory Moore, "The Dilemma of Stereotypes: Theodore Roosevelt and China, 1901–1909" (Ph.D. diss., Kent State University, 1978), p. 73; TR to Hay, 13 May 1903, *Letters*, 3:474.

35. Edward H. Zabriskie, *American-Russian Rivalry in the Far East: A Study in Diplomacy and Power Politics, 1895–1914* (Philadelphia: University of Pennsylvania Press, 1946), pp. 88–89; TR to Hay, 22 May 1903, *Letters*, 3:478.

36. Taylor Stults, "Roosevelt, Russian Persecution of Jews, and American Public Opinion," *Jewish Social Studies* 33 (Jan. 1971): 17.

37. TR to Francis B. Loomis, 1 July 1903, *Letters*, 3:508.

38. TR to Lucius N. Littauer, 22 July 1903, ibid., p. 526.

39. Tyler Dennett, *Roosevelt and the Russo-Japanese War* (Garden City, N.Y.: Doubleday, Page, 1925), p. 27 n.

40. TR to Hay, 1 July 1902, *Letters*, 3:284; Dwight C. Miner, *The Fight for the Panama Route: The Story of the Spooner Act and the Hay-Herrán Treaty* (New York: Columbia University Press, 1940), p. 159.

41. *Autobiography*, pp. 508, 509.

42. Richard L. Lael, *Arrogant Diplomacy: U.S. Policy toward Colombia, 1903–1922* (Wilmington, Del.: Scholarly Resources, 1987), p. 6.

43. "The Panama Canal Treaty," *Literary Digest* 26 (31 Jan. 1903): 142.
44. *Autobiography*, p. 509.
45. Miner, *Fight for the Panama Route*, p. 242.
46. John Hay to A. M. Beaupre, 9 June 1903, in U.S., Senate, Committee on Foreign Relations, *Background Documents Relating to the Panama Canal*, 95th Cong., 1st sess. (Washington, D.C.: Government Printing Office, 1977), p. 228.
47. TR to John T. Morgan, 13 Aug. 1903, *Letters*, 3:565; David G. McCullough, *The Path between the Seas: The Creation of the Panama Canal, 1870–1914* (New York: Simon & Schuster, 1977), p. 339 (Cullom); Miner, *Fight for the Panama Route*, p. 340 (Hay).
48. TR to Hay, 19 Aug. 1903, *Letters*, 3:567.
49. The *World* article of 13 June 1903 appears in *The Story of Panama: Hearings on the Rainey Resolution before the Committee on Foreign Affairs of the House of Representatives* (Washington, D.C.: Government Printing Office, 1913), p. 345.
50. Philippe Bunau-Varilla, *Panama: The Creation, Destruction, and Resurrection* (New York: McBride, Nast, 1914), p. 311; TR to Albert Shaw, 10 Oct. 1903, *Letters*, 3:628.
51. TR to John Bigelow, 6 Jan. 1904, *Letters*, 3:689.
52. *Background Documents Relating to the Panama Canal*, pp. 266 (naval orders), 307 (army officers' report); Bunau-Varilla, *Panama*, p. 318.
53. *Background Documents*, p. 252.
54. "The Panama Revolution," *Literary Digest* 27 (14 Nov. 1903): 650.
55. John Major, "Who Wrote the Hay–Bunau-Varilla Convention?" *Diplomatic History* 8 (Spring 1984): 115–23.
56. Major, "Who Wrote," p. 121.
57. Bunau-Varilla, *Panama*, p. 378.
58. "The Panama Revolution," p. 649.
59. TR to Spring Rice, 9 Nov. 1903, *Letters*, 3:651; *Addresses*, pp. 425, 453.
60. TR to William Bayard Hale, 26 Feb. 1904, *Letters*, 4:740.

CHAPTER 5
THE SQUARE DEAL, 1903–1904

1. TR to Maria Longworth Storer, 8 Dec. 1902, *Letters*, 3:392. This section draws on information in William Seale, *The President's House: A History*, 2 vols. (Washington, D.C.: White House Historical Association, 1986), 2:653–78.
2. Abby G. Baker, "Social Duties of Mrs. Roosevelt," *Pearson's Magazine* 10 (Dec. 1903): 525; *The Letters of Archie Butt, Personal Aide to President Roosevelt*, ed. Lawrence F. Abbott (Garden City, N.Y.: Doubleday, Page, 1924), pp. 54, 126.
3. Baker, "Social Duties," pp. 526, 527.
4. Sylvia Jukes Morris, *Edith Kermit Roosevelt: Portrait of a First Lady* (New York: Coward, McCann & Geoghegan, 1980), p. 233.
5. TR to Kermit Roosevelt, 17 Jan. 1903, *Letters*, 3:406.
6. TR to Corinne Roosevelt Robinson, 23 Sept. 1903, ibid., p. 605.
7. Stacy A. Rozek, " 'The First Daughter of the Land': Alice Roosevelt as

Presidential Celebrity, 1902–1906," *Presidential Studies Quarterly* 19 (Winter 1989): 57; TR to Theodore Roosevelt, Jr., 20 Jan. 1903, *Letters*, 3:408.

8. Rozek, " 'The First Daughter,' " p. 51; see also E. Alexander Powell, *Yonder Lies Adventure* (New York: Macmillan, 1932), pp. 310–11.

9. Morris, *Edith Kermit Roosevelt*, pp. 237, 265.

10. TR to Kermit Roosevelt, 4 Dec. 1902, *Letters*, 3:389.

11. Mark Sullivan, *Our Times*, vol. 2: *America Finding Herself* (New York: Scribner's, 1927), p. 445 n. 2.

12. *Addresses*, pp. 347, 348–49, 350.

13. Ibid., pp. 351, 357.

14. Ibid., p. 351.

15. Philander C. Knox to George Frisbie Hoar, 3 Jan. 1903, in *Reply of the Attorney General Dated January 3, 1903 to a Communication Dated December 20, 1902, from the Hon. George F. Hoar, Chairman of the Committee on the Judiciary, United States Senate*, Senate Document 73, 57th Cong., 2d sess. (Washington, D.C.: Government Printing Office, 1903), p. 20.

16. TR to Lawrence Fraser Abbott, 3 Feb. 1903, *Letters*, 3:417.

17. TR to George W. Perkins, 26 Dec. 1902, ibid., p. 399.

18. William C. Beer to George W. Perkins, 11 Jan. 1903, George W. Perkins Papers, Special Collections, Nicholas Murray Butler Library, Columbia University, New York City.

19. Hans B. Thorelli, *The Federal Antitrust Policy: Origination of an American Tradition* (Baltimore, Md.: Johns Hopkins Press, 1955), pp. 552, 553; TR to Lawrence Fraser Abbott, 3 Feb. 1903, *Letters*, 3:417.

20. TR to Abbott, 3 Feb. 1903, *Letters*, 3:416, 417.

21. *New York Times*, 8 Feb. 1903; "How Congress Has Treated the Trusts," *Literary Digest* 26 (21 Feb. 1903): 255.

22. *New York Times*, 10 Feb. 1903.

23. Thorelli, *Federal Antitrust Policy*, p. 548; TR to Joseph B. Bishop, 17 Feb. 1903, *Letters*, 3:429; "How Congress Has Treated the Trusts," p. 255.

24. "James R. Garfield as Trust Investigator," *Literary Digest* 26 (28 Feb. 1903): 295; Seale, *President's House*, 2:687–89.

25. Diary entry of 13 Feb. 1903, James R. Garfield Papers, box 6, MD, LC.

26. Henry Cabot Lodge to Henry L. Higginson, 23 Mar. 1903, Henry L. Higginson Papers, Baker Library, Graduate School of Business Administration, Harvard University, Cambridge, Mass.; TR to Nelson Aldrich, 25 Feb. 1903, *Letters*, 3:433–34.

27. TR to David B. Henderson, 4 Mar. 1903, *Letters*, 3:438.

28. *Addresses*, pp. 121, 144.

29. Addison C. Thomas, *Roosevelt among the People* (Chicago, Ill.: L. W. Walter Co., 1910), pp. 150, 283.

30. Paul Russell Cutright, *Theodore Roosevelt: The Making of a Conservationist* (Urbana: University of Illinois Press, 1985), p. 223.

31. *Autobiography*, p. 402.

32. "Government Scandals as an Issue," *Literary Digest* 27 (12 Sept. 1903): 309.

33. TR to J. H. Woodward, 10 Mar. 1903, *Letters*, 3:444.

34. Dorothy Ganfield Fowler, *The Cabinet Politician: The Postmaster General, 1829–1909* (New York: Columbia University Press, 1943), p. 274; TR to Payne, 23 May 1903, *Letters*, 3:479.

35. TR to Payne, 6 Aug. 1903, *Letters*, 3:543.

36. TR to Payne, 27 Feb. 1904, in William W. Wight, *Henry Clay Payne: A Life* (Milwaukee, Wis.: Burdick & Allen, 1907), p. 136; Fowler, *Cabinet Politician*, p. 276.

37. TR to Cortelyou, 26 Aug. 1903, *Letters*, 3:576–77; "Presidential Trains and Yachts," *Literary Digest* 27 (12 Sept. 1903): 314.

38. Michael Herbert to Lord Lansdowne, 8 May 1903, FO 800/144, Lansdowne Papers, Public Record Office, London; TR to William Howard Taft, 9 June 1903, *Letters*, 3:486.

39. TR to Cortelyou, 13 and 14 July 1903, *Letters*, 3:516.

40. TR to Cortelyou, 13 July 1903, ibid., pp. 514, 515.

41. TR to James S. Clarkson, 16 July 1903, ibid., p. 519.

42. "U.S. and Union Constitutions," *Public Opinion* 35 (30 July 1903): 134 (citing *New York Tribune*); Willard B. Gatewood, Jr., *Theodore Roosevelt and the Art of Controversy: Episodes of the White House Years* (Baton Rouge: Louisiana State University Press, 1970), p. 153 (*Wall Street Journal*); TR to Albert Shaw, 1 Aug. 1903, *Letters*, 3:537.

43. TR to Ebenezer J. Hill, 21 July 1903, *Letters*, 3:522.

44. Richard Todd McCulley, "The Origins of the Federal Reserve Act of 1913: Banks and Politics during the Progressive Era, 1897–1913" (Ph.D. diss., University of Texas at Austin, 1980), pp. 172–73.

45. Ibid., p. 185; Orville H. Platt to John H. Flagg, 29 July 1903, Orville H. Platt Papers, Connecticut State Library, Hartford; TR to Cannon, 13 Aug. 1903, *Letters*, 3:565.

46. Platt to Albert J. Beveridge, 14 Sept. 1903, Platt Papers; TR to Joseph B. Bishop, 28 Aug. 1903, and TR to Lodge, 3 Sept. 1903, *Letters*, 3:578, 587.

47. TR to Winfield T. Durbin, 6 Aug. 1903, *Letters*, 3:540–43.

48. TR to Carl Schurz, 24 Dec. 1903, ibid., p. 679.

49. Gatewood, *Theodore Roosevelt and the Art of Controversy*, p. 84; TR to Silas McBee, 3 Feb. 1903, *Letters*, 3:419.

50. TR to James S. Clarkson, 29 Sept. 1902, *Letters*, 3:333.

51. Gatewood, *Theodore Roosevelt and the Art of Controversy*, p. 99.

52. Ibid., p. 102.

53. TR to James Adger Smyth, 26 Nov. 1902, *Letters*, 3:384; James E. Haney, "Theodore Roosevelt and Afro-Americans, 1901–1912" (Ph.D. diss., Kent State University, 1971), p. 86.

54. Joel Williamson, *The Crucible of Race: Black-White Relations in the American South since Emancipation* (New York: Oxford University Press, 1984), p. 352.

55. Pearl Kluger, "Progressive Presidents and Black Americans" (Ph.D. diss., Columbia University, 1974), p. 114.

56. TR to Lemuel Clarke Davis, 20 Aug. 1903, and TR to Lodge, 3 Sept. 1903, *Letters*, 3:567, 587.

57. "General Miles's Retirement," *Public Opinion* 35 (13 Aug. 1903): 202; *Addresses*, p. 364.

58. Stephen Skowronek, *Building a New American State: The Expansion of National Administrative Capacities, 1877–1920* (Cambridge, Eng.: Cambridge University Press, 1982), p. 221.

59. TR to Root, 24 Aug. 1903, *Letters*, 3:572.

60. *Addresses*, p. 30.

61. Judith Rene McDonough, "William Henry Moody" (Ph.D. diss., Auburn University, 1983), p. 82.

62. Elting E. Morison, *Admiral Sims and the Modern American Navy* (Boston, Mass.: Houghton Mifflin, 1942), p. 103; TR to William S. Cowles, 12 Dec. 1901, *Letters*, 3:207.

63. Albert Shaw to TR, 4 Nov. 1903, TRP.

64. Shelby M. Cullom, *Fifty Years of Public Service: Personal Recollections* (Chicago: A. C. McClurg, 1911), p. 375.

65. "President Roosevelt's Position," *Public Opinion* 35 (17 Dec. 1903): 776.

CHAPTER 6
"HOW THEY ARE VOTING FOR ME!"

1. Alexander Dana Noyes, *The Market Place: Reminiscences of a Financial Editor* (Boston, Mass.: Little, Brown, 1938), p. 214.

2. William Allen White to Cyrus Leland, 15 Aug. 1901, William Allen White Papers, MD, LC.

3. Henry Adams to Elizabeth Cameron, 26 Jan. 1902, in *Letters of Henry Adams (1892–1918)*, 2 vols., ed. Worthington Chauncey Ford (Boston, Mass.: Houghton Mifflin, 1938), 2:370.

4. Herschel V. Jones to TR, 24 Mar. 1902, TRP; Adams to Cameron, 2 Mar. 1902, *Letters of Henry Adams*, pp. 375–76.

5. John Morton Blum, *The Republican Roosevelt* (Cambridge, Mass.: Harvard University Press, 1954), p. 38.

6. Thomas M. Anderson, "Theodore Roosevelt and Colorado Politics, 1901–1904: A Roosevelt-Hanna Rivalry?" (Master's report; University of Texas at Austin, 1973).

7. Albert J. Beveridge to L. H. Lasater, 31 May 1902, Albert J. Beveridge Papers, MD, LC.

8. Marcus A. Hanna to N. B. Scott, 20 Aug. 1902, Hanna-McCormick Family Papers, MD, LC.

9. Hanna to TR, 8 Apr. 1902, enclosing Charles Emory Smith, "The Week at Washington," TRP; Louis T. Michener to James S. Clarkson, 12 Mar. 1903, James S. Clarkson Papers, MD, LC.

10. Everett Walters, *Joseph Benson Foraker: An Uncompromising Republican* (Columbus: Ohio History Press, 1948), p. 202; Joseph B. Foraker, *Notes of a Busy Life*, 2 vols. (Cincinnati, Ohio: n.p., 1916), 2:110.

11. Herbert D. Croly, *Marcus Alonzo Hanna: His Life and Work* (New York: Macmillan, 1912), p. 425; *New York Tribune*, 26 May 1903.

12. Walters, *Joseph Benson Foraker*, p. 203; Orville H. Platt to Albert J. Beveridge, 30 May 1903, Orville H. Platt Papers, Connecticut State Library, Hartford.

13. TR to Henry Cabot Lodge, 27 May 1903, *Letters*, 3:482.

14. N. B. Scott to Hanna, 23 Dec. 1903, Hanna-McCormick Family Papers, ed. Bascom N. Timmons, *A Journal of the McKinley Years by Charles G. Dawes*, (Chicago: R. R. Donnelley, 1950), p. 362.

15. William Loeb to James R. Sheffield, 11 Jan. 1904, James R. Sheffield Papers, Sterling Memorial Library, Yale University, New Haven, Conn.; Sheffield to TR, 30 Jan. 1904, TRP.

16. TR to Elihu Root, 16 Feb. 1904, and TR to Theodore Roosevelt, Jr., 19 Feb. 1904, *Letters*, 4:730, 732.

17. TR to Joseph B. Bishop, 27 Apr. 1903, ibid., 3:471.

18. TR to Jacob Riis, 10 May 1904, ibid., 4:795.

19. Oliver Wendell Holmes, Jr., to Frederick Pollock, 9 Feb. 1921, in *Holmes-Pollock Letters: The Correspondence of Mr. Justice Holmes and Sir Frederick Pollock, 1874–1932*, 2 vols., ed. Mark DeWolfe Howe (Cambridge, Mass.: Harvard University Press, 1941), 2:63–64.

20. TR to Root, 7 June 1904, *Letters*, 4:822–23.

21. TR to Orville H. Platt, 25 May 1904, ibid., p. 804.

22. Frank H. Platt to Charles W. Fairbanks, 23 June 1904, Charles W. Fairbanks Papers, Lilly Library, Indiana University, Bloomington; TR to Theodore Roosevelt, Jr., 14 May 1904, *Letters*, 4:798–99.

23. TR to Henry Cabot Lodge, 13 June 1904, *Letters*, 4:833.

24. Entry for 23 June 1904, James R. Garfield's diaries, MD, LC.

25. M. W. Blumenberg, comp., *Official Proceedings of the Thirteenth Republican National Convention Held in the City of Chicago, June 21, 22, 23, 1904* (Minneapolis, Minn.: Harrison & Smith, 1904), p. 137; Peter Larsen, "Theodore Roosevelt and the Moroccan Crisis, 1904–1906" (Ph.D. diss., Princeton University, 1984), p. 25.

26. William James Hourihan, "Roosevelt and the Sultans: The United States Navy in the Mediterranean, 1904" (Ph.D. diss., University of Massachusetts, 1975), p. 108.

27. William Roscoe Thayer, *The Life and Letters of John Hay*, 2 vols. (Boston, Mass.: Houghton Mifflin, 1915), 2:383; Hourihan, "Roosevelt and the Sultans," p. 205.

28. Fred C. Shoemaker, "Alton B. Parker: The Image of a Gilded Age Statesman in an Era of Progressive Politics" (Master's thesis, Ohio State University, 1983), p. 41.

29. Ibid., p. 48.

30. Milton W. Blumenberg, comp., *Official Report of the Proceedings of the Democratic National Convention Held in St. Louis, Mo., July 6, 7, 8, and 9, 1904* (New York: Publisher's Printing Co., 1904), p. 277.

31. Ibid., p. 279; TR to John Hay, 11 July 1904, *Letters*, 4:852.

32. Henry A. Fisk to Elmer Adams, 29 July 1904, Elmer Adams Papers, Archives/Manuscript Division, Minnesota Historical Society, St. Paul.

33. TR to Lodge, 14 July 1904, *Letters*, 4:858.

34. TR to Cannon, 12 September 1904, ibid., pp. 921, 936, 942.

35. Mortimer Durand to Lord Lansdowne, 11 Aug. 1904, FO 5/2550, Public Record Office, London.

36. Jonathan P. Dolliver to S. W. Rathbun, 6 Sept. 1904, Jonathan P. Dolliver Papers, State Historical Society of Iowa, Iowa City.

37. "Democratic Objections to Democratic Possibilities," *Literary Digest* 28 (19 Mar. 1904): 398.

38. Louis A. Coolidge to George D. Perkins, 8 Sept. 1904, George D. Perkins Papers, Iowa State Department of History and Archives, Des Moines.

39. Republican Canvass Book for 1904, Newcomb, N.Y., author's collection.

40. *New York Daily Tribune*, 30 Sept. 1904; *Leslie's Weekly*, 17 Nov. 1904, clipping in TRP.

41. TR to Edward H. Butler, 8 Sept. 1904, TR to Lodge, 20 Sept. 1904, and TR to Edward H. Harriman, 10 Oct. 1904, *Letters*, 4:919, 948, 979.

42. John Hay to Joseph Hodges Choate, 23 Sept. 1904, Joseph Hodges Choate Papers, MD, LC; Henry L. West, "American Politics," *Forum* 36 (Oct. 1904): 165; William Boyd Allison to George D. Perkins, 2 Nov. 1904, Perkins Papers.

43. *Washington Post*, 24 Oct. 1904.

44. Oswald Garrison Villard, *Fighting Years: Memoirs of a Liberal Editor* (New York: Harcourt, Brace, 1939), p. 181.

45. TR to Harriman, 10 Oct. 1904, and TR to Cortelyou, 26 Oct. 1904, *Letters*, 4:979, 995–96.

46. TR to Cortelyou, 26 and 29 Oct. 1904, ibid., pp. 996, 1004–5.

47. TR to Cortelyou, 2 Nov. 1904, and TR to Root, 5 Nov. 1904, ibid., pp. 1009, 1014; *Washington Post*, 1 and 5 Nov. 1904.

48. Shoemaker, "Alton B. Parker," p. 84.

49. TR to Kermit Roosevelt, 8 Nov. 1904, *Letters*, 4:1018.

50. *New York Tribune*, 9 Nov. 1904.

51. TR to Anna Lodge, 10 Nov. 1904, *Letters*, 4:1025.

52. "What The Election Showed," *World's Work* 9 (Dec. 1904): 5561.

53. Orville H. Platt to Nelson W. Aldrich, 12 Nov. 1904, Platt Papers; TR to Philander Knox, 10 Nov. 1904, *Letters*, 4:1023.

54. TR to Knox, 10 Nov. 1904, *Letters*, 4:1023; John Coit Spooner to John Hicks, 11 Nov. 1904, John Coit Spooner Papers, MD, LC.

55. "Mr. Roosevelt's Safeness," *World's Work* 8 (June 1904): 4832.

CHAPTER 7
ROOSEVELT AND REGULATION, 1905–1906

1. Elihu Root to TR, 16 Nov. 1904, TRP; R. L. McCabe to Charles W. Fairbanks, 2 Nov. 1904, Charles W. Fairbanks Papers, Lilly Library, Indiana University, Bloomington.

2. TR to Joseph Wharton, 22 Nov. 1904, *Letters*, 4:1039; *New York Press*, 20 Nov. 1904.

3. TR to Joseph G. Cannon, 30 Nov. 1904, *Letters*, 4:1052–53.

4. *American Economist*, 27 Jan. 1905, p. 41.

5. Roosevelt to Lyman Abbott, 11 Jan. 1905, *Letters*, 4:1100.

6. Orville H. Platt to Albert J. Beveridge, 14 Nov. 1904, Orville H. Platt Papers, Connecticut State Library, Hartford; *New York Herald*, 7 Jan. 1905.

7. Shelby M. Cullom, *Fifty Years of Public Service: Personal Recollections* (Chicago: A. C. McClurg, 1911), p. 399.

8. TR to Ernest H. Abbott, 6 Feb. 1905, TR to Shelby M. Cullom, 10 Feb. 1905, TR to Silas McBee, 16 Feb. 1905, and TR to Joseph B. Bishop, 23 Mar. 1905, *Letters*, 4:1117, 1118, 1122, 1143; Jacob H. Gallinger to James O. Lyford, 12 Feb. 1905, James O. Lyford Papers, New Hampshire Historical Society, Concord.

9. *State Papers*, p. 226.

10. Charles A. Prouty to TR, 24 Oct. 1904, TRP; TR to E. H. Harriman, 30 Nov. 1904, *Letters*, 4:1054.

11. *State Papers*, p. 226.

12. Walker D. Hines, "Unfair Railroad Regulation: The Case for the Companies," *Saturday Evening Post* 177 (1 Apr. 1905): 18.

13. Ray Stannard Baker, "The Railroad Rate: A Study in Commercial Autocracy," *McClure's Magazine* 26 (Nov. 1905): 59.

14. *New York Herald*, 22 Dec. 1904.

15. *New York Herald*, 1 Feb. 1905; Joseph B. Bishop, *Theodore Roosevelt and His Times Shown in His Own Letters*, 2 vols. (New York: Scribner's, 1920), 1:427.

16. Orville H. Platt to Charles Hopkins Clark, 13 Feb. 1905, Platt Papers.

17. *World's Work* 9 (Mar. 1905): 5885; TR to George Otto Trevelyan, 9 Mar. 1905, *Letters*, 4:1132, 1133, 1134.

18. Lincoln Steffens, *The Autobiography of Lincoln Steffens* (New York: Literary Guild, 1931), p. 510; Albert Henry George Grey to John St. Loe Strachey, 8 May 1906, John St. Loe Strachey Papers, House of Lords Record Office, London.

19. Edward Bok, *The Americanization of Edward Bok: An Autobiography* (New York: Scribner's, 1920), pp. 273–75.

20. William Loeb to George B. Cortelyou, 17 Oct. 1905, and Cortelyou memorandum, 18 Oct. 1905, box 62, George B. Cortelyou Papers, MD, LC.

21. Walter E. Clark to Erastus Brainerd, 26 Jan. 1906, Erastus Brainerd Papers, University of Washington Library, Seattle.

22. TR to George H. Lorimer, 12 May 1906, *Letters*, 5:265.

23. *World's Work* 9 (Apr. 1905): 5997; TR to John Hay, 2 Apr. 1905, *Letters*, 4:1156.

24. James Bryce to Edward Grey, 29 May 1907, FO 371/357, Public Record Office, London.

25. Albert B. Cummins to Albert J. Beveridge, 12 Nov. 1906, Albert B. Cummins Papers, Iowa State Department of History and Archives, Des Moines.

26. "Railroad Authorities on Rate Control," *Literary Digest* 30 (27 May 1905): 767–68; *Remarks of Lucius Tuttle on the Relation of the National Government to the Railways before the Commercial Clubs of Cincinnati, Boston, Chicago and St. Louis at*

Cincinnati, Friday Evening May 26, 1905 (n.p., 1905), pp. 6–7, pamphlet in author's collection.

27. Theodore Roosevelt, speech at Banquet of Iroquois Club, 10 May 1905, TRP.

28. William H. Moody to Stephen B. Elkins, 5 May 1905, in *Regulation of Railway Rates: Hearings before the Committee on Interstate Commerce, Senate of the United States, December 16, 1904, to May 23, 1905 on Bills to Amend the Interstate Commerce Act,* 59th Cong., 1st sess., Senate Document 243, 5 vols. (Washington, D.C.: Government Printing Office, 1905), 5:1666; "Railroad Authorities on Rate Control," p. 768.

29. Paul Morton to C. L. Wellington, 6 July 1904, copy in author's collection; TR to Henry Cabot Lodge, 24 May 1905, *Letters,* 4:1192. For the documents on the Morton case see *Departure from Published Rates by the Atchison, Topeka and Santa Fe Railway Company, etc.,* 59th Cong., 1st sess., Senate Document 140 (Washington, D.C.: Government Printing Office, 1905).

30. TR to Ray Stannard Baker, 13 Nov. 1905, 20 Nov. 1905 (first quotation), *Letters,* 5:76, 83; Henry Cabot Lodge to Winthrop Murray Crane, 27 Nov. 1905, Henry Cabot Lodge Papers, Massachusetts Historical Society, Boston.

31. *State Papers,* pp. 275, 277.

32. *New York World* is quoted in *Current Literature* 40 (Jan. 1906): 11.

33. Jonathan P. Dolliver to J. J. Ryan, 26 Jan. 1906, Jonathan P. Dolliver Papers, Iowa State Historical Society, Iowa City.

34. Dolliver to Shelby M. Cullom, 26 Feb. 1906, Dolliver Papers.

35. Dolliver to A. L. Ames, 6 Jan. 1906, Dolliver Papers; Henry Beach Needham, "Railroad Senators Unmask," *Collier's* 36 (24 Mar. 1906): 20.

36. Thomas Richard Ross, *Jonathan Prentiss Dolliver: A Study in Political Integrity and Independence* (Iowa City: State Historical Society of Iowa, 1958), p. 211.

37. TR to Kermit Roosevelt, 1 Apr. 1906, *Letters,* 5:204.

38. Entries for 31 Mar., 5, 9, and 11 Apr. 1906, William E. Chandler's diary, New Hampshire Historical Society, Concord.

39. TR to William Boyd Allison, 12 Apr. 1906, *Letters,* 5:211.

40. *American Problems,* p. 416.

41. Ibid., p. 421.

42. Henry Cabot Lodge to Lucius Tuttle, 5 June 1906, Lodge Papers; TR to W. F. Hill et al., 6 May 1906, *Letters,* 5:260.

43. Walter E. Clark to Erastus Brainerd, 8 May 1906, Brainerd Papers; Mark Sullivan, *Our Times,* vol. 3: *Pre-War America* (New York: Scribner's, 1930), pp. 260–61.

44. Clark to Brainerd, 15 May 1906, Brainerd Papers.

45. TR to Kermit Roosevelt, 13 June 1906, TRP; Albert J. Beveridge to Albert Shaw, 20 May 1906, Albert J. Beveridge Papers, MD, LC; John C. Spooner to Elisha W. Keyes, 4 June 1906, Elisha W. Keyes Papers, Wisconsin State Historical Society, Madison.

46. William Z. Ripley, *Railroads: Rates and Regulation* (New York: Longmans, Green, 1912), p. 505; Beveridge to Shaw, 20 May 1906, Beveridge Papers.

47. Gabriel Kolko, *Railroads and Regulation, 1877–1916* (Princeton, N.J.: Princeton University Press, 1965), saw the railroads as favoring regulation. Albro Martin, *Enterprise Denied: Origins of the Decline of American Railroads, 1897–1917* (New York: Columbia University Press, 1971), took the view that regulation crippled the rail companies.

48. *State Papers,* p. 326. James Harvey Young, *Pure Food: Securing the Federal Food and Drugs Act of 1906* (Princeton, N.J.: Princeton University Press, 1989), is excellent on the background and passage of the act.

49. Donna J. Wood, "The Strategic Use of Public Policy: Business Support for the 1906 Food and Drug Act," *Business History Review* 59 (Autumn 1985): 420.

50. Charles R. Williams to Charles W. Fairbanks, 7 June 1906, Delavan Smith Papers, Indiana Historical Society, Indianapolis; Oscar E. Anderson, Jr., *The Health of a Nation: Harvey W. Wiley and the Fight for Pure Food* (Chicago: University of Chicago Press, 1958), p. 188.

51. TR to James Wilson, 12 Mar. 1906, *Letters,* 5:176.

52. TR to the Senate and House of Representatives, 4 June 1906, *Conditions in Chicago Stock Yards,* 59th Cong., 1st sess., House Document 873 (Washington, D.C.: Government Printing Office, 1906); John Braeman, *Albert J. Beveridge: American Nationalist* (Chicago: University of Chicago Press, 1971), p. 103.

53. TR to James Wadsworth, 26 May 1906, *Letters,* 5:282.

54. TR to Wadsworth, 31 May 1906, ibid., p. 291; TR to the Senate and House of Representatives, 4 June 1906, *Conditions in Chicago Stock Yards;* Young, *Pure Food,* pp. 241–42.

55. TR to Wadsworth, 15 June 1906, *Letters,* 5:298; Young, *Pure Food,* pp. 246–47.

56. Braeman, *Albert J. Beveridge,* p. 107; TR to Beveridge, 16 June 1906, *Letters,* 5:300; Henry C. Adams to Ben C. Adams, 19 June 1906, Henry C. Adams Papers, State Historical Society of Wisconsin, Madison.

57. TR to Beveridge, 30 June 1906, *Letters,* 5:327.

58. TR to Lyman Abbott, 1 July 1906 (second quotation), and TR to Benjamin Ide Wheeler, 3 July 1906 (first quotation), ibid., pp. 328, 329; John Braeman et al., eds., *Change and Continuity in Twentieth Century America* (Columbus: Ohio State University Press, 1964), p. 75.

59. David Sarasohn, "The Democratic Surge: Forging a Progressive Majority" (Ph.D. diss., University of California, Los Angeles, 1976), p. 28.

CHAPTER 8
PRESIDENT OF A GREAT NATION

1. TR to George von Lengerke Meyer, 26 Dec. 1904, *Letters,* 4:1079; *State Papers,* p. 267.

2. *State Papers,* p. 256.

3. TR to Meyer, 7 July 1905, *Letters,* 4:1263; Elihu Root, "Roosevelt's Conduct of Foreign Affairs," in *American Problems,* p. xiii.

4. Richard Hume Werking, *The Master Architects: Building the United States*

Foreign Service, 1890–1913 (Lexington: University Press of Kentucky, 1977), pp. 125–42.

5. *State Papers*, p. 257.

6. TR to Root, 20 May and 7 June 1904, *Letters*, 4:801, 821–22.

7. TR to Joseph B. Bishop, 23 Feb. 1904, ibid., p. 734.

8. Dana G. Munro, *Intervention and Dollar Diplomacy in the Caribbean, 1900–1921* (Princeton, N.J.: Princeton University Press, 1964), pp. 90 (first quotation), 92 (second quotation); TR to Charles William Eliot, 4 April 1904, *Letters*, 4:770.

9. Dexter Perkins, *The Monroe Doctrine, 1867–1907* (Baltimore, Md.: Johns Hopkins Press, 1937), p. 429.

10. John Hay to Thomas C. Dawson, 30 Dec. 1904, and Dawson to Hay, 23 Jan. 1905, in *Papers Relating to the Foreign Relations of the United States, 1905* (Washington, D.C.: Government Printing Office, 1906), pp. 298, 312.

11. For Roosevelt's message see ibid., pp. 341, 342.

12. William Stull Holt, *Treaties Defeated by the Senate: A Study of the Struggle between President and Senate over the Conduct of Foreign Relations* (Baltimore, Md.: Johns Hopkins Press, 1933), p. 216.

13. Ibid., p. 220, for both quotations.

14. TR to Joseph B. Bishop, 23 Mar. 1905, and TR to Hay, 30 Mar. 1905, *Letters*, 4:1145, 1150; Dawson to Hay, 25 Mar. 1905, *Papers Relating to Foreign Relations, 1905*, p. 359.

15. TR to Charles J. Bonaparte, 4 Sept. 1905, *Letters*, 5:10.

16. Holt, *Treaties Defeated*, p. 226.

17. TR to Edward Grey, 28 Feb. 1907, *Letters*, 5:602.

18. TR to George von Lengerke Meyer, 26 Dec. 1904, ibid., 4:1079.

19. TR to Theodore Roosevelt, Jr., 10 Feb. 1904, TR to Hay, 26 July 1904, and TR to Meyer, 26 Dec. 1904, ibid., pp. 724, 865, 1079.

20. John Hay to Mr. ——, 20 Feb. 1904, in U.S., House of Representatives, *Papers Relating to the Foreign Relations of the United States, 1904*, 58th Cong., 3d sess., Document 1 (Washington, D.C.: Government Printing Office, 1905), p. 2; TR to Cecil Spring Rice, 19 Mar. 1904, *Letters*, 4:760.

21. TR to Spring Rice, 13 June 1904, *Letters*, 4:830.

22. TR to Meyer, 26 Dec. 1904, ibid., p. 1079.

23. Raymond A. Esthus, *Double Eagle and Rising Sun: The Russians and Japanese at Portsmouth in 1905* (Durham, N.C.: Duke University Press, 1988), p. 21.

24. TR to Hay, 2 Apr. 1905, *Letters*, 4:1158.

25. Esthus, *Double Eagle and Rising Sun*, p. 32.

26. B. F. Barnes to William Loeb, 18 Apr. 1905, conveying the note from Japan, in Tyler Dennett, *Roosevelt and the Russo-Japanese War* (Garden City, N.Y.: Doubleday, Page, 1925), p. 177; TR to Spring Rice, 13 May 1905, *Letters*, 4:1179.

27. TR to Kentaro Kaneko, 31 May 1905, *Letters*, 4:1198; Count Komura to Minister Takahira, 31 May 1905, in Dennett, *Roosevelt*, p. 215.

28. TR to Meyer, 5 June 1905, in TR to Lodge, 5 June 1905, *Letters*, 4:1203, 1204.

29. TR to Meyer, 5 June 1905, ibid., p. 1204.

30. TR to Meyer, 8 June 1905, and TR to Hay, 12 June 1905, ibid., pp. 1216, 1224.

31. *London Morning Post*, 12 June 1905, is quoted by Eugene P. Trani, in *The Treaty of Portsmouth: An Adventure in American Diplomacy* (Lexington: University of Kentucky Press, 1969), p. 61; TR to Kermit Roosevelt, 11 June 1905, *Letters*, 4:1210.

32. TR to Whitelaw Reid, 30 June 1905, *Letters*, 4:1258.

33. TR to Victor Metcalf, 16 June 1905, ibid., p. 1235.

34. TR to William W. Rockhill, 22 Aug. 1905, and TR to George C. Perkins, 31 Aug. 1905, ibid., pp. 1310, 1327.

35. TR to John Hay, 28 Jan. 1905, ibid., p. 1112; John Edward Wilz, "Did the United States Betray Korea in 1905?" *Pacific Historical Review* 54 (Aug. 1985): 244.

36. John Gilbert Reid, "Taft's Telegram to Root, July 29, 1905," *Pacific Historical Review* 9 (Mar. 1940): 66–70.

37. TR to William Howard Taft, 31 July 1905, *Letters*, 4:1293.

38. Esthus, *Double Eagle and Rising Sun*, p. 77; Joseph B. Bishop, *Theodore Roosevelt and His Times*, 2 vols. (New York: Scribner's, 1920), 1:405.

39. TR to Whitelaw Reid, 3 Aug. 1905, *Letters*, 4:1298.

40. TR to Herbert H. D. Pierce, 29 Aug. 1905, and TR to John C. O'Laughlin, 31 Aug. 1905, ibid., p. 1326, 1328.

41. *Outlook* 81 (9 Sept. 1905): 58.

42. TR to Francis Vinton Greene, 5 Sept. 1905, *Letters*, 5:12.

43. TR to Charles Joseph Bonaparte, 15 Nov. 1905, and TR to T. C. Friedlander, 23 Nov. 1905, ibid., pp. 77, 90.

44. TR to William Howard Taft, 11 Jan. 1906, ibid., p. 133.

45. TR to Whitelaw Reid, 28 Apr. 1906, ibid., p. 230. Roosevelt's long letter to Reid provides a thorough review of U.S. participation in the Algeciras episode.

46. TR to Taft, 20 Apr. 1905, ibid., 4:1162.

47. TR to Reid, 28 Apr. 1906, ibid., 5:234, 236. The German memorandum of 11 June 1905 is included in Roosevelt's letter.

48. Ibid., p. 236.

49. Peter Larsen, "Theodore Roosevelt and the Moroccan Crisis, 1904–1906" (Ph.D. diss., Princeton University, 1984), p. 131; Speck von Sternburg to TR, 28 June 1905, *Letters*, 5:241; TR to Lodge, 11 July 1905, ibid., 4:1273. How Sternburg handled messages from the kaiser is discussed by Stefan H. Rinke, in "Between Success and Failure: The Diplomatic Career of Ambassador Hermann Speck von Sternburg and German-American Relations, 1903–1908" (Master's thesis, Bowling Green State University, 1989), pp. 134–36, 156–57.

50. TR to Joseph Hodges Choate, 16 Aug. 1905, *Letters*, 4:1302; Raymond A. Esthus, *Theodore Roosevelt and the International Rivalries* (Waltham, Mass.: Ginn-Blaisell, 1970), p. 85.

51. Larsen, "Theodore Roosevelt," p. 256.

52. Luella J. Hall, *The United States and Morocco, 1776–1956* (Metuchen, N.J.: Scarecrow Press, 1971), p. 565.

53. TR to Reid, 28 Apr. and 27 June 1906, *Letters*, 5:250, 319.

54. TR to Shelby M. Cullom, 26 June 1906, ibid., p. 317.

55. *State Papers*, p. 398; Ronald Francis Reter, "The Real versus the Rhetorical: Theodore Roosevelt in Foreign Policy-Making" (Ph.D. diss., University of Georgia, 1973), p. 131.

56. TR to Charles William Eliot, 22 Sept. 1906, *Letters*, 5:421.

CHAPTER 9
ROOSEVELT THE ADMINISTRATOR, 1905–1909

1. *Autobiography*, p. 346.

2. Ibid., pp. 347, 348.

3. Charles E. Perkins to Henry L. Higginson, 17 June 1907, Henry L. Higginson Papers, Baker Library, Harvard Business School, Boston, Mass.

4. William Dudley Foulke, *Fighting the Spoilsmen: Reminiscences of the Civil Service Reform Movement* (New York: Putnam's, 1919), p. 257.

5. *Autobiography*, p. 397; James L. Penick, Jr., *Progressive Politics and Conservation: The Ballinger-Pinchot Affair* (Chicago: University of Chicago Press, 1968), p. 190.

6. *State Papers*, pp. 237, 238; Gifford Pinchot, *Breaking New Ground* (New York: Harcourt, Brace, 1947), p. 259.

7. *Autobiography*, p. 385; Stephen R. Fox, *John Muir and His Legacy: The American Conservation Movement* (Boston, Mass.: Little, Brown, 1981), p. 130.

8. Pinchot, *Breaking New Ground*, p. 257.

9. Ibid., p. 305, quoting Roosevelt's *Autobiography*; Stephen E. Ponder, "Executive Publicity and Congressional Resistance, 1905–1913: Congress and the Roosevelt Administration's PR Men," *Congress and the Presidency* 13 (Autumn 1986): 177–86.

10. James D. Richardson, comp., *A Compilation of the Messages and Papers of the Presidents*, 10 vols. (Washington, D.C.: Bureau of National Literature, 1911), 10:7315, creating a forest reservation in the state of Montana; hereafter cited as *Messages and Papers*.

11. *State Papers*, p. 315.

12. Pinchot, *Breaking New Ground*, pp. 271–72.

13. TR to Ethan Allen Hitchcock, 29 June 1906, *Letters*, 5:324; Richardson, *Messages and Papers*, 10:7682.

14. TR to Hitchcock, 4 Dec. 1906, and TR to Philip B. Stewart, 22 Dec. 1906, *Letters*, 5:519 (first quotation), 534 (second quotation).

15. *State Papers*, p. 376; *Congressional Record*, 59th Cong., 2d sess. (18 Feb. 1907), p. 3188 (Senator Fulton).

16. Francis E. Warren to W. E. Chaplin, 21 Feb. 1907, Francis E. Warren Papers, Western History Research Center, University of Wyoming, Laramie; G. Michael McCarthy, *Hour of Trial: The Conservation Conflict in Colorado and the West, 1891–1907* (Norman: University of Oklahoma Press, 1977), p. 206.

17. Memorandum, 2 Mar. 1907, *Letters*, 5:604.

18. TR to Theodore E. Burton, 14 March 1907, ibid., pp. 619, 620.

19. Samuel P. Hays, *Conservation and the Gospel of Efficiency: The Progressive Conservation Movement, 1890–1920* (Cambridge, Mass.: Harvard University Press, 1959), p. 117.

20. TR to James Wilson, 7 June 1907, *Letters*, 5:682.

21. *American Problems*, p. 126; Pinchot, *Breaking New Ground*, p. 347.

22. *State Papers*, p. 129.

23. Frederick E. Hoxie, *A Final Promise: The Campaign to Assimilate the Indians, 1890–1920* (Lincoln: University of Nebraska Press, 1984), p. 106; *State Papers*, p. 526.

24. Hoxie, *Final Promise*, p. 165; Sean J. Flynn, "Western Assimilationist: Charles H. Burke and the Burke Act," *Midwest Review* 11 (Spring 1989): 1–15; Donald L. Parman, "Francis Ellington Leupp, 1905–1909," in *The Commissioners of Indian Affairs, 1824–1977*, ed. Robert M. Kvasnicka and Herman J. Viola (Lincoln: University of Nebraska Press, 1979), pp. 221–32.

25. TR to the Isthmian Canal Commission, 8 Mar. 1904, *Letters*, 4:745–46.

26. Alfred D. Chandler, Jr., "Theodore Roosevelt and the Panama Canal: A Study in Administration," in *Letters*, 6:1548.

27. Miles P. Du Val, Jr., *And the Mountains Will Move: The Story of the Building of the Panama Canal* (Stanford, Calif.: Stanford University Press, 1947), p. 211.

28. TR to Taft, 27 Aug. 1906, *Letters*, 5:385.

29. TR to Kermit Roosevelt, 20 Nov. 1906, ibid., p. 497.

30. Joseph B. Bishop, *The Panama Gateway* (New York: Scribner's, 1913), p. 176.

31. TR to Shonts, 26 Feb. 1907, and TR to Edward Grey, 28 Feb. 1907, *Letters*, 5:599, 602.

32. *Autobiography*, p. 517.

33. Ibid., pp. 414, 422.

34. *State Papers*, p. 224.

35. Ida M. Tarbell, *The Life of Elbert H. Gary: The Story of Steel* (New York: D. Appleton, 1925), p. 184.

36. Gabriel Kolko, *The Triumph of Conservatism: A Reinterpretation of American History, 1900–1916* (New York: Free Press, 1963), p. 80.

37. TR to James R. Garfield, 9 Mar. 1905, James R. Garfield Papers, MD, LC.

38. Thomas Roger Wessel, "Republican Justice: The Department of Justice under Roosevelt and Taft, 1901–1913" (Ph.D. diss., University of Maryland, 1972), p. 172.

39. *Report of the Commissioner of Corporations on the Transportation of Petroleum, May 2, 1906*, House Document 812, 59th Cong., 1st sess. (Washington, D.C.: Government Printing Office, 1906), pp. xx, xxi.

40. Kolko, *Triumph of Conservatism*, p. 121 (Smith quotation); TR to Charles J. Bonaparte, 22 Aug. 1907, *Letters*, 5:763.

41. Harvey W. Wiley, *The History of a Crime against the Food Law* (Washington, D.C.: Harvey W. Wiley, 1929), pp. 162, 163.

42. Oscar E. Anderson, Jr., *The Health of a Nation: Harvey W. Wiley and the Fight for Pure Food* (Chicago: University of Chicago Press, 1958), p. 214.

43. Ibid., p. 217.

44. *State Papers*, pp. 129, 215; *Autobiography*, p. 356.

45. TR to Charles Hallam Keep, 2 June 1905, *Letters*, 4:1201, 1202.

46. Oscar Kraines, "The President versus Congress: The Keep Commission, 1905–1909; First Comprehensive Presidential Inquiry into Administration," *Western Political Quarterly* 23 (Mar. 1970): 35; *State Papers*, p. 293.

47. Kraines, "President versus Congress," p. 39.

48. *Autobiography*, p. 345.

CHAPTER 10
KEEPING THE LEFT CENTER TOGETHER

1. Esme Howard to Edward Grey, 6 Apr. 1907, Edward Grey Papers, FO 800/81, Public Record Office, London, for both quotations.

2. Charles B. Landis to Joseph B. Foraker, 31 July 1907, Joseph B. Foraker Papers, Cincinnati Historical Society, Cincinnati, Ohio.

3. TR to Anna Lodge, 20 Sept. 1907, *Letters*, 5:799.

4. *The Letters of Archie Butt, Personal Aide to President Roosevelt*, ed. Lawrence F. Abbott (Garden City, N.Y.: Doubleday, Page, 1924), p. 380.

5. Ibid., p. 232.

6. *State Papers*, p. 461.

7. Helen Nebeker Tomlinson, "Charles Lang Freer: Pioneer Collector of American Art," 2 vols. (Ph.D. diss., Case Western Reserve University, 1979), 2:429.

8. TR to Melville W. Fuller, 19 Dec. 1905, *Letters*, 5:117, 118. For a thorough discussion of the Freer gift see Richard H. Collin, *Theodore Roosevelt, Culture, Diplomacy, and Expansion: A New View of American Imperialism* (Baton Rouge: Louisiana State University Press, 1985), pp. 66–91.

9. TR to Leslie M. Shaw, 27 Dec. 1904, *Letters*, 4:1088. The best treatment of this episode is by Willard B. Gatewood, Jr., in *Theodore Roosevelt and the Art of Controversy: Episodes of the White House Years* (Baton Rouge: Louisiana State University Press, 1970), pp. 213–35.

10. Gatewood, *Theodore Roosevelt*, pp. 224, 232.

11. Ida Tarbell, *All in the Day's Work: An Autobiography* (New York: Macmillan, 1939), p. 211.

12. Again, Gatewood, *Theodore Roosevelt*, pp. 175–212, gives an excellent examination of this unhappy episode.

13. TR to Bellamy Storer, 11 Dec. 1905, enclosing TR to Maria Storer, 11 Dec. 1905, *Letters*, 5:107–11.

14. Gatewood, *Theodore Roosevelt*, p. 210.

15. The controversies over simplified spelling and "nature fakirs" are handled with skill and humor by Mark Sullivan, in *Our Times*, vol. 3: *Pre-War America* (New York: Scribner's, 1930), pp. 146–62 (nature fakirs), 155 (quotation), 162–90

(simplified spelling); TR to George Gray, 6 Oct. 1905, *Letters*, 5:46 (football quotation).

16. Richard Cleveland Baker, *The Tariff under Roosevelt and Taft* (Hastings, Nebr.: Democrat Printing Co., 1941), p. 55; Henry Wallace to William Boyd Allison, 18 Feb. 1905, box 355, William Boyd Allison Papers, Iowa State Department of History and Archives, Des Moines.

17. Baker, *The Tariff under Roosevelt and Taft*, p. 56.

18. TR to Leslie M. Shaw, 4 Aug. 1905, *Letters*, 4:1301; and TR to Curtis Guild, Jr., 12 Nov. 1905, ibid., 5:75.

19. TR to Richard Watson Gilder, 26 June 1906, ibid., 5:317.

20. Joseph B. Foraker to A. Maurice Low, 30 May 1906, Foraker Papers.

21. William Jennings Bryan, "Has the President the Courage to Be a Reformer?" *Public Opinion* 38 (15 Apr. 1905): 559; "Mr. Bryan, Mr. Hearst, and the White House," *Literary Digest* 33 (21 July 1906): 69.

22. "Organized Labor in Politics," *Independent* 61 (26 July 1906): 175–76.

23. TR to Lodge, 6 and 9 Aug. 1906, *Letters*, 5:347, 350.

24. TR to Lodge, 15 Aug. 1906, and TR to Root, 18 Aug. 1906, ibid., pp. 361, 367.

25. TR to James E. Watson, 18 Aug. 1906, ibid., pp. 372, 373, 375, 376, 377–78.

26. Albert J. Beveridge to TR, 21 Aug. 1906 (second quotation), TRP; James E. Watson to John F. Lacey, 20 Aug. 1906 (first quotation), and N. E. Kendall to Lacey, 14 Sept. 1906 (third quotation), John F. Lacey Papers, Iowa State Department of History and Archives, Des Moines.

27. TR to Lodge, 4 Sept. 1906, *Letters*, 5:397.

28. *New York Tribune*, 6 Sept. 1906 (Taft quotation); *Des Moines Register Leader*, 4 Oct. 1906 (Beveridge); Cannon to Roosevelt, 17 Aug. 1906, TRP.

29. TR to Calvin Cobb, 16 June 1906 (first quotation), and TR to Gifford Pinchot, 15 Sept. 1906 (second quotation), *Letters*, 5:302, 413. For the later development of the Haywood case and Roosevelt's attitude toward labor agitators see Syed M. Habibuddin, *Civil Liberties and Democracy: Attitude of a President* (Calcutta, India: Scientific Book Agency, 1977), p. 167.

30. *American Problems*, pp. 71, 73; *Des Moines Register Leader*, 10 Oct. 1906; *Washington Star*, 18 Oct. 1906; James A. Tawney to John Coit Spooner, 25 Sept. 1906, John Coit Spooner Papers, MD, LC.

31. *Des Moines Register Leader*, 29 July 1906.

32. TR to Alice Roosevelt Longworth, 7 Nov. 1906, *Letters*, 5:488–89.

33. Albert J. Beveridge to William Loeb, 9 Nov. 1906, Albert J. Beveridge Papers, MD, LC; TR to Charles Evans Hughes, 7 Nov. 1906, and TR to Taft, 8 Nov. 1906, *Letters*, 5:491.

34. Ann J. Lane, *The Brownsville Affair: National Crisis and Black Reaction* (Port Washington, N.Y.: Kennikat Press, 1971), p. 20.

35. *American Problems*, pp. 345, 346.

36. James E. Haney, "Theodore Roosevelt and Afro-Americans, 1901–1912" (Ph.D. diss., Kent State University, 1971), p. 149.

37. *American Problems*, pp. 352, 353–54.

38. TR to Owen Wister, 27 Apr. 1906, *Letters*, 5:226, 227.

39. Lane, *Brownsville Affair*, p. 22.

40. Pearl Kluger, "Progressive Presidents and Black Americans" (Ph.D. diss., Columbia University, 1974), pp. 175–76; TR to William Howard Taft, 21 Nov. 1906, *Letters*, 5:498.

41. TR to Taft, undated, but 28 Nov. 1906, *Letters*, 5:517.

42. TR to Taft, 5 Dec. 1906, ibid., p. 521.

43. James D. Richardson, comp., *A Compilation of the Messages and Papers of the Presidents*, 10 vols. (Washington, D.C.: Bureau of National Literature, 1911), 10:7709, 7710, 7711, 7712, 7714, 7716, hereafter cited as *Messages and Papers*.

44. Joseph Benson Foraker, *Notes of a Busy Life*, 2 vols. (Cincinnati, Ohio: Stewart & Kidd, 1916), 2:240; Everett Walters, *Joseph Benson Foraker: An Uncompromising Republican* (Columbus: Ohio State Archaeological and Historical Society, 1948), p. 237; TR to Brooks Adams, 22 Dec. 1906, *Letters*, 5:534.

45. Richardson, *Messages and Papers*, pp. 7717, 7721.

46. TR to George F. Spinney, 22 Jan. 1907, *Letters*, 5:560.

47. Foraker, *Notes of a Busy Life*, 2:251, 255, reprints a letter from Foraker to his son of 29 Jan. 1907 and a *Washington Post* news story of the same date; John D. Weaver, *The Brownsville Raid* (New York: Norton, 1970), p. 139.

48. Foraker, *Notes of a Busy Life*, 2:256.

49. Weaver, *Brownsville Raid*, p. 143; Foraker, *Notes of a Busy Life*, 2:257.

50. Foraker, *Notes of a Busy Life*, 2:298.

51. TR to John Carter Rose, 21 Dec. 1906, *Letters*, 5:533.

52. "A Week of Presidential Messages," *Literary Digest* 33 (29 Dec. 1906): 964.

53. *State Papers*, pp. 342, 356, 358; "How the President's Message Is Received," *Literary Digest* 33 (15 Dec. 1906): 890.

54. *State Papers*, pp. 359, 360.

55. TR to Edward Grey, 28 Feb. 1907, *Letters*, 5:602.

56. "Wall Street and the President," *World's Work* 13 (Apr. 1907): 8708; TR to Jacob Schiff, 25 Mar. 1907, *Letters*, 5:631.

57. Morgans's statement is in *Washington Star*, 12 Mar. 1907, quoted in *Letters*, 5:617, n. 1.

58. TR to Henry L. Higginson, 28 Mar. 1907, *Letters*, 5:633; the Harriman letter was TR to James S. Sherman, 8 Oct. 1906, *Letters*, 5:447–52; Rita E. Loos, "President Theodore Roosevelt and Eastern Businessmen: A Divergence of Views" (Ph.D. diss., St. John's University, 1971), p. 124.

59. *American Problems*, pp. 80–81, 83, 84.

60. Ibid., p. 84; *State Papers*, p. 357.

61. TR to Charles J. Bonaparte, 4 Nov. 1907, *Letters*, 5:830–31.

62. *Investigation of United States Steel Corporation*, U.S., House of Representatives, House Report 1127, 62d Cong., 2d sess. (Washington, D.C.: Government Printing Office, 1912), p. 205, quoting Roosevelt's testimony.

63. TR to Hamlin Garland, 23 Nov. 1907, *Letters*, 5:855; *State Papers*, p. 426; James Bryce to Edward Grey, 28 Nov. 1907, FO 371/357, Public Record Office, London.

64. TR to Arthur Lee, 26 Dec. 1907, *Letters*, 6:875.

65. *State Papers*, p. 477.

CHAPTER 11
"WE WERE AT ABSOLUTE PEACE"

1. TR to William Howard Taft, 21 Aug. 1907, *Letters*, 5:761.

2. Root is quoted by Dana G. Munro in *Intervention and Dollar Diplomacy in the Caribbean, 1900–1921* (Princeton, N.J.: Princeton University Press, 1964), p. 116.

3. TR to George O. Trevelyan, 9 Sept. 1906, *Letters*, 5:401.

4. TR to Don Gonzalo de Quesada, 14 Sept. 1906, ibid., p. 412.

5. TR to William Howard Taft, 22 and 28 Sept. 1906, ibid., pp. 419, 434.

6. TR to Whitelaw Reid, 28 Apr. 1906, ibid., p. 242.

7. *State Papers*, pp. 296, 298, 300.

8. TR to Andrew Carnegie, 6 Aug. 1906, and TR to Whitelaw Reid, 7 Aug. 1906, *Letters*, 5:345, 348–49.

9. *British Documents on the Origins of the War, 1898–1914*, vol. 8: *Arbitration, Neutrality and Security*, ed. G. P. Gooch and Harold Temperley (London: His Majesty's Stationery Office, 1932), p. 195; TR to Eugene Hale, 27 Oct. 1906, and TR to Root, 2 July 1907, *Letters*, 5:475, 700.

10. TR to Arthur Lee, 20 Dec. 1908, *Letters*, 6:1432.

11. TR to Root, 8 Aug. 1908, ibid., p. 1164.

12. TR to Hermann von Hatzfeldt-Wildenburg, 24 Aug. 1908, and TR to William II, 26 Dec. 1908, ibid., pp. 1196, 1441.

13. Charles E. Neu, *An Uncertain Friendship: Theodore Roosevelt and Japan, 1906–1909* (Cambridge, Mass.: Harvard University Press, 1967), p. 31.

14. TR to Kaneko, 26 Oct. 1906, and TR to Eugene Hale, 27 Oct. 1906, *Letters*, 5:473–75.

15. TR to Victor H. Metcalf, 27 Nov. 1906, ibid., p. 510.

16. *State Papers*, pp. 386, 387; Neu, *An Uncertain Friendship*, p. 49.

17. TR to Joseph G. Cannon, 27 May 1906, *Letters*, 5:286.

18. Raymond A. Esthus, *Theodore Roosevelt and Japan* (Seattle: University of Washington Press, 1966), p. 161.

19. Thomas A. Bailey, *Theodore Roosevelt and the Japanese-American Crises* (Stanford, Calif: Stanford University Press, 1934), p. 165.

20. TR to Kentaro Kaneko, 23 May 1907, *Letters*, 5:671.

21. TR to Henry Cabot Lodge, 10 July 1907, ibid., p. 709.

22. *Autobiography*, p. 536.

23. TR to Taft, 21 Aug. 1907, *Letters*, 5:762.

24. Neu, *An Uncertain Friendship*, p. 152.

25. Esthus, *Theodore Roosevelt and Japan*, p. 216.

26. TR to Arthur Lee, 8 Apr. 1908, *Letters*, 5:995.

27. James R. Reckner, *Teddy Roosevelt's Great White Fleet* (Annapolis, Md.: Naval Institute Press, 1988), p. 23.

28. *State Papers*, p. 472.

29. TR to Albert L. Key, 10 Apr. 1908, *Letters*, 6:1001.

30. James D. Richardson, comp., *A Compilation of the Messages and Papers of the Presidents*, 10 vols. (Washington, D.C.: Bureau of National Literature, 1911),

pp. 7528, 7530; TR to Richmond P. Hobson, 16 Apr. 1908, *Letters*, 6:1008.

31. TR to Samuel H. Piles, 22 Apr. 1908, *Letters*, 6:1014.

32. Neu, *An Uncertain Friendship*, p. 250; TR to Henry White, 27 Apr. 1908, *Letters*, 6:1017 18.

33. Elting E. Morison, *Admiral Sims and the Modern American Navy* (Boston, Mass.: Houghton Mifflin, 1942), pp. 204, 205; TR to Truman H. Newberry, 28 Aug. 1908, *Letters*, 6:1199.

34. *State Papers*, p. 543; TR to Alfred Thayer Mahan, 27 Jan. 1909, *Letters*, 6:1487.

35. *The Letters of Archie Butt, Personal Aide to President Roosevelt*, ed. Lawrence F. Abbott (Garden City, N.Y.: Doubleday, Page, 1924), p. 354.

36. Esthus, *Theodore Roosevelt and Japan*, p. 282.

37. TR to James N. Gillett, 16 Jan. 1909, *Letters*, 6:1478; Neu, *An Uncertain Friendship*, p. 293.

38. TR to Kermit Roosevelt, 23 Jan. 1909, *Letters*, 6:1481.

39. TR to James N. Gillett, 4 Feb. 1909, and TR to Philip A. Stanton, 8 Feb. 1909, ibid., pp. 1502, 1510.

40. TR to Philander C. Knox, 8 Feb. 1909, TR to Gillett, 10 Feb. 1909, TR to Theodore Roosevelt, Jr., 13 Feb. 1909, and TR to William Howard Taft, 3 Mar. 1909, ibid., pp. 1513, 1517, 1520, 1543.

41. *Autobiography*, p. 544.

CHAPTER 12
"THERE IS NO ONE LIKE THEODORE"

1. TR to Frederic Harrison, 18 Dec. 1907, *Letters*, 6:866.

2. William Howard Taft to C. M. Heald, 25 Dec. 1907, William Howard Taft Papers, MD, LC; TR to George O. Trevelyan, 19 June 1908, *Letters*, 6:1085.

3. TR to William Allen White, 30 July 1907, *Letters*, 5:735.

4. TR to Benjamin Ide Wheeler, 3 July 1906, ibid., p. 329.

5. TR to White, 11 Aug. 1906, ibid., p. 354.

6. TR to Taft, 15 Mar. 1906, ibid., pp. 184, 185, 186.

7. Helen Taft to Taft, 27 Oct. 1906, Taft Papers; TR to Taft, 5 Nov. 1906, *Letters*, 5:486.

8. TR to George von Lengerke Meyer, 16 Mar. 1907, and TR to White, 30 July 1907, *Letters*, 5:625, 735; "Conference between Secretary Taft, Mr. Burton, and Mr. Vorys," 8 June 1907, Taft Papers.

9. Entry for 16 Nov. 1907 in James R. Garfield's diaries, MD, LC.

10. *State Papers*, p. 416; TR to Charles J. Bonaparte, 2 Jan. 1908, *Letters*, 6:889.

11. Mark Sullivan, *Our Times, 1900–1925*, vol. 4: *The War Begins, 1909–1914* (New York: Scribner's, 1936), p. 304.

12. TR to James E. Watson, 18 Aug. 1906, *Letters*, 5:376; "Special Message of the President of the United States," ibid., 6:1572.

13. "Special Message," ibid., 6:1577.

14. Ibid., pp. 1582, 1585, 1587, 1588, 1590.

15. Joseph B. Foraker to Edward L. Buchwalter, 5 Feb. 1908, Joseph B. Foraker Papers, Cincinnati Historical Society, Cincinnati, Ohio; John J. Esch to Earle Welch, 4 Feb. 1908, John J. Esch Papers, Wisconsin State Historical Society, Madison; TR to Kermit Roosevelt, 2 Feb. 1908, *Letters*, 6:922.

16. TR to Kermit Roosevelt, 2 Feb. 1908, *Letters*, 6:922.

17. George W. Perkins to J. P. Morgan, 16 Mar. 1908, George W. Perkins Papers, Columbia University Library, New York City; J. Hampton Moore, *Roosevelt and the Old Guard* (Philadelphia, Pa.: Macrae Smith, 1925), p. 219; TR to Albert Shaw, 22 May 1908, *Letters*, 6:1033.

18. Richard Todd McCulley, "The Origins of the Federal Reserve Act of 1913: Banks and Politics during the Progressive Era, 1897–1913" (Ph.D. diss., University of Texas at Austin, 1980), p. 249.

19. Perkins to J. P. Morgan, 7 May 1908, Perkins Papers.

20. TR to Kermit Roosevelt, 30 May 1908, and TR to Elmer H. Youngman, 2 June 1908, *Letters*, 6:1044, 1046.

21. "Special Message," ibid., p. 1577.

22. Martin J. Sklar, *The Corporate Reconstruction of American Capitalism, 1890–1916: The Market, the Law, and Politics* (Cambridge, Eng.: Cambridge University Press, 1988), pp. 204, 228.

23. TR to John Carter Rose, 30 Mar. 1908, *Letters*, 6:984, Roosevelt's emphasis.

24. TR to Seth Low, 28 Mar. 1908, ibid., pp. 983–84.

25. "The President's Program," *Literary Digest* 26 (4 Apr. 1908): 466; Arthur M. Johnson, "Antitrust Policy in Transition, 1908: Ideals and Reality," *Mississippi Valley Historical Review* 48 (Dec. 1961): 428; TR to Seth Low, 9 Apr. 1908, *Letters*, 6:997.

26. TR to Kermit Roosevelt, 30 May 1908, *Letters*, 6:1044.

27. Thomas Roger Wessel, "Republican Justice: The Department of Justice under Roosevelt and Taft, 1901–1913" (Ph.D. diss., University of Maryland, 1972), p. 282; TR to Joseph G. Cannon, 29 Apr. 1908, *Letters*, 6:1019; "An Unpopular Congress," *Literary Digest* 36 (6 June 1908): 811.

28. TR to John Sparks, 4 Jan. 1908, *Letters*, 6:896.

29. TR to the Department of Justice, 20 Mar. 1908, ibid., p. 977; Syed M. Habibuddin, *Civil Liberties and Democracy: Attitude of a President* (Calcutta, India: Scientific Book Agency, 1977), p. 46.

30. TR to William Alden Smith, 24 Apr. 1908, *Letters*, 6:1017.

31. John D. Weaver, *The Brownsville Raid* (New York: Norton, 1970), pp. 192–99.

32. TR to John Henry Patterson, 20 Mar. 1908, *Letters*, 6:979.

33. TR to Lyman Abbott, 29 May 1908, ibid., pp. 1041, 1042.

34. George B. Lockwood to Charles W. Fairbanks, 9 June 1908, Charles W. Fairbanks Papers, Manuscripts Department, Lilly Library, Indiana University, Bloomington.

35. Henry F. Pringle, *The Life and Times of William Howard Taft*, 2 vols. (New York: Farrar & Rinehart, 1939), 1:352.

36. Richard Cleveland Baker, *The Tariff under Roosevelt and Taft* (Hastings, Nebr.: Democrat Printing Co., 1941), p. 73.

37. TR to Frank B. Kellogg, 16 June 1908, and TR to George Otto Trevelyan, 19 June 1908, *Letters*, 6:1078, 1085; Milton W. Blumenberg, comp., *Official Report of the Proceedings of the Fourteenth Republican National Convention* (Columbus, Ohio: Press of F. J. Heer, 1908), p. 117.

38. *Taft and Roosevelt: The Intimate Letters of Archie Butt*, 2 vols. (Garden City, N.Y.: Doubleday, Doran, 1930), 2:551.

39. Judson C. Welliver to John C. Keely, 21 Aug. 1908, Albert B. Cummins Papers, Iowa State Department of History and Archives, Des Moines.

40. TR to Taft, 7 and 21 July, 7 Aug. 1908, *Letters*, 6:1113, 1140, 1157.

41. TR to Liberty Hyde Bailey, 10 Aug. 1908, ibid., pp. 1167, 1169.

42. George S. Ellsworth, "Theodore Roosevelt's Country Life Commission," *Agricultural History* 34 (Oct. 1960): 164.

43. *American Problems*, p. 133.

44. *Chicago Tribune*, 7 Oct. 1908.

45. TR to Taft, 5 Sept. 1908, *Letters*, 6:1210.

46. TR to Conrad Kohrs, 9 Sept. 1908, and TR to Nicholas Longworth, 21 Sept. 1908, ibid., pp. 1218, 1246.

47. TR to Taft, 19 Sept. 1908, ibid., p. 1244; Everett Walters, *Joseph Benson Foraker: An Uncompromising Republican* (Columbus: Ohio State Archaeological and Historical Society, 1948), p. 279.

48. Entry of 29 Sept. 1908, George von Lengerke Meyer's Diary, MD, LC; TR to William Jennings Bryan, 23 Sept. 1908, *Letters*, 6:1252; entry of 23 Sept. 1908, James R. Garfield's diaries, MD, LC.

49. TR to John D. Pringle, 30 Oct. 1908, *Letters*, 6:1325.

50. *The Letters of Archie Butt, Personal Aide to President Roosevelt*, ed. Lawrence F. Abbott (Garden City, N.Y.: Doubleday, Page, 1924), p. 153; Jean Jules Jusserand, *What Me Befell: The Reminiscences of J. J. Jusserand* (Boston, Mass.: Houghton Mifflin, 1933), p. 337.

51. Taft to Roosevelt, 7 Nov. 1908, Taft Papers; Lucius B. Swift to Mrs. Swift, 8 July 1910, Lucius B. Swift Papers, Indiana State Library, Indianapolis.

52. *Letters of Archie Butt*, p. 205.

53. Ibid., p. 338; Meyer's diary, 4 Jan. 1909.

54. TR to Taft, 4 Jan. 1909, *Letters*, 6:1457; *Letters of Archie Butt*, p. 338; Pringle, *Life and Times of William Howard Taft*, 1:388.

55. *State Papers*, pp. 498, 503, 508; TR to William Allen White, 30 Nov. 1908, *Letters*, 6:1393.

56. *State Papers*, p. 528.

57. John E. Wilkie to Kirt W. DeBelle, 27 June 1908, Charles J. Bonaparte Papers, box 131, MD, LC; Willard B. Gatewood, Jr., *Theodore Roosevelt and the Art of Controversy: Episodes of the White House Years* (Baton Rouge: Louisiana State University Press, 1970), p. 254.

58. TR to Oscar S. Straus, 22 Dec. 1908, Oscar S. Straus Papers, MD, LC.

59. James D. Richardson, comp., *A Compilation of the Messages and Papers of*

the Presidents, 10 vols. (Washington, D.C.: Bureau of National Literature, 1911), 10:7628, hereafter cited as *Messages and Papers.*

60. TR to Eugene Hale, 5 Jan. 1909, and TR to Kermit Roosevelt, 10 Jan. 1909, *Letters,* 6:1461, 1472.

61. "At Sword's Point in Washington," *Literary Digest* 38 (16 Jan. 1909): 79.

62. TR to Theodore Roosevelt, Jr., 31 Jan. 1909, *Letters,* 6:1499.

63. TR to Kermit Roosevelt, 10 Jan. 1909, ibid., p. 1473; "A Review of the World," *Current Literature* 46 (Mar. 1909): 238.

64. James Wyman Barrett, *Joseph Pulitzer and His World* (New York: Vanguard Press, 1941), p. 228.

65. TR to William Dudley Foulke, 1 Dec. 1908, *Letters,* 6:1396; Barrett, *Joseph Pulitzer,* p. 231.

66. TR to Henry L. Stimson, 9 Dec. 1908, *Letters,* 6:1415.

67. *Messages and Papers,* 10:7729, 7730.

68. Clyde Peirce, *The Roosevelt Panama Libel Cases* (New York: Greenwick Book Publishers, 1959), p. 81.

69. TR to Jacob H. Schiff, 25 Dec. 1908, and TR to Paul Morton, 2 Mar. 1909, *Letters,* 6:1440, 1541.

70. TR to Taft, 26 Feb. 1909, ibid., p. 1538.

71. *Letters of Archie Butt,* p. 369; Henry Cabot Lodge to Corinne Roosevelt Robinson, 18 Sept. 1921, Corinne Roosevelt Robinson Papers, Houghton Library, Harvard University, Cambridge, Mass., quoted with the permission of the Houghton Library.

72. Pringle, *Life and Times of William Howard Taft,* 1:393, 394, 396.

73. W. S. Hinman to W. H. Cathcart, 21 Feb. 1909, author's collection; *Letters of Archie Butt,* p. 323.

74. William R. Thayer to Henry Cabot Lodge, 1 June 1916, Henry Cabot Lodge Papers, Massachusetts Historical Society, Boston.

75. TR to Richard Derby, 12 Sept. 1918, *Letters,* 8:1370.

76. *Autobiography,* p. ix; TR to E. A. Van Valkenburg, 5 Sept. 1916, *Letters,* 8:1113–14; Gifford Pinchot, "Roosevelt as President," *State Papers,* p. xxix.

77. Lodge to Robert L. O'Brien, 9 Jan. 1909, Lodge Papers; Sydney Brooks, "President Roosevelt's Record," *Living Age* 261 (1 May 1909): 261; "A Short Measure of What President Roosevelt Has Done," *World's Work* 17 (Mar. 1909): 11314; Lyman Abbott, "A Review of President Roosevelt's Administration: IV—Its Influence on Patriotism and Public Service," *Outlook* 91 (27 Feb. 1909): 434; Harry Thurston Peck, "President Roosevelt," *Bookman* 29 (Mar. 1909): 29.

BIBLIOGRAPHICAL ESSAY

MANUSCRIPTS

The primary sources on Theodore Roosevelt's presidency are extensive and rich; a brief survey of them can only suggest how much material exists. The Theodore Roosevelt Papers, Manuscript Division, Library of Congress (hereafter LC) are a rich resource for a study of Roosevelt's years in the White House. The collection is available in a microfilm edition of 485 reels. It contains Roosevelt's outgoing letters, incoming correspondence, speeches, scrapbooks, and appointment records. The *Index to the Theodore Roosevelt Papers*, 3 vols. (Washington, D.C.: Library of Congress, 1969), is a convenient and efficient guide to the president's thoughts, writings, and statements. There are other original Roosevelt letters and documents at Harvard University, Cambridge, Massachusetts, and at Theodore Roosevelt's birthplace in New York City.

The papers of members of Roosevelt's cabinet are voluminous and important. The Library of Congress holds the papers of Charles J. Bonaparte, George B. Cortelyou, James R. Garfield, John Hay, Philander C. Knox, William H. Moody, Elihu Root, Oscar S. Straus, and William Howard Taft. The Ethan Allen Hitchcock Papers are at the National Archives, Washington, D.C., RG (record group) 316. The Massachusetts Historical Society has the papers of George von Lengerke Meyer; his diaries are at the Library of Congress. The papers of Truman H. Newberry are at the Detroit Public Library. Collections for Paul Morton, Victor H. Metcalf, and James Wilson remain in private hands or have been lost.

Among the papers of governmental officials who were close to Roosevelt but below the cabinet level, the Gifford Pinchot Papers (LC) are the largest in scope. The Henry White Papers (LC), the Joseph Hodges Choate Papers (LC), the Whitelaw Reid Papers (LC), and the Francis B. Loomis Papers, Stanford

University Library, are illuminating on the diplomatic aspects of the administration. The Library of Congress also holds the papers of James S. Clarkson, George W. Goethals, Fredrick H. Newell, and Leonard Wood. The Charles W. Fairbanks Papers, in the Lilly Library at Indiana University, Bloomington, and also at the Indiana Historical Society, Indianapolis, reveal a vice-president who had large ambitions and little to do.

For private citizens who were close to Roosevelt at various times during his presidency see the Nicholas Murray Butler and George W. Perkins papers, Columbia University Library, New York City; the Albert Shaw Papers, New York Public Library; and the William Allen White Papers (LC). The William E. Chandler Papers (LC), the Eugene Ganoe Hay Papers (LC), the Moreton Frewen Papers (LC), and the Halstead Family Papers, Cincinnati Historical Society, were helpful on specific aspects of the Roosevelt years.

Because of the ample documentation that existed on the presidential level for Roosevelt, I did not pursue research into the materials for individual agencies of the government. The National Archives contain rich resources in the records of the Department of Justice, RG 60; the files of the Bureau of Corporations, in the Records of the Federal Trade Commission, RG 122; and the records of the Department of Commerce, RG 40. For foreign policy, there are the Records of the Department of State, RG 59; the Department of the Navy, RG 45; and the War Department, RG 165.

The papers of members of Congress were indispensable to this study. The Nelson W. Aldrich Papers (LC) are large but not as helpful as might be expected. The William Boyd Allison Papers, Iowa State Department of History and Archives, Des Moines, are enlightening, especially on the early years of the administration. The Albert J. Beveridge Papers (LC) recount the development of a Republican progressive. The La Follette Family Papers (LC) show the increasing tension between the Wisconsin senator and the president. The John Coit Spooner Papers (LC) reveal a conservative perspective. Also important are the Henry Cabot Lodge Papers, Massachusetts Historical Society, Boston; the Jonathan P. Dolliver Papers, Iowa State Historical Society, Iowa City; and the Orville H. Platt Papers, Connecticut State Library, Hartford. The Joseph B. Foraker Papers, Cincinnati Historical Society, are useful for Roosevelt's opposition in Congress.

The reports of the British ambassadors, contained in the Public Record Office, London, are often quite revealing about events in the United States. For Roosevelt's press relations, the Erastus Brainerd Papers, University of Washington Library, Seattle, contain the comments of Walter Clark, who covered the president's activities. The records of the attorney general of Minnesota shed new light on the origins of the *Northern Securities* case.

DOCUMENTS, PERIODICALS, AND SECONDARY WORKS

Theodore Roosevelt was a prolific writer as president, and the documentary record of his presidency is large. The most important of all published sources is

Elting E. Morison et al., *The Letters of Theodore Roosevelt*, 8 vols. (Cambridge, Mass.: Harvard University Press, 1951–54), which prints about ten thousand of the hundred thousand letters that Roosevelt sent during his life. A superb and well-edited selection, the *Letters* are a basic guide to the key events of the White House years. For Roosevelt's public statements, *The Works of Theodore Roosevelt*, 20 vols. (New York: Scribner's, 1926), provide an excellent place to begin, because they contain the president's annual messages and major speeches. For individual addresses during the first term, *Addresses and Presidential Messages of Theodore Roosevelt, 1902–1904* (New York: Putnam's, 1904), is convenient. James D. Richardson, comp., *A Compilation of the Messages and Papers of the Presidents*, 10 vols. (Washington, D.C.: Bureau of National Literature, 1911), is important for Roosevelt's many special messages to Capitol Hill.

For Roosevelt's actions in foreign affairs, *Papers Relating to the Foreign Relations of the United States, 1901–1909* (Washington, D.C.: Government Printing Office, 1902–9) provide the official record of what the government did. In addition to the annual reports of the War Department, the Navy Department, the Treasury Department, the Interior Department, the Civil Service Commission, and the Bureau of Corporations, there are special publications of documents that are useful for Roosevelt's administration. The *Report to the President on the Anthracite Coal Strike of May–October 1902 by the Anthracite Coal Strike Commission* (Washington, D.C.: Government Printing Office, 1903), contains enlightening material on this crucial labor dispute. *Report of the Commissioner of Corporations on the Transportation of Petroleum*, House Document 812, 59th Cong., 1st sess. (Washington, D.C.: Government Printing Office, 1906), and *Departure from Published Rates by the Atchison, Topeka and Santa Fe Railway Company, etc.*, Senate Document 140, 59th Cong., 1st sess. (Washington, D.C.: Government Printing Office, 1905), are important for Roosevelt's policy toward the regulation of corporations. The *Congressional Record*, as well as other House and Senate documents, were of continuing value for a grasp of Roosevelt's relations with Congress.

Newspapers in this period covered politics closely. The *Washington Star* and the *New York Tribune* were well informed about affairs at the White House. The *Washington Post*, the *New York Times*, the *Chicago Tribune*, and the *Iowa State Register* were consulted for specific topics. A broad sense of press opinion emerges from the surveys that the *Literary Digest* regularly conducted. Such periodicals as the *American Monthly Review of Reviews*, *Independent*, *Outlook*, *Forum*, and *World's Work* provide a rich source of commentary and insight into the events of the day.

The printed literature on Theodore Roosevelt is vast, but there is not yet a single bibliographical publication that surveys it in a comprehensive way. A place to start is with the revised second edition of Albert Bushnell Hart and Herbert Ronald Ferleger's *Theodore Roosevelt Cyclopedia* (Westport, Conn.: Meckler Corporation and Theodore Roosevelt Association, 1988). Updated with a new bibliography and chronology by John Gable, the *Cyclopedia* is very helpful. Wallace Finley Dailey's "Theodore Roosevelt in Periodical Literature, 1950–1981," *Theodore Roosevelt Association Journal* 8 (Fall 1982): 4–15, covers the writing about Roosevelt in most scholarly publications.

The best one-volume biography of Roosevelt is William H. Harbaugh's *The Life and Times of Theodore Roosevelt* (New York: Oxford University Press, 1975). There are also rewarding passages in Henry F. Pringle's *Theodore Roosevelt: A Biography* (New York: Harcourt, Brace, 1931). The most-important and most-influential interpretive treatment of Roosevelt is John Morton Blum's *The Republican Roosevelt* (Cambridge, Mass.: Harvard University Press, 1954). Blum's perceptive insights, impressive research, and graceful prose have deservedly shaped Roosevelt scholarship for almost four decades. *The Warrior and the Priest: Woodrow Wilson and Theodore Roosevelt* (Cambridge, Mass.: Belknap Press of Harvard University Press, 1983), by John Milton Cooper, Jr., is a comparative study of Roosevelt and his major historical rival.

For the years before the presidency, three books are essential. Carleton Putnam's *Theodore Roosevelt: The Formative Years, 1858–1886* (New York: Scribner's, 1958) provides a detailed narrative of Roosevelt to the age of twenty-eight. Edmund Morris's *The Rise of Theodore Roosevelt* (New York: Coward, McCann & Geoghegan, 1979) is a dramatic and compelling narrative from Roosevelt's own point of view. David G. McCullough's *Mornings on Horseback* (New York: Simon & Schuster, 1981) takes a thoughtful look at how Roosevelt's character was shaped in his youth. Also very informative on these years is Kathleen Dalton's "The Early Life of Theodore Roosevelt" (Ph.D. diss., Johns Hopkins University, 1979).

The six years that Roosevelt spent as a civil-service commissioner have not received detailed attention. Jay Stuart Berman's *Police Administration and Progressive Reform: Theodore Roosevelt as Police Commissioner of New York* (Westport, Conn.: Greenwood, 1987) considers Roosevelt's impact on the city's policemen. G. Wallace Chessman's *Governor Theodore Roosevelt: The Albany Apprenticeship, 1898–1900* (Cambridge, Mass.: Harvard University Press, 1965) shows the continuity between Roosevelt's career in Albany and his approach to the presidency.

Among the memoir literature on Roosevelt, the best account is his own *Autobiography*, which is included in his *Works*, cited earlier. In part a critique of Taft's record as president, the autobiography also sets forth what Roosevelt thought was important about his administration by 1913. *The Letters of Archie Butt, Personal Aide to President Roosevelt*, edited by Lawrence F. Abbott (Garden City, N.Y.: Doubleday, Page, 1924), prints the thoughts of the president's military aide about the last phase of the presidency. Gifford Pinchot's *Breaking New Ground* (New York: Harcourt, Brace, 1947) is important for conservation policy. M. A. DeWolfe Howe's *George von Lengerke Meyer: His Life and Public Services* (New York: Dodd, Mead, 1920) contains extracts from Meyer's letters and diaries. Oscar S. Straus's *Under Four Administrations, from Cleveland to Taft: Recollections of Oscar S. Straus* (New York: Houghton Mifflin, 1922) is interesting on Straus's cabinet service. William Dudley Foulke's *Fighting the Spoilsmen: Reminiscences of the Civil Service Reform Movement* (New York: Putnam's, 1919) presents information on Roosevelt's style of governing. Jean Adrien Antoine Jules Jusserand's *What Me Befell: The Reminiscences of J. J. Jusserand* (Boston, Mass.: Houghton Mifflin, 1933) and Stephen Gwynn's edition of *The Letters and*

Friendships of Sir Cecil Spring Rice: A Record (Boston, Mass.: Houghton Mifflin, 1929) provide the perspective of two of Roosevelt's diplomatic friends.

While there is no book-length examination of Roosevelt's presidency as a whole, a number of authors have written informative volumes on specific topics that deal with the whole administration. Howard K. Beale's *Theodore Roosevelt and the Rise of America to World Power* (Baltimore, Md.: Johns Hopkins Press, 1956) is rich in information, but there is still room for a new examination of Roosevelt's handling of foreign policy. Willard B. Gatewood, Jr.'s *Theodore Roosevelt and the Art of Controversy: Episodes of The White House Years* (Baton Rouge: Louisiana State University Press, 1970) looks at individual episodes within the framework of broad research and informed analysis of Roosevelt's performance. Raymond A. Esthus's *Theodore Roosevelt and the International Rivalries* (Waltham, Mass.: Ginn-Blaisdell, 1970) is based on an impressive knowledge of American and foreign sources. Frederick W. Marks III's *Velvet on Iron: The Diplomacy of Theodore Roosevelt* (Lincoln: University of Nebraska Press, 1979) is a staunch defense of Roosevelt, but it is a more episodic treatment than its title suggests. Richard H. Collin's *Theodore Roosevelt, Culture, Diplomacy, and Expansion: A New View of American Imperialism* (Baton Rouge: Louisiana State University Press, 1985) offers a cultural interpretation of Roosevelt's foreign-policy record. Collin's *Theodore Roosevelt's Caribbean: The Panama Canal, the Monroe Doctrine, and the Latin American Context* (Baton Rouge: Louisiana State University Press, 1990) came out while this book was in press. Paul Russell Cutright's *Theodore Roosevelt: The Making of a Conservationist* (Urbana: University of Illinois Press, 1985) is strongest for the years before Roosevelt became president.

The members of Roosevelt's cabinet have been the subjects of a number of impressive biographies. Tyler Dennett's *John Hay: From Poetry to Politics* (New York: Dodd, Mead, 1933) remains the best account of the secretary of state. Kenton J. Clymer's *John Hay: The Gentleman as Diplomat* (Ann Arbor: University of Michigan Press, 1975) offers a more critical modern interpretation. Philip C. Jessup's *Elihu Root*, 2 vols. (New York: Dodd, Mead, 1938), has held up well, but a new biography of Root would be an important contribution. Henry F. Pringle's *The Life and Times of William Howard Taft*, 2 vols. (New York: Farrar & Rinehart, 1939), covers Taft's cabinet career well. Other treatments of cabinet members include James Brown Scott's *Robert Bacon: Life and Letters* (Garden City, N.Y.: Doubleday, Page, 1923), Naomi Wiener Cohen's *A Dual Heritage: The Public Career of Oscar S. Straus* (Philadelphia, Pa.: Jewish Publication Society of America, 1969), and Wayne A. Wiegand's *Patrician in the Progressive Era: A Biography of George von Lengerke Meyer* (New York: Garland Publishing, 1988). Dissertations shed light on other members of the official family. Allen Walker Rumble's "Rectitude and Reform: Charles J. Bonaparte and the Politics of Gentility, 1851–1921" (Ph.D. diss., University of Maryland, 1970), Benjamin Temple Ford's "A Duty to Serve: The Governmental Career of George Bruce Cortelyou" (Ph.D. diss., Columbia University, 1963), Jack M. Thompson's "James R. Garfield: The Career of a Rooseveltian Progressive, 1895–1916" (Ph.D. diss., University of South Carolina, 1958), Anita Torres Eitler's "Philander Chase Knox,

First Attorney-General of Theodore Roosevelt, 1901–1904" (Ph.D. diss., Catholic University of America, 1959), and Judith Rene McDonough's "William Henry Moody" (Ph.D. diss., Auburn University, 1983) are all very useful contributions.

A favorable overview of Roosevelt's administration emerges from George E. Mowry's *The Era of Theodore Roosevelt, 1900–1912* (New York: Harper & Row, 1958). More critical of Roosevelt's political style is Lewis L. Gould's *Reform and Regulation: American Politics from Roosevelt to Wilson* (New York: Alfred A. Knopf, 1986).

On specific policy issues, the administration's trust program is analyzed in Hans B. Thorelli's *The Federal Antitrust Policy: Origination of an American Tradition* (Baltimore, Md.: Johns Hopkins Press, 1955), William Letwin's *Law and Economic Policy in America: The Evolution of the Sherman Antitrust Act* (New York: Random House, 1965), and Thomas Roger Wessel's "Republican Justice: The Department of Justice under Roosevelt and Taft, 1901–1913" (Ph.D. diss., University of Maryland, 1972).

For related aspects of the trust issue, Arthur M. Johnson's "Theodore Roosevelt and the Bureau of Corporations," *Mississippi Valley Historical Review* 45 (Mar. 1959): 571–90, examines Roosevelt's administrative agency that conducted the regulation of trusts. Johnson's "Antitrust Policy in Transition, 1908: Ideal and Reality," *Mississippi Valley Historical Review* 48 (Dec. 1961): 415–34, examines the effort to reform the Sherman Antitrust Act in 1908. That struggle is the main focus of Martin J. Sklar's *The Corporate Reconstruction of American Capitalism, 1890–1916: The Market, the Law, and Politics* (Cambridge, Eng.: Cambridge University Press, 1988). Gabriel Kolko's *The Triumph of Conservatism: A Reinterpretation of American History, 1900–1916* (New York: Free Press, 1963) is very critical of Roosevelt's record on regulation. Robert H. Wiebe's "The House of Morgan and the Executive, 1905–1913," *American Historical Review* 65 (Oct. 1959): 49–60, details the administration's negotiations over regulation with a major corporate interest.

On the pure-food-and-drug issue see *The Health of a Nation: Harvey W. Wiley and the Fight for Pure Food* (Chicago: University of Chicago Press, 1958), by Oscar E. Anderson, Jr. Donna J. Wood's "The Strategic Use of Public Policy: Business Support for the 1906 Food and Drug Act," *Business History Review* 59 (Autumn 1985): 403–42, and Jack High and Clayton A. Coppin's "Wiley and the Whiskey Industry: Strategic Behavior in the Passage of the Pure Food Act," *Business History Review* 62 (Summer 1988): 286–309, consider the motives of those who were being regulated. James Harvey Young's *Pure Food: Securing the Federal Food and Drugs Act of 1906* (Princeton, N.J.: Princeton University Press, 1989) is a definitive treatment of the law and its enactment.

The railroad question is examined in two contrasting volumes. Gabriel Kolko's *Railroads and Regulation, 1877–1916* (Princeton, N.J.: Princeton University Press, 1965) contends that the railroads endorsed national regulation. Albro Martin's *Enterprise Denied: Origins of the Decline of American Railroads, 1897–1917* (New York: Columbia University Press, 1971) argues that the rail companies suffered under regulation. Rita E. Loos's "President Theodore Roosevelt and

Eastern Businessmen: A Divergence of Views" (Ph.D. diss., St. John's University, 1971) looks at how the railroad, trust, and financial policies of the administration were received.

Robert J. Cornell's *The Anthracite Coal Strike of 1902* (Washington, D.C.: Catholic University of America Press, 1957) is a comprehensive account of this major episode in Roosevelt's labor record. It should be supplemented with Robert H. Wiebe's "The Anthracite Coal Strike of 1902: A Record of Confusion," *Mississippi Valley Historical Review* 48 (Sept. 1961): 229–51. The general situation of labor in Roosevelt's day is well outlined in David Montgomery's *The Fall of the House of Labor: The Workplace, the State, and American Labor Activism, 1865–1925* (Cambridge, Eng.: Cambridge University Press, 1987).

For the banking problem and its political impact, Richard Todd McCulley's "The Origins of the Federal Reserve Act of 1913: Banks and Politics during the Progressive Era, 1897–1913" (Ph.D. diss., University of Texas at Austin, 1980) was more informative than the more theoretical work that is offered in James Livingston's *Origins of the Federal Reserve System: Money, Class, and Corporate Capitalism, 1890–1913* (Ithaca, N.Y.: Cornell University Press, 1986). Historians have essentially neglected the tariff issue during the Roosevelt period. The best survey of the subject remains Richard Cleveland Baker's *The Tariff under Roosevelt and Taft* (Hastings, Nebr.: Democrat Printing Co., 1941). There is additional information on the tariff in Robert H. Wiebe's *Businessmen and Reform: A Study of the Progressive Movement* (Cambridge, Mass.: Harvard University Press, 1962).

The issue of race relations engaged Roosevelt's time and thought throughout most of his presidency. James E. Haney's "Theodore Roosevelt and Afro-Americans, 1901–1912" (Ph.D. diss., Kent State University, 1971) and Pearl Kluger's "Progressive Presidents and Black Americans" (Ph.D. diss., Columbia University, 1974) are very helpful accounts. Joel Williamson's *The Crucible of Race: Black-White Relations in the American South since Emancipation* (New York: Oxford University Press, 1984) is critical of Roosevelt's performance. Thomas G. Dyer's *Theodore Roosevelt and the Idea of Race* (Baton Rouge: Louisiana State University Press, 1980) supplies an overview of the president's racial thought. John D. Weaver's *The Brownsville Raid* (New York: Norton, 1970) and Ann J. Lane's *The Brownsville Affair: National Crisis and Black Reaction* (Port Washington, N.Y.: Kennikat Press, 1971) began the reappraisal of Roosevelt's actions in this controversial case. Pete Daniel's *The Shadow of Slavery: Peonage in the South, 1901–1969* (New York: Oxford University Press, 1973) looks at the administration's campaign to deal with this social problem.

Roosevelt's conservation policy has been examined in a number of works. The place to start is Samuel P. Hays's important contribution *Conservation and the Gospel of Efficiency: The Progressive Conservation Movement, 1890–1920* (Cambridge, Mass.: Harvard University Press, 1959). James L. Penick, Jr.'s *Progressive Politics and Conservation: The Ballinger-Pinchot Affair* (Chicago: University of Chicago Press, 1968) is enlightening in regard to Roosevelt's resource policies. G. Michael McCarthy's *Hour of Trial: The Conservation Conflict in Colorado and the West, 1891–1907* (Norman: University of Oklahoma Press, 1977) describes the opposition to Pinchot and Roosevelt. Stephen R. Fox's *John Muir and His Legacy: The American Conservation Movement* (Boston, Mass.: Little, Brown, 1981) deals with Roosevelt in the context of conservation in general.

Roosevelt's efforts to reshape the administrative structure of the government are treated in Oscar Kraines's "The President versus Congress: The Keep Commission, 1905–1909; First Comprehensive Presidential Inquiry into Administration," *Western Political Quarterly* 23 (Mar. 1970): 5–54, which is more detailed than Harold T. Pinkett's "The Keep Commission, 1905–1909: A Rooseveltian Effort for Administrative Reform," *Journal of American History* 52 (Sept. 1965): 297–312. George S. Ellsworth's "Theodore Roosevelt's Country Life Commission," *Agricultural History* 34 (Oct. 1960): 155–72, traces the work of a famous presidential advisory panel. Stephen E. Ponder's "Executive Publicity and Congressional Resistance, 1905–1913: Congress and the Roosevelt Administration's PR Men," *Congress and the Presidency* 13 (Autumn 1986): 177–86, deals with the reaction to Pinchot's promotional methods. Syed M. Habibuddin's *Civil Liberties and Democracy: Attitude of a President* (Calcutta, India: Scientific Book Agency, 1977) offers a critical appraisal of Roosevelt's record toward dissenters, the press, and his political opponents. Richard Hume Werking's *The Master Architects: Building the United States Foreign Service, 1890–1913* (Lexington: University Press of Kentucky, 1977) reviews the changes that Root and his associates made in the diplomatic service.

Relations with the press during the Roosevelt presidency have received growing attention. George Juergens's *News from the White House: The Presidential-Press Relationship in the Progressive Era* (Chicago: University of Chicago Press, 1981) offers an overview that draws primarily on published sources. Robert C. Hilderbrand's *Power and the People: Executive Management of Public Opinion in Foreign Affairs, 1897–1921* (Chapel Hill: University of North Carolina Press, 1981) contains some perceptive passages about Roosevelt.

Changes in the operation and organization of the military services constituted an important feature of Roosevelt's administration. Gordon Carpenter O'Gara's *Theodore Roosevelt and the Rise of the Modern Navy* (Princeton, N.J.: Princeton University Press, 1943) is a useful starting point. William R. Braisted's *The United States Navy in the Pacific, 1897–1909* (Austin: University of Texas Press, 1958) covers Asiatic strategy. Albert C. Stillson's "Military Policy without Political Guidance: Theodore Roosevelt's Navy," *Military Affairs* 25 (Spring 1961): 18–31, is critical of Roosevelt's style. Richard D. Challener's *Admirals, Generals, and American Foreign Policy, 1898–1914* (Princeton, N.J.: Princeton University Press, 1973) contains much information about the navy. For the army see Eldridge Colby's "Elihu Root and the National Guard," *Military Affairs* 23 (Spring 1959): 28–34, and Philip L. Semsch's "Elihu Root and the General Staff," *Military Affairs* 27 (Spring 1963): 16–27. There are good chapters on army reform in Stephen Skowronek's *Building a New American State: The Expansion of National Administrative Capacities, 1877–1920* (Cambridge, Eng.: Cambridge University Press, 1982).

The partisan politics of the period are covered in several of the sources cited earlier, but for more information on the party battles see Horace Samuel Merrill and Marion Galbraith Merrill's *The Republican Command, 1897–1913* (Lexington: University Press of Kentucky, 1971), which does not exhaust the subject, and David Sarasohn's *The Party of Reform: Democrats in the Progressive Era* (Jackson: University Press of Mississippi, 1989), which includes several interesting chapters on Roosevelt. Michael E. McGerr's *The Decline of Popular Politics: The American North, 1865–1928* (New York: Oxford University Press, 1986) is excellent on changes in campaign styles.

Helpful on specific aspects of the politics of Roosevelt's day were David Crosson's "James S. Clarkson and Theodore Roosevelt" (Master's report, University of Texas at Austin, 1972), Thomas M. Anderson's "Theodore Roosevelt and Colorado Politics, 1901–1904: A Roosevelt-Hanna Rivalry?" (Master's report, University of Texas at Austin, 1973), and Walter J. Gaffield's "Theodore Roosevelt and Nicholas Murray Butler: An Evaluation of Party Leadership" (Master's report, University of Texas at Austin, 1974). Fred C. Shoemaker's "Alton B. Parker: The Image of a Gilded Age Statesman in an Era of Progressive Politics" (Master's thesis, Ohio State University, 1983) is informative on the 1904 election. Joel A. Tarr's "President Theodore Roosevelt and Illinois Politics, 1901–1904," *Journal of the Illinois State Historical Society* 58 (Autumn 1965): 245–64, indicates the possibilities in studies of Roosevelt's patronage policies.

The members of Roosevelt's family have not yet received much interpretive attention for the presidential years. Sylvia Jukes Morris's *Edith Kermit Roosevelt: Portrait of a First Lady* (New York: Coward, McCann & Geoghegan, 1980) is a sound start, but more needs to be done about the first lady's influence on her husband. Stacy A. Rozek's " 'The First Daughter of the Land': Alice Roosevelt as Presidential Celebrity, 1902–1906," *Presidential Studies Quarterly* 19 (Winter 1989): 51–70, shows what thorough research and sound analysis can do with Roosevelt's most famous child.

For the general cultural and social background in which Roosevelt and his administration moved, Mark Sullivan's *Our Times*, vol. 2: *America Finding Herself* and vol. 3, *Pre-War America* (New York: Scribner's, 1929, 1930) are a storehouse of helpful data. William Seale, *The President's House: A History*, 2 vols. (Washington, D.C.: White House Historical Association, 1986), looks at Roosevelt's impact on the White House.

Any discussion of the available sources on Roosevelt and foreign policy must be highly selective; only a few relatively important titles can be mentioned. For the problems of the Philippines see Oscar M. Alfonso's *Theodore Roosevelt and the Philippines, 1897 1909* (New York: Oriole, 1974), which covers the entire administration in workmanlike fashion. Frank T. Reuter's *Catholic Influence on American Colonial Policies, 1898–1904* (Austin: University of Texas Press, 1967) is valuable for the friars and their land problems. Frederick Zwierlein's *Theodore Roosevelt and Catholics* (St. Louis, Mo.: V. T. Suren, 1956) does not do justice to its subject.

The amount of writing on the Venezuelan issue is substantial. Edmund Morris's " 'A Few Pregnant Days': Theodore Roosevelt and the Venezuelan Crisis of 1902," *Theodore Roosevelt Association Journal* 15 (Winter 1989): 2–13, is the most-recent defense of Roosevelt's recollections of his actions. Paul S. Holbo's "Perilous Obscurity: Public Diplomacy and the Press in the Venezuelan Crisis, 1902–1903," *Historian* 32 (May 1970): 428–48, looks at how the administration used public disclosures as part of its policy. Manfred Jonas's *The United States and Germany: A Diplomatic History* (Ithaca, N.Y.: Cornell University Press, 1984) and Holger H. Herwig's *Germany's Vision of Empire in Venezuela, 1871–1914* (Princeton, N.J.: Princeton University Press, 1986) are instructive on the German side of the episode.

The Canadian boundary issue has been considered in a number of larger studies. Charles Callan Tansill's *Canadian-American Relations, 1875–1911* (New Haven, Conn.: Yale University Press, 1943) and Charles S. Campbell, Jr.'s *Anglo-American Understanding, 1898–1903* (Baltimore, Md.: Johns Hopkins Press, 1957) supply the basic information about what took place. *The Alaska Boundary Dispute,* edited by John A. Munro (Toronto, Can.: Copp-Clark, 1970), collected diverse opinions on the controversy.

For the Far Eastern policy of Roosevelt's first term see Raymond A. Esthus's *Theodore Roosevelt and Japan* (Seattle: University of Washington Press, 1966), Edward H. Zabriskie's *American-Russian Rivalry in the Far East: A Study in Diplomacy and Power Politics, 1895–1914* (Philadelphia: University of Pennsylvania Press, 1946) and A. Gregory Moore's "The Dilemma of Stereotypes: Theodore Roosevelt and China, 1901–1909" (Ph.D. diss., Kent State University, 1978); see also Michael H. Hunt's *The Making of a Special Relationship: The United States and China to 1914* (New York: Columbia University Press, 1983).

The literature on Roosevelt and the Panama Canal is extensive and complex. David G. McCullough's *The Path between the Seas: The Creation of the Panama Canal, 1870–1914* (New York: Simon & Schuster, 1977) is a well-written synthesis. Dwight C. Miner's *The Fight for the Panama Route: The Story of the Spooner Act and the Hay-Herrán Treaty* (New York: Columbia University Press, 1940) is an older study that is critical of Roosevelt. Also critical is Richard L. Lael's *Arrogant Diplomacy: U.S. Policy toward Colombia, 1903–1922* (Wilmington, Del.: Scholarly Resources, 1987). Philippe Bunau-Varilla, in *Panama: The Creation, Destruction, and Resurrection* (New York: McBride, Nast, 1914), claims a large role in these events, as does Gustave A. Anguizola's *Philippe Bunau-Varilla: The Man behind the Panama Canal* (Chicago: Nelson-Hall, 1980). John Major's "Who Wrote the Hay–Bunau-Varilla Convention?" *Diplomatic History* 8 (Spring 1984): 115–23, plays down Bunau-Varilla's importance in one key aspect of the controversy. Terence Graham's *The 'Interests of Civilization'?: Reaction in the United States against the 'Seizure' of the Panama Canal Zone, 1903–1904* (Lund, Sweden: Esselte Studium, 1983) looks at the reaction to Roosevelt's policy.

For the actual construction of the Canal and the resulting problems, Miles P. Du Val, Jr.'s *And the Mountains Will Move: The Story of the Building of the Panama Canal* (Stanford, Calif.: Stanford University Press, 1947) and Gerstle Mack's *The Land Divided: A History of the Panama Canal and Other Isthmian Canal Projects* (New York: Alfred A. Knopf, 1944) are still informative.

Tyler Dennett's *Roosevelt and the Russo-Japanese War* (Garden City, N.Y.: Doubleday, Page, 1925) prints some documents in a convenient form. Eugene P. Trani's *The Treaty of Portsmouth: An Adventure in American Diplomacy* (Lexington: University of Kentucky Press, 1969) looks closely at Roosevelt's role. More international in scope is Raymond A. Esthus's *Double Eagle and Rising Sun: The Russians and Japanese at Portsmouth in 1905* (Durham, N.C.: Duke University Press, 1988).

Other foreign-policy issues of the second term are examined in William Stull Holt's *Treaties Defeated by the Senate: A Study of the Struggle between President and Senate over the Conduct of Foreign Relations* (Baltimore, Md.: Johns Hopkins Press, 1933), Dexter Perkins's *The Monroe Doctrine, 1867–1907* (Baltimore, Md.: Johns Hopkins Press, 1937), Dana G. Munro's *Intervention and Dollar Diplomacy in the Caribbean, 1900–1921* (Princeton, N.J.: Princeton University Press, 1964), Ronald Francis Reter's "The Real versus the Rhetorical: Theodore Roosevelt in Foreign Policy-Making" (Ph.D. diss., University of Georgia, 1973), which is critical of Roosevelt's actions toward Congress, and Brenda Loudermilk's "Theodore Roosevelt and the Arbitration Treaties of 1905" (Master's report, University of Texas at Austin, 1972). Serge Ricard's *Theodore Roosevelt et la justification de l'imperialisme* (Aix-en-Provence, France: Publications de l'Université de Provence, 1986) is informative on several aspects of Roosevelt's foreign relations.

On the Algeciras Conference, Peter Larsen's "Theodore Roosevelt and the Moroccan Crisis, 1904–1906" (Ph.D. diss., Princeton University, 1984) is a thorough study that merits publication. Stefan H. Rinke's "Between Success and Failure: The Diplomatic Career of Ambassador Hermann Speck von Sternburg and German-American Relations, 1903–1908" (Master's thesis, Bowling Green State University, 1989) adds new information on the conduct of German policy. Also helpful on this topic are Luella J. Hall's *The United States and Morocco, 1776–1956* (Metuchen, N.J.: Scarecrow Press, 1971) and William James Hourihan's "Roosevelt and the Sultans: The United States Navy in the Mediterranean, 1904" (Ph.D. diss., University of Massachusetts, 1975).

For the Asian policy that Roosevelt pursued from 1905 to 1909, the following works were most helpful. Thomas A. Bailey's *Theodore Roosevelt and the Japanese-American Crises* (Stanford, Calif.: Stanford University Press, 1934) offers an older interpretation of this climactic foreign-policy event. Charles E. Neu's *An Uncertain Friendship: Theodore Roosevelt and Japan, 1906–1909* (Cambridge, Mass.: Harvard University Press, 1967) blends well both foreign and domestic considerations. Neu's work and the analysis of Raymond Esthus on the same subject, cited earlier, offer excellent coverage of Roosevelt's dealings with Japan. John Edward Wilz's "Did the United States Betray Korea in 1905?" *Pacific Historical Review* 54 (Aug. 1985): 243–70, delivers an affirmative answer. James R. Reckner's *Teddy Roosevelt's Great White Fleet* (Annapolis, Md.: Naval Institute Press, 1988) replaces earlier treatments of this celebrated episode.

Finally, the biographies of Roosevelt's friends, rivals, and colleagues that could be mentioned would make an unwieldy list. The following volumes are ones that helped me in preparing this book or that influenced my thinking about Roosevelt. Nathaniel Wright Stephenson's *Nelson W. Aldrich: A Leader in American Politics* (New York: Scribner's, 1930) is instructive about legislative matters but is written in a sometimes opaque style. Leland L. Sage's *William Boyd Alli-*

son: A Study in Practical Politics (Iowa City: State Historical Society of Iowa, 1956) is important for midwestern political currents. John Braeman's *Albert J. Beveridge: American Nationalist* (Chicago: University of Chicago Press, 1971) shows how Beveridge evolved into a progressive. Louis W. Koenig's *Bryan: A Political Biography of William Jennings Bryan* (New York: Putnam's, 1971) is the place to begin with the Democratic leader. Leon Burr Richardson's *William E. Chandler, Republican* (New York: Dodd, Mead, 1940) has much to offer about the Hepburn Act and other Republican issues. Thomas Richard Ross's *Jonathan Prentiss Dolliver: A Study in Political Integrity and Independence* (Iowa City: State Historical Society of Iowa, 1958) is also informative about Republican responses to Roosevelt. Herbert D. Croly's *Marcus Alonzo Hanna: His Life and Work* (New York: Macmillan, 1912) is still the best study of Roosevelt's rival during the first term. Several books on Hanna are under way, and a new biography is very much needed. For Henry Cabot Lodge, the best work is John A. Garraty's *Henry Cabot Lodge: A Biography* (New York: Alfred A. Knopf, 1953), and a stimulating interpretation of Lodge's foreign-policy ideas, which sheds light on Roosevelt as well, is William C. Widenor's *Henry Cabot Lodge and the Search for an American Foreign Policy* (Berkeley: University of California Press, 1980). John A. Garraty's *Right-Hand Man: The Life of George W. Perkins* (New York: Harper, 1960) is enlightening on trust policy and the Panic of 1907. Martin Nelson McGeary's *Gifford Pinchot, Forester-Politician* (Princeton, N.J.: Princeton University Press, 1960) is a thorough biography, but there is room for a new study of the Roosevelt-Pinchot relationship. Elting E. Morison's *Admiral Sims and the Modern American Navy* (Boston, Mass.: Houghton Mifflin, 1942), a classic in U.S. naval biography, was of great value for understanding Roosevelt's policies. Louis R. Harlan's *Booker T. Washington: The Wizard of Tuskegee, 1901–1915* (New York: Oxford University Press, 1983) is revealing and insightful about Washington himself and the plight of black people in Roosevelt's day.

For those interested in further examples of writing about Theodore Roosevelt, the *Theodore Roosevelt Association Journal*, published in Oyster Bay, New York, is an excellent source for the latest findings and projects about his life and times.

INDEX

Abbott, Lyman, 296
Adams, Henry C., 168–69
Adams, Samuel Hopkins, 155, 166
Addicks, J. Edward, 21
African-Americans. *See* Blacks
Aguinaldo, Emilio, 42, 56
Alaska, boundary of, 73, 81–86, 91, 139, 298
Alcohol, tax on, 170
Aldrich, Nelson Wilmarth, 10, 25, 26, 37, 53, 65, 66, 108, 109, 117, 152, 156, 159–60, 162, 163, 166, 265, 276
Aldrich-Vreeland Act (1908), 277–78, 281
Algeciras Conference (1906), 171, 189–95, 250, 270
Allison, William Boyd, 25–26, 53, 65, 66, 141, 160, 161, 162, 165, 231
Alverstone, R. E. W., 85, 86
American Federation of Labor (AFL), 35, 116, 232–33, 279, 285, 286
American Medical Association, 165, 166
American Protective Association, 37
American Protective Tariff League, 148
American Tobacco Company, 27–28, 217–18
Ananias Club, 20, 154
Anarchism, 31, 282
Anglo-Japanese Alliance (1902), 88
Annual messages: 1901, 19, 28–45, 220; 1902, 104–5, 122; 1903, 86, 98; 1904, 148–49, 150, 174, 199, 213, 220, 254; 1905, 158–59, 165, 188, 201, 231, 254; 1906, 194, 203, 244–45, 247, 258–59; 1907, 227, 250, 263, 274–75; 1908, 291

Anthracite coal strike, 65, 66–71, 115, 298
Arbitration, international, 149
Arizona, 109, 170
Atchison, Topeka, and Sante Fe Railroad, 157
Aylesworth, A. B., 85

Bacon, Augustus O., 192, 194
Bacon, Edward P., 150
Bacon, Robert, 70, 248, 250–51
Bailey, Joseph Weldon, 162, 163
Bailey, Liberty Hyde, 286–87
Baker, Ray Stannard, 162
Balfour, Arthur James, 81, 83, 85
Ballinger, Richard A., 203
Barnes, Benjamin F., 15
Beale, Howard K., 299
Beavers, George W., 113
"Beef Trust," 53, 150
Beer, William C., 106, 107
Beveridge, Albert J., 130, 164, 167, 169, 234, 236, 265, 284
Bishop, Joseph B., 128, 149, 299
Blacks, 22–24, 30; Brownsville, 42, 300; and Republicans, 118–22, 140. *See also* Brownsville; Lynching
Blaine, James G., 4, 5
Bliss, Cornelius N., 134, 142
Blum, John Morton, 299

347

Hill, James, 119
Hill, James J., 49
Hitchcock, Ethan Allen, 17, 111, 203–4, 216, 236
Hitchcock, Frank H., 220, 286
Hitt, Robert R., 135
Hoar, George Frisbie, 56, 64, 105
Holleben, Theodore von, 74, 75–76, 77–78, 80
Holmes, Oliver Wendell, Jr., 63–64, 85–86, 134
Howells, William Dean, 10
Hughes, Charles Evans, 155, 235, 236, 272–73, 274, 275, 284, 288, 298
Hunter, Robert, 34

Immigration, 36–37, 87–88, 170, 245, 257–58, 260, 262, 298
Immigration Restriction League, 36
Income tax, 37, 245, 275
Indianapolis News, 294–95
Indianola, Miss., 119
Indians. *See* Native Americans
Industrial Workers of the World (IWW), 35, 234–35
Inflation, 34, 150–51, 155–56
Inheritance tax, 162, 245, 275
Injunctions, 275, 281, 285
Insular Cases, 56, 63
International Brotherhood of Bookbinders, 115
International Harvester Co., 213, 217–18
Interstate Commerce Act (1887), 28, 33
Iowa, 24–25, 150
"Iowa Idea," 24–25, 64, 133
Ireland, John, 59, 60, 229
Irrigation, 41–42, 61–62
Italy, 176, 177–78

James, Henry, 227
Japan, 14, 87; and Korea, 185–86; and United States, 189, 250, 257–63, 267–68, 269; and war with Russia, 90–91, 180–88
Jetté, L. A., 85
Jews, in Russia, 89–90, 189
Jones, Thomas Goode, 22
Jungle, The (Sinclair), 167
Jusserand, Jean Jules, 74, 190–91, 192–94, 195, 219, 253, 289, 296
Jutaro, Komura, 181, 186, 187

Kaneko, Kentaro, 74, 180, 182, 258, 260
Kasson, John A., 24

Katsura, Taro, 185
Keep, Charles Hallam, 220–22
Keep Commission, 220–22
Kerens, Richard, 21
King, William Lyon MacKenzie, 263
Knickerbocker Trust Company, 248
Knox, Philander C., 18, 67, 135, 145, 150, 163, 269, 272, 273; and Northern Securities Company, 50, 51, 52–53
Korea, 185, 186, 188, 268

Labor unions, 34–35, 116, 280. *See also* American Federation of Labor; Industrial Workers of the World
La Farge, John, 227
La Follette, Robert M., 135, 156, 164, 198, 265, 272, 277, 278, 285
Laurier, Wilfred, 82, 85, 86
Lee, Arthur, 74, 254, 255, 263
Leland, Cyrus, 21
Lesseps, Ferdinand Marie de, 93
Leupp, Francis E., 114, 208–10
Littauer, Lucius N., 90
Littlefield, Charles E., 107–8, 233
Lodge, Henry Cabot, 2, 4, 6, 25, 48, 56, 57, 58, 63, 65, 66, 83, 118, 122, 138, 284, 297, 299; and arbitration treaties, 149; and Canadian boundary, 85, 86; on Roosevelt, 178, 192; and 1906 election, 232, 234; and immigration, 36, 259, 260; and navy, 261, 265; and railroad regulation, 158, 163; and tariff, 231
Loeb, William, Jr., 15–16, 128, 153, 274, 291
Lomax, John A., 296
Long, Chester I., 160–61
Long, John D., 6, 18, 19, 48
Longworth, Alice Roosevelt, 4, 5, 76, 101, 103, 185, 226, 236
Longworth, Nicholas, 226, 239
Loomis, Francis B., 95
Lorimer, William, 135
Lurton, Horace H., 273
Lynching, 23, 57, 118, 238, 245

McCullough, David, 299
McKim, Charles F., 102, 228
McKinley, William, 1, 8, 12, 17, 18, 19, 20, 22, 29, 31, 32, 35, 36, 43, 51, 56, 58, 66, 120, 127, 128, 229, 235, 238, 273; Open Door policy of, 45; as president, 6, 15, 74, 121, 129, 130, 142, 144, 170, 220, 269, 300; and tariff, 24, 25, 26; and trusts, 29
McLaurin, John L., 120